ROTH FAMILY FOUNDATION

Music in America Imprint

Michael P. Roth

and Sukey Garcetti

have endowed this

imprint to honor the

memory of their parents,

Julia and Harry Roth,

whose deep love of music

they wish to share

with others.

The publisher gratefully acknowledges the generous contribution to this book provided by the AMS 75 PAYS Endowment of the American Musicological Society, funded in part by the National Endowment for the Humanities and the Andrew W. Mellon Foundation.

Blowin' the Blues Away

MUSIC OF THE AFRICAN DIASPORA

Guthrie P. Ramsey, Jr., Editor

Samuel A. Floyd, Jr., Editor Emeritus

Blowin' the Blues Away

Performance and Meaning on the
New York Jazz Scene

Travis A. Jackson

UNIVERSITY OF CALIFORNIA PRESS
Berkeley · *Los Angeles* · *London*

Center for Black Music Research
Columbia College Chicago

University of California Press, one of the most
distinguished university presses in the United States,
enriches lives around the world by advancing
scholarship in the humanities, social sciences, and
natural sciences. Its activities are supported by the UC
Press Foundation and by philanthropic contributions
from individuals and institutions. For more information, visit www.ucpress.edu.

University of California Press
Berkeley and Los Angeles, California

University of California Press, Ltd.
London, England

Center for Black Music Research
Columbia College Chicago

Early versions of portions of chapters 5 and 6 appeared
as "Jazz Performance as Ritual: The Blues Aesthetic
and the African Diaspora" in *The African Diaspora: A
Musical Perspective*, ed. Ingrid Monson, 23–82 (New
York: Garland, 2000).

Library of Congress Cataloging-in-Publication Data

Jackson, Travis A.
  Blowin' the blues away : performance and meaning
on the New York jazz scene / Travis A. Jackson.
     p. cm. — (Music of the African diaspora)
  Includes bibliographical references and index.
     ISBN 978-0-520-27044-2 (cloth : alk. paper) —
ISBN 978-0-520-27045-9 (pbk. : alk. paper)
     1. Jazz—New York (State)—New York—History
and criticism.   I. Title.
  ML3508.8.N5J33 2012
  781.6509747'109049—dc23
                                        2011042263

Manufactured in the United States of America

20   19   18   17   16   15   14   13   12
10   9   8   7   6   5   4   3   2   1

In keeping with a commitment to support environmen-
tally responsible and sustainable printing practices,
UC Press has printed this book on 50-pound
Enterprise, a 30% post-consumer-waste, recycled,
deinked fiber that is processed chlorine-free. It is
acid-free and meets all ANSI/NISO (Z 39.48)
requirements.

*To Lawrence Jackson Sr. and to the memory of
Sherryl L. Jackson, Rev. Chalmers Jackson Sr.,
and Robert Thomas Hodge—each of whom
opened a way for me*

Contents

Illustrations

Acknowledgments

Although the cover and title page indicate that this book has one author, it is in fact the result of a wide-ranging series of relationships—with musicians, colleagues, friends, and family—spanning a life, several cities, and three academic institutions. Indeed, the number of intellectual and spiritual gifts I have received over that time and in those places has left me with an obligation to reciprocate that I will fulfill gladly, though many of my return gifts, sadly, will be prestations to the universe rather than to those who shared with me their time and their perspectives, who let me into their worlds, and who gave me their support.

In particular, it saddens me that neither Mark Tucker, one of my stalwart supporters during my time at Columbia University and afterward, nor James Williams, who saw potential in my work and opened doors for his fellow Tennessean, lived to see this book published. Both of them, prematurely felled by cancer, were the kinds of people, as the cliché goes, one doesn't meet every day. Eminently skilled and widely esteemed in their respective fields, they both exhibited a capacious humanity, trying always to make the world a better place for those around them. I doubt that any of this book's merits would be what they are without their profound influence.

Equally important are the musicians who, in sometimes only fleeting conversations, made observations or shared insights that turned my head just enough to make me see things in fresh and productive ways. I mention most of them by name throughout this book, listing them prominently in

chapters 2 and 4. Bruce Barth, Peter Bernstein, Antonio Hart, Sam Newsome, Leon Parker, and Steve Wilson were especially helpful. They invited
me into their homes and to their recording sessions and their gigs, even
after my fieldwork was done. Like James Williams, they had little to
nothing to gain from me, but they offered me nearly everything via their
candid, thoughtful responses and their friendship. To this day, seeing
them perform on my returns to New York City or when they are touring
as leaders or sidemen remains a revelatory delight for me.

In addition to the musicians, my scholarly interlocutors have contributed immensely to the style and substance of this book. At the University
of Michigan I had the pleasure of sharing ideas about music making and
scholarship with a broad range of individuals affiliated with the School
of Music, the American Culture Program, the Atlantic Studies Initiative,
and the Center for Afroamerican and African Studies. In particular, the
research support provided by former dean of the School of Music, Paul
Boylan, and by senior vice-provost for Academic Affairs, Lester P. Monts,
was crucial in this project's early stages. My colleagues in Music History and Musicology, the School of Music, and the Music in the United
States of America project office—including Naomi André, Gregory Bar-
nett, Judith Becker, James Borders, Evan Chambers, Mark Clague, David
Crawford, Hugh de Ferranti, Joseph Lam, Beth Levy, Stefano Mengozzi,
Marcello Piras, Gillian Rodger, Louise Stein, Amy Stillman, Steven M.
Whiting, and Roland John Wiley—provided as nurturing an environment
as any junior professor might have desired. Likewise, my conversations
with varied performance faculty—Gerald Cleaver, Ellen Rowe, Ed Sarath,
and the late Donald Walden—helped to keep me anchored in the particu-
lars of music making even as I made my way, again, through the broad and
varied literature on jazz, improvisation, and American culture. I am
also grateful to the Julie and Parker Hall Endowment for Jazz and
American Popular Music at the University of Chicago, whose support
made it possible for me to use Jack Vartoogian's photograph of Steve
Wilson on this book's cover. Beyond there, Paul A. Anderson, Santiago
Colás, Frances Aparicio, Kevin Gaines, Frank Gunderson, Sandra Gun-
ning, Martha S. Jones, Marlon Ross, Carroll Smith-Rosenberg, Lucia
M. Suárez, and Penny M. Von Eschen were among my favorite interlocutors in the broader university community. A number of people who
were graduate students during those years have also contributed significantly to this work. Among them are Tamar Barzel, John Behling, Kate
Brucher, Charles Gentry, Mark Kirschenmann, Caroline Kovtun, LaTis-
sia Mitchell, Shani Mott, Michal Rahfaldt, Matthew Shippee, Wilson

Valentín-Escobar, and Carla Vecchiola. I am particularly indebted to Ryan Snyder Ananat and Stephanie Heriger, whose research assistance in two critical periods freed me to concentrate on writing.

Still, my experience at Michigan owed its particular luster to the polish provided by three special colleagues. Richard Crawford, who also served as Mark Tucker's mentor, warmly welcomed me from the beginning of my campus visit in 1997. His sage guidance and his unflappable (and sometimes unflattering) humor were a constant during my time in Ann Arbor and have continued since my departure in 2003. He was the person who introduced me to Samuel A. Floyd Jr. and set me on the path to publishing this book in the Music of the African Diaspora series. Even more, it is through Crawford's influence as well as Tucker's that I learned about the constant work that good writing requires. I'm still trying to emulate his example, but he's pushed me farther than I thought I could go. Albin J. Zak III and Erik Santos were (and remain) the best friends and colleagues I could have hoped for. Through countless dinners, drinks, impromptu jams, discussions of recordings, late-night listening sessions, and reading suggestions (as well as through performances with other members of the short-lived Ann Arbor Noise Collective), they made life seem like an endlessly gratifying voyage of discovery. I feel privileged to have been able to share so much with and learn so much from them. Many of the same observations are true of their wives, Victoria von Arx and Toko Shiiki-Santos, respectively. Their collective friendship is one of the greatest gifts I have ever received.

At the University of Chicago, my home since 2003, I have had an unparalleled interdisciplinary *and* collegial experience. In particular, my contact with faculty and staff across the university, some of whom have now taken positions elsewhere, has been both invigorating and positively challenging. Although I am certain to omit some people inadvertently, I have particularly grown through my association with (from the music department) Melvin L. Butler, Thomas Christensen, Martha Feldman, Philip Gossett, Berthold Hoeckner, Robert L. Kendrick, Kaley R. Mason, Marta Ptaszynska, Steven P. Rings, Anne Robertson, and Lawrence W. Zbikowski (with special thanks to Kathy Holmes) and (from the university more broadly) Lauren Berlant, Bill Brown, James Chandler, Cathy Cohen, Nicole M. Guidotti-Hernández, Deborah L. Gillaspie, Robert von Hallberg, Melissa Harris-Perry, Elise M. LaRose, Waldo Johnson, Scott Landvatter, David Levin, and Jacqueline Stewart. Among those whom I first encountered as graduate students, Nathan Bakkum, Vicki Brennan, Eric Brinkmann, M. Celia Cain, Sinan Dora, Byron

Dueck, Luis-Manuel Garcia, Donald James, Jaime Jones, Kristen McGee, Kevin McKenna, Andrew Mall, Marina Peterson, Rumya Putcha, Melissa Reilly, Peter Shultz, Greg Weinstein, and Mark Yeary have been invaluable conversation partners and good friends. In my time at Chicago, though, Philip V. Bohlman and Martin Stokes (now at King's College London) were my greatest sources of inspiration, both because of the breadth and depth of their intellects and because of their unfailing generosity of spirit. For good reason, they remain exemplars of what ethnomusicologists are and can do as scholars and human beings.

My ten-year-plus association with the Jazz Study Group at Columbia University also widened my horizons and expanded my acquaintance with some of the leading scholars working today. Spearheaded in its first incarnation by Robert G. O'Meally, to this day one of my most cherished mentors, the group was a place where I first tried out some of the ideas presented here and garnered feedback that helped me to hone them further. The group's scholars and staff over the years have my undying gratitude. They include Herman Beavers, Gerald Early, Brent Hayes Edwards, Krin Gabbard, John Gennari, Farah Jasmine Griffin, William J. Harris, Robin D.G. Kelley, Sue Laizik, George E. Lewis, Bill Lowe, Timothy R. Mangin, Ingrid Monson, Fred Moten, Richard J. Powell, Guthrie P. Ramsey, David Lionel Smith, John F. Szwed, Jeffrey Taylor, Salim Washington, and many others. The varied fruit of the group's work is on display in two volumes: *The Jazz Cadence of American Culture* (1995), edited by O'Meally and curated by the group, and *Uptown Conversation: The New Jazz Studies* (O'Meally, Edwards, and Griffin 2004), featuring contributions from the group and its affiliates. I would be remiss in not extending warm thanks to James C. "J.C." Sylvan, whose administrative expertise and wry humor helped to make the time I spent at Columbia's Center for Jazz Studies in 2000 and 2001 all the more rewarding. That sabbatical year was funded in part by a Ford Foundation Postdoctoral Fellowship.

In the much broader worlds of academia and the jazz scene, I have been enriched by my experiences with Paul Austerlitz, Gage Averill, Amy Bauer, Mellonee V. Burnim, Aaron Cohen, Scott DeVeaux, Kate Dumbleton, Daniel Ferguson, Kai Fikentscher, Aaron A. Fox, Alyssa Garcia, Melissa Gonzalez, Jocelyne Guilbault, Harold J. Haskins, Cheryl L. Keyes, Donna L. Kwon, Ferentz Lafargue, Steven Mamula, Portia K. Maultsby, Robin D. Moore, Zachary Ross Morgan, Michelle Nasser, Katherine S. Newman, Danielle Pacha, Steven F. Pond, Lewis Porter,

Michelle Smith-Bermiss, Gabriel Solis, Nicole Stahlmann, George L. Starks Jr., Maurice Stevens, Michael E. Veal, Bonnie L. Wade, Richard Wang, Jeremy Wallach, Christopher J. Washburne, Christopher A. Waterman, Peter Watrous, and Cynthia P. Wong-Lippe. A stellar group of friends dating back three decades, especially Charles B. Adams, Jennifer Clary, Jeffrey Fracé, Adam Glaser, Beverly James, Stephen Lapointe, Carmen Maldonado, Jerusha Ramos, Roberto B. Vargas, and Paula Young, has also provided loving moral support through the years.

More so than most projects, this book has had a long development. It was delayed at some points by my unwillingness to declare it done and at others by the disciplinary disagreements that various drafts have occasioned. Some of the arguments contained herein will likely engender further disagreement and commentary, but both are welcome and, in fact, necessary. Through the whole process, Mary C. Francis has been a perceptive and accommodating editor. Taking over from Lynne Withey shortly after I signed my contract, she has guided this project through sometimes difficult straits with grace and seemingly endless patience. Eric Schmidt, Sharron Wood, and Mari Coates likewise have helped me work through the most intricate issues in the production process with skill and aplomb.

Miriam Tripaldi came into my life late in my work on this project, and she has quickly become a loving supporter and a true partner, making my life fulfilling and the work of finishing this book enjoyable in ways I never could have imagined: I owe her debts a lifetime will be too short to repay. But I look forward to that lifetime.

Most importantly, however, my extended family, centered in Nashville, Tennessee, has kept me going. In a world where many increasingly delay marriage and child rearing, having the opportunity to know one's great-grandparents or even grandparents past one's early years is a privilege. Because I was lucky on both counts, my great-grandparents in rural Tennessee and rural Louisiana, present mostly in memory over the last few decades, are a constant reminder of what struggle, strategic planning and creative improvisation can mean beyond the individual life. My grandparents, and especially my grandfathers, have been exemplars, people who taught me more about being in and hearing the world than I ever realized it was possible to know. On a more day-to-day level, my siblings, Lawrence Jackson Jr. and Melody Morris, as well as their children have always been only a phone call away and ready to remind me both that I am loved and do love and that there is a world beyond work. In the same way, my parents, Lawrence Sr. and the late Sherryl L. Jackson, were ever-interested, ever-supportive, ever-loving, even when the child who always wanted to be a pediatrician suddenly declared an interest in some strange thing called ethnomusicology. Without them nothing you read here would have been possible. The faults in this book are all mine, but any celebration or congratulations should be all theirs.

PART ONE

Black, Brown and Beige

CHAPTER I

Studying Jazz

As the second decade of the twenty-first century begins, we are undoubtedly at a pivotal moment in the development of jazz. Major and independent record labels and a number of cultural institutions have, particularly since the early 1980s, presented jazz to varied publics in ways that promote both its essential "Americanness" and its supposed universality. They have devoted considerable resources to preserving and promulgating the music via new recordings, reissues of older ones, sponsorship of concert and lecture series, the mounting of museum exhibits, and the production of documentaries as well as syndicated radio and television programs. Popular publications and their advertisers, moreover, have also shown interest in the music, as evidenced by feature articles on jazz and jazz musicians in periodicals as diverse as the *New York Times,* the *Washington Post, Newsweek, GQ, Essence, Out,* and *Rolling Stone* and by the appearance of jazz musicians in stylish advertisements for Johnston & Murphy shoes and Movado watches, among other products.[1] Two further indicators of the increased importance of jazz have been its designation by the House of Representatives and the United States Senate as a "rare and valuable national American treasure" in 1987 and frequent references to its status as "America's classical music."[2] At the same time, after the high points of the 1980s and 1990s, younger audiences seem less interested in jazz,[3] and the music seems to be receding from mass public consciousness—receding so far, at least in the United States, that commentators such as Stuart Nicholson (2005, xi) have asserted that continued performance of jazz may require the kinds of public subsidy more common in Europe.

In the midst of these activities and alongside such arguments, academics have also had their say. Sociologists, psychologists, literary scholars, art historians, and cultural critics have found ways to see jazz through the lenses of their respective fields. Indeed, even those scholars working in the normally conservative and slow-to-change subdisciplines of musicology took notice: historical musicologists, ethnomusicologists, and music theorists have added their voices to an expanding discourse, using jazz to confirm, extend, and challenge the validity of paradigms of musical analysis and musicological research. All involved—whether they were trying to find the essence of American culture, trying to account for the impact that the music has had on its listeners, or attempting to understand how canonical musicians achieved their status—seemed fixed on jazz almost as though it might hold answers to some of life's most intractable mysteries, as though it might help them to make sense of the modern world and how it came to be.

In the outpouring of work that has accompanied "the modern resurgence" of jazz (Nicholson 1990), however, views of the music, the musicians, and the world that they inhabit have rarely risen above the myopic or the romantic. On one hand, musicologists have spoken of jazz primarily in the terms they developed for European concert music. Thus meticulous transcriptions and analyses of jazz, focused on the "immanent and recurrent properties" (Nattiez 1990, 10–11) of "music itself," and nearly obsessive attention to discographical detail have made much jazz scholarship seem a replication of score-based analysis and sketch studies. In such research, sometimes defensively oriented toward the elevation of the music, jazz often appears as an imperfect version of classical music rather than as something vital and examinable in its own right.[4] Ethnomusicologists have, over the last couple of decades, widened the horizon, emphasizing the roles of culture and musical interaction, but, like other academically trained music researchers, they have tended to rely exclusively on commercially released recordings for their music analytical work. Those academics approaching jazz from other disciplines have refracted it through the prisms of their respective fields, for example, occupational and organizational behavior, deviance, musical taste/preference, political protest, and social interaction, among other things (e.g., Becker 1951; Winick 1960; Katz and Longden 1983; Gridley 1987; Kofsky 1970; Sharron 1985). On the other hand, those writers concerned with reaching a lay audience have focused on the personal triumphs and foibles of musicians, who either overcome misfortune and tragic circumstances or succumb to them. In either case, only rarely do the writers connect their hypotheses convincingly to the lives or work of the musicians or their supporters. Jazz, as a result, has become a facile metaphor for American democratic ideals, a paradigmatic instance of racial/cultural integration, and/or the most singular contribution of the United States to the world.[5]

Blowin' the Blues Away was conceived, in part, as a response to those alternatives. Rather than confront jazz using a loose biographical approach or conventional musicological techniques, this study instead focuses attention on the kinds of "interpretive moves" (Feld 1994b, 86–89) that performers and other participants in musical events make as they engage with music. What kinds of aesthetic—normative and evaluative—criteria do they bring to their engagement? How have those criteria developed, and how do they change with the passage of time? Such questions remind us that the meanings of jazz are not simply *in* the music; rather, they are constructed from the ongoing, dynamic relationship between what one encounters in musical events, the dispositions one brings to those events, and the relationships between the two. In short, this book examines the way that "strictly musical" parameters of performance constrain but don't completely determine the kinds of interpretations that might emerge (Jackson 2000; DeNora 2000, 27–31).

An exploration of the meanings and interpretation of jazz cannot proceed, however, without an examination of the contested nature of the term in both scholarly and popular writing. One major question is how inclusive a definition of jazz can be. Can or should it embrace entities as disparate as the free improvisations of Derek Bailey, the meticulous arrangements of New York Voices, and the recordings of Norah Jones? Although scholars have attempted to address these questions using a number of criteria to distinguish jazz from nonjazz, or the more jazzlike from the less jazzlike (Gridley et al. 1989; Jackson 2002), their results have not always been illuminating. Such questions, responses aside, go directly to the heart of the struggle over who can lay claim to the title "jazz" or have their music labeled thus. For some musicians and other social actors, the stakes are high, since jazz, starting in the 1950s, has increasingly come to be viewed as a prestigious art music in American society (DeVeaux 1991; Gabbard 1995).

During my research, two radio stations in the New York City metropolitan area, WBGO-FM (Newark, New Jersey) and WQCD-FM (Manhattan), both of which were self-described jazz stations, illustrated this struggle.⁶ WBGO programmed those styles that nearly any scholar or layperson would define as jazz, styles commonly referred to as "traditional," "mainstream," "straight-ahead," "bop," "neo-bop," and, in some cases, "free bop."⁷ These styles are played primarily on acoustic instruments by small groups of three to seven musicians; make frequent use of thirty-two-bar song forms, twelve-bar blues, and "modal" frameworks, as well as various modifications of them; and are historically rooted in the practices of paradigmatic jazz musicians in general and African American jazz musicians in particular. WBGO at times used the phrase "real jazz" in its on-air promotional spots to distinguish itself from WQCD, which programmed what its own advertisements referred to as "smooth jazz" or sometimes "contemporary jazz." Smooth or contemporary styles are highly dependent on electronic instruments and have developed more self-consciously from the practices of rhythm and blues, soul, funk, and fusion musicians from the mid-1970s forward. In fact, many of the artists programmed on smooth jazz stations—such as Anita Baker and Sade— also appear in "urban contemporary" or "quiet storm" radio formats, which cater to audiences for soul and rhythm and blues classics from the 1970s and 1980s. In any event, people listening to either station might potentially have prided themselves on being culturally informed members of society who listened to jazz.

My focus here is on the styles that would be programmed on WBGO. Those styles are also distinct from smooth as well as experimental ones in a number of other respects, including the training, background, and philosophies of the musicians and other musical event participants; the venues in which performances take place; and the publications and media channels that promote them. That is, other styles, such as jazz-rock fusion, various forms of free jazz, and those styles associated with cocktail-lounge combos, may use harmony in similar ways, place great emphasis on improvisation, or have a repertoire comprising popular tunes drawn from Tin Pan Alley and American musical theater—all characteristics that one might attribute to straight-ahead jazz performance. But those styles exhibit such features under different circumstances and in different venues from those that characterize the straight-ahead New York jazz scene. In the interest of ethnographic depth, I chose to focus primarily on the latter. Therefore, in the remainder of the book, when I refer to the "jazz scene," I am writing primarily about the mainstream scene rather than its counterparts.⁸

My project has been to understand how participants in the jazz scene, and especially musicians, construct and construe meaning in *musical events.* As Ruth M. Stone (1982, 3, 4) describes them, such events are complexes of activity that are "set off and made distinct from the world of everyday life" and whose participants include "both the individuals producing music and the people experiencing the music performance as listeners or audience." In part, her aim is to situate music amid a host of other activities that might accompany and frame it, such as speech, dance, and kinesic-proxemic factors. While Stone's focus is on the direct, face-to-face interactions of participants, her formulation might also encompass those situations in which one, alone or with others, hears only the sonic traces of such events as she construes them (as on a recording; see Horn 2002, 19–21). In either situation, musical events, understood as dynamic and processual, are a space in which performers and other participants interact and negotiate their relationships with each other as well as with other events that have occurred in the past. In those moments, as well, they condition themselves, consciously and unconsciously, for future events.

In contrast, many of the writers whose histories, essays, and analyses I have read have either been interested primarily in musical analysis focused on "great men" in jazz history (Schuller 1968, 1989), have concerned themselves with exploring connections between music and cultural history (Tirro 1977; Collier 1978; Kenney 1993; Stowe 1994), or—in extreme cases—have subjected musicians to psychoanalytic scrutiny (Collier 1987; cf. Carner 1991). In other words, these writers have taken as their object a static conception of "the music" and/or the individual and have relied upon the standard tools and methodologies of musicological and historical investigation. If they have widened their scope to encompass anything comparable to musical events, to see music ontologically as process as well as product (Bohlman 1999), they have done so only as a secondary concern. Their modes of inquiry are heavily dependent on documents, entities whose isolatability and seeming fixity make them amenable to textual interpretation.

As such documents, audio recordings have been valuable sources for scholars interested in jazz performance. By facilitating repeated listening, they enable a researcher to grasp performative and textu(r)al nuances that might otherwise pass unnoticed. They also make possible comparative projects, so that one might examine the two complete takes of "Parker's Mood" from *Charlie Parker: The Complete Savoy Sessions* or use Thelonious Monk's numerous takes of "'Round Midnight" on *Thelonious Monk: The Complete Riverside Recordings* as a basis for understanding jazz improvisation as practice and process.[9] At the same time, recordings also minimize the importance of the researcher being in close physical proximity to the musicians at a given performance, "live" or recorded, and that lack of proximity often creates interpretive blind spots. Performances, after all, are multitextured events, filled with proxemic, kinesthetic, visual, and other contextual stimuli and information. Recordings containing only the audio information are unique but ultimately incomplete representations of them.

Despite such obvious limitations, some of jazz's most influential analysts have written as though recordings were transparent windows into the past or into performance practice. In the preface to *Jazz: Its Evolution and Essence* (1956), for example, André Hodeir explains his reliance on recordings for research by emphasizing their fixity: "The judgments of jazz in this book are based on recordings, which have reached a state of technical perfection that makes such an approach valid. Besides, the recording is the most trustworthy witness we have in dealing with an art form of which nothing that is essential can be set down on paper. The reader should not be surprised, therefore, if the words *work* and *record* are used interchangeably throughout" (2). While acknowledging the limited efficacy of notation, Hodeir asserts that recordings are similar to written scores in that they offer analysts access to musical *works*.[10] Like Hodeir, Gunther Schuller posits an equivalence between recordings and works when he writes that the jazz historian must evaluate "the only thing that is available to him: the recording" (1968, x).[11] Schuller does question whether such "one-time affairs" can be viewed as definitive, but he feels that—in absence of other texts—they, as "primary source[s]," are all that historically minded analysts have at their disposal. And since the most prominent methods of musical analysis were developed for notated music, jazz researchers who want their work to be intelligible have to transcribe music from a recording—to transform it into a score/work, and in the process reduce complex sonic events to the parameters of pitch, rhythm, and volume—before analyzing it.[12]

The work perspective, though, founders partly because recordings are not "acoustic window[s] giving access to how the music really sounded" (Rasula 1995, 135). Or, as Anthony Seeger explains, "[no recording] preserves sounds. What it preserves are [selective] *interpretations* of sounds—interpretations made by the people who did the recordings and their equipment" (Seeger 1986, 270, emphasis in original; see Jairazbhoy and Balyoz 1977). Microphone selection and placement, recording media, room construction, frequency equalization, dynamic range compression, and countless other choices affect what we hear on a recording.

A change in any one of them can appreciably alter the final product.[13] Each of these choices constitutes a human decision, whether a producer's, engineer's, or performer's, oriented toward getting a specific kind of sound, doing something in one way rather than in others.[14]

Indeed, based on evidence from a number of recordings in the 1990s, one might assert that the now-standard reliance on multitrack recording and on digital editing has led to a broader anxiety regarding the fidelity of recordings to a live performance ideal.[15] In the notes for pianist Jacky Terrasson's 1995 release *Reach,* for example, Mark Levinson offers the following account of the CD's recording:

> Years ago, musicians recorded music as they played—informally, in close physical proximity, without much editing. What they played was what people heard on the record. Today that approach has been all but lost. Studios separate the musicians, put them behind glass booths, give them headphones and cue tracks, and leave most of the production decisions to engineers in the post-production process—mixing, editing, and mastering.... [In my approach, only] two microphones are used, positioned carefully in the optimum location. The balance between instruments is therefore created by the musicians themselves. There is no opportunity later to change this balance.... Musicians and engineer are in the same room with no glass windows or partitions between them. No headphones or monitors are used by the musicians.[16]

Here, again, the assumption is that recordings, at least when done well, can provide direct access to what musicians do. Many other releases from the 1980s and '90s contain similar statements, such as "recorded live to 2-track," perhaps intended to make them seem more authentically representative of live jazz performance and more accurate as historical documents.

In that capacity, they might also give us privileged access to the authorial intentions of individual musicians. This second kind of fidelity is compromised when we take account of how musicians decide what and when to record (see DeVeaux 1988, 127, 135). In his autobiography *Reminiscing in Tempo* (1990), for example, producer Teddy Reig explains that he allowed Charlie Parker to choose all of the tunes recorded during his sessions for Savoy—provided they were "original" compositions, that is, ones that did not require the record label to pay royalties to other composers. Orrin Keepnews, however, took a more hands-on approach in recording Thelonious Monk for Riverside:

> My partner [Bill Grauer] and I had decided that our initial goal was to try to reverse the widely held belief that our new pianist was an impossibly obscure

artist; therefore, we would start by avoiding bebop horns and intricate original tunes. We proposed an all-Ellington trio date: certainly Duke was a universally respected figure and major composer. . . . [Monk] agreed without hesitation, despite claiming to be largely unfamiliar with Ellington's music. I insisted that Thelonious pick out the specific repertoire, and eventually he requested several pieces of sheet music. (Keepnews 1988, 122–23)

Monk's second session for Riverside produced another album of jazz standards, again at the request of Grauer and Keepnews. It was only with his third release that Monk was allowed to record his own compositions.[17] Likewise, Joshua Redman (1995a) told me that his decision to record Eric Clapton's "Tears in Heaven" for the album *Wish* (1993) came after he listened to a cassette compilation suggestively given to him by Matt Pierson, his producer.[18]

Finally, it is rarely clear whether the compositions on a given release were rehearsed by a band prior to recording or whether they were created in the studio. Charlie Parker's most celebrated quintet—with Miles Davis, Duke Jordan, Tommy Potter, and Max Roach—was a working band that almost certainly had performed some of the tunes they recorded in live settings before entering the studio. At the very least, they had performed tunes with similar harmonic progressions. But according to both Teddy Reig (Reig and Berger 1990, 22) and Miles Davis (Davis and Troupe 1989, 88–89), there were also numerous tunes recorded by Parker and his groups whose melodies were composed and learned by musicians on the spot. Such instant composition and performance were certainly affected by the time constraints of recording. As Helen Oakley Dance and James Patrick point out, prior to the 1950s it was standard practice to record four tunes in a three-hour recording session.[19] Up to forty-five minutes then, on average, could be allotted to the recording of each three-minute tune. Such generous amounts of time, however, could be diminished by in-studio rehearsal, by false starts and mistakes, or by decisions to change repertoire or modify arrangements. Alternatively, Robert Palmer (1985) suggests that the high quality of recordings on the Blue Note label in the 1960s was due to the label's policy of financing two to three days of rehearsal prior to each recording session.[20]

These examples make clear that one cannot definitively say whether an individual recording truly represents a first-time, improvisationally brilliant performance.[21] For those writers interested in locating such performances, the use of commercially released live recordings is not a viable corrective, for such releases are as subject to post-performance manipulation as studio recordings. When artists like Joshua Redman and Joe

Lovano made their live recordings at the Village Vanguard in the 1990s, it was likely as apparent to other audience members as it was to me that these were *not* typical performances. Intricate networks of wires and cables ran from the stage to other areas of the club and up the stairs to large mobile recording units parked in front of the club on both occasions. If that weren't evidence enough, the musicians took care to inform us in each case that the evening's performance was being recorded for commercial release.[22] Moreover, as is standard with studio recordings, some recorded material, such as the intervals between songs or "extraneous" audience noise, didn't appear on the final releases. Finally, audience applause was recorded on separate microphones to be mixed in later, and the individual tunes chosen for inclusion on the final recordings were sequenced in a manner that didn't replicate their order on the evening(s) of performance.[23]

Where musical analysis is concerned, the process of transcribing those same recordings strips dense sonic phenomena of all that cannot be translated into a particular notational system, discourages study of musics not easily transcribed, and privileges the aspects of sound that researchers dependent on Western notation have been trained to emphasize (Tagg 1982, 41–42).[24] Consequently, through notational dependence the analysis of jazz has come to resemble the analysis of Western concert music (see Walser 1995, 170–71, for a strategic use of notation-centered analysis). As a result, the majority of jazz analytical work concentrates on the improvised solos of historically prominent musicians, with most writers being content to focus their attention solely on the structural and melodic parameters of those solos.

Following Potter (1990), one can loosely group the analytical approaches to jazz in the categories represented in table 1. Analyses mapping pitch onto harmony or mode examine, moment to moment, what pitch choices are common or idiomatic for a particular improviser. Those analyses classed as "thematic/motivic/formulaic" have attempted to show how specific improvisers such as Charlie Parker, Sonny Rollins, and John Coltrane developed themes or motives in individual improvisations or consistently used the same melodic shapes (formulae) over specific harmonic progressions. Schenkerian analyses have been applied to show that "instantaneous composers—improvisers . . . think in long-range terms" (Potter 1990, 66) similar to those of the concert music composers on whom Heinrich Schenker based his work. The schemata under reductive techniques/pitch-class set analysis apply the implication-realization models of Eugene Narmour and Leonard Meyer or set analysis to melodic

TABLE I   ANALYTIC APPROACHES

Analytic Framework	Representative Examples
Relation of pitch to harmony or mode	Published transcriptions in *Down Beat,* listed by Koger 1985
Thematic/motivic/formulaic	Williams 1958; Schuller 1958; Owens 1974; Tirro 1974; Gushee 1981; Kernfeld 1983; Smith 1983; Spring 1990; Van der Bliek 1991
Schenkerian/harmonic	Owens 1974; Stewart 1979, 1982; Larson 1993, 1998, 2009; Martin 1996; Julien 2003; Waters and Williams 2010
Reductive techniques / pitch-class set analysis	Pressing 1982; Williams 1982; Block 1990, 1993
Linguistic	Perlman and Greenblatt 1981; Steedman 1984; Suhor 1986
Stylistic	Williams 1982; Wildman 1985; Strunk 1979; Stein 1977; Koch 1985
Signification—derived from the work of Henry Louis Gates Jr. (1988)*	Murphy 1990; Floyd 1991, 1993, 1995; Walser 1995
Performance interaction	Katz and Longden 1983; Porter 1985; Stewart 1986; Rinzler 1988; Bastien and Hostager 1991; Washburne 1991; Jackson 1992; Berliner 1994; Monson 1996; Borgo 2005; Benadon 2006; Butterfield 2000, 2006, 2010

* Gates reaches into the African past to ground his concern with "Signifyin(g)," and, like Houston A. Baker Jr. (1984), he sees the African American vernacular as a source of new tools for literary criticism. "Signifyin(g)"—Gates explains his spelling of the term on page 46—defined as "repetition, with a signal difference" (1988, 51), is for him the master trope of the black English vernacular: "Black formal repetition always repeats with a difference, a black difference that manifests itself in specific language use. And the repository that contains the language that is the source—and the reflection—of black difference is the black English vernacular tradition" (xxii–xxiii). The importance of "Signifyin(g)" for literary criticism is its naming of a kind of intertextuality: "All texts Signify upon other texts, in motivated and unmotivated ways" (xxiv). Noting that "one does not signify something . . . one signifies in some way" (54), Gates delineates a number of ways in which Signifyin(g) is used by African American speakers, writers, and musicians, especially through the repetition, revision, blurring, and inversion of formal structures; pastiche; parody; and reinterpretation. In addition to numerous language-based examples, Gates provides music-based ones to support his assertions: "When playing the blues, a great musician often tries to make musical phrases that are elastic in their formal properties. These elastic phrases stretch the form rather than articulate the form. Because the form is self-evident to the musician, both he and his well-trained audience are playing and listening with expectation. Signifyin(g) disappoints these expectations; caesuras, or breaks, achieve the same function. This form of disappointment creates a dialogue between what the listener expects and what the artist plays. Whereas younger, less mature musicians accentuate the beat, more accomplished musicians do not have to do so. They feel free to imply it" (123).

entities. Although reductive analyses attempt to show that certain melodic moves require or imply their own continuation, pitch-class set analyses reveal the relations between vertical or horizontal collections of pitches. Those studies termed "linguistic" have explored parallels between spoken language and jazz improvisation and have borrowed linguistic techniques and concepts, such as generative grammar, competence, and performance. The stylistic category encompasses analyses that are essentially descriptive, aimed at elucidating stylistic parameters such as harmonic or melodic usage. Studies of performance interaction focus on the ways in which performers interact with each other in the course of performance, particularly through their manipulation of harmony, rhythm, timbre, and other musical parameters.

To some degree, the analytical projects outlined above have been important in convincing an older generation of scholars that jazz was indeed worthy of study. But because of their intentions or target audiences, many of those researchers privileged (and privilege) categories, concepts, and methodologies drawn from the study of Western concert music and derive their research questions from them. One might gain useful knowledge from such strategies, but it is clear that they might fail to engage other important issues. Indeed, much promise for the future of jazz studies and jazz analysis lies in developing analytical schemata that are more capable of accounting for what is distinctive about jazz (see Walser 1995; 179; Butterfield 2000). Studies based on ethnographic fieldwork and performance interaction, though in their infancy, seem to be positive steps in that direction.

Such studies require a more direct engagement of the scholar with music, performers, listeners, *and* the cultures and contexts that support their interaction. The perspectives gained through fieldwork and personal knowledge are, of course, not inherently superior to other perspectives, but they open a space for improving and refining analysis as well as avoiding all-too-common pitfalls (see Horowitz 1982). They allow a researcher to investigate issues that audio recordings and published sources alone cannot illuminate. By situating themselves in the context(s) of performance and allowing the data gathered to shape their analyses, researchers studying living performers emphasize what they might learn from *people,* particularly the individuals and groups who perform and otherwise participate in musical events.[25]

Indeed, one might argue that attempts to assert jazz's status as an art music in the academy have depended on the erasure of the "extramusical" from its study, an erasure that deemphasizes the music's roots in and continued interactions with African diaspora cultures and other African American musics (Radano 1993, 15–21; Horn 2002, 28). As a result, works by African American writers whose perspectives on the music and its relation to African American and American cultures have been critical in illuminating the music's cultural functions have until recently been overlooked by jazz scholars. To be sure, the work of Baraka (1963, 1967a), Ellison (1964c, 1986), and Murray (1970, 1976) contains historical errors and misapprehensions of specific musical-technical matters, but its importance lies in its ability to articulate the spirit of the music, not only via cultural foundations but also via the music's meanings within and inseparability from the African American communities that have nurtured it.[26] In other words, these writers raise questions about the meaning of jazz performance that are concerned with, in saxophonist Antonio Hart's charged phrase, "what the music is really about" (Hart 1995) for one group of people intimately involved with it. And as writing on and the study of jazz have become ensconced in the academy and in conservatories, particularly since the 1950s, those writings that come from outside established academic disciplines or mainstream jazz criticism have, like the music's cultural connections, been underemphasized (for further discussion, see Gennari 1991; Gabbard 1995; Ramsey 1999).

Drawing inspiration from those writers' cultural focus, I have used ethnographic methods as well as the theories and methods of ethnomusicology to try to get at one version of what the music is "really about." Particularly inspirational for me have been Alan Merriam's model of cyclical relationships between concept, behavior, and sound (1964, 32–35); Timothy Rice's focus on formative processes—how music is historically constructed, socially maintained, and individually created and experienced (1987, 472–80); and issues pertinent to the ethnography of musical performance (McLeod and Herndon 1980; Béhague 1984). The authors of these models individually and collectively propose ways of viewing music as a dynamic process, including but not limited to a sound object. Though I do not make explicit reference to these concepts at every point, they are embedded in the arguments in subsequent chapters, especially those related to the value of "native" categories in understanding music making, the importance of musical events, and the ways in which musicians and fans respond strategically to questions about music making.

How do participants in musical performances or events engage with the various cultural matrices that surround and inform, and are surrounded and informed by, musical performance?[27] One might argue, as Steven Feld does, that as they attend to or participate in a musical event, they come to comprehend it, to understand its meanings, through a series of "interpretive moves" (1994b, 86–89). Such moves, which he describes as locational, categorical, associational, reflective, and evaluative, can be highly individual and idiosyncratic, for they draw upon each individual's past experiences.[28] By extending Feld's argument, one comes to see that such individual understandings become social or cultural meanings when they are shared among and/or debated by participants. That is, "Collective systems of meanings are created as individuals reveal their individual understandings to one another . . . through [their] input into the shared perspective from individual experience. . . . The collective system of meanings is also cumulative, like the individual consciousness. It expands as individuals face new experiences together, inform each other of individual perceptions against the background of what they already have in common, or discover additional facets of their individual systems of meanings to be shared" (Hannerz 1980, 284).

The musical event, participation in it, responses to it, and talk about it force participants to face new experiences together, share perceptions, and discover new ways to share their understandings. The resultant meanings, then, are never wholly fixed. They are constantly emerging and being shaped through the interpretive moves of various participants in musical events and the contribution of those moves to and their acceptance (or rejection) in larger systems of meaning. For my purposes, then, musical meaning is what emerges from the shared and variable understandings that participants bring to and create through participation in musical events (see Jackson 2000).

Moreover, as the wording above indicates, meanings never emerge ex nihilo. Individuals who participate in musical events bring with them understandings from other kinds of musical events and other realms of activity; they bring ways of deploying interpretive moves that may have as much to do with jazz performance as with other kinds. In that sense, the discourses of meaning that surround jazz performance and its interpretation are inseparable from and overlap in significant ways with other discourses about meaning, the nature of "artistic creation," and the functions of music, for example. Attempting to understand the meanings that are attached to and emerge from jazz performance, then, means entering into a complex discourse always and already in progress (Williams 1977, 35–42; Lipsitz 1990, 99–100), one that has tangible connections to other discourses.

My method of understanding that process of discourse merging and development has been to focus on the jazz scene in New York City, where

I conducted fieldwork continuously between July of 1994 and December of 1995 and more sporadically from 1997 to 2001. Some aspects of my fieldwork were informed by the research I did between January and July of 1992, also in New York City, for a master's thesis (Jackson 1992). The contacts I made with musicians for the earlier project allowed me to begin understanding and mapping the jazz scene and to see it and the performances that take place on it as the most appropriate unit of investigation (rather than an era, an individual musician, or a body of recordings). Through following some of those musicians in the time between my first fieldwork period and my second, I gained access to and an understanding of the larger network of individuals, venues, record labels, educational institutions, and media that comprise the scene that I describe in chapters 3 and 4.

In the summer of 1994 I began contacting some of the musicians I had met previously, such as guitarist Peter Bernstein, saxophonist Antonio Hart, and drummer Gregory Hutchinson, to interest them in my new project. I explained to them that I was interested in observing their performances and recording sessions to gain a better understanding of the workings of the scene and their place in it. In addition, I told them that I would welcome suggestions for other musicians whose perspectives they thought I should seek. I also reestablished the few relationships I had with recording industry personnel, most notably Sharon Blynn, then at Verve Records. In addition, to acquaint myself with what was happening on the New York scene and beyond, I started systematically reading the national and local jazz periodicals (*Down Beat, JazzTimes,* and *Cadence*) as well as jazz-related articles in newspapers such as the *New York Times* and the *Village Voice.* I focused not only on feature articles and short news items but also on reviews of recordings and advertisements. In the process I familiarized myself with a number of performers, producers, and recording industry personnel of whom I had not previously been aware; learned something of the current activities of ones about whom I already was aware; and gained greater understanding of their backgrounds and relationships to one another and the scene. Through these different forms of inquiry, I started to develop a picture of the variety of jazz activity occurring in the city. Each individual with whom I was personally acquainted led or introduced me to others. They also kept me apprised of performances, recordings, recording sessions, and other information about the functioning of the scene.

Particularly toward the end of August 1994, I started regularly attending the performances of musicians I knew as well as the performances of others. During breaks, I would introduce myself to the musicians and to interested audience members and tell them about my study.[29] I informed them that I was a graduate student studying jazz performers on the New York scene and was interested in finding out "what makes this music so powerful and important." I told the musicians that participation in the study would require my seeing them perform and record as well as my interviewing them. Most responded favorably and exchanged phone numbers with me. Not all, however, responded to my phone calls or agreed to become part of the study. In particular, my attempt to include female musicians in my sample was hampered by their tacit refusals, even in those situations where other musicians or scene participants vouched for me.[30]

My entry into some areas of the scene was easier because of another contact I made in August of 1994. Through Robert G. O'Meally of Columbia University I met Peter Watrous, then the only full-time jazz critic for the *New York Times*. I served as Watrous's intern from September of 1994 to August of 1995. My duties consisted of helping him to catalog and file the dozens of recordings and books he received on a weekly basis. In exchange for that work I was able to accompany him to nearly every performance he attended (when my own plans did not conflict with his) and was introduced to musicians, club owners, booking agents, publicists, photographers, record label personnel, and writers whom he knew. I also gained insight both into the role of the media in the scene's functioning and into the music editorial procedures of the *New York Times*. Sometimes that understanding emerged from direct conversation with Watrous. At other times it came more obliquely, through attending and discussing shows with him and comparing the verbal "drafts" of his reviews with what eventually was—or was not—published.

My primary method was participant observation: I made observations at musical events—rehearsals, live performances, and recording sessions—in which I functioned as a participant in some capacity. I also made observations in those settings in which I listened to or discussed recorded music with other individuals. Evaluations of recordings generally included conversation about the background of the artists and the conditions under which recordings were made, if such information was known to anyone present. I kept chronological field notes recording the observations I made at musical events as well as my impressions from listening sessions. Among the data recorded were the date, place, time, and relative length of musical events or sessions; the role(s) of specific individuals or groups in those events; narration of moment-to-moment communication and interaction among the participants (see Jackson 1992); listings of the musicians present and the songs played; the responses of audience members to a musical event; records of conversations with other participants; and my own impressions and evaluations. During musical events I produced handwritten "scratch notes" that, combined with my recollections and other "headnotes" (see Sanjek 1990; Ottenberg 1990), were the basis for typed field notes. I typed these notes as soon as possible after a musical event, generally before going to sleep or, when that was not feasible, upon awakening later in the day. In the typewritten notes I attempted to capture as much as I could remember of what I observed but had not written down, mingling reporting with interpretation and evaluation. In addition, my chronological field notes contain records of phone conversations and other discussions that were not tape-recorded, appointments, phone numbers, contact information, biographical sketches, and any other information directly related to or drawn from the participant observation portion of my fieldwork—both at and away from musical events.

The central activities that comprised my fieldwork entailed progressively deeper involvement with the functioning of the scene. In the first couple of months I limited my activities to attending live performances alone and making contact with musicians and other participants. I used this time to establish myself as a regular on the scene, to be recognized as a participant in it. That process required major shifts in my lifestyle, particularly my sleeping habits. I quickly found myself waking between noon and 1 PM and retiring between 4 and 5 AM. Such a schedule made it easier for me to hang out with the musicians I knew and was coming to know. Being able to stay through the last set of a musical performance (such as the 2 AM set at Bradley's) and, more importantly, for the socializing that took place after it ended allowed me to participate in conversations that the most casual scene participants—or those with day jobs—typically miss. In part because of that schedule, my involvement with friends and colleagues not related to my research became largely nonexistent. By the end of my fieldwork period, the jazz scene had become my social world: whenever I went to live performances I would see someone I knew well in the audience, whether or not I knew the musicians who were performing. I'd frequently sit through a set or two with whomever I met and go with them afterward to Bradley's for the late set.

During those times I engaged in conversation with musicians and others about aspects of performances and got recommendations about upcoming performances that I should attend as well as certain "blessed records" that they liked or felt had exerted great influence on them.[31] In some cases, discussion of such recordings was triggered by the music that happened to be playing on the stereo system in the venue.[32] Sometimes musicians who didn't know me well would test me by asking me to identify the performer(s) on a recording by listening attentively. Making both my own choices about performances and following the recommendations of musicians and Peter Watrous, I generally attended no fewer than four live performances per week during the fieldwork period, sometimes going to three venues in the course of one evening. By attending performances and studying blessed recordings, I gained more insight into the criteria that distinguished good performers and recordings. I also enhanced my ability to recognize songs from the standard jazz repertoire and to analyze performances instantly, discerning elements of form, feel, meter, harmony, and substitutions as well as other parameters.

After this early period I started attending performances with the musicians and other individuals whose acquaintance I had made. The conversations that resulted from our reactions to what we were hearing and experiencing helped me to understand the evaluative criteria of individuals on the scene and to compare those criteria with my own. Among the many things that I learned in this process was that my criteria were not significantly different from those of the musicians and listeners with whom I interacted. Like them, I was listening, for example, for aspects of form, arrangement, style, creativity, and play in individual performance and group interaction.

In late September I started attending recording sessions sporadically as well as spending time with musicians outside of performance contexts, such as in their apartments or on social outings. These activities, combined with the observation of numerous performances, helped me to ascertain the "communicative norms" of individuals on the scene. Charles L. Briggs (1986) recommends that one attempt to learn these norms in the early phases of fieldwork, paying particular attention to how queries are framed, who has the right to ask questions, of whom, and on which topics. Based on that investigation, one can then design an interview methodology that takes into account what one has discovered.

In late October I started reviewing my field notes to see which issues had been prominent during my field experience. In those notes I had included potential questions to ask in interviews, such as questions about the role of various people in the recording industry, the importance of audience interaction, and conflicts among musicians in touring groups. I also noticed topics on which I needed more information. In comparing the issues raised in my notes with my central questions, I began to formulate an interview schedule focused on the dynamics of the scene, its various agents and actors, and interactive parameters of performance. I started conducting tape-recorded formal interviews with musicians in November 1994 and continued until September 1995. Although some interviews were conducted in restaurants, cafés, or offices, the majority were conducted in the homes of the musicians. Conducting interviews in musicians' homes generated other questions regarding their record collections and memorabilia.[33] (I also conducted a series of informal interviews with recording industry personnel, most frequently in performance venues, that allowed me to understand the work they did and its function in the scene.) I prepared for musicians' interviews by reviewing whatever notes I had taken on performances by them, reviewing comments that had been made about them by other musicians or in the press, and listening to a sample of their recordings to generate questions specifically geared toward them. When interviewing non-musicians, my questions focused on their work, their pathways to it, and their knowledge and understanding of music.

The musicians' interviews, although guided by the schedule, were open-ended. A few lasted as little as ninety minutes. More typically, they lasted from two to four hours, and some had to be done in multiple sittings. I reviewed each of the tapes and took detailed notes. In comparing the notes, I identified common concerns and selectively transcribed relevant portions. Those excerpts were then combined in word-processing documents so that I could look at individual comments on the same topic in close proximity to one another and thus make comparisons and further refine the concepts that emerged from them. The data gathered from the interviews provided more questions for observation in the last phases of fieldwork, particularly regarding the ways in which performers actualized their normative statements about performance. I rendered my transcriptions as literally as possible, making no attempts to convert the grammatical irregularities of speech into the regularities readers are accustomed to seeing. My reason for doing so was to preserve the moments of "interpretive time" that characterized the interviewees' and my attempts to "force awareness to words" (Feld 1994b, 93).

In the spring of 1995, while I continued attending live performances, observing recording sessions, and conducting interviews, my involvement with the scene became deeper as I became a freelance writer, researching a two-page sketch of jazz past and present for the *New York Times Magazine* (Jackson 1995) as well as writing a number of artist biographies, brochures, and record reviews for various labels and publications. These activities exposed me to more of the behind-the-scenes work that led not only to writing about record releases and public performances but to the recordings or performances themselves. I had already begun to learn, through my internship with Watrous, the kinds of information that record labels provided to writers, but by becoming one myself, I participated in the creation and dissemination of such information.[34] I also learned more about the role that publicity firms, record release parties, and other promotional activities play in the day-to-day functioning of the scene by fostering familiarity and contact among critics, recording industry personnel, and musicians.

Through engaging in all these activities over an eighteen-month period, I gained an understanding of the complexity of the interactions that comprise the scene. The roles of specific individuals on the scene were often multiple and overlapping. Writers whom I associated only with the popular press sometimes had serious commitments to the recording industry. At least one of them, Jeff Levenson, moved from a job as a writer (jazz editor at *Billboard* magazine) to a position at a record label (Warner Brothers). I also noted the cyclical nature of the scene, which was characterized by the prolonged absence of many performers from the city during the summer festival season, the opening and frequent closing of clubs, the launching and failure of jazz labels, and the signing and dropping of performers from those labels' rosters.

My fieldwork in the mid-1990s and in 2000–2001 forms the basis for this book, which has three major sections. The first, "Black, Brown, and Beige," which includes this chapter and the next, examines the issues raised by the study of jazz in the 1990s and, more importantly, directly engages the issues of race, culture, history, memory, education, and experience that are integral to (and frequently debated with regard to) the making of jazz. Indeed, one of the most trenchant questions in chapter 2 is whether jazz is African American music, American music, or something else altogether. My response hinges on problematizing notions of race/culture and history/memory, seeing them as constructs that have been strategically deployed by various commentators. While the writings of these commentators frequently conflate race and culture with one another, they stake their claims to authority by valorizing history at the expense

of memory without seeing the two as related rather than opposed entities. As a corrective, I consider the pathways taken by various musicians
to performing, recording, and listening to jazz. In doing so, I draw attention to the roles of practical activity, lived experience, and notions
of social, economic, and cultural capital to argue that there are compelling reasons to consider jazz African American.

The second section, "Scenes in the City," builds on the first by examining the convergence of musicians' and other participants' pathways on
the New York jazz scene. I argue that one cannot have a comprehensive
understanding of the meanings that might be attached to the music without relating it to the geographic, economic, and social contexts in which
it is performed and evaluated. In chapter 3, therefore, I suggest that consideration of space and spatiality enhances a jazz historical narrative that
generally renders geography as inert and subservient to time. In particular, those two concepts highlight the impact that attempts to regulate the
use of space in cities has had on jazz historically—determining, among
other things, where jazz musicians can perform, how often, and for whom.
Zoning laws, uneven spatial development, and a shift from an industrial
to a service economy over the last several decades have been just as crucial as developments in musical style for the making and interpreting of
jazz. Toward the end of chapter 3, I argue that jazz performance is inseparable from a loose and shifting assemblage of agents and institutions—
the jazz scene—that facilitates (and inhibits) the public presentation of the
music and musicians in live performance and on recordings. In chapter 4,
I examine in more detail the contours of the New York scene in the 1990s,
describing its network of agents and institutions and their relation to one
another.

The first two sections provide the context in which one might most
fruitfully understand the book's title and the framework developed in
the third section, "Blowin' the Blues Away." Chapter 5 focuses on the
normative and evaluative statements that my interviewees made about
performing and learning to perform jazz. I use those statements to hy-
pothesize a "blues aesthetic" that encompasses what performers are trying to do and how they evaluate musical events. In chapter 6, I argue that
discourses on race and culture as well as history and memory work with
a blues aesthetic to frame jazz performance as a spiritually oriented ritualized activity. In chapter 7, I analyze three studio recordings and three
live performances to illustrate the efficacy of seeing jazz through the
lenses of a blues aesthetic and ritualization. In the final chapter, I consider

the implications that the perspective presented here might have for future research and writing on jazz as well as other forms of music. Finally, noting the ways that the scene has changed since I conducted the research, I speculate on the directions in which the musicians may head in the future.

CHAPTER 2

History and Memory, Pathways and Practices

The African Americanness of Jazz

History will either off you or make you valid. . . . I think
the idea now is for blacks to write about the history of our
music. It's time for that because whites have been doing it all
the time. It's time for us to do it ourselves and tell it like it is.
The whites have a whitewash look at our music. Naturally,
they're going to try to ooze off as much as they can to the
whites, but they can't, because we're documented in records
and the truth will stand.

—Dizzy Gillespie, quoted in Taylor (1993, 126–27)

There are perhaps no issues more vexed in discussions of jazz than the concepts of race and culture. Whenever one encounters them, whether those offering their opinions are musicians, critics, historians, or musicologists, what is arguably at stake is legitimation: who can rightfully lay claim to jazz and on what grounds? Is it African American music, America's classical music, or just music (Walser 1995)? When stories about jazz, however conceived, are told, which narratives receive priority: those transmitted in historical writing, those produced by critics, or those based in memory and orally transmitted among musicians and aficionados of the music? In differing ways, anyone concerned with answering these questions has to turn the past into something usable. It becomes a charter variously interpreted to authorize (or invalidate) cultural practices (Appadurai 1981; Trouillot 1995; Sider and Smith 1997).

Even without consideration of jazz, race and culture are highly contested terms in the United States. Many lay commentators use the two interchangeably. Both, after all, are rough-and-ready ways of explaining and understanding the myriad differences between individuals and social groups. For most people, substituting one for the other perhaps seems unobjectionable. Scholars, however, have often thought it better to distinguish the terms. In recent academic writing, then, race is a sociopolitical construction (Holt 2000), an emergent result of processes of "racial formation" (Omi and Winant 1994) derived from visual markers: based on physical appearance (i.e., phenotype) any person might be ascribed membership in one of a number of groups that can ultimately trace their ancestry to specific geographic locales (Asia, Africa, and Europe, for example). For its part, culture, particularly as used by anthropologists, is a term that focuses on the widely varying practices that distinguish human groups from one another.

So defined, these terms are not without their difficulties. What happens, for example, when we heed the scientists who have convincingly argued that as a matter of biology and/or genetics race does not exist? Do we then also conclude that those who see race as a social construction mean to discount the effects that race—in the non-academic sense—might have on people's daily lives?[1] Does a focus on constructedness support assertions that, in the twenty-first century, the United States is postracial? One need not go that far, for it is certainly possible to disentangle seeing race as an arbitrary construction from seeing it as lacking any real function or meaning. More than likely, constructionists hope that emphasizing race's social and political valence, rather than its "naturalness," may give everyone—scholars, politicians, and laypeople—tools to understand and minimize the negative effects of policies and beliefs derived from simplistic notions centered on phenotypes.

Where culture is concerned, anthropologists, at least since the 1970s, have questioned whether it is a useful way to understand the ways that human beings relate to one another and the world around them. At worst, some uses of the culture concept draw attention away from the cumulative, processual nature of human interaction. Rather than seeing human groups as dynamic and adaptive, such usage encourages us to see them as static, reductively described via an inventory of habits, customs, foodways, moral codes, and the like. Similarly, by focusing on culture as something shared, some anthropologists' writings have had the (unintended?) effect of deemphasizing the conflicts between members of cultural groups—for example, those situations where behavioral and moral matters are contested (Abu-Lughod 1991). As a result, those researchers interested in addressing the complexity and variability of different groups' practices have increasingly had to suggest conceptual alternatives that carry fewer of the homogeneous, utopian connotations that culture has accrued.[2]

To people outside academia, these debates may appear precious and disconnected from common sense. Race and culture aren't constructions: they are real things that people see and live every day (Hall 1980). As categories, they draw attention to the similarities that allow us to group people and concepts together. In other words, race and culture, if they are constructions, are relational ones. Whether or not points of similarity are specified by a particular writer or speaker, color-based labels such as black, white, yellow, and red presuppose commonalities among *races* that in the academic sense are attributable to *cultures*. That is, by substituting a racial or color designation for a cultural one, an individual implicitly says that those terms signify roughly the same thing and assumes that others equate them as well. In such cases, laypeople and scholars' statements alike reveal that race per se has less to do with how people look (as the visual markers would suggest) than it does, in the Geertzian sense, with culture: those practices and frameworks for interpretation they share.[3]

Where race and culture are collapsed into one another, history and memory are frequently kept apart despite their similarities. "Both processes," Geneviève Fabre and Robert G. O'Meally have written, "involve the retrieval of felt experience from the mix and jumble of the past. . . . [But at] least until quite recently, many observers would agree that while history at its finest is a discipline, . . . memory is something else again, something less. Memory, these same observers would say, is by definition a personal activity, subject to the biases, quirks, and rhythms of the individual's mind" (Fabre and O'Meally 1994, 5). That is, where people's memories are variable and fallible at best, historians' focus on facts and responsible interpretation raises their work to a presumably more objective level. The process through which certain events and social actors come to be regarded as historically significant, however, is not in the end drastically different from the reconstruction and sense-making processes of memory. After all, the "balanced and sober modes of analysis" (Fabre and O'Meally 1994, 6) that characterize the writing of history are equally selective and interpretive. In Michel-Rolph Trouillot's characterization (1995), historians base their conclusions on data gathered from archives of various kinds, specially maintained repositories of papers and artifacts, to be sure, but more generally from whatever records remain from the past: newspapers, magazines, books, photographs, and audio and video recordings, for example. Archivists of whatever kind cannot fully document and preserve every bit of potential historical data. They must continually decide which items to keep and which to discard. Furthermore, they must develop aids for researchers who might use the materials they have kept: Which materials do they group together? Which criteria do they employ in determining what those groupings will be? The evidence of the archive and its documents, then, are necessarily filtered through the biases, quirks, and rhythms of the minds of archivists and historians before they reach readers or auditors.[4]

Debates over the relative importance of race and culture in jazz's development and performance are intimately tied to those over the relative importance of history and memory as evidence for whatever claims one makes about the music. Those writers who favor particular visions of jazz—as African American music or America's classical music, for example—frequently appeal to history to support their assertions. In the process, they attempt to raise their understandings to a level higher than the supposedly ideological, selective memories of others. One clear example of how the dyads race/culture and history/memory are relationally connected is the ongoing debate about the nature and constitution of the jazz tradition, a debate that was both fresh and resonant during my fieldwork. Both sets of categories provide the means through which understandings of tradition and claims over legitimacy are configured in written and musical discourse, as Gillespie's previously quoted comment suggests.[5]

The jazz tradition, one might say, is the invention of Martin Williams, who in 1970 first published a collection of essays that put the definite article in front of the words *jazz* and *tradition*.[6] Williams further solidified his conception of a coherent tradition with the release of the multi-LP *Smithsonian Collection of Classic Jazz* in 1973. Whether he intended this outcome or not, his choices for that compilation became for a time the de facto standard repertoire in the teaching of jazz history, the "classic" recordings made by the most important performers. Partially because of the Smithsonian's imprimatur, numerous municipal and school libraries purchased the original set as well as its later revisions. Moreover, given the collection's wide availability up to the late 1990s, the authors of a number of jazz textbooks, including Tirro (1977), Porter (1993), and Gridley (1997), chose the majority of their listening examples from the Smithsonian set.[7]

The tradition as Williams understands it emerges from the work of a series of exemplary figures. Great improvisers like Louis Armstrong and Charlie Parker "reassessed the music's past, gave it a new vocabulary, or at least repronounced its old one," while great composers like Duke Ellington and Thelonious Monk "gave the music a synthesis and larger form" (1983, 5). Williams's tradition also has clear racial and gendered dimensions. He writes, "Jazz is a music evolved by black men in the United States. It has been in general best played by [them], and its development has been dependent upon their artistic leadership. But at the same time, it is a music which men of other races, and men in other countries, can play and sometimes play excellently" (249; see also Wilmer 1970, 3). Because of his language, one can't help but wonder whether he is conflating race and culture (were these musicians capable of providing artistic leadership simply because they had dark skin?). In addition, his (tacked-on) acknowledgment that blacks aren't the only skilled performers might leave some nonblack musicians and listeners wondering about the legitimacy of their involvement with jazz. Williams's masculinist version of tradition rests on the belief that the deeds of African American men are central to any understanding of jazz. Indeed, the narrative he presents has its support in what he sees as the determining roles of race and culture and in the play of history and memory: he chose outstanding African American male performers and composers from the much wider universe of musicians whose work he knew (remembered) and, through writing and argumentation, fashioned them into a now foundational account.

Williams's invented tradition is, of course, not the only one: writers like André Hodeir (1956) and Gunther Schuller (1968) had already assembled similar pantheons of greats to support their own visions of a jazz tradition. Interestingly, all three brought to their work ideas and prescriptions originating outside the music they discussed. Williams, a former English student enamored of the New Criticism he read in college, was interested in the degree to which close reading of recordings could illuminate jazz's artistic qualities (Gennari 1991, 2006). Hodeir and Schuller both brought concert music backgrounds to their encounters with and writings on jazz. Whatever their backgrounds, these three writers molded what they saw as primarily African American musical practices in the image of Western literary and musical traditions.[8] Along with a number of others (e.g., Baraka 1963; Tirro 1977; Collier 1978; Sales 1984; Porter et al. 1993; Gridley 1997), moreover, they have created what we might call the master narrative of jazz history—one concerned with rapid advances in harmonic and rhythmic vocabulary and successive stylistic permutations spearheaded by a number of "great men," Ferdinand "Jelly Roll" Morton, Louis Armstrong, Duke Ellington, Charlie Parker, John Coltrane, and Ornette Coleman, among them. Taken together, those musicians and their body of recordings form the central core of jazz: without due consideration of their work, the argument might go, no understanding of the music is possible.

Other writers have convincingly pointed out all there is to critique in the resulting narrative (DeVeaux 1991; Tomlinson 1991; Gabbard 1995; Tucker 2000). In effect, such writing can do little more than present a view of jazz history as selective as the memories it attempts to organize. The point is not that being selective is inherently bad. No single historical work can be truly comprehensive: some stories, some figures, some styles have to be omitted or discussed less extensively. Selective or not, though, the wide acceptance of Williams, Hodeir, and Schuller's interpretations has allowed them to become a baseline for discussions of the roles of race, culture, history, and memory in jazz. At one and the same time, they provide evidence for both those who endorse their visions and those who might take a different view.

Although it is impossible to say how widely Williams's work informed subsequent debates, by the late 1970s the nature of the jazz tradition was also being discussed publicly by musicians and critics, who prominently featured the catchphrase "in the tradition." Indeed, the phrase might have entered wide circulation as the title of a 1979 LP by saxophonist Arthur Blythe.[9] Blythe was among a number of musicians based in New York City in the 1970s who developed their craft in semicommercial loft spaces in Lower Manhattan. At the time and since, performances in these spaces were celebrated for wide-ranging, exploratory music that frequently fell outside the stylistic parameters that club owners and record executives thought marketable.[10]

In that context, Blythe's work is notable for its eclectic but respectful embrace of the past. In an interview published shortly after the album's release, he explained why he chose the approach he did: "What prompted me to do that album now was not an attempt to be part of any trend, because several players are going back to the tradition, but just a sense that now the feeling would be right for an album like this. . . . The music on *In the Tradition* is basic and fundamental to so-called jazz. If you don't acknowledge anything of that nature then what are you doing?" (Blumenthal 1980, 64). Indeed, he amplifies his comment later in assessing his own work as well as that of like-minded performers: "People don't have to be innovative to be creative. For a while everybody was trying to be innovative, but everybody isn't. I've always felt that the innovative thing comes about when one does his homework being creative.... You don't have to reject everything that has been dealt with already and go look for the new horizons, because you could be out in the dark where you don't see shit" (Blumenthal 1980, 64).[11] On the recording he leads his quartet through compositions by Duke Ellington, John Coltrane, and Fats Waller. His repertoire choices repeat, in a different medium, the canonizing gestures of earlier writers, but with a signal difference. Through the inclusion of two original compositions, one might say that Blythe sees himself as someone capable not only of playing *in* the tradition, but also of *adding to it*. One result of his recording, as Francis Davis suggested in a piece originally published in 1983, was the addition of a new phrase to the discourse on jazz: "When Arthur Blythe formed a quartet . . . and began mixing tunes by Ellington, Waller, Monk, and Coltrane in with his originals, he gave a movement—or more precisely, a moment—its name and unintentionally became its figurehead. Any performance that swings or follows a chord sequence or makes an overt reference to the past is now said to be in the tradition. And any performance which doesn't do any of those things isn't" (Davis 1986, 194–95).

Thus, although many commentators have associated a "neoconservative" return to traditional playing with the rise of Wynton Marsalis in the early 1980s (Pareles 1984; Sancton 1990), Blythe's comments make clear that other musicians were motivated to explore previous styles without the prompting of the young trumpeter. Indeed, many of the issues that would be part of the debate regarding tradition and conservatism in the 1980s and '90s are prefigured in Blythe's statement and his work.[12]

Through the 1980s, greater investment by major recording labels, more extensive media coverage, and the institutionalization of jazz in schools and performing arts institutions strengthened the related visions of tradition presented by Williams, Blythe, and, eventually, Marsalis. Many of the musicians who would become prominent figures in the mid-1990s had their interest in acoustic jazz sparked by the evidence of a venerable jazz tradition around them. Critic Tom Piazza describes the era in this way: "At the beginning of the 1980s, it would have been hard to imagine young musicians who were playing demanding acoustic jazz being signed to major labels.... But by 1990 they were appearing constantly, and at an amazing rate" (Piazza 1997, 96). While the interest young musicians and fans were displaying might have been regarded as a sign of the music's vitality, there were critics who were less sanguine about the new-comers. "Predictably," Piazza continues,

> the phenomenon ... stirred up a backlash among reviewers ... with odd racial overtones, as many of the music's young players were, for the first time in quite a while, African-American. The gist of the attacks was that the young musicians, instead of making a Coltrane-like, self-immolatory jour-ney of self-discovery, were focusing too much energy studying previous work in the idiom. Along with this, the attacks ran, they paid entirely too much attention to their appearance—dressing in suits and ties with a sophis-tication that hadn't been seen in jazz musicians since the Miles Davis of the mid-1960s[,] and this effort was taken to be symptomatic of the superficial-ity of the Yuppie '80s. There was a sneering, hostile quality to many of the attacks; the young musicians were being characterized as "neo-conservative," "reactionary," and "Reaganite." ... Some enlightened soul even came up with the snide phrase "young black men in suits" to characterize the move-ment. (97)[13]

As the decade ended and Lincoln Center chose Wynton Marsalis to be the artistic director of its summer "Classical Jazz" series, the attacks grew more vicious. Critics regarded young black men in suits as some-thing more pernicious than conservative: they were antiwhite.

In a widely cited *Down Beat* interview (Crouch 1987), Marsalis had stressed the need for budding jazz musicians to study the work of the masters. And, since all of the masters he named were African American (as had been the case with Williams), many commentators saw his vision of tradition as racially exclusive. Even more, Marsalis's seeming refusal to feature tributes to white musicians in Lincoln Center's programs and the absence of white musicians in various young black bandleaders' bands were prima facie evidence that Marsalis and his acolytes were militantly rejecting white musicians.[14] Likewise, the record labels that seemed to be favoring young black musicians such as trumpeter Roy Hargrove and guitarist Mark Whitfield for presumably lucrative recording contracts were also—and quite paradoxically—regarded as antiwhite. It mattered little that the same label that promoted Hargrove also put significant promotional energy behind a white saxophonist named Christopher Hol-lyday or that Harry Connick Jr., Joey DeFrancesco, Benny Green, and Ryan Kisor were also signed to major labels at that time (for a more complete list, see DiMartino 1991). Furthermore, comments by African American musicians to the effect that jazz was a form of African Ameri-can music would lead writers like James Lincoln Collier, Gene Lees, and Terry Teachout by the mid-1990s to level charges of "reverse racism" at them. In other words, those young players were not only denying the contributions of white musicians to jazz, they were also denying white musicians the opportunity to support themselves playing a music they too loved and, as Americans, should receive equal credit for having created.[15]

The crux of the argument, then, was that jazz was historically an *American* music rather than an African American one. In differing ways, these writers each conceded that jazz had (partial) roots in African American musics or resulted from a mixture of European and African elements (Collier 1993, 183–224; Lees 1994, 187–246; Teachout 1995).[16] That is, where African Americanness *might once* have been an important factor in the development of jazz, its impact registered only in the past: in post–Civil Rights–era America, it no longer mattered. In fact, labeling jazz as African American ran counter to the music's democratic, integrationist spirit and was a *politically correct* attempt to elevate black musicians while erasing the contributions of white ones. The introduction of Richard M. Sudhalter's *Lost Chords: White Musicians and Their Contribution to Jazz* (1999b) places it squarely in this ideological camp. He writes, for example,

> The rage for "multiculturalism" in the arts—as in society at large—has led to the reassessment of, and often elevation of, artistic traditions of non-European and non-white cultures. With it has come recognition of many black artists and writers whose achievements long stood hidden from public sight. . . . Applied to jazz history, such thinking has spawned a view of early white efforts as musically insignificant and—particularly in the 1920s and '30s—vastly overpublicized. Jazz, says the now-accepted canon, is black: there have been no white innovators, few white soloists of real distinction; the best white musicians (with an exception or two) were only dilute copies of black originals, and in any case exerted a lasting influence only on other white musicians. (xvi)

Such a state of affairs leads him to lament the resulting distortion, for in truth "in at least one important field, black and white once worked side by side, often defying the racial and social norms of their time to create a music whose graces reflected the combined effort." Jazz represents, then, true, nonpoliticized multiculturalism, "living proof that the races and ethnic groups *can* cooperate to the common good" (xvii).

Drawing inspiration from the work of Arthur Schlesinger Jr., Sudhalter asserts that his work is grounded in historical facts and therefore both ideologically neutral and capable of correcting the sins of those who have forgotten the role that whites have played in the music's development. In his estimation writers who have unduly stressed the African Americanness of jazz and players who hire musicians presumably based only on their color are betraying the music's mandate to be a model of interracial cooperation. (Exactly who gave the music this mandate is never clearly specified; unlike other elements singled out for historical investigation, this assertion has gone largely unexamined.)[17] Sudhalter and the others contrast their views with those put forward by Albert Murray, Stanley Crouch, and Wynton Marsalis, prominent figures on the board of Jazz at Lincoln Center.[18] These latter three they accuse of overlooking the importance of figures like Bix Beiderbecke, Benny Goodman, Gil Evans, and Bill Evans through programming that focuses almost exclusively on the work of African American performers and composers. Furthermore, they assert that the aesthetic judgments of Murray and the others, which foreground blues playing and swing, implicitly exclude white musicians from meaningful and publicly sanctioned participation in jazz.

Although many of these arguments have been stated in almost identical terms for decades (see, for example, Hentoff 1961a), they had a particular resonance near the close of the twentieth century. The use of words and phrases such as *meritocracy, reverse racism,* and *politically correct* connected the project of Collier, Sudhalter, Teachout, and Lees to the affirmative action debates of the 1990s and perhaps constitutes an attempt to resist any reframing of historical narrative.[19] Even worse, in a move reminiscent of the era's conservative politicians and radio talk show hosts, Collier, Lees, Teachout, and Sudhalter placed selected black musicians and scholars in roles similar to those voluntarily assumed by black conservatives such as Clarence Thomas, Shelby Steele, and Ward Connerly, making Louis Armstrong, Duke Ellington, and Gerald Early, for example, unwitting yes-men for arguments they might never have independently endorsed. Toward the end of "The Color of Jazz," for example, Teachout quotes Duke Ellington as having told an interviewer in 1945, "Twenty years ago when jazz was finding an audience *[sic]*, it may have had more of a Negro character. The Negro element is still important. But jazz has become a part of America. There are as many white musicians playing it as Negro. . . . We are all working along more or less the same lines. We learn from each other. Jazz is American now. *American* is the big word" (Teachout 1995, 53; see also Tucker 1993, 254).

Teachout then comments, "Five decades later, this spirit is being undermined by cultural politicians for whom the word 'American' has validity only when it lies on the far side of a hyphen. That jazz, the ultimate cultural melting pot and arguably America's most important contribution to the fine arts, would have fallen victim to such divisive thinking is an especially telling index of the unhappy state of our culture at the end of the 20th century" (Teachout 1995, 53). One wonders, however, what Ellington, who often insisted on calling his work "Negro music" rather than jazz (Ellington 1939), might have thought of his words being so characterized, particularly without the context of his comments being considered. He was, after all, speaking near the end of the Second World War; was talking to an unidentified, but presumably white, interviewer; and knew that his words would appear in *PM,* a "liberal newsmagazine" whose "readership [was] more accustomed to [reading about] opera, symphonies, and art museums" than jazz (Kelley 2009, 132). When one remembers how important dissembling has been for African American survival in the United States (Hine 1989; Roberts 1989) and how few negative opinions Ellington ever expressed publicly, his intentions become germane. His repeated references to jazz's modern, American qualities (he likens the music to the automobile and the airplane) make it seem that he might have been self-consciously striving to present a patriotic view, whether or not it expressed all that he thought (see Cohen 2010, 227–28, 232, 239, 242). Teachout's interpretation, however, doesn't leave room for that possibility.

In the collective work of Collier, Lees, Teachout, and Sudhalter, then, to mention race is to be divisive and to delay the arrival of a truly color-blind society. Like the conservative cultural critics with whom I've aligned them, they have effectively turned the rhetoric of the 1950s and 1960s American civil rights movement against it. A clear example of this rhetorical strategy is Teachout's plea for a world in which "artists are judged not by the color of their skin but by the content of their choruses" (Teachout 1995, 53).[20] In short, even though Collier, Lees, Teachout, and Sudhalter defend their project as neutral historical recuperation, their ideology is just as apparent as the one they seek to expose.

In fact, the writers and musicians they single out for criticism share some of their assumptions regarding the primacy of skill and the relative importance of race. Murray (1976), Crouch, and Marsalis, to be sure, feel that the essence of jazz lies in the "fire" of its fundamentals: blues feeling, timbral nuance, and rhythmic swing. These immutable fundamentals (see DeVeaux 1997, 17; Rudinow 1994)[21] are most profoundly audible in the work of a group of musical masters like Morton, Armstrong, Ellington, Monk, and Coltrane. One might infer, as Teachout does, that the fundamentals were chosen to exclude white musicians. I see no other way to understand his inference beyond seeing in it a conflation of race and culture. He assumes, based on their programming choices and their list of masters, that Marsalis, Crouch, and Murray believe that blues and swing are the exclusive province of black men and that they attribute the excellence of African American jazz musicians to their skin color (cf. Lock 1988, 115–16). Teachout used as evidence esteemed *New Yorker* critic Whitney Balliett's assertion (1977) that Murray's view of jazz history in *Stomping the Blues* (1976) was racist, for Murray allegedly discussed only one white musician (Gene Krupa) in main text of the book.

It is difficult to substantiate these charges when one carefully examines the writing in question. Indeed, it seems as though Teachout and Balliett have grossly misread Murray, seeing in his work only that which seems to support their opposition to him. Murray, in fact, is primarily concerned with asserting that jazz performance is about skill and nuance rather than racial essences or inborn gifts, particularly when, using blues as a synonym for jazz, he writes:

> No matter how deeply moved a musician may be, whether by personal, social, or even aesthetic circumstances, he must always play notes that fulfill the requirements of the context, a feat which presupposes far more skill and taste than raw emotion. . . . [Such skill and taste] represent . . . not natural impulse but the refinement of habit, custom, and tradition become second nature. . . . Indeed on close inspection what was assumed to have been unpremeditated art is likely to be largely a matter of conditioned reflex, which is nothing other than the end product of discipline, or in a word, training. (Murray 1976, 98)

More than anything, Murray is trying to disentangle those cultural and practical concerns that he feels are actually operative in performance from racist assumptions. His focus is on an *approach* to music making. When he later writes of those "conditioned by the blues idiom in the first place" as having certain advantages over those who were not, writers like Teachout read that argument as racial, focusing attention on dark persons rather than on what Murray foregrounds: skill, conditioning, and discipline. Murray is ultimately concerned with musical competence, as Benjamin Brinner (1995, 1) would later describe it: "an integrated complex of skills and knowledge upon which a musician relies within a particular cultural context" (see also Stanyek 2004).

Though his position is harder to defend, Stanley Crouch likewise maintains what I consider a focus on practice and action rather than race or phenotypical notions of it. Indeed, he has no shortage of negative criticisms of hip-hop or rhythm and blues or of African American musicians who fail to work within the tradition as he understands it (see Crouch 1990a). Writing about Miles Davis's *The Birth of the Cool* recordings, for example, he excoriates Davis, implicitly condemns arranger Gil Evans, and questions the discernment of other jazz critics in one magisterial sweep:

> Davis's nonet of 1948–50 played little in public and recorded only enough to fill an album, but it largely inspired what became known as "cool" or "West Coast" jazz, a light-sounding music, low-keyed and smooth, that disavowed the Afro-American approach to sound and rhythm. This style had little to do with blues and almost nothing to do with swing.... Heard now, the nonet recordings seem little more than primers for television writing.... The overstated attribution of value to these recordings led the critical establishment to miss Ellington's "The Tattooed Bride," which was the high point of jazz composition in the late 1940s. Then, as now, jazz critics seemed unable to determine the difference between a popular but insignificant trend and a fresh contribution to the art. (Crouch 1990b, 31)

The suggestion that Crouch is thinking only in racial terms is difficult to support when one asks what he means by an "Afro-American approach to sound and rhythm" that one might disavow. Might it not be possible for Crouch to recognize whites who adhere to that approach? For all the insults contained in the passage, Crouch still seems to be asserting something about a *way* of doing things, about a particular form of musical competence. Implicit in his work as well as that of Murray and Marsalis is the notion that musicians of whatever background must *learn* to be jazz performers.

Part of the difficulty Murray and Crouch's critics have is that they reductively interpret "Afro-American" as denoting color rather than culture. The highly publicized moves of black leaders in the 1980s to have "Afro-American" and then "African American" replace "black" were intended in part to separate phenotype and practice, that is, to relocate the commonalities of those once described racially as black to a historically and geographically based narrative of shared practices and worldviews. While the aesthetic formulations of Murray, Crouch, and Marsalis have, to their credit, deemphasized an outmoded racial discourse, they are, nonetheless, like those of their critics, rooted in claims of historical objectivity, give short shrift to memory, and don't go far enough into the realm of practice. In other words, these figures offer a particular historical interpretation to support their vision. But in saying that blues, swing, and sonic invention are and have always been important, they perhaps foreclose on a more textured investigation of the practices that might support their project.

One possible way for them to refigure the terms of the debate would lie in their focusing more detailed attention on the ways in which individuals have come to jazz performance as well as their understandings of its meanings. For many jazz musicians, there is a wide world of music making and many ways to move through it. Although they may at times enter strategically into the debates in which scholars and critics engage, their work is more concerned with the ins and outs of performance, composition, interaction, and financial survival. An examination of the paths they have taken to become jazz musicians and the activities and practices that sustain them in this endeavor may, in fact, offer a useful way to resolve questions about jazz's pedigree.

In the jazz master narrative mentioned previously, the linkages between jazz and other African American (and African diaspora) musics are primarily restricted to the past. They surface only in cursory mentions of jazz's birth, along with spirituals and the blues, from a seemingly passive "mixture" of European and African elements in the late nineteenth and early twentieth centuries (see, e.g., Brothers 1994). At some point after this hazy period of origins—generally with the emergence of bebop in the 1940s—the historical narrative continues with jazz becoming an autonomous stream whose connections to more popular manifestations of African American music become problematic (Levine 1977). Those connections are bracketed, or set aside, in favor of understanding jazz as a species of modernist art that transcends its humble, racially bound origins.[22]

The musicians I interviewed during my fieldwork questioned the rightness of separating jazz as musical form and structure from African American culture, both in their talk about music and through their performances. Saxophonist Donald Harrison, for example, expressed disappointment when I told him of a debate on whether jazz was "African American music" that took place in a New York University classroom where I lectured in October of 1994. He invoked the words of drummer Art Blakey, who said he didn't care what the music was called as long as everyone "gave credit to the music's creators and innovators," whom he felt were primarily African American. Numerous other statements by performers and listeners in my field notes express a similar view, one that is summarized by the late pianist James Williams's assertion that there's no separation between jazz and other forms of African American music: "It all comes from the same place. I have no problem playing religious songs in the clubs or playing [John] Coltrane in the church, as long as I play with the proper spirit and attitude. [Jazz and gospel] run in parallel. They not only criss-cross, they often come together" (field notes, 11 October 1994). All African American musics, he argues, are linked together and are different facets of the same entity.

One way to explore Harrison and Williams's assertions is to focus on the pathways and practices of jazz musicians, showing that whatever motivation jazz performers or listeners may have to categorize what they perform and consume as "art," the sounds and their choices of sound configurations emerge most strongly from African American performative strategies. Songs, structures, and ways of manipulating them in performance become mechanisms for the regulation of group identity and collective memory (Bourdieu 1977, 78; Giddens 1979, 2; Gilroy 1991b, 211). There is, of course, value in approaches that see jazz as a complex system examinable in its own right. But when those approaches radically decontextualize the music, we might be moving toward realizing the state of affairs about which Dizzy Gillespie warned drummer Arthur Taylor in this chapter's epigraph.

In evoking musicians' pathways, I am drawing on Ruth Finnegan's *The Hidden Musicians* (1989), a book that examines a specific locality, the English town Milton Keynes, and attempts to make sense of the variety of music-making activity in it: choral music, brass band music, jazz, rock, and country, among others. For Finnegan, the pathways that individuals follow in musical performance and their negotiation of urban life are the "known and regular routes which people [choose]—or [are] led into—and which they both [keep] open and [extend] through their actions" (305). Pathways, moreover, are meaningful beyond their offering familiar routes that one can follow or sets of musical practices that one can learn or adapt: "They also [have] symbolic depth. One common impression given by many participants was that their musical pathways were of high value among the various paths in their lives" (305). The importance of these pathways lies in their providing a "framework for people's participation in urban life, something overlapping with, but more permanent and structured than, the personal networks in which individuals also participate" (323).

Moreover, she argues, "Entry on to particular musical pathways [was] dependent . . . on family membership [and] partly related to that family's social and economic resources. Certain activities needed money, transport, or access to specific kinds of venues or networks, or were perhaps related to particular kinds of educational achievements, material possessions, cultural interests, or social aspirations. All these were thus likely to play some part in the selection of particular pathways—though differently in different contexts and for different individuals" (311–12). These varied constellations do not map easily onto notions of class, however. Her data showed that the encouragement and support of parents, siblings, and friends were often more significant for young musicians than their guardians' incomes, occupations, or education. Gender and age in particular proved more crucial than parental resources or attainment in shaping or constraining the musical pathways chosen by young people (315–16), making it difficult for boys to become involved in classical music or girls in rock bands, for example. In any event, she asserts that "the continuance of . . . pathways—so often ignored or taken for granted as 'just there'— depends not on the existence in some abstract sphere of particular musical 'works', but on people's collective and active practice on the ground" (325; see also Goehr 1992, 102–15).

Although Finnegan's pathways are largely ready-made templates that frame and enable collective and individual practice, her notion may be extended to include the literal pathways taken by individuals to musical performance. How, indeed, have jazz's most highly praised practitioners typically learned their craft? What elements have been integral to the process of performing jazz, and what is the role of education, formal or informal, in making young musicians aware of and conversant with those elements? To what degree do class, age, and gender constrain one's ability to enter a jazz pathway? And how does a musician's deployment of what he or she has learned affect performance or our understandings of what jazz is? Too often commentators equate education with formal institutions and ignore the other salient ways in which people acquire knowledge. For jazz musicians, as Paul Berliner's *Thinking in Jazz* (1994) shows, there are at least as many paths to knowledge as there are individuals willing to embark on them. In the course of a musician's lifetime, he or she may glean important insights from friends and relatives, private teachers, fellow musicians, books and other pedagogical materials,[23] audio and video recordings, and close observation of live performance, as well as from classroom instruction in history, music theory, and performance practice.

None of these activities has to be focused specifically on the different musical approaches generally subsumed by the label "jazz." Indeed, at the most basic level, singers and instrumentalists need to find ways to use their respective tools. In some cases they can proceed admirably by learning to deal with the practical issue of generating sound without much reference to the aesthetic parameters of jazz or African American musics.

Nor do musicians' educational activities always have to concern music. Much work in ethnomusicology and anthropology since the 1960s has focused on the interconnectedness of different domains of experience. Writings dealing with musics as diverse as those from Papua New Guinea, the Amazonian rainforest, Liberia, and Nigeria as well as those most easily labeled jazz, country, and European concert music all stress the importance of knowledge of history, ecology, and social and cultural codes for music making (Feld 1994a; Seeger 1987; Stone 1982; Waterman 1990; Monson 1996; Kingsbury 1988; Fox 2004). Thus, learning about music requires engagement with a wide range of materials that may not be part of formalized instruction or simplistic understandings of race and history.

Mark Tucker's description of Duke Ellington's musical education (1991) encompasses what Ellington learned from musicians like Willie "The Lion" Smith, Will Marion Cook, and Bubber Miley, as well as what he gained from studying piano rolls such as James P. Johnson's "Carolina Shout." John Coltrane's education includes what he took from studying at the Ornstein School of Music in Philadelphia and playing with Eddie "Cleanhead" Vinson, Miles Davis, and Thelonious Monk alongside what he gathered from immersion in African American religious rituals, listening to recordings of Indian and African music (Weinstein 1993, 60–72; Porter 1998, 25–34, 41–53, 63–72), and reputedly practicing with Nicolas Slonimsky's *Thesaurus of Scales and Melodic Patterns* (1947). And, in a more contemporary example, Joshua Redman's musical education combines early experiences playing gamelan, rhythm and blues, and ska with those gained from playing in the jazz band at Berkeley High School in California and touring with his father, saxophonist Dewey Redman, in the late 1980s. A thorough and usable jazz education, therefore, is more often than not idiosyncratic and encompasses more than what might be typically taught in a classroom (see Reed 1979).

Classroom settings, however, were not foreign or inimical to jazz even before the beginning of formalized college-level jazz education in the late 1940s.[24] Hsio Wen Shih's description of the backgrounds of influential 1920s jazz musicians (1959) highlights the degree to which seeing these musicians as untutored omits crucial information. The typical 1920s innovator, he writes,

> was born about 1900, into a Negro family doing better than most, possibly in the Deep South, but more likely on its fringe; in either case, his family usually migrated North in time for him to finish high school. If he had gone to

college, and he often had, he had gone to Wilberforce or a . . . school like Howard or Fisk. He might have aimed at a profession and fallen back on jazz as a second choice. He was, in any case, by birth or by choice, a member of the rising Negro middle class; he was Fletcher Henderson, or Don Redman, or Coleman Hawkins, or Duke Ellington. (174)

Moving forward in time, we discover that the "young lions"[25] who emerged in the late 1980s and early 1990s are not the only ones to have had significant formal schooling in music. Among the prominent examples, saxophonist Joe Lovano studied at the Berklee College of Music in Boston; pianist Cecil Taylor at the New England Conservatory; saxophonists Joe Henderson and Julian "Cannonball" Adderley at Detroit's Wayne State University and Florida A&M University, respectively; and keyboardist Lyle Mays at the University of North Texas.

These examples show that the ways in which one learns to be a jazz musician are extremely varied. No one is actually *born* a jazz musician, even those who are phenotypically black. Instead, she or he must acquire the necessary skills through a lifetime of engagement with music making in general and by gathering as much information as possible from diverse sources. Young women have traditionally had a more difficult time acquiring such skills, given the extreme homosocial and masculinist practices that characterize the discourse and social world of jazz musicians (Tucker 2004). Formalized jazz education, complemented by antidiscrimination laws, has ameliorated the situation somewhat by functioning as a surrogate for the neighborhood bars and the numerous performance venues that dotted American cities prior to the 1970s. Before that time, musicians acquired their skills primarily, but not exclusively, in a performance world that limited opportunities for women. From the large corpus of musical and performative skills that musicians develop in either setting, a few merit more extensive consideration: developing proficiency and individual style; developing the ability to perform with other musicians and improvise in real time; and learning to navigate the professional world of music making.

Musical proficiency can most simply be glossed as the ability to produce the sounds that are in one's head with whatever musical tools are at one's disposal. Such proficiency is a function of knowing the capabilities and limitations of one's instrument so well that the conduit from concept to execution seems almost direct. The fluidity and ease with which exceptional performers such as Charlie Parker have plied their craft typically leads the outsider to think that musicians are playing without reference to conscious knowledge. More accurately, though, they are exhibiting in such moments a mastery of their instruments and the structural, interactive, and textural parameters of performance that makes what they do *seem* natural. The ability to speak furnishes a useful comparison. In one's adult years, the specific steps taken in acquiring that ability may have receded from consciousness, but one's skill at deploying it, even while carrying out other activities simultaneously, is the result of having deeply internalized it.

For developing proficiency, education has a great role to play, particularly when we remember that education can happen effectively both within and outside institutional walls. Although guitarists Wes Montgomery, Allan Holdsworth, and Russell Malone learned to play with little or no formal instruction, they are indeed exceptions. Almost always, someone somewhere has been crucial to the young musician's ability to navigate his or her instrument, tease appropriate and inappropriate sounds from it, and use them in a group performance context. At nearly every point in jazz's development, young musicians have been eager to mine whatever they could from the accumulated wisdom of experienced musicians, teachers, and bandleaders. Since the 1970s, formalized study at institutions such as the New England Conservatory, William Paterson University, the University of North Texas, and Berklee has afforded young players apprenticeship opportunities with faculty such as David Berger, Loren Schoenberg, Joe Chambers, Jim Hall, James Williams, Rodney Whitaker, and Reggie Workman. Few aspiring players would pass up the chance to have the harmonic and rhythmic intricacies of their most prized recordings revealed to them in courses that deal with the development of particular jazz styles. Where sound is concerned, those institutions perhaps cannot and should not be expected to foster the development of individual style. Learning to improvise and learning to play with other musicians in real time are also skills that musicians can develop in a number of settings, from practicing with recordings that provide accompaniment or using functionally similar MIDI-based software like Band-in-a-Box to participating in jam sessions with like-minded musicians or performing in school or professional ensembles. In any event, musicians are constantly faced with having to listen and to think critically about what they're hearing and how they're contributing to it. What formalized institutions provide are spaces where musicians can practice, rehearse, perform, and assimilate a wide body of knowledge in an arena where the stakes are considerably lower than they are in professional performances.

According to the musicians I interviewed, the area in which institutions are perhaps the most deficient is the teaching of improvisation. In the decades after the appearance of George Russell's *The Lydian Chromatic Concept of Tonal Organization for Improvisation* (1959),[26] a number of improvisation primers were published that stressed what jazz educators commonly refer to as the chord-scale approach to improvisation (e.g., Reeves 1989). In an simplest terms, improvisers using this approach associate a particular scale with each harmony in a composition, so that upon encountering a G major seventh chord, they think, for example, "play a G Lydian scale or an F# minor pentatonic." Such an approach, on one hand, makes it much easier for novice educators to teach jazz improvisation and, on the other, potentially encourages musicians to play scale patterns over harmonies rather than address the varied ways that expert players improvised in similar situations.[27] Indeed, one inside joke among jazz musicians is that schooled musicians are easy to identify, for in improvising they instinctively employ the melodic minor scale a half step up from the root of a dominant chord whenever one appears on a lead sheet. Saxophonist Sam Newsome said that Terence Blanchard would always yell, "Get out of there!" when he heard his bandmates falling back on such clichés in performance (Newsome 1995).

Many musicians told me that educators work more effectively when they inculcate in students the idea that learning the conventions and rules of jazz performance constitutes a base for further exploration rather than a rigid formula to be applied. Jazz improvisation requires not only having the theoretical materials at hand: it also requires knowing how to use them. As vibraphonist Gary Burton has observed, jazz education such as that offered at Berklee "allows [the young musician] to go further faster" (Helland 1995, 24). Burton explains, "A typical classical musician studies how music works, how harmony works, what the grammar of this music is in order to play better. You study your instrument with a master player. You study these same things as a jazz musician, but instead of using as an example a piece by Beethoven, you use a piece by Monk or Ellington. You're still learning musical information, which helps you to be a more knowledgeable, proficient player" (quoted in Helland 1995, 23). Through courses in harmony, improvisation, composition, and arranging and participation in ensembles, students are presented with the opportunity to assimilate the advances of the past in a systematic manner.

When it comes to negotiating the professional world, there are a number of ways in which formal and informal settings are again complementary. Professional musicians need, in addition to performance knowledge, an understanding of copyrights, music publishing, recording processes, booking, promotion and marketing, and survival on the road. In the past, the only way for musicians to learn such things was by gleaning them from conversation, trial and error, and experience. Jazz education in no way obviates the need for musicians to actually have such experiences, reflect upon them, and develop their own strategies for coping with them. What it does do, however, is to give them more reasonable expectations and the opportunity to benefit systematically from others who have already made and worked through mistakes. Perhaps the most significant, and perhaps unintended, consequence of jazz education is its contribution to the formation of musical networks that I discuss in chapter 4.

Despite differences in age, geographical background, cultural identity, and musical training, each of the musicians I interviewed stressed the importance of various African American musics and cultural practices in their education and experience as jazz artists. Pianist James Williams, for example, was born in Memphis, Tennessee. His early musical education included lessons focused on Western piano repertoire. His training included his work as a pianist and organist in church. In my interviews and subsequent conversations with him, he stressed the profound influence 1960s free-format radio stations in Memphis had on him. In addition to programming a variety of rhythm and blues, doo-wop, blues, and Motown-produced music, those stations played rock and roll that drew largely upon African American musical practices. Williams studied music at Memphis State University, dividing his time between jazz performance, classical performance, and music education. Upon graduation in the early 1970s, he took a teaching position at the Berklee College of Music. He left there toward the end of the decade to join Art Blakey's Jazz Messengers in the version of the group that included an eighteen-year-old Wynton Marsalis. Williams left Blakey's group in the early 1980s and, over the next several years, established himself as a reputable composer, sideman, and producer of recordings for other jazz musicians. Through his production company, Finas Sound Productions, he hosted concerts in the mid- and late 1990s that paid tribute to (then) living jazz legends like Milt Jackson and John Lewis. From the late 1990s until his death in 2004, he was director of the jazz studies program at William Paterson University.

Pianist Bruce Barth was born in Pasadena, California, in the late 1950s. His family moved to New York state when he was seven. Like that of Williams, his early musical training included classical piano lessons, which he continued through the end of high school. He also spent time playing guitar and learning rock and jazz songs by ear in his preteen and teen years. His serious engagement with jazz started with a Mose Allison record, *Back Country Suite,* that he received as a gift when he was fourteen.[28] Through Allison's music, and later through engagement with the work of pianists like Bud Powell, Thelonious Monk, Oscar Peterson, Wynton Kelly, and Red Garland, Barth learned to play jazz.[29] He earned a bachelor's degree in music from the University of Michigan and a master's degree in music from the New England Conservatory. Since the late 1980s, he has performed with Stanley Turrentine, Terence Blanchard, and Danilo Pérez among others; made recordings under his own name; and produced recordings for other jazz musicians, particularly singers.

Saxophonist Steve Wilson was born in Hampton, Virginia, in the early 1960s. His father sang in a group that traveled and performed spirituals in the area around Hampton and exposed his son to a wider world of African American music. The younger Wilson developed an interest in jazz through listening to his father's copy of Ahmad Jamal's *But Not for Me: Live at the Pershing* and through seeing saxophonists Eddie Harris and Rahsaan Roland Kirk at the Hampton Jazz Festival in the early 1970s. He took lessons on the alto saxophone and the oboe through high school and developed as a performer through playing in his school's concert band, in funk and rhythm and blues bands in Hampton, and in the horn section of singer Stephanie Mills's band. He attended Virginia Commonwealth University, where he studied with Doug Richards, who introduced him to the music of Duke Ellington, Jelly Roll Morton, and Fletcher Henderson. After graduating in the mid-1980s and moving to New York City, he played with the collective Out of the Blue and, in addition to leading his own ensembles, has been in demand as a saxophonist since then, performing with Lionel Hampton, Buster Williams, Chick Corea, Claudia Acuña, Bruce Barth, Maria Schneider, Mulgrew Miller, and Leon Parker.

Parker, who is a drummer, was born in White Plains, New York, in the mid-1960s. His parents had a record collection that not only spanned jazz history—from Lionel Hampton and Count Basie to Art Blakey, Miles Davis, and John Coltrane—but also included important Latin jazz recordings by artists such as Tito Puente and Mongo Santamaria. His musical training was less formal than Williams's or Barth's but no less extensive. He involved himself in the musical life of Westchester in the 1970s, playing in his high school's jazz ensemble as well as in gospel groups and blues and rock bands. During this time he started performing in jazz clubs in Westchester and turned down a scholarship to Fordham University to start playing full-time in New York City. He began studying classical percussion around that time. In the late 1980s he became associated with some of the young musicians who were part of the New School for Social Research's jazz program and started to develop his reputation on the jazz scene. Since then, he has recorded and performed with Kenny Barron, Jesse Davis, David Sánchez, Jacky Terrasson, Bruce Barth, and Steve Wilson. He has also released four CDs under his own name and collaborated with choreographers on various "body percussion" works.

Lastly, guitarist Peter Bernstein was born in New York City in the late 1960s. Because of the demands of his father's work as a journalist, his family moved frequently—to Chicago shortly after he was born, back to New York for a few years, then to Israel for four years before finally returning to New York. Public interest in Scott Joplin's work in the early 1970s—inspired by the film *The Sting*—inspired a six-year-old Bernstein to learn to play piano. While his family was in Israel, he started exploring his parents' record collection, which included recordings by Simon and Garfunkel and James Taylor as well as the Dizzy Gillespie Big Band and Charles Mingus. Bernstein started taking guitar lessons there, mostly learning to play Bob Dylan tunes and songs like "Proud Mary."[30] His world changed, however, when he heard Jimi Hendrix and began to explore the blues-based conceptions of guitarists such as B.B. King, Freddie King, Albert King, and Eric Clapton. Hearing them eventually led him to Pat Metheny, George Benson, Kenny Burrell, Wes Montgomery, and Grant Green and cemented his interest in jazz. He attended Rutgers University, where he studied with Ted Dunbar and Kevin Eubanks. Like Leon Parker, he became associated with the jazz program at the New School in the late 1980s and started performing publicly in the city. Since then, he has recorded and performed with Jesse Davis, Lou Donaldson, Larry Goldings, Joshua Redman, and Diana Krall, among others.

It might be obvious what broad racial/cultural identities one might ascribe to these musicians. Without my making those ascriptions (or the musicians' own self-identifications) explicit, there are tangible regularities in the paths they have taken to jazz performance. All are men who have benefited from the support of their parents, siblings, and teachers. Two of them have had extensive training in European instrumental techniques and repertoire, while two more have had less serious engagement and the remaining musician almost none. Regardless of their knowledge of concert music and its performance practices, however, their approaches to learning and developing have primarily entailed engagement with the work of African American musicians and various kinds of African American musics: jazz, in particular, but also gospel, rhythm and blues, blues, and funk. As musics that draw from a common fund of musical practices, these styles have been pivotal in each musician's development. Indeed, they have all learned to play jazz through close listening and through performance. Many of them have concentrated on keeping central in their performances and choice of repertoire the African Americanness of the music.

Although these issues will be explored in more depth in chapter 5, their importance here lies in musicians' foregrounding of an African American approach to music making, one that has been most aptly described in scholarly writing by composer Olly Wilson. In 1974, he proposed that "a black-music cultural sphere exists which includes the music of the African and African-descendant peoples of the following geographic areas: the Atlantic Ocean in the center, bounded by West Africa on the east with the northern part of South America and the Carribean [sic] Islands on the south-west and the United States on the north-west" (6). Within that sphere, various musics are connected to each other via common conceptual approaches to music making: use of (overlapping) call-and-response techniques, off-beat phrasing of melodic accents, percussive approaches to performance, timbral heterogeneity, use of polymetric frameworks, and the integration of environmental factors into performance.[31] Wilson summarizes his argument as follows:

> The relationship between African and Afro-American music consists not only of shared characteristics, but importantly, of shared conceptual approaches to music making, and hence is not basically quantitative but qualitative. Therefore the particular forms of black music which evolved in America are specific realizations of this shared conceptual framework which reflects the peculiarities of the American black experience. As such the essence of their Africanness is not a static body of something which can be depleted but rather a conceptual approach, the manifestations of which are infinite. The common core of this Africanness consists of the way of doing something, not simply something that is done. (20)

These approaches are manifest in jazz performance in the ways in which jazz performers choose and adapt material, sometimes originating in other forms of African American music. Moreover, they are evident in the way that musicians adapt and play with those materials, regardless of source.

In experiential terms, then, jazz is a form inseparable from other African American musics. The pathways that musicians traverse in coming to it and continuing to develop necessitate engagement with more than the technical aspects of jazz performance. Arguments that, through selective historical interpretation, reduce jazz to technical parameters and render it as a neutral and expansive *American* tradition are perhaps arguments that paint over African Americanness to assuage European American anxiety. Although asserting that jazz is an African American music is equally ideological, it is not simply an argument about race or even one that makes a simplistic appeal to historical precedent. It is instead a statement about the relationship of culture and experience, an understanding that emerges from examining the way that musicians of varying backgrounds have *learned* to perform the music. Each of them has had to marry whatever musical skills they had—however they acquired them—with the conventions and aesthetic priorities of jazz performance, which remain consistent with the aesthetic imperatives of other African American and African-derived musical forms. On their pathways, in other words, these musicians have explored the changing cultural and musical practices of African Americans beyond the years of jazz's emergence. Complaints about the relative valence of race and culture or history and memory surely have a part to play, but the work of musicians is less about the ideas associated with those dyads—integration, racial exclusion, expansive Americanness, or fiery fundamentals—than it is about strategies for negotiating structure and performance that emerge from and are consistently enriched by other African American musics. To the degree that there is a unified jazz tradition, it is predicated on cultural practice and memory-based reconstruction, both of which are decidedly oriented more toward the future than the past.

PART TWO

Scenes in the City

CHAPTER 3

Jazz and Spatiality

The Development of Jazz Scenes

On many nights during my fieldwork, I would leave my apartment on 119th Street and walk to the 1/9 train station at 116th and Broadway. After descending the stairs on the downtown side, I would proceed to the far end of the station in order to get a seat in the front car. Upon arriving at 14th Street, I'd exit the station on the downtown side and walk up the stairs into the New York night. Turning 180 degrees toward 7th Avenue South, I'd orient myself by looking for St. Vincent's Hospital and then looking right, where I could see the now-fallen twin towers of the World Trade Center dominating the southern horizon. Walking down 7th Avenue in their direction, I would soon encounter the red awning of the Village Vanguard stretching over the sidewalk. If I continued in that direction, I could look to the right at 10th Street, as I passed under the sign for Dix et Sept, and see patrons waiting to enter Smalls. Going further down, past Christopher Street, I might also see the enclosed sidewalk café of Sweet Basil (later Sweet Rhythm), through whose windows I could gauge the number of patrons within and perhaps catch a glimpse of the performers. Alternatively, I might have turned left at Christopher and headed toward 6th Avenue and West 3rd Street, where by going to the left I could choose between performances at the Blue Note and Visiones in a single block.

Other potential routes might have taken me north and east toward Bradley's on University Place, north and west toward Zinno on 13th Street, or much further south, into Tribeca, where the Knitting Factory was located on Leonard Street. Regardless of my destination on a given night, the proximity of those venues to one another, as well as to Russ Musto's Village Jazz Shop (at 163 West 10th Street), made that area of Greenwich Village a jazz neighborhood. More accurately, my walks through the city on those evenings, my routes and routines (Certeau 1984, 97–110; Román-Velázquez 1999, 64–65), created a jazz-related understanding of the neighborhood through my deemphasizing spaces that equally characterized the area: piano bars like Rose's Turn, rock clubs like the Lion's Den and the Bitter End on Bleecker Street, or the various pizza shops, cafés, lounges, restaurants, and bars that might have attracted other people. Indeed, in discussing the neighborhood with friends who had a stronger interest in other aspects of New York nightlife, I was generally astonished to find that we had wildly divergent conceptions of the same terrain.

Such experiences reinforced for me the notion that space, in its geographic and theoretical dimensions, is a crucial component for understanding and conceptualizing jazz. Accounts of the music's development, usually starting in New Orleans, moving to Chicago, and finally settling in New York—with brief side trips to Kansas City, Los Angeles, Philadelphia, and other locales—generally acknowledge the role of space, but, like race, its importance registers in such accounts primarily in jazz's past. Those locales figure in the historical narrative only as backdrops for the supposed real action: the development of musical style as exemplified in the work of the music's masters. The places where Louis Armstrong, Duke Ellington, or Ornette Coleman, for example, spent their childhood years (in New Orleans, Washington, D.C., and Fort Worth, respectively) are important only because they initially shaped musical lives that seemed less affected by geography once those individual musicians' styles were formed. In other words, rather than being considered constitutive of musical or historical development or being viewed dynamically, the locales in which jazz musicians have flourished were a scrim in front of which they marched on their way to making history. Even those works that have explored the role played by various cities, states, and regions in jazz's development (e.g., Ostransky 1978; Gordon 1986; Pearson 1987; Gioia 1992; Oliphant 1996; Björn and Gallert 2001; Suhor 2001) see space as subsidiary to time, devoting less space to geography after jazz styles or musicians have emerged.

In differing ways, these writings describe the built environments, legal structures, and migration patterns that make certain places attractive and fertile (temporary) destinations or points of embarkation for musicians. Each city, state, or region (with New York City as a notable exception) experiences a rise and fall (cf. Kruse 2003, 14), so that New Orleans ceases to be important after the closing of the Storyville red-light district; Chicago loses much of its centrality once New Orleans migrants and other musicians, following a crackdown on speakeasies in the late 1920s, depart for New York; Kansas City "fades out" with the end of the Pendergast political machine; and Detroit's lively jazz scene is eclipsed by the rise of Motown Records. Studies of jazz outside the United States (Godbolt 1984, 1989; Kater 1992; Starr 1994; Atkins 2001, 2003) act as supplements that mildly challenge the standard narratives without necessarily expanding the role of geography. Those nations and regions are simply other places whose roles in jazz's development merit consideration. The master narrative itself, however, remains intact—at least in the United States—and isn't subject to modification or elaboration.

Careful observers, however, might notice the threads linking local stories and might see as well what many of those tales tend not to emphasize: that jazz activity does not disappear from those localities after their supposed declines. The elements that comprise a given scene—musicians, educational institutions, performance venues, and the like—continue operating long afterward, if only on a muted level. After all, New Orleans from the 1970s to the '90s nurtured the careers of Wynton and Branford Marsalis, Terence Blanchard, Donald Harrison, Nicholas Payton, Peter Martin, and Brian Blade. Detroit did the same for Robert Hurst, Kenny Garrett, Geri Allen, James Carter, Jaribu Shahid, and Craig Taborn, just as Chicago earlier did for Sun Ra, various members of the Association for the Advancement of Creative Musicians, Steve Coleman, and Lonnie Plaxico or as Los Angeles did for Charles Mingus, Horace Tapscott, Charles McPherson, Arthur Blythe, and David Murray, among others. Even those places that might seem peripheral in the development of jazz, like St. Louis and Memphis, have done similar work for musicians such as Lester Bowie, Julius Hemphill, James Williams, Mulgrew Miller, and Donald Brown. Although some of those musicians might have moved to specific metropolitan areas as young adults, the role played by their previous homes in their development is unassailable.

These observations suggest another way of examining jazz's development, one that devotes greater attention to the roles of *space* and *spatiality* over time and addresses the ways in which jazz musicians and other interested parties have sought to negotiate them. As developed in the work of Marxist geographers (e.g., Harvey 1989b; Soja 1989), inspired by the work of Henri Lefebvre (1974), those terms draw our attention to the variability and contingency of geography. Although literal space might be taken as a given, seen in commonsense terms as an arrangement of physical elements or a particular landscape, spatiality is something different, a function of how people manipulate space and make it useful for their own ends. As a concept, then, spatiality is—like society—a dynamic product of the relationships between individuals and groups and is, as a result, instrumental in the way that they navigate both space and time.

Edward W. Soja writes that, for its part, spatiality is distinct from both the "physical space of material nature and the mental space of cognition and representation, each of which is used and incorporated into the social construction of spatiality but cannot be conceptualized as its equivalent" (1989, 120). He argues further that human activity (e.g., the construction of buildings, the paving of streets, and the passage of laws regulating the use of them) and representations of geography (e.g., Greenwich Village as a jazz neighborhood, New York as "the city that never sleeps") transform material space into something that transcends our most simplistic understandings of it. Spatiality is a direct result of these transformative processes, but it is neither static nor a one-time result of them: it "always remains open to further transformation. . . . It is never primordially given or permanently fixed" (122). The complex of factors that has allowed jazz to flourish in particular spaces at different times, therefore, argues for a history that takes account of the built environment and human uses and representations of it as more than silent partners to presumably more vocal historical processes. A jazz scene, provisionally understood as a spatial formation, is not something that was constructed in the 1920s, for example, and subsequently became a self-sustaining entity, the interrelationship of whose elements did not change.[1]

In a dramaturgical sense, we might conceive a scene in complementary ways that encompass both space and time. On one hand, the term references space: it denotes a backdrop, background, or context, something that provides a setting for action. In this sense, a scene constrains and conditions the kinds of interactions that can take place among those positioned or performing in it. It is thus more than an inert setting for musical activity: through both their actions in and representations of that space, musicians and other participants transform it into something usable (Cohen 1999, 247; see also Olson 1997, 275). On the other hand, a scene can signify time: a brief episode in the larger unfolding of a narrative, an identifiable, bounded temporal space that is not fully meaningful when removed from its narrative context. Either way, studying scenes allows a researcher to place various relations between groups and their negotiation of space and time at the center of inquiry and to move beyond the oppositions between musicians and various others. Moreover, the frequent use of the term *scene* by jazz musicians and critics gives it an emic valence and specificity missing from other formulations.[2]

Perhaps the first sustained meditation on musical scenes in popular music studies is an article published by Will Straw (1991). In it, he begins by defining musical communities as entities that are presumed to have stable populations and to be exploring one or more musical forms within a specific geographical heritage. Musical communities are most effective, he writes, when they link contemporary musical practices with a specific heritage that renders those practices meaningful. In contrast, a musical scene "is that cultural space in which a range of musical practices coexist, interacting with each other within a variety of processes of differentiation and according to widely varying trajectories of change and cross-fertilization" (373). For him, rather than working as an exploration of a particular style over time or in terms of a specific heritage, a musical scene operates on the principles of alliance building and musical boundary drawing through varied forms of communication. Participants in a musical scene are involved not only in the exploration of a style, but also in the active defining of that style's parameters through relations with other musics, musicians, and audiences. As such, they both observe and modify conventions through their practical action.

As processes of internationalization and globalization have become more central in the recording industry, and as ownership of recording companies has become the province of a few large conglomerates (including Universal, Sony, and Time Warner), processes occurring on the national and international levels can and do have a significant impact on positionings and articulations within localized musical scenes (Erlmann 1993; Garofalo 1993; Guilbault 1993; Negus 1992, 1999; Román-Velázquez 1999). In describing the constant spatio-temporal circulation of recordings and live performances, however, Straw rules out the possibility of a particular local scene having a significant effect on the nature or composition of other local scenes: "The relationship of different local or regional scenes to each other is no longer one in which specific communities emerge to enact a forward movement to which others are drawn" (1991, 378). Instead, he says, musicians are easily able to circulate from one local scene to another without having to adapt themselves to local circumstances (374; see also Florida et al. 2010, 786).

Although Holly Kruse (1993) agrees with much of what Straw has written, she is highly critical of his last point. She argues that the emergence of highly influential local rock scenes originating in Champaign, Illinois; Minneapolis, Minnesota; and Seattle, Washington, in the 1980s and '90s undermines Straw's conclusion. She is critical as well of two other studies that focus on local musical communities: Ruth Finnegan's *The Hidden Musicians* (1989) and Sara Cohen's *Rock Culture in Liverpool* (1991). She feels that both writers "overlook an important way in which musicians and others involved in local scenes understand their own involvement: as something that differentiates them from individuals and groups in other communities" (Kruse 1993, 38). She admits, despite her critique of localized inquiry, that "*local* musical scenes are the sites at which we may first want to look . . . in order to understand the relationship between situated musical practices and the construction of identity" (39), especially since, as Straw suggests, many musicians do not always find it possible to circulate easily from one scene to another (40). The common thread in the work of Straw and Kruse, nonetheless, is the advantage that the study of musical scenes has over that of musical communities. Rather than resting on static conceptions of style or geography, a scholar focused on a particular scene has to engage with the interactions among actors and institutions on both local and translocal levels over time.

In this context, Barry Shank's 1994 study of the "rock'n'roll" scene in Austin, Texas, is exemplary. He sees its emergence as the result of both local practices and modes of identification reaching back to the late nineteenth century and larger interactions with the recording industry and other nonlocal agents and institutions. For him, a musical scene is a "signifying community," "a necessary condition for the production of . . . music capable of moving past the mere expression of locally significant cultural values and generic development—that is, beyond stylistic permutation—toward an interrogation of dominant structures of identification, and potential cultural transformation" (122).[3] Although Shank might be accused of uncritically grafting the subcultural work of Hebdige (1979) onto American cultural forms, he is on more solid ground in describing musical scenes as systems capable of producing meaning, ones that allow for varied associations to be made among "cultural signifiers [e.g., musical signs and individual bodies] of identity and community" (125). Scenes for Shank are thus predicated on the interaction between older notions of community—geographically and historically rooted—and extralocal processes of communication and identification. Musicians involved with local scenes are concerned simultaneously with the construction and maintenance of local *and* translocal identities and their attendant boundaries (see also Kruse 1993, 38).

Choosing the scene as the unit of study, therefore, involves enlarging one's focus within a single locale as well as beyond it. Shank's inquiry highlights the important roles played by musicians as well as various social movements, economic factors, publications, record stores, zoning regulations, and performance spaces in the constitution of a scene on the local level. In addition, he links those local activities to the larger national and international activities of the recording industry and various musical forms. All of them are important in the constitution of the Austin scene and, by extension, other local scenes.

Drawing upon popular music writing, as well as those local jazz studies cited earlier, one might begin to glimpse the general contours of *jazz* scenes. Each one consists of groups of participants (musicians, audiences, teachers, venue owners, managers, recording industry personnel, critics, and historians), as well as educational institutions, performance venues, record labels, and publications, which collaborate to present, develop, and comment upon musical events in both recorded and live forms. The specific shape of any local scene is dependent upon the participation of different combinations of these groups of agents and institutions. Their collective work, moreover, is both enabled and constrained by accommodations to and modifications of the built environments in which they are situated. The regulation of public space expressed in zoning laws, for example, determines whether, when, and where performance venues can exist. The emergence and eventual demise of jazz districts in specific places at specific times—Storyville in the 1910s, the South Side of Chicago from the 1920s through the 1950s, Harlem in the 1920s, or Central Avenue in Los Angeles in the 1930s and 1940s—are a function of such interactions on the local level (Ogren 1989; Lopes 2002).

In *Steppin' Out: New York Nightlife and the Transformation of American Culture, 1890–1920* (1984), for example, Lewis Erenberg discusses the changes in public entertainment occurring in New York City at the turn of the twentieth century. He describes the novel forms of social interaction centered on cabarets and rathskellers, particularly in the

Times Square area in the 1910s. Although rathskellers were associated primarily with public drinking and vice, cabarets, often lavishly decorated, were conceived as a respectable alternative for well-heeled patrons. Both kinds of venues had high cover charges, served expensive food and drink, and offered their patrons floor shows and opportunities for dancing (119). The atmosphere in cabarets differed in one major respect: it brought men and women "into a more intimate relationship than was possible in conventional theatres. . . . Performers appeared on the floor at eye level, standing or moving amid the diners seated in a semi-circle. . . . The audiences were close enough to touch the performers, and they often did so in specially designed numbers and rituals" (124–25). The sociability encouraged in cabarets, which catered primarily to audiences who had seen theatrical performances earlier in the evening, led to the establishment of the nightclub:

> In order to allow patrons to remain undisturbed by the 2:00 a.m. curfew laws and police harassment, promoters began buying the charters of defunct private social organizations in the fall of 1914 and turned special rooms of their establishments into so-called clubs. . . . When the regular portion of the restaurant closed, members adjourned to the room set aside for the club. . . . Some establishments adhered to strict rules of membership and dues, but most merely declared those remaining after the legal closing hours as members. Writing their names on cards supplied by the management, customers henceforth had proof of membership. The night "club" remained open as long as the desire for enjoyment prevailed, rather than as the law or the duration of the play demanded. (129–30)

Legally sanctioned as places where alcohol could be served, cabarets and their attendant nightclubs encouraged their patrons to lower their inhibitions in pursuit of pleasure and afforded them limited opportunities to mingle with less respectable people (like gangsters and gamblers) without threatening their social status. In other words, a change in the definition and use of public space was a crucial component in the transformation of cultural life for at least one group of people in New York City.

New York, however, was not unique in this respect. Kathy Ogren (1989, 56–86) details the way in which similar scenarios played out in other metropolitan centers in the early decades of the twentieth century. Transitional areas and vice districts—particularly after the passage of the Volstead Act, which prohibited the sale of alcohol, in 1920—became the primary locus for cabaret-style entertainment. Ogren observes that "residential zoning laws designed to regulate commercial development and racial segregation often combined . . . and forced blacks and other inner-city residents to live in the same areas that supported vice" (1989, 60; see also Ostransky 1978, 63, 85–86). Wherever they existed, and however they came into being, such spaces proved crucial in the development of jazz, for they gave professional musicians opportunities to perform and allowed audiences the opportunity to hear them. Moreover, the work of publishing and recording companies as well as coverage in newspapers and other contemporary publications, both local and national, helped not only to create scenes but also to generate public interest in them. Additionally, the success of early jazz and blues recordings beginning in the late 1910s helped to cement interest in the emerging musical styles in New York, Chicago, Detroit, San Francisco, Los Angeles, and other places.

Many musicians were drawn to New York City in the 1910s and 1920s by increasing opportunities to perform and record, as Samuel Charters and Leonard Kunstadt show in *Jazz: A History of the New York Scene* (1962). The authors present a richly detailed account of the early jazz scene in New York City, discussing musicians, various performance venues, and the spaces in Harlem and near Times Square that were the centers of music-related activities through the 1950s. In their chronicle of the careers of musicians such as James Reese Europe, Scott Joplin, Fletcher Henderson, and Bix Beiderbecke and the fortunes of venues in different parts of the city, they continually remind their readers of the importance of seeing jazz's development as encompassing more than progressively more intricate musical arrangements:

> By 1923 and 1924 it had become fashionable to listen to jazz. Not the rough, crude jazz of a few years before, but the new "symphonic" jazz. Just as in the 1950s, another of jazz's brief moments of stylish attention, there were lectures on jazz, "concerts," lengthy articles in slick magazines, and some interest from [music] publishing houses. . . . Carl Van Vechten, Abbe Niles, Henry Osgood, Virgil Thomson, and Don Knowlton were contributing articles to magazines like *Harper's, Literary Digest,* and *New Republic.* The Negro revues, with their jazz orchestras and blues vocalists, were playing to large and enthusiastic audiences along Broadway. (131–32)

> The real rush to Harlem began about 1926, and by 1927 and 1928 it was one of the fashionable places in New York. The night life began to have some of the glitter that [Jazz Age] novels described. There were nightly radio programs from the larger clubs, the bands were getting frequent notices from the magazines and newspapers, and there was a noisy parade of musicians through most of the small clubs. (196)

> [During the swing era, the] expenses of organizing and advertising a band were so high that the successful leaders had to enter into complicated financial

arrangements with outside backers. Everything about the new bands cost money, from hiring soloists away from their present bands to buying uniforms and music stands. . . . Newspapers and trade magazines were flooded with press-agent releases. As the publicity grew more insistent, the personalities became more and more the centers of attraction. They were given nearly as much publicity as successful movie stars. If the promotion caught the public's eye, the investment could be made highly profitable. Willard Alexander's M.C.A. booking office handled the very slick and very expensive promotions of both Benny Goodman and Count Basie and realized a small fortune on the percentage of the bands' gross take. . . . Behind the elegant face that swing presented to the public was a nervous, tensely competitive entertainment industry that was exploiting the new style. (242)

In short, a number of factors drew musicians to New York City, provided opportunities for them to perform in different parts of the city, and made the public aware of their activities. In addition to musicians, moreover, critics, publicists, venues, and fans played prominent roles. Together they entered a stage framed by the scene, commented upon it, and, through their actions, sustained and transformed it. The development of jazz, then, was not simply a function of developments in musical style; it was also a function of developments in the *use of urban space*—the peregrinations of European American "cultural tourists" to largely African American areas for entertainment, the continued movement of African American musicians (but not non-performers) to downtown performance spaces (which were presumably safer for middle-class white patrons), and the use of nascent broadcasting technologies both to attract audiences to those spaces and to allow them to experience, at least vicariously, what occurred in them without actually being present.[4]

Paul Chevigny's *Gigs: Jazz and the Cabaret Laws in New York City* (1991) shows how incomplete any history of the New York scene is without consideration of the municipal regulations that determined who could perform in the city's venues, how many musicians and what instrumental combinations were permitted, and where venues could be located. These regulations, collectively known as cabaret laws (after the early twentieth-century venues that inspired them), imposed what now seem absurd strictures on venue owners. As legally defined in 1926, a cabaret was "any room, place or space in the city in which any musical entertainment, singing or dancing or other similar amusement is permitted in connection with the restaurant business or the business of directly or indirectly selling the public food or drink" (quoted in Chevigny 1991, 56). Anyone operating such an establishment was required to have a cabaret license. Initially, only venues were required to be licensed, but following the transfer of licensing functions to the police department in 1931, anyone who worked in a cabaret was required to be licensed as well. After 1940, both potential performers and regular employees of such venues were required to be fingerprinted and undergo police background checks. Depending on the results of the investigations, applicants were either issued identification cards signifying their suitability to work in cabarets or denied them in an effort to minimize the corrupting influence on cabaret patrons of "criminals and other undesirables . . . who come into contact with patrons under conditions conducive to criminality" (58).

The requirement of identification cards, Chevigny observes, was based on a preemptive logic that was not, at least according to existing records, supported by any actual cases of criminal conduct by musicians in or near clubs. Those musicians who were denied cabaret cards typically had criminal records, frequently for drug possession, though few, if any, arrests took place at performance venues. Rooted in fears about intimate contact between the public and (black) musicians or left-leaning comedians such as Lord Buckley, the cabaret and cabaret card laws were both paradoxical and hypocritical. As Chevigny (1991, 59–64) explains, the laws were arbitrarily enforced, so that Billie Holiday, denied a cabaret card after being convicted for narcotics possession and imprisoned in 1947, could still perform in concert in Central Park in 1948, and Frank Sinatra worked frequently at venues such as the Copacabana in the 1950s without ever obtaining a card.

Although the laws requiring identification cards were rescinded in 1966,[5] other laws regulating the clubs continued to have an effect on jazz performers' fortunes into the late 1980s. Dismayed by provisions in the city's zoning regulations that forbade live performance in restaurants outside the areas where entertainment was permitted, lobbyists from Local 802 of the American Federation of Musicians (AFM) and later the owners of Greenwich Village coffeehouses convinced the mayor and the City Planning Commission to amend the existing laws in 1955 and 1961, to allow "incidental musical entertainment" performed by "up to three musicians, playing strings or keyboards" in restaurants (Chevigny 1991, 70–74). Because incidental entertainment could not feature horns or percussion instruments (including the vibraphone), in part to comply with noise regulations, this exception was damaging to venue owners who favored jazz but didn't have the capital to obtain a cabaret license in addition to the other permits required to operate a business in New York City. As a result, many of them

tried to tailor their music to the . . . exception. The Burgundy Café . . .
stopped using saxophones and began to emphasize the piano and hire singers. At Gregory's, Warren Chiasson stopped playing vibraphone and switched
to piano in the Chuck Wayne trio on Tuesday nights. Discovery, in 1985 a
new place at Broome and Mercer Streets in Soho, took the ingenious approach of offering a trio of Reggie Workman on bass, Stanley Cowell on
piano, and violinist Ali Akbar. . . . [But when] Bob Belden, a young saxophonist fresh from the big bands, tried to play his demonstration tape at the
West End Bar . . . the management told him they could not hire sax players.
Belden heard the same story at 55 Christopher Street, a small place in Greenwich Village. (84)

Chevigny chronicles the absurdity of the regulations and the varied
legal strategies employed by the AFM, musicians, attorneys, and venue
owners to have them overturned starting in the 1960s. Those efforts culminated in the incidental musical entertainment exception being ruled
unconstitutional in January of 1988 by judge David Saxe, though actual
change still lagged behind (86–131). The repeal of the laws was welcome,
but Chevigny and a number of the people he interviewed felt that irrepa-
rable damage had been done to the scene. Indeed, the prospects for musicians seemed not to change markedly. Established performers, the very
ones who could draw larger audiences, might have been less inclined to
play in the venues that opened in the wake of the repeal of cabaret laws,
preferring instead to devote their energies to teaching as well as performing in the dwindling number of clubs outside New York and in jazz festivals in the United States and abroad. Younger, less-established musicians
perhaps benefited most from the repeal, for they found themselves with
more opportunities to perform in restaurants in various parts of the city
(154–66). For those reasons and many others, the economic climate for
jazz venues was increasingly volatile in the 1980s and '90s.

Some of the difficulties have a direct connection to many cities' shifting toward neoliberal strategies to spur growth and derive tax revenue
through the regulation of public space beginning with the fiscal crises
of the 1970s (Sites 1997, 540). For much of the twentieth century and
especially in the aftermath of the Second World War, the United States
and other capitalist nations experienced unparalleled economic pros-
perity based on their ability to manufacture goods for domestic and
foreign consumption (Harvey 1989a, 129). Indeed, the military and financial power of the United States led to the Bretton Woods agreement
of 1944, which "turned the dollar into the world's reserve currency and
tied the world's economic development firmly into U.S. fiscal and mon-

etary policy" (Harvey 1989a, 137). In this climate, ever more efficient, scientifically managed American corporations found ways to liquidate surplus goods overseas and to pass the benefits of their profitability along to their employees, especially those who were members of unions.

Between 1965 and 1973, however, signs that the postwar boom was coming to an end were ever more apparent. During that time, David Harvey writes, U.S. corporate productivity and profitability were declining; inflation accelerated to the point where the dollar's stability as a reserve currency was called into question; and Western European nations and Japan challenged U.S. manufacturing dominance—all with the result that the dollar was devalued (Harvey 1989a, 141). One additional result of these changes, exacerbated by OPEC's raising of oil prices in 1973, was that leaders in major municipalities had to acknowledge more directly that their tax bases were eroding. That is, the postwar boom had perhaps made it easier for them to ignore the fact that, beginning in the late 1940s, not only had affluent and middle-class dwellers (including white male heads of household who enjoyed the benefits of union membership) had chosen to move to more spacious and presumably safer suburbs (leaving other residents to deal with declining services, increased joblessness, and an attendant increase in crime; see Sugrue 1996), but corporations were also progressively transferring their manufacturing operations to more remote areas within and outside the United States as they struggled to remain competitive.

No longer able to depend on the tax revenues of the boom years, municipal leaders like those in New York City turned their attention toward the reconfiguring and regulation of space as a way of attracting capital investment from corporations and real estate developers, particularly in parts of Lower Manhattan (Sites 1997, 542–45; Hudson 1987). One related manifestation of this shift, with direct effects on jazz scenes, was those same leaders' increased reliance on the revenue that could be derived from tourism. That is, municipal governments invested significant resources in building convention centers, improving roads in, around, or leading to central business districts, renovating or creating parks on riverfronts, revitalizing entertainment areas, providing incentives for professional sports teams to relocate, and emphasizing—sometimes even *inventing*—their unique cultural heritages in an attempt to attract business travelers and other visitors (Blank 1996; Zukin 1997; Hoffman 2003; Judd et al. 2003), despite little evidence that such schemes would result in the desired outcomes.

This same period witnessed the establishment of annual jazz festivals in New Orleans, Detroit, New York, and other cities (see, for example, Atkinson 1997), as well as shifts in locations where one might prominently find performing venues. As David Grazian observes in his study of blues clubs in Chicago, the cultural tourism of prior decades, which often entailed white patrons going into predominantly black areas to hear blues and jazz, was replaced by the relocation of venues to whiter, more centrally located areas—the very ones that might more easily draw visitors on vacation or on business. And as musicians realized there was more money to be made in these newer locations, it became increasingly difficult for venues located in lower-income or crime-ridden areas to remain solvent (Grazian 2003, 165–96). In New York, a similar process was underway as the aggregate number of venues decreased and the "slow march downtown" (Szwed 2000, 73), which had begun in the 1930s, continued. As a result, venues came to be more concentrated in and on the fringes of Greenwich Village. By the end of the twentieth century, even the lofts that had seemed a viable alternative in the 1970s were "done in by gentrification and new city laws that drove . . . musicians out. It was . . . a dry period for jazz, and only the oldest and most stable clubs survived. There would be other clubs coming along, but . . . most of the new ones were either supper clubs modeled on an old-time idea of social class, tourist sites aimed specifically at foreign clientele (and sometimes owned by foreign money), or eclectic new takes on '60s-styled loft clubs" (Szwed 2000, 74–75; see also Deutsche and Ryan 1984). In such a climate, musicians increasingly turned to alternative ways of supporting themselves, including teaching in emerging jazz studies programs and competing for grants from the National Endowment for the Arts as well as a number of local and regional agencies (Anderson 2002).

Indeed, even the media channels that had provided one means for musicians, venues, and labels to promote jazz began to decline during this period. The recording industry, feeling the effects of the economic downturn, was in a slump toward the end of the 1970s, with the result that many labels, including CTI, Atlantic, Elektra, and Columbia trimmed their (jazz) artist rosters and laid off employees in an attempt to remain viable. To the degree that they managed to profit from sales of recordings, they did so largely with fusion-oriented releases rather than more traditional forms of acoustic jazz. As Ricky Schultz, the national promotion manager for Warner Brothers' jazz and progressive music department, told one reporter, his label was being more cautious about investment and expenditures: "All areas are going to be scrutinized carefully . . . and areas like tour support and advertising are definitely going to be affected. Also, instead of an extensive marketing campaign up front, there will be more of a wait-and-see attitude" (Paikert 1979, 44–45).

Given such grim news from the labels, the demise in 1980 of WRVR (106.7 FM), New York City's last commercial jazz radio station, should have come as no surprise. Originally established at the Riverside Church in 1961, the station had always presented an eclectic mix of music. In a move spearheaded by Robert A. Orenbach, WRVR switched in 1974 to an all-jazz format that was dependent on advertising revenue from labels and venues. After losing money for a couple of years, the station was sold to the Sonderling Broadcasting Corporation, which altered the format to include more fusion- and pop-oriented jazz (Gans and Tusiewicz 1978). Despite the changes initiated by Sonderling's program directors and signs that the prospects for jazz were improving by 1979, the station, then owned by Viacom, was unable to generate either solid ratings or sufficient revenue and abruptly switched to a country music format on 8 September 1980 ("WRVR-FM Switches" 1980; Jeske 1980).

Although a number of noncommercial stations, like WNYU-FM and WEVD-FM, increased their jazz programming, and others, including WBGO-FM, lengthened their broadcast days, many musicians, record industry executives, music retailers, and event promoters presumed WRVR's format switch would have a chilling effect on the economy of the jazz scene, predicting that, compensatory measures aside, the markets for jazz recordings and performance would suffer. Vernon Slaughter, then vice president for progressive/jazz marketing at CBS Records, was quoted in the *New York Times* saying, "The whole idea of WRVR . . . was that it was a commercial outlet that allowed us to sell jazz. The problem is that now we don't have a target market that's into jazz that we can direct our advertising to directly. . . . New York is the largest market for jazz in the United States and when you take away WRVR it hurts" ("Radio Tries" 1980).[6] John F. Szwed confirms some of Slaughter's fears: "Understanding the directions taken by jazz since the '80s is not easy. The continued diffusion of various jazz styles, the disappearance of regular reviews in most newspapers and magazines, an economic slump in the record business, the shift of some of the most vital recording activity to small recording labels and to overseas, the confusion that followed the change in record formats from vinyl to CD, all contributed to the difficulty" (2000, 269). Indeed, over the next two decades even public radio stations, forced to get more of their operating revenue from listeners, joined the exodus, abandoning jazz (and classical music) in favor of the news, talk, and special interest programs that radio consultants such as David Giovannoni guaranteed would shore up their listener bases (Freedman 2001).[7]

In short, changes in international and municipal economic policy had long-lasting effects on the viability of jazz in American cities like New York. Although conventional wisdom says that the uprisings in urban African American neighborhoods in the late 1960s were largely responsible for so-called white flight, it should be clear that the conditions that made the uprisings possible had their roots in an earlier era (Sugrue 1996). The policies implemented by municipal authorities in the 1970s and 1980s, however, had that conventional wisdom as well as an economically changed world at their root. They invoked fears about safety as well as the need to attract tourist and corporate revenue (Warren 1993; Zukin 1995) to justify certain alterations of the spatial configuration of urban environments. As bars and clubs presenting live jazz in African American neighborhoods, unable to depend on the leisure dollars of industrial workers, grew less numerous, they were replaced by venues in whiter, more affluent areas, ones that could pay even poorly compensated musicians more money. Likewise, the media outlets that benefited from venues' promotional needs had to find new ways to attract advertising revenue. As a result, record labels, promoters, and musicians all found themselves scrambling to adjust to a changed, less economically stable environment.

These examples show that the development of jazz in a particular locale is always and everywhere a story of a musical style's dependence on the work of a number of individuals as well as their accommodation to the ways that space is transformed and controlled. A similar perspective emerges from Nat Hentoff's *The Jazz Life* (1961b). He focuses attention on the jazz scene in the late 1950s. His collected essays take a wide view, offering in turn discussions of the motivations and backgrounds of audiences, the role of formal and informal education in musicians' development, the benefits and disadvantages of membership in the music union, the economics and atmosphere of jazz clubs, the constraints imposed on performers by recording contracts, and the involvement of musicians with drugs and the underworld. Likewise, Martin Williams's essays in *Jazz Heritage* (1985) and elsewhere bring the picture into sharper focus, providing glimpses of musicians at work, in the recording studio and at rehearsals. By concentrating his critical eye on the

nature of jazz composition and improvisation, as well as the accommodations musicians necessarily make with performance venues and various other intermediaries, Williams implicitly suggests the importance
of a scene-based perspective. The work of W. Royal Stokes (1991) and
Stuart Nicholson (1990) helps to complete a picture of what has happened since the end of the 1960s. None of these works, however, explicitly takes the interconnected roles of a variety of actors and institutions
as its subject.

Not surprisingly, some of the most insightful work on the constitution of jazz scenes has come from journalists employed by national newspapers and international jazz magazines. Because they are of necessity
more concerned with the day-to-day and month-to-month functioning of
the scene, their work can be useful in exploring present-day phenomena.
Magazines like *JazzTimes* and *Down Beat* from time to time include
issue-based articles (Jones 1995; Corbett 1995; Gavin 2001; Milkowski
2001)—alongside news items, artist features, record reviews, and advertisements for recordings and instruments. The *New York Times,* the
Philadelphia Inquirer, the *New Yorker,* and the *Atlantic,* among others,
also publish occasional articles, performance reviews, and artist features.
There are, of course, easily discernible biases and distortions of fact in
the press. Among musicians and the critical establishment, it is somewhat expected that national and international magazines, whose main
advertisers are record companies, might shy away from being overly
critical of the recording industry from which they receive a great deal of
their advertising revenue.

In any event, any responsible discussion of jazz is incomplete without consideration of the varied factors that make it possible. A modern
jazz scene in New York City, or anywhere else, is properly understood
as a socially constructed arena (see Spradley 1988, 102) within which
jazz performance occurs and is made possible. The processes that bring a
scene into being and modify it over time differentiate jazz from musics in
other scenes as well as distinguish straight-ahead performers from those,
for example, who might be classified as "avant-garde" or "fusion" performers. A scene is a fluid space within which a variety of actors and institutions negotiate their relationships to each other and those outside
their networks (Barth 1978; Bender 1982, 3–11) as well as the various
legal structures that enable and constrain their activities. In the process,
these actors and institutions form shifting alliances, negotiate the boundaries of the scene—what can legitimately be considered jazz and who can

legitimately be considered a participant in the scene—and construct one central context that renders jazz's meanings intelligible. The jazz scene is therefore not a stable or neatly isolatable entity: its shape and constitution are constantly in flux. Sometimes its actors and institutions work together seamlessly; at other times (or even simultaneously) they may be at cross-purposes. The apparent complexity of the scene, however, is not an indication of chaos: it merely underscores the contestation and negotiation characteristic of human groups and relationships.[8]

The actors and institutions whose changing relationships constitute the processes that create and sustain the jazz scene include broad groups of musicians, audiences, performance venues, educational institutions, the recording industry, and radio, print, and television media, among others. In the next chapter I'll consider each of these groups in turn and discuss some of the ways in which they interact with each other. While I separate these groups for the sake of discussion, it is impossible to examine any of them divorced from the others without distorting the resulting picture. They are all part of a social field, conceived as "the product of [a] continuous and changing relationship between the 'system' under observation and the 'external' world" (Comaroff 1985, 3). An exclusive focus on any component of the system might tend to overstate its autonomy or understate its interaction with other elements in the social field.

The scene is, in this sense, inherently *spatial* and *historical*. It is a product not only of the interactions of its participants with one another *in* space and time but also of their interactions *through* space and time. Through purposive action, they create the scene and conceive it as both a physical manifestation of space and a cognitive construct. It is centered on particular physical spaces, to be sure, but not necessarily bound by them. The activities of musicians and other participants in those locales are not only affected by the given elements of geography; they also have the potential to substantially alter that geography through their movements as well as their responses to and attempts to control it. Likewise, their conceptions of that geography influence the ways in which they understand themselves as beings in the world, based in a local scene but not isolated from others. Formative experiences in other locales, to be sure, condition the ways in which participants conceive a scene as both distinct from and related to others in the same locale or to similar ones in other places. But those experiences and the conceptions that result from them are subject to reinterpretation in light of new experiences as one moves both in time and space. In the end, conceiving jazz's development and existence as spatial emphasizes the inseparability and contingency of history and geography, drawing our attention to the importance of human interaction and away from abstractions that disguise such activities or elide their continued shaping force.

CHAPTER 4

The New York Jazz Scene in the 1990s

Jazz in the 1990s, as in the 1920s and the 1950s, enjoyed a particularly high public profile, one that perhaps culminated with the airing of Ken Burns's *Jazz* on PBS in 2001. Interest in jazz, however, was still centered more on the personalities of musicians and the abstract development of musical style than on the contours and effects of a temporally and spatially located scene. Building on the previous discussions of history, memory, race, culture, and practices, on one hand, and spatiality, on the other, I offer as a corrective a focus not only on the people moving through and populating the scene, but also on the spaces and institutions they manipulate (and that manipulate them) in the process of making jazz. Central here are the relationships between all involved as the scene changes and develops, even in the course of one decade. In the pages that follow, I will rapidly sketch the major elements of the jazz scene in and since the 1990s. Toward the end of the chapter I devote more attention to the interaction of those differing elements to show how, together, they have as much impact on the making of jazz as ready-made notions of musical or historical progress.

MUSICIANS

The number of New York–based musicians active on the jazz scene is difficult to determine. Reliance on the data one could gather from the membership rolls of Local 802 of the American Federation of Musicians

(AFM) would probably be misleading, undercounting musicians who might be said to be part of the New York scene.[1] An alternative approach, using data taken from the most recent United States census, might be misleading as well, as it would include all those who claim "jazz musician" as their profession and perhaps not include those who simply describe themselves as a "musician." One government-funded report relied on union membership, questionnaires, and sophisticated sampling methods to estimate that there are more than seven thousand musicians in the New York metropolitan area who derive at least part of their living from jazz performance (Jeffri 2003). These and other factors make choosing a statistically representative sample of musicians for a study such as this one extremely difficult, if not impossible. Among the variables that one might have to account for in attempting to construct such a sample are race, gender, ethnicity, age, geographic background, instrument(s) played, training, performance style(s), and status on the scene.

What can be said with certainty is that new musicians arrive in the city every day from different parts of the United States and the world. Like musicians conversant with other musical styles (see Florida et al. 2010, 800–801), many of them are seeking to establish themselves: to make themselves known to other musicians, to get gigs, and perhaps to attract the attention of critics and recording industry personnel. At the same time, many other musicians leave New York City, some moving across the Hudson River to New Jersey, some to areas immediately north of New York City or further north in New York state, and still others to parts of northeastern Pennsylvania, other states, and even other countries. In many cases the musicians who leave are those who have grown tired of the pace or expense of the city, are advancing in age, or have young children (Milkowski 2001).

The musicians who remain in the city live primarily in three of the city's boroughs: Manhattan, Brooklyn, and Queens.[2] As in many other cities, one's income largely determines where one can reside. Typically, only those musicians with the most prestige and/or the most stable financial portfolios can afford to reside in the more expensive Manhattan locales, which include Central Park West, Midtown Manhattan, and some areas of Chelsea, Greenwich Village, and SoHo. Residing in those areas tends to afford musicians easier access to Manhattan recording studios, performance venues, recording company offices, and other important sites. Other musicians living in Manhattan typically reside in less expensive areas: on the Lower East Side or further "uptown," on the Upper West Side, in Harlem, and in Washington Heights. Anecdotal evidence, however, suggests that the majority of musicians live in Brooklyn, having been drawn there by lower rents and the presence of other musicians. Many of the Brooklyn neighborhoods favored by musicians, particularly areas like Park Slope, Fort Greene, and Clinton Hill, are conveniently situated close to Manhattan-bound subway trains, which facilitate getting to the island for performance and recording opportunities. In addition, those neighborhoods afford more convenient access to important locations in Brooklyn, such as the recording studio Systems Two and various bars and restaurants that have served as sites for jam sessions.[3]

Wherever they reside in the city, the many musicians who are part of the New York scene play in a variety of styles and are connected to each in a number of ways. Many have come from the same regions of the United States, have studied in the same music schools or conservatories, have had common performing experiences in various groups, have familial relationships with others on the scene, play the same instruments, frequent the same venues, live in the same neighborhoods, or possess some combination of these and other factors (see Wilmer 1980, 144). One can therefore speak of Memphis pianists, the New School crowd, Art Blakey alumni, the Jones brothers, alto players, the Smalls scene, or Brooklyn cats, with each designation demarcating differing but sometimes overlapping mini-networks.[4] Each of these methods of identification offers potential for the formation of alliances among performing musicians.

In this sense, the musicians on the jazz scene constitute a network of networks. Knowledge of the various mini-networks of musicians as well as membership in any of them helps to confirm one's place on the scene. Each of those mini-networks might be utilized under various circumstances—such as when there is a vacancy in a band, or when one wants to organize a tribute to a particular musician, inquire about setting up residence in a certain neighborhood, or find the best night to go to a particular musician's engagement. Even more, those alliances, based as they are on shared experiences or shared characteristics, allow musicians to establish affective ties among themselves and to break a largely heterogeneous and shifting community into more manageable units.

Those alliances also roughly correspond with groups of musicians who "hang" with each other or with other scene participants. "Hanging" is what Ingrid Monson described as "public visibility," attending jazz events and being recognized by other participants as part of the scene (1991, 357). It is possible to see "jazz events" as including any events at which scene participants may gather, including birthday celebrations, music-related art openings, master classes, or even nonjazz musical events. Musicians can hang at various clubs that stay open particularly late (such as the now-closed Bradley's or Smalls), at certain bars or restaurants, or even at the residences of other musicians. In any of those situations, one's place in the scene is confirmed when one is recognized as part of the scene and included in conversations that may arise regarding performers, performances, or other issues related to the scene's daily functioning. Still, musicians who do not hang can be considered valuable participants in the scene to the extent that they are linked to it by the other types of alliances described above.

Issues of race, ethnicity, gender, and sexuality also form bases on which boundaries can be constructed that include or exclude certain musicians. One might assert that, on a gross level, African American musicians tend to hang with other African American musicians; that European American musicians tend to hang with other European Americans; that female musicians rarely get the same level of encouragement or work that male musicians do; and that, with a few notable exceptions, many homosexual musicians tend not to discuss their sexuality openly (Robinson 1994; Gavin 2001; Davis 2002). It would be a mistake, however, to assume that the exclusivity of such alliances could be explained merely by racism, reverse racism, sexism, or homophobia. That is, the alliances that musicians form—based on their home cities or regions, where they went to school, what bands they have played in, what instruments they play, and where they tend to hang—might leave the impression that racism or sexism or homophobia is a driving force when other factors might be more salient. Saxophonist Joshua Redman made this point clear and revealed some of its complexity when I questioned him about the composition of his band:

> *TJ:* I'm sure that someone has commented to you at some point about, you know, um, you know, looking . . . Kevin [Hays], Brad [Mehldau], Jonny [King], Peter [Martin]: all white pianists.[5] Um, and someone might try to argue that that's by design.
>
> *JR:* Right. Um, I would say . . . I mean, it's *not*. It's . . . not at all. Uh, I mean . . . Before I even get into it, I'll just say, you know, one thing that throws a wrench into all that is that there was . . . The first time that Brad had to sub out a gig was in May of last year [1994]. He couldn't do two weeks with me. And I got Eric Reed to do it. Eric is black. So, you know, at least that throws a little wrench into the pattern. And that was exactly the same situation [with a white substitute]. It just happened to be for less time . . . When I realized that Brad had to take time off from the band, and I was looking for a sub, the order of the piano players . . . in which I

called them—let me get this right for the record—were [he names, in succession, three black pianists] . . . I called those three . . . Did I call [an-
other white pianist]? I don't know. Oh, [the sub I chose] was somewhere
right after . . . but I called those three first. And that doesn't necessarily
say that much because the order in which I call people, you know, wasn't
necessarily the order in which . . . who I thought the best person for the
gig was. It had to do with a lot: who I thought might be available, who I,
you know, who I happened to flip to in the Rolodex first, or whatever.
But I will say that, you know, I mean, I love [the subsitute], and with all
due respect to him . . . [The three black piansists]—I knew [the first of
them] couldn't do it. But they were my first choices. Oh, I know who I
called [fourth]. I called [another white player] . . . It's definitely not by
design. (Redman 1995a)

Redman's response suggests that the appearance of racist thinking doesn't
fully reveal the processes that might be responsible for that appearance.
Moreover, he asserts that some propositions that might be considered
racist, particularly by writers like Lees, can have reasoned, nonracist
explanations.[6]

The foregoing is in no way an attempt to minimize the impact of racism, sexism, and homophobia on the jazz scene or the real ways in
which they affect the daily lives of many of its participants. I am, however, arguing that there is a need for much more nuanced, historically
aware research on these topics—particularly research that sees them as
the products of various relationships between individuals and groups.
Paul Gilroy (1991b) argues that most commonsense ideas about racism—
and, by extension, those about sexism and homophobia—tend to focus
on it as a problem to be solved or to focus on ways of compensating its
victims. The problem with such thinking, however, is that "the oscillation
between black as problem and black as victim has become, today, the
principal mechanism through which 'race' is pushed outside of history
and into the realm of natural, inevitable events" (11). In being viewed as
part of the natural landscape, race (or ethnicity, or gender, or sexuality) is
configured as something that is peripheral to the concerns of daily life: it
is merely there, in the background. When it comes forward, one need
merely deal with its current manifestation—with the problem or the
victims—and send it back to the background, without ever addressing
the historical conditions that support it as an ideology.[7]

With an eye to the differences that characterized the backgrounds of
musicians within the scene, I sought out individuals for this study who
were born and came of age in different eras, who come from different

parts of the United States, who play different instruments, who have followed different educational paths, and who participate in the scene to varying degrees. Understanding the jazz scene and the musicians who are part of it requires engagement with the histories of each of the musicians and the relationships that they have with other actors on the scene. Only by being attentive to those issues might one come to fruitful conclusions about the scene's makeup and the relative status of various groups within it.

The musicians formally interviewed for this book (listed by primary instrument) were alto saxophonists Donald Harrison, Antonio Hart, and Steve Wilson; tenor saxophonists Joe Lovano, Sam Newsome,[8] and Joshua Redman; singer Maria DeAngelis; pianists Bruce Barth and James Williams; guitarist Peter Bernstein; and drummer Gregory Hutchinson. Other musicians were informally interviewed in connection with an article I researched for the *New York Times Magazine* (Jackson 1995). They were pianists Hank Jones, Harold Mabern, and Mulgrew Miller; bassist Milt Hinton; and drummer Elvin Jones. Numerous other musicians were valuable sources of information in conversation. Among them were saxophonists Lou Donaldson and Craig Handy; pianists George Colligan, Charles Craig, James Hurt, Jonny King, Eric Reed, and Anthony Wonsey; organist Larry Goldings; guitarists Howard Alden, Russell Malone, and Mark Whitfield; cellist Lesa Terry; bassists Christian McBride and Christopher Thomas; and drummers Brian Blade, Curtis Boyd, Leon Parker, Clarence Penn, Marvin "Smitty" Smith, and Kenny Washington. Finally, I interviewed saxophonist James Carter and trombonists Wycliffe Gordon and Ronald Westray after the official fieldwork period and in connection with work I did for Atlantic Records.[9]

These musicians enjoy varying levels of status on the scene reckoned in a number of overlapping ways. One might distinguish well-respected and influential musicians from those who are less so. One might attribute higher status to older musicians who have been playing the music longer and presumably know it better than younger musicians. Those who have played with other influential musicians may be of higher status than those who haven't. Musicians who lead their own bands generally have a higher status than those who are primarily sidemen. Musicians with recording contracts have certain material advantages over those who do not. And those with major-label contracts—and thus presumably benefit from better distribution, marketing, and promotion—have, in a sense, a higher status than those with minor or independent label contracts.

Likewise, one might distinguish the conservatory-trained from the "self-taught" musicians, but it is not clear which group would have the higher status.

These status distinctions, as well as the other ways in which I have suggested that alliances might be built and boundaries constructed, have important implications for a musician's daily experiences. If one considers a musician's main goals (cf. Becker 1951) to be getting income-producing gigs, developing artistically, enhancing his or her reputation on the scene, and perhaps getting public or financial recognition, it should be clear how such statuses or boundaries might affect a musician's prospects. Those who have major-label contracts, significant public reputations, and "drawing power," for example, have greater access to lucrative gigs at well-known venues. Some have argued—and trends in signings since the mid-1980s might be cited as evidence—that younger musicians are favored for the most lucrative recording contracts while older musicians are typically signed by smaller labels (Heckman 1990; Masland 1990; Woodard 1990; McCormick 1992; Moon 1992).[10] Whatever differences obtain between the musicians I consulted, there are observations that apply to all of them as well as to many others living and working in New York City. There is a core of central activities that make up their daily lives and work: performing "live," making recordings, practicing, rehearsing, composing, and performing other tasks related to career development.

Most of the musicians devote themselves to all of these activities at one time or another, but gigs and recordings take precedence over all other activities. Specific income figures for engagements or recording sessions (or individual musicians) are difficult to come by, if only because most musicians negotiate their salaries and contracts independently. A performer might make as little as $40 or $50 for a night in a restaurant as a sideman and between $100 and $200 for better attended and financed engagements in nightclubs. But a well-placed musician, even without a recording contract, can make a comfortable wage.[11] Part of that income comes from major-label recording sessions, at which AFM regulations have to be strictly observed. Under those regulations, the least one can make for each "session" is $339.20.[12] Some musicians may command above-scale wages for recording sessions. Those same musicians may also, as a favor to others, work at (or below) scale.[13] Each commercially released recording requires a minimum of two sessions, as defined by the union, to complete. When agreeing to do record dates or gigs, musicians have to be careful about scheduling, being sure not to commit themselves to events that are occurring simultaneously. Musicians who make a habit of "double booking" jeopardize their future opportunities for work by appearing disorganized and unreliable.

Practicing and rehearsing are more conditional. Frequently the time-consuming demands of touring, doing record dates, or performing live make it nearly impossible for musicians to practice as much as they might deem ideal. Likewise, groups tend to rehearse only when there are new tunes or arrangements to be learned or when record dates or other important engagements are pending. In any event, the deciding factor is often money. If one calls a rehearsal but cannot guarantee compensation, there can be little complaint if the other musicians opt not to attend and take paying work instead. Moreover, while some musicians may consciously work on the craft of composition on a regular basis, an approaching record date is often sufficient motivation for greater compositional activity. Again, a major factor motivating such a choice would be its income-producing potential.

Lastly, the varied career development activities include sending out notices to those on one's mailing list informing them of upcoming engagements or record releases; meeting with record industry personnel; meeting with or talking to club owners or booking agents to secure gigs; and being interviewed by various media or publicity organizations, among other things. For some musicians, such as pianist Bruce Barth, these activities can almost completely consume the time that one would ideally devote to practicing and playing. He does the work on his own because the 15 percent that a manager might command, before transportation and lodging expenses, is prohibitive for musicians like him who are less well-known or play as headliners infrequently. In contrast, musicians such as Joshua Redman and Joe Lovano have major-label support and play frequently enough to justify and profit from the work of managers and booking agents. They benefit as well from a star system that emphasizes bandleaders. As Barth points out, recordings are generally labeled with the name of the bandleader rather than his or her group, for example, with "Joshua Redman" rather than "Miles Davis Quintet."

If the foregoing discussion seems overly focused on economic concerns, it merely serves to show that these are professional musicians who, in addition to satisfying their artistic imperatives, have to make a living. With limited resources, they have to find the most effective ways of allocating their time. Some supplement their income by giving private lessons, teaching music at area institutions, or playing in pit orchestras for Broadway and symphonic shows. But all of the daily activities of the musicians are informed by the myriad ways in which they have formed alliances with others and by the way the boundaries of their networks have been constructed. Those groupings help to determine who is called for record dates or live performances, whose tunes will be included on a record date, and which musicians will be favored for recording contracts, lucrative gigs, or positions in repertory groups like the Lincoln Center Jazz Orchestra.

AUDIENCES

If identifying and profiling jazz musicians is difficult, then characterizing the jazz audience raises even more issues. Does the jazz audience comprise those individuals who purchase jazz recordings? Those who listen to jazz on the radio? Those who attend live performances? Or is the jazz audience some combination of those categories of participation? And however one constructs the audience, how can one characterize it?

Many of these issues have been addressed in Scott DeVeaux's *Jazz in America: Who's Listening?* (1995). His monograph is an interpretation of data gathered in the 1992 Survey of Public Participation in the Arts (SPPA) sponsored by the National Endowment for the Arts, for which 12,739 people from various regions of the United States were contacted (28). He describes several difficulties he encountered in interpreting the SPPA's data. The aggregate jazz audience that emerges from the survey includes those who attended live performances, listened to radio and recordings, and watched performances on television—broadcast live or taped—in addition to those who performed jazz. In other words, the survey "represents the broadest possible interpretation . . . including casual, passive, or even unintentional listening to jazz through any medium." He concludes that "the more purposeful supporters of [jazz]—the regular concert goers, record buyers, and radio listeners that one ordinarily associates with the concept of 'audience'—undoubtedly constitute a fraction of the total reported jazz audience, and probably a small fraction at that" (5).

The SPPA's findings are further complicated by their reliance on "respondent identification," that is, by their sidestepping the question of what jazz is and allowing each respondent to "apply his or her own definition of jazz" to the questions posed. Indeed, only at the end of the survey, when the respondents were questioned about their preferences for different types of music, were they given any clue that jazz was "a genre distinct from . . . 'blues [or] rhythm and blues,' 'soul,' 'big band,' or 'rock'" (6). In other words, the audience described by the report includes supporters of jazz as I have defined them, as well as supporters of various forms of "contemporary jazz" and jazz-influenced popular music such as those recorded and performed by Kenny G and Anita Baker, for example.

Still, some interesting conclusions emerge from DeVeaux's analysis of the data, which describe the characteristics of the most optimistically large jazz audience (1995, 16–21). Those with an annual income of $50,000 or greater are disproportionately represented in the jazz audience, as are those who have had at least some college education. The audience, particularly for live performance, is relatively youthful, with the majority clustering in the age range twenty-five to forty-four years of age. The jazz audience is also predominantly white, but DeVeaux offers a few cautionary notes about that observation:

> White Americans make up 81 percent of the jazz attenders, 78 percent of those watching jazz on television or listening to jazz recordings, and 79 percent of those listening to jazz on the radio. This simply reflects the numerical predominance of whites in the population. African Americans, who account for 11 percent of the population as a whole, make up 17 percent of jazz attenders, 18 percent of the radio audience, 19 percent of the television audience, and nearly 20 percent of those who listen to jazz recordings. . . . African Americans consistently participate in jazz at a higher rate than white Americans: they are one and a half times as likely to attend jazz performances and even more likely to participate in jazz through the media . . . Figures from 1982 show the same pattern: blacks participating in jazz at significantly higher rates than whites, while participating in other art forms at significantly lower rates. (23)

The jazz audience is also more male than the audiences for any of the other arts activities—classical music, ballet, opera, musicals, and plays—covered by the survey. Most interesting is the assertion, based on figures for frequency of attendance at live events, that as the jazz audience becomes "more dedicated, it becomes more male and more African American" (27).[14]

Although it might have been informative to compare figures from the SPPA with ethnographic or other local data, my attempt to do so was complicated by a number of factors. Chief among them was the unwillingness of record labels and other private recording, broadcast, and media concerns to furnish me with audience or listener profiles. In a phone interview, for example, Stuart Pressman, then director of marketing for Polygram Classics and Jazz, described the average jazz record buyer as ranging in age from twenty to seventy. He sidestepped other specific questions about audience demographics by saying, "There is no particular ethnic or income group that has a monopoly on the music" (1995). Other record company officials were similarly unwilling to divulge such information, partly because providing it might have made it possible for competing labels to use sales figures or audience demographics against them. Equally uninformative statistics about the demographics of the jazz audience are cited by Jeff Levenson (1992).

The only manner in which local survey data was available was via one radio station's listenership profile. During my fieldwork, the metropolitan New York City area was served by three radio stations that claimed to be jazz stations: WBGO-FM (88.3), a National Public Radio affiliate located in Newark, New Jersey; WKCR-FM (89.9), a station based at Columbia University; and WQCD-FM (101.9), which is privately owned. Of the three, WBGO focused most explicitly on the styles played by the musicians who are the focus of this book. WKCR played a great deal of jazz but also programmed a variety of other types of music, in keeping with its status as a college radio station. Perhaps because it was less dependent on individual donors or commercial sponsors to stay on the air, it presented a great deal more historical and "avant-garde" jazz than WBGO. For the same reason, audience demographics seemed to be of less (public) significance to it. WQCD, better known then as "CD 101.9," specialized in styles labeled by the recording industry as "contemporary jazz" or "smooth jazz." Its programming included artists like George Howard, Kenny G, Sade, and Anita Baker—all of whose music falls outside the boundaries established for this study.[15] Its demographic information was available primarily to potential advertisers.

The information on WBGO's web site, however, was quite fascinating. Its audience was described as being "24% African American, 6.23% Latino, and 75% not black or Hispanic." The station description also informed readers that more than four hundred thousand individuals, clustered between the ages of twenty-five and fifty-four and with an average household income of $100,000 per year, comprised its listenership. In addition, the page included a table detailing the percentage of its listeners "above market average" who had certain characteristics or engaged in activities that might have been attractive to underwriters, for example, those with postgraduate degrees, who worked in sales, owned homes with values greater than $1,000,000, played golf, attended performances at Lincoln Center, or read the *New York Times*.[16] Although it was not mentioned how those figures were obtained, they perhaps do argue for high participation by upscale African Americans and Latinos, variously defined. They also offer a few pieces of information that facilitate comparison with data from the SPPA: that African Americans are a disproportionately large part of the audience, which also happens to be well educated and financially well-off.

Fieldwork observations did little to make more detailed comparisons easy. In eighteen months of attending events at the most prominent mainstream jazz venues in New York City, I was unable to identify any regular audience members. That is, I was unable to identify individuals who regularly attended live performances and who were connected to the scene *only* as fans. Those individuals whom I did see frequently were all attached to the jazz scene via some more primary connection. They attended live events as relatives of other participants or as musicians, writers, record industry personnel, booking agents, publicists, and the like. Identifying them in terms of racial, ethnic, or gender categories was not possible based on strict observation. The audiences in clubs in Greenwich Village were primarily white American, if one considered only non-musicians as audience members. The cases became more complex once musicians were added. There were also occasions when many European and East Asian tourists—my ascription is based on the languages I heard—were in attendance.

There were many individuals in any of the clubs on a given night, particularly if an advance article or favorable review had appeared in the *New York Times*. On the many occasions when I struck up conversations with other attendees seated near me, the ensuing discussion would always lead to one of three conclusions: that those individuals had come because they sought a different kind of social activity; because they wanted to hear "some jazz," but had very little understanding of the musicians or the music (cf. Berliner 1994, 456–57); or because they possessed some degree of knowledge about the music and were connected to the scene in one of the ways mentioned above.

I came to consider the first two groups to be more casual, occasional consumers of live jazz, who were sometimes guided by the dictates of tourism (Watrous 1996a), jazz's higher profile in the media since the mid-1980s, and the music's ability to cement the position of its listeners as educated, culturally aware members of society (cf. Bourdieu 1984; Small 1987a). Although the latter group shares some of the motivations of the former two, its dedication to the music was more apparent to me, especially since I eventually saw many people in the latter group at other events (although I cannot recall having seen any individuals from the former two groups after my initial encounters with them). Using De-Veaux's phrase from the previous discussion, these individuals were the "more purposeful" supporters of jazz, ones who were critically engaged in listening to jazz radio, purchasing jazz recordings, and, importantly, going to hear live jazz performances.

The distinction between the latter group and the two former ones perhaps corresponds to the one between fans and spectators, respectively. Barry Shank (1994) describes the difference in terms of identification with the musicians and the scene. He quotes one of his informants describing the motivation of a fan: "There was always that pressure that if you didn't go out, you were missing something. You had to do it regularly. You had to keep in touch" (131). Being a fan entails consistent, purposeful participation in musical events or other activities comprising life on the scene (see, for example, Cavicchi 1998). Although the fans whose acquaintance I made frequently expressed sentiments similar to those of Shank's informant, those spectators whose attachment to the scene was more ephemeral seemed to feel less pressure, viewing live jazz performances as occasional diversions. Such a view, of course, is only an ascription. And by presenting it, I am not asserting that the categories are not permeable or that one's membership in either group is not subject to change. In other words, spectators can become fans when they have the desire and the financial resources to do so. Likewise, fans can become spectators under appropriate circumstances.

What emerged from my interactions with dedicated jazz fans was a feeling of camaraderie. In conversation, we would discuss recordings; other live performances that we had witnessed; upcoming performances; our opinions of various musicians, writers, or other individuals or institutions on the scene; places to buy recordings; different sources of information about the music; and other issues. In other situations, the feeling of camaraderie was tacitly expressed through the exchange of glances in response to remarkable aspects of a performance event. Whether our responses were verbal or tacit, through them we as audience members would confirm our participation in and knowledge of the scene. Likewise, we were participating in a process where individual understandings were molded into a larger system of social and cultural meaning.

Once a performance started, conversation was kept to a minimum. As knowledgeable participants, our primary concern was experiencing an event as it unfolded, making associations between it and past ones, cross-referencing sounds heard in the present with those in our memories—in short, making various interpretive moves. That this process was occurring for other listeners was made apparent to me by post-performance conversations. Frequent topics would be the provenance of particular musical quotations, the names of particular tunes, and assessments of the success of a performance based on a number of evaluative criteria (see chapter 5). In that sense, we were approaching the music as something that required active and constant attention (see Kivy 1990, 68–73; Marshall 1982, 165) filtered through a shared body of knowledge and interpretive frames. Berliner's description of the listening and response of knowledgeable audience members was confirmed by my observations: "Knowledgeable jazz audience members respond to exceptional improvisations with bursts of applause, shouts of praise, and whistle calls. Some join in the delineation of the beat by swaying, nodding, finger snapping, and—when the style of jazz, the occasion, or room permits it—dancing. Others mark its course by singing silently to themselves. . . . At the very least, polite audience members listen attentively, typically offering applause after solos and at the conclusion of each piece" (Berliner 1994, 456).

It is important to note here that those same types of responses can and do accompany exceptional moments of group interaction. One interesting example, which illustrates the degree to which performance interaction can engender audience response and interaction, comes from a performance by the Ahmad Jamal Trio at the Blue Note in February of 1995. I was accompanied by a friend whom I had told about Jamal's performances. Throughout the set that we participated in, we kept looking at each other in astonishment, responding to different interactions taking place among the musicians. At the same time, however, we were also exchanging approving and amazed glances with two other audience members unknown to us before that evening. When the set ended, they came to us, introduced themselves, and thanked us for having seen and shared the show with them.

In the end, the jazz audience is to some degree composed of all of the groups of potential participants mentioned at the beginning of this section. The audience as it is conceived here, however, comprises a specific subset: the group that engages in all three types of participation—musical event attendance, record buying, and radio listening—regularly and frequently and goes to great lengths to keep up with the happenings on the scene. Although it may be true that many of them do so because of their professions, in conversation many of them also noted that they chose their jobs precisely because their positions allowed them to maintain links to the music and the musicians. The major function that audience members serve is to provide economic and social support to the musicians via payment of cover charges or ticket prices, purchasing recordings, enthusiastic and respectful responses to their performances, and support of radio stations that play the music (which in turn generates royalties for musicians).

EDUCATIONAL INSTITUTIONS

The role played by educational institutions in the constitution and maintenance of the jazz scene is important, but its impact has frequently been misunderstood. The ones that seem to have the most importance for the scene are New York's New School for Jazz and Contemporary Music, the Mannes College of Music, and the Manhattan School of Music; New Jersey's William Paterson College; and Boston's Berklee College of Music. Each of these institutions serves as a conservatory for jazz musicians in training, taking young men and women recently graduated from high school and giving them instruction in harmony, composition, instrumental technique, and improvisation. In addition, they get performance experience in various required and optional performing ensembles. Pianist Bruce Barth characterizes such programs as

> imperfect substitute[s] for a jazz scene that was once here, but is no longer with us . . . the way . . . it used to be in every city across the country. People in high school, you know, maybe not in every city, but most of the cities—whether they were—like Detroit, Philly [Philadelphia], Chicago, the main jazz towns. People in high school were playing bebop. That was the music of their day . . . Jazz was the popular music of the time. People were playing, and there were all these opportunities to learn . . . So they didn't have to go to school to study jazz 'cause they were really immersed in it. And now, of course, times have changed, and jazz is no longer a popular music. And it's a music that, like, a small percentage of the population tries to listen to or play or buy records. And so, you really won't find it *everywhere* like you did in the past. And so, I think the schools can give students some of the basic foundation that they, in the past, . . . would have gotten hanging out on the scene. (1994; see also Reed 1979; Gottlieb 1957)[17]

In a similar vein, those institutions now serve as primary places where alliances are formed among young musicians. Through their studies and extracurricular performance activities they form bonds that often last beyond the school experience. Roy Hargrove and Antonio Hart, for example, met at Berklee; Hart, as result of their friendship, was asked to be the saxophonist in Hargrove's first quintet. Peter Bernstein be-friended organist Larry Goldings in a high school music camp and later became associated with musicians like Goldings, saxophonist Jesse Da-vis, and pianist Brad Mehldau, all of whom were students in the New School's jazz program in the late 1980s. Bernstein has since recorded and performed frequently with all of them.

In addition, educational institutions also function as places where older musicians make the acquaintance of younger ones whom they might hire through their peers on the faculty at those schools. They may also meet young musicians who play similar instruments in clinics and master classes at those institutions. In any event, after making the ac-quaintance of a young musician, an older performer has another poten-tial player to hire or to recommend to someone else. Drummer Jimmy Cobb, for example, after meeting Peter Bernstein during his time as an instructor at the New School, later enlisted Bernstein and Mehldau for an early version of Cobb's Mob. Jackie McLean did the same with stu-dents from the Hartt School in West Hartford, Connecticut.

Although study at these institutions may make it easier for musicians to make their way into the networks that constitute the scene, it is not the only path of entry for young musicians. Many young musicians have come into contact with others through sitting in with famous musicians playing in their hometowns or via the recommendations of local musi-cians to touring ones, especially when substitute players are needed on an emergency basis. Saxophonist James Carter, for example, did not attend a conservatory but came out of a vibrant local scene in Detroit in the 1980s and enriching summer experiences, like the one provided by the Blue Lake Arts Camp. Likewise, saxophonist Joshua Redman did not follow the conservatory path, but, while attending Harvard University, took summer courses at Berklee and befriended musicians such as Antonio Hart, Seamus Blake, Paul LeDuca, and Jorge Rossy (all of whom have been significant young musicians on the New York scene). The time he spent playing with those musicians and others to whom they introduced him provided contact, albeit limited, with the social aspect of conserva-tory life. Moreover, when he came to New York City in the fall of 1991, he became a roommate of Rossy and LeDuca.

As I noted in chapter 2, some critics and older musicians have in re-cent years criticized younger conservatory-trained musicians for sound-ing sterile and emotionless.[18] Such criticisms partially ignore the long history that some of these institutions have in training young musicians, particularly those who have come of age since the 1950s. Some of the older musicians consulted for this study, like Joe Lovano, studied at Berklee in the 1970s, while Antonio Hart and Sam Newsome, among the younger ones, studied there in the 1980s.[19] Likewise, those critics don't always acknowledge the enormous influence of older, well-respected musicians who teach or have taught at those institutions, such as saxophonists Joe Viola, Andy McGhee, and Billy Pierce and the late drummer Alan Dawson, all of whom have been or were longtime members of the Berklee faculty.

The actual objects of those criticisms seem to be each school's methods of instruction. As I observed in chapter 2, particularly singled out for criticism is the chord-scale approach to improvisation, in which one is taught a series of scales that are appropriate for improvising over certain harmonies. Jamey Aebersold's Music Minus One recordings—sometimes used by young musicians—came, for example, with lead sheets that presented the pitches or scales that one might superimpose on a particular chord.[20] Saxophonist Joshua Redman noted that using the Aebersold records and pattern books as pedagogical tools helped him in some ways, but they "messed up" his playing at a time when he should have been focusing more on how to play within the jazz idiom rather than via a theoretical approach (Redman 1995a). Guitarist Peter Bernstein expresses their limitations succinctly, noting how they can close off inquiry and exploration: "All those Jamey Aebersold things where you have a chart of a tune, every time you see an altered chord, he writes the scale out for you. Like that's the only scale that's worth really checking" (Bernstein 1995a).

Still, the instruction offered by jazz education programs, in keeping with Barth's previously cited comments, is invaluable. Saxophonist Antonio Hart reminds us that degrees provide educational institutions with a means to evaluate the credentials of those they might hire. On the scene, however, the degrees are much less important. Hart, laughing, asserted if Art Blakey had called him to play in one of the Jazz Messengers groups, he would not have asked whether the saxophonist had a degree (Hart 1994). Writer Ralph Ellison's comments on the learning process of jazz musicians are instructive and similar in spirit to those of the musicians:

> Although since the twenties many jazzmen have had conservatory training and were well grounded in formal theory and instrumental technique, when we approach jazz we are entering quite a different sphere of training. Here it is more meaningful to speak, not of courses of study, of grades and degrees, but of apprenticeship, ordeals, initiation ceremonies, of rebirth. For after the jazzman has learned the fundamentals of his instrument and the traditional

techniques of jazz—the intonations, the mute work, manipulation of timbre, the body of traditional styles—he must then "find himself," must be reborn, must find, as it were, his soul. . . . In this his instructors are his fellow musicians, especially the acknowledged masters, and his recognition of manhood depends upon their acceptance of his ability as having reached a standard which is all the more difficult for not having been rigidly codified. (1964e, 209)

Indeed, although some younger musicians may think themselves ready for careers as professional jazz performers when they complete their studies, older players such as pianist James Williams (1994) generally consider them to be technically skilled young musicians who need "more seasoning," which they can get only through apprenticeship to older musicians (Jackson 1993a, 1993b). In the bands of older musicians, young performers learn not only what is required of them musically but also how to manage their lives while traveling.[21] Some workers in the recording industry diluted or eliminated such seasoning by convincing some young musicians, signed to major contracts before or upon college graduation in the late 1980s, that they were already sufficiently well formed. Following a backlash against the signing of "young lions" and what some heard as lackluster recordings in late 1980s, in the early 1990s some of the labels started channeling their efforts into supporting their young artists' needs for growth via apprenticeship (Moon 1992).

The efficacy of educational institutions is limited. At best, they help young musicians develop specific skills that will help them negotiate some of the musical challenges they will face as professionals. In other words, they complement the educational systems of various scenes. They also give young musicians the opportunity to meet and form alliances with other young musicians—ensuring some generational unity on the scene—and to meet older musicians to whom they might be informally apprenticed. Beyond that, educational institutions serve as sites for preserving and disseminating certain kinds of knowledge about the music, its history, and its performance.

PERFORMANCE VENUES

The sheer number and variety of performance venues in New York City is astounding. The October 1994 issue of *Hot House,* for example, included forty-four nightclubs, restaurants, theaters, and concert halls in its listings of upcoming events in Manhattan. Those venues perhaps comprise the majority of major performance spaces in Manhattan, but the publication's listing is limited to those spaces that submitted information to *Hot House* staff. Several then-active uptown and Harlem venues, like Birdland, La Famille, and Perks, were not included in the list. Also omitted were small bars in Brooklyn and Manhattan, like Augie's Pub (now known as Smoke). Included or not, all of these venues are important, for they constitute the arena in which jazz musicians perform before and interact with audiences, providing central places for performers and other scene participants to enjoy music, to meet, and to form alliances.

Among those venues are nightclubs, such as the Village Vanguard, and bars, like Smoke and St. Nick's Pub, that cater strictly to audiences wanting to hear jazz performances. Other venues, like Sweet Rhythm (formerly Sweet Basil), Zinno, and Iridium, market themselves to jazz audiences and double as restaurants. Beyond those, there are clubs that occasionally present jazz performers but also book a number of rock, blues, folk, and world music acts. All of these venues have music spectators and fans as their clientele. Other venues are primarily restaurants or bars where the presentation of jazz performers is incidental. In those places, such as Eamonn Doran and Sfuzzi during my fieldwork, the musicians provide ambiance for dining or drinking and can sometimes barely be heard above the conversations of patrons. Jazz performers are also booked into concert halls, either in conjunction with established concert series, as at Lincoln Center, or on a more ad hoc basis, as at Town Hall.

Even these possibilities do not exhaust the opportunities that jazz musicians have to perform in public. Various cultural and arts organizations in New York City sponsor summer outdoor concerts at various parks and piers. One such organization, the Jazzmobile, sponsors concerts nearly every summer weeknight, taking jazz performances into different parks throughout New York City. The highlight of each week is a Wednesday-night concert at Grant's Tomb, located near the Riverside Church in Upper Manhattan. Moreover, many corporations and museums mount concerts in public plazas and other spaces. Corporate-sponsored summer jazz festivals in the 1990s, all of which were intended, in part, to draw New York residents and visitors to Lower Manhattan, presented further performance opportunities and another means to attract tourist revenue. Thus, the Panasonic Village Jazz Festival combined a free concert in Washington Square Park with a series of paid events at Greenwich Village clubs in 1994; the annual J&R Downtown Music Festival, also free, drew patrons to City Hall Park and its adjoining streets; the annual Charlie Parker Festival showcased live jazz in Tompkins Square Park; and even the JVC Jazz Festival featured a series of free concerts in a newly vibrant and sanitized Bryant Park (Zukin 1997) in 1996. And jazz performers are even called upon to play for corporate banquets, private parties, and other occasions when those organizing the events prefer them to club date musicians, who are normally first-call performers for such events and for wedding receptions (MacLeod 1993).

Most of the dedicated jazz clubs are clustered in the Greenwich Village area, where five of them—the Village Vanguard, Smalls, Sweet Basil, the Blue Note, and Visiones—were within easy walking distance of each other during my fieldwork. Iridium and Birdland were the only major venues located outside the Village during that time. The numerous restaurants and bars are scattered throughout the city's five boroughs, while the concert halls are located primarily in Midtown Manhattan.

To a large degree, the location of each venue determines the artists who will play in it as well as its clientele and pricing structure. Clubs in Greenwich Village tend to be the most expensive, but they also are the only ones that consistently book major artists with recording contracts and bankable reputations. Their steep cover charges and drink prices are to some degree justified by the costs of running a jazz club in an expensive neighborhood. Those prices, however, almost always ensure that only those who are willing and able to spend $20 to $50 for forty-five to sixty minutes of music and those who are dedicated fans attend their sets. Some commentators have suggested that such economic factors may account for the overwhelming "whiteness" of the jazz audience (DeVeaux 1995, 23). By contrast, Harlem venues such as St. Nick's Pub and the Lenox Lounge are cheaper than Greenwich Village clubs, offer less compensation to performers than their downtown counterparts, and, until recently, were rarely frequented by white patrons.[22] These second-tier clubs tend to feature musicians who have contracts with independent labels or are well-known sidemen who perform with major artists. At different points, however, the owners of second-tier venues, such as the Lenox Lounge, have tried to position themselves as first-tier clubs, doing whatever they could to attract tourist groups and others to their establishments, sometimes alienating neighborhood regulars in the process (Richardson 2000). There are generally no cover charges at the various restaurants and bars that feature jazz as incidental entertainment, though one may be required to purchase a minimum amount of food or drink. These venues tend to feature even less well-known musicians.

For any venue that is privately owned and receives no local, state, or federal arts funding, staying in business is a constant struggle. A number of clubs that had been in existence for ten years or more closed in the mid-1990s, among them the Village Gate and Fat Tuesday's. Another, Bradley's, closed in October of 1996, when its proprietor, Wendy Cunningham, could not pay debts stemming from a fire that necessitated her closing the club for several months while remodeling took place (Watrous 1996c). Perhaps most revealing with regard to the volatility of the jazz club business are newspaper and magazine articles heralding the "jazz renaissance(s)" of recent years. Many of these articles focus on the openings of new clubs catering to jazz audiences. Of the six new clubs cited in articles in 1994, only two were still in business and booking jazz performers at the end of 1995 (Blumenfeld 1994; Watrous 1994c), and only one now remains.[23] Numerous reasons are cited for the failure of venues, among them poor capitalization, poor management, and lax promotion. Even those that manage to break even—after compensating musicians and staff and paying their rent and fees for various required licenses—generally have little cash on hand for emergencies. These difficulties, of course, are not unique to jazz performance venues. As Strauss (1996), Rothman (1999), and Navarro (2001) indicate, the situation for other venues in New York City is just as dire.

The venues that are most successful maintain solvency through charging relatively steep prices, having certain engagements or portions of them underwritten by major record labels or corporations, booking only the most popular or established musicians, advertising aggressively in the *Village Voice* and *New York Times,* and cultivating tourist audiences, particularly from Europe (Watrous 1996a). The result, however, is a system that makes it difficult for any but the best-known musicians to be booked in the most prestigious clubs. Bruce Barth told me that pianist Monty Alexander remembers a time when "if the club owner liked what you were doing, and if he saw that an audience dug it, he would give you a gig. Now, that's not enough. It has to be . . . the label, the *big* label. It's not even enough to have your own CDs . . . It seems like you have to be on a major label" (Barth 1994). He further explained that major-label artists are typically the only ones who get significant press coverage, even in dedicated jazz publications.

Beyond the musicians they book and the audiences they attract, there are certain commonalities among jazz venues with regard to physical layout and decor. The Village Vanguard, the longest running and perhaps oldest jazz venue, has certain design characteristics that appear in other venues as well. Patrons descend from street level to enter the performance space. Inside, the stage is raised above floor level to make the musicians more visible. The walls of the club are adorned with pictures of musicians who have played in the Vanguard as well as famous jazz musicians not necessarily connected to the club's history. And nearly every possible place where tables and chairs might be positioned is filled. In fact, the tables and chairs are positioned so closely as to make maneuvering to certain tables nearly impossible once others are seated.

The layout and decor of other venues are similar to that of the Vanguard in varying ways. Other clubs that require (or required) a descent from street level include Fat Tuesday, Fez under Time Cafe, Iridium, Metropolis, and Smalls. Some venues that are not situated below street level have some sort of transitional area that separates the outside world from the performance space proper. Portraits of famous musicians and album covers adorn (or adorned) the walls of Birdland, Bradley's, Smalls, Iridium, Sweet Basil, and many other venues. All of them allow in some way for the physical separation of performers from audiences, either via a raised stage or an area off-limits to non-performers.

The dedicated jazz venues are also similar in terms of their scheduling and the performance atmosphere they project. Most artists are booked for weeklong engagements beginning on Tuesday night and running through Sunday in the major clubs (the schedule at Bradley's was displaced by a day: engagements started on Monday and ended on Saturday). The free night between weeklong engagements is usually dedicated to regular performances by big bands, one-night engagements, showcases by new artists, or jam sessions.[24] Many of the second-tier clubs book different artists on a daily basis, generally having one artist play on both Friday and Saturday evenings. The clubs typically feature two sets on weeknights, the first starting between 9 and 9:30 and the second between 11 and 11:30 PM. On Friday and Saturday an additional set may be added.[25] Each set usually lasts from forty-five minutes to an hour and is followed by a break of equal or greater length during which patrons for earlier sets are cleared to admit new ones. Sometimes audience members from one set are allowed to stay for a later one with no additional cover charge, although they may be required to observe a drink or food minimum during each subsequent set. Lastly, each club has instituted a quiet policy, which requires patrons to "keep their conversation to a minimum" during a performance. And in the event that they haven't read the cards on tables alerting them to the policy, all patrons are verbally reminded of it as the lights are being dimmed for a set.

These different types of venues attract knowledgeable audience members to varying degrees, but each has the potential to allow such listeners feel the camaraderie alluded to previously. Musicians devote a considerable amount of their time trying to secure gigs in these venues. The importance of the clubs cannot be overstated, for they provide a space where all of the scene's varied participants—regardless of their specific connections—can converge and converse. Concert halls are less important for the day-to-day maintenance of the scene, for the concerts at Lincoln Center and Carnegie Hall cater to an even more exclusive set of audience members and diminish the degree to which performers can interact with listeners and to which listeners can interact with one another.

RECORDING INDUSTRY

The recording industry provides another conduit through which audiences become acquainted with musicians, though only via the projection of their "sonic personae" (Shank 1994, 183–87). Between the musicians' conception and performance of music and its reception by record buyers is an elaborate network of individuals working in various capacities at record labels, recording studios, entertainment law offices, publicity firms, and record stores (Negus 1992, 1999). As I argued in chapter 1, the many steps in the production of a recording, largely unknown to consumers, make the uncritical use of recordings in musical analysis problematic in a number of ways. Still, our discussion of the scene would be incomplete without some explication of the way in which recordings are made and the way they function for those on the scene.

There are three primary paths that one might take toward the production of a recording: one can make a recording with major-label support, with minor/independent label support, or without any label support. In the first scenario the musician works more or less closely with someone in Artists and Repertoire (A&R). At the major jazz labels during my fieldwork—Warner Brothers, Sony, Verve, Impulse!, Atlantic, and Blue Note—there was generally one individual, though sometimes more than one, charged with most of the responsibility for signing artists and producing their recording sessions. There would be a series of meetings during which personnel from the record company would meet with the artist to discuss what type of recording the artist would make, which and how many musicians they might use, the ratio of original compositions to jazz standards, and the budget for the project, among other topics.[26] Such meetings could be highly charged, depending on the artist's relationship with the label, the openness of each party to the other's ideas, and sales figures for the artist's previous recording(s). Once those details were negotiated, the artist would receive an advance against royalties—as little as $500 for minor label acts to $10,000 or more for those on major labels—and devote time to composing and arranging tunes for the recording. At the same time, individuals at the record label would start production coordination: securing studio time, choosing a producer, contracting recording engineers and assistants, and making other arrangements.[27] There might have been additional meetings, primarily between the artist, producer, and A&R representative, to check the artist's progress in preparing for the session and to begin the process of securing legal permission to record the works of other musicians not in the public domain. The process for minor labels was similar, though anecdotal evidence indicated a more "hands-off" approach in that scenario. That is, there was generally less collaboration between record label personnel and the artist prior to the recording session, less talk of album concept, previous sales figures, or target audience (Suter 1979; Gray 1988). Artists producing recordings without label support made all of their decisions independently prior to (or during) the recording session.

In general, the amount of money invested in a project declines as one moves from major label support to independent production. The budget for a recording made by one of the major-label artists I interviewed was slightly over $40,000. As this musician was approaching the end of a multi-album deal, this figure was much larger than the label's outlay for his previous projects. It was my impression from conversations with him and others, moreover, that this investment was exceptional. My impression was partially confirmed early in 2001, when Richard Woodward quoted Warner Brothers A&R representative Matt Pierson as saying, "It costs between 15 to 60,000 to make a recording, depending on how much you pay the sidemen. But with touring, advertising and promotion, you're talking about at least another 30 to 50,000 to market a record you hope will sell 10,000 units. You have to place your bets very carefully and believe that in the long run [they] will pay off in someone becoming a major artist" (2001, 50). A recording will generally have eighteen months to sell enough units to recoup the label's investment or risk being deleted from its catalog. Minor labels, which are not required to observe AFM regulations, invest much smaller sums—frequently less than $10,000—in recording and promotion and therefore have to sell fewer units to break even.

As the recording date or dates approach, the artist may elect to have rehearsals. Major labels will frequently rent space and pay the musicians for the time spent rehearsing. When Terence Blanchard was recording in December of 1994, for example, Sony allowed his ensemble the luxury of alternating days of rehearsal with days of recording.[28] Minor labels may or may not pay the musicians for time spent rehearsing. As is the case for recordings produced independently, rehearsals for minor label recordings are likely to be paid for by the artist. Rehearsals, consequently, are likely to take place at the home of one of the musicians rather than in a rented space.

Once the musicians are in the studio, the process is nearly the same regardless of the path taken. The major difference is the amount of time the musicians have to record. Major labels generally pay for up to three days of recording time, and sometimes even more. Minor label recordings, such as those made for Enja and Criss Cross, are generally made in a day. The number of days spent recording independent projects varies based on the funds at the artist's disposal. Each day generally consists of six hours of recording time, not including a meal break.

In the earliest stages of a session, the positioning of and sight lines for the musicians are determined; microphones and headphones are set up by the engineer and assistants in the studio along with any baffles necessary to prevent unwanted sounds from bleeding into other microphones; and the microphones are assigned to specific tracks on the mixing console and labeled. To varying degrees, musicians depend on visual cues in negotiating the formal parameters of tunes. Sensitive engineers and producers work with the artists to facilitate visual communication in the recording studio, particularly since instruments such as bass and drums are frequently placed in isolation booths to keep the sounds they make distinct from those produced by other instruments. Drums in particular are isolated not only to keep their volume from overwhelming other microphones but also to keep the overhead microphones that capture cymbal sounds as well as the "room sound" of the drum kit from being affected by other, non-drum sounds.[29] Such sound isolation is less important when a group is recording "live" to two-track digital tape, meaning that there will be no mixing of sounds from different tracks or overdubbing in the post-production phase. After setting up microphones, the engineer sets the levels and, if desired, the amount of reverberation and other effects to be applied to individual instruments during recording. The positioning optimally takes into account the vantage point of the producer and engineer, ensuring that they can see the musicians from the control room. Throughout the session, the assistant will be charged with starting and stopping the tape or reels and labeling each completed one. There are at least two tapes running simultaneously at each session to guard against equipment failure. In some cases an additional recorder or digital audio tape (DAT) machine will be running to generate a recording for the session's leader to take home to evaluate.

Once the recording session proper has started, the musicians record tunes in succession, monitoring their playing and that of the other musicians through headphones. They precede the recording of each tune with discussion of the arrangement and the number and order of solos. Likewise, and particularly if there are difficult passages in an arrangement, they do a run-through, during which they play the entire head and any interludes that may present problems during recording. The producer, engineer, assistant engineer, and any onlookers observe the proceedings from the control room, where the recording console is situated. Those onlookers might include record company personnel, fellow musicians, or friends. Once the musicians are ready for a take, they inform the producer. The engineer instructs the assistant to start rolling tape, and the producer gives the artists the cue to start when they are ready. During each take or portion thereof, the producer takes notes, writing down the title of the tune, any mistakes that have been made during that take, and, most importantly, the approximate length of the take. The length is important, for the musicians have to produce a finished product that fits the target total time for the project (usually between forty-five and sixty minutes for a single disc).

After each complete or aborted take, there is discussion about whether that take will be sufficient or whether additional attempts are necessary. If another take is necessary, the musicians may choose to change the tempo, modify the number of solos or change their order, make alterations to the arrangement, or work on problem areas in the tune. Afterward, the musicians will record additional takes until they are satisfied or the producer recommends that they move on. Those with the most limited studio time tend to do at most three takes of a given tune. In major label sessions, the leeway for additional takes is considerably wider. When only a portion of the tune, such as the head or the coda, needs to be redone, the musicians might do an *insert* rather than a full take. During the mixing process, this corrected portion will be inserted into an otherwise complete but flawed take.[30] To be sure, opinions differ on whether inserts are suitable on jazz recordings. Many musicians favor a "live" interactive sound that might be compromised by using inserts, though they are sometimes the most practical and efficient solution. Inserts are almost never done for mistakes in solos, although one recording session I attended in 1995 was an exception. There, one musician was dissatisfied with his one portion of his solo. Realizing, however, that it would be difficult to clean up that one part, he chose, after consulting with the engineer and producer, to redo the entire solo, while listening to the playback of the other musicians with his earlier solo deleted. Another performer on that track thereafter opted to redo his solo as well.

Once a recording session is done, the musician and the producer decide which takes and inserts will be used for the finished recording. The musician(s), producer, and engineer collaborate on making the rough mixes from the recording session sound more polished by further adjusting dynamic levels and frequency content as necessary, sometimes on a moment-to-moment basis, to help individual elements stand out in the mix. In some cases mixing takes as much time as recording. After the mix has been completed, but before the recording can be sent off to be mastered for mass production, other issues have to be decided, such as the sequencing of the record—the order in which tunes will be presented. For major label artists, meetings are held to discuss, if necessary, possible titles for the record and to decide on aspects of package design, including photographs and liner notes. Some minor labels, like Criss Cross, keep their costs down by investing very little in packaging or photo shoots. Those who are producing records independently may make many of these decisions themselves before shopping their records to potential buyers (like Enja or Evidence).

Once all of these decisions have been made, the project is largely in the hands of the record label. The marketing staff of the label creates a plan to market the recording, sometimes in consultation with the musician. The label's publicity department or an outside vendor (like Don Lucoff's DL Media or Helene Greece's Third Floor Media) produces (or commissions) an artist biography, generally one to four pages in length, detailing the artist's history, the concept of the record, the musicians playing on the recording, and aspects of the artist's musical philosophy. The label then sends out promotional copies of the recording along with the biography to the music press, ideally no fewer than three months before the official release, to get advance reviews (Petlin 1995). Those charged with publicizing the record also make contact with their networks of radio stations to ensure that the recording gets airtime, even prior to its formal release. The label and/or the musician's management will typically arrange for him or her to perform in a New York club near the album's release date. These procedures are for the most part mechanical and may be neglected when the label has little faith in the artist's product or little desire to continue a relationship with that musician. When labels do give special attention to promotion, their efforts are sometimes reflected in high sales. Alternatively, when promotion is given little attention—such as when field staff fail to follow up on their initial promotional efforts with phone calls—sales tend to suffer (Keepnews 1979).[31]

In the same way that label officials are guarded about the demographics of their audiences, they are reluctant to divulge sales figures. Inquiries to SoundScan, a Long Island–based organization that tracks record sales at various retail outlets throughout the United States, indicate that in terms of gross figures, jazz constituted a mere 4.3 percent of total record sales during my research period.[32] Of that small percentage, one commentator (Jeffrey 1992) has suggested that reissues of previously released recordings, which are much cheaper for the labels to market, accounted for 40 to 50 percent of total jazz record sales at major labels (see also Kofsky 1977; Richardson 1990). As Michael Cuscuna of Blue Note put it, "When Joe Lovano puts out a new record, he's not only competing with his contemporaries for sales. . . . He's also up against Gene Ammons and Coltrane and every record ever made. The whole history of the music is now available on CD, and that's a problem for anyone who hopes to break through" (quoted in Woodward 2001, 51). New jazz recordings don't sell as well as new recordings in other styles or (generally cheaper) reissues. Such low sales figures might partially account for the limited funds put into promoting and distributing new jazz records, especially when one considers the greater potential profit in marketing new rock bands or hip-hop or pop performers.

With most releases averaging around five thousand units,[33] only the best-known artists earn money from record sales; most others record for different reasons. They use recordings to present their music to a wider audience, to gain exposure in the press, and to convince club owners and promoters to give them gigs in an increasingly competitive market (Orgill 1995). In many cases, recordings on minor labels also help artists attract the attention of major labels (Stein 1993; Watrous 1996b), with standout sidemen in major-label artists' groups generally getting attention from independent or major labels.[34] In addition, recordings help musicians document what they are doing at particular points in time, show different facets of their musical personae, and/or present their compositions to others who might potentially record them.

For their part, record labels are primarily involved in producing jazz records to generate income. Many of the major labels, however, maintain their jazz divisions because they bring the label a certain degree of prestige, particularly when they can publicize their "discovering" and signing new musicians or rediscovering and signing older ones. If nothing else, such signings may indicate to those on the scene that a particular label maintains a commitment to jazz. In 1979, Peter Keepnews (1979) expressed doubt about whether signing artists in itself was indicative of commitment: without promotion and extensive attention to marketing and building an audience, such signings might mean a series of releases receives poor distribution, little airplay, and therefore low sales. Indeed, one strategy employed by some labels during the late 1970s recording industry slump was to put significant effort behind only those projects that seemed to take off without label intervention (Paikert 1979).

The dissolution of the RCA, Atlantic, and Sony jazz divisions, however, is a discouraging sign. In an industry now dominated by a portfolio management style (Negus 1999), which requires that each unit of a label cover its own costs and realize a profit, promoting new jazz artists in the interests of prestige may not be viable. There is simply more money to be made reissuing older recordings than there is in promoting new artists. As Woodward rhetorically asks, "Why risk [$25,000] touring a quintet who haven't a prayer of airing on MTV when you can mine your catalog of Miles and Coltrane for nothing?" (2001, 50). Indeed, Woodward suggests that Columbia's last-ditch reorganization of its jazz division in 2000, when it put Jeff Jones, the director of the Legacy reissue label, at the head, said a great deal about where jazz at major imprints was headed:

> Jones has no experience producing new records, but neither has he been losing Sony's money. He makes all the right noises about "our commitment to stay in jazz business." . . . At the same time, Jones talks about finding the "most commercial and credible artists we can" and making jazz "fun, so that it's not just for the critics. The trend everywhere is more urban and teen-oriented. I don't think it's just jazz." Every jazz label to survive must embrace artists who fit a "smooth" format or who create hybrids of pop, fusion, New Age, techno and rap. . . . Jones sounds as perplexed as other executives about the future of straight-ahead jazz within this market. (2001, 50; see also Giddins 2001)

The label fired its jazz staff, released Wynton Marsalis and most other artists from their contracts, and focused more energy on acts such as Richard Bona and Angelique Kidjo, retaining only Branford Marsalis, David Sánchez, and Jeff "Tain" Watts as clearly straight-ahead jazz artists on its roster (Graybow 2001). By 2005, none of the latter artists was still with the label.

Apart from such reshuffling, dedicated fans on the scene have mixed opinions about recordings and the industry that produces them. Although many have gained knowledge of the music's history through recordings (and radio programs), they seem less important to those engaged in day-to-day life on the scene. If one has limited resources and must choose between purchasing a recording and attending a live performance, generally the latter is the preferred option. Lisa Michel, one fan and musician with whom I had frequent conversations, told me in October of 1994 that she now hates recordings, in part because of her knowledge of how they are made: "I learned about music through them, but the ones they make now just don't have any edge" because so much effort goes into making them "perfect" products. But she also dislikes them because they aren't as stimulating to her as live performances, which have an edge that recording—because it reduces a multisensory experience to sound—cannot capture. Other fans have a more benign view of recordings, finding them useful for learning repertoire, tracing influences, and discovering musicians about whom they'd known very little.

CRITICS AND THE MEDIA

Critics and commentators on jazz in the popular press and on television serve a mediating function on the jazz scene. In some cases, they insert themselves between musicians and the recording industry on one hand and between musicians and jazz audiences on the other. In this capacity, they choose to endorse some recordings as worthy of purchase while withholding that endorsement from others. Likewise, they mediate between musicians, performance venues, and potential audiences for performances, again recommending certain engagements while not commenting on others. Their work, therefore, is primarily promotional and evaluative.

Critics on the jazz scene have a number of outlets for reaching members of the jazz audience. They do so through weekly and monthly publications, such as *Billboard, Cadence, Down Beat,* and *JazzTimes,* as well as locally produced weekly and daily publications, such as the *Village Voice,* the *New Yorker,* the *New York Times,* the *New York Daily News,* and *Newsday.* None of these publications is dedicated strictly to happenings on the New York scene. One monthly publication, *Hot House,* is aimed directly at New York audiences. It is available only in performance venues, at selected record stores, or via subscription (only those who subscribe pay for the magazine).

In their writings, these critics reveal varying degrees of partisanship and knowledge about the music. Some, like Stanley Crouch and Kevin Whitehead, have at times displayed almost unbroken allegiance to particular styles and even particular musicians, allegiances that have sometimes precluded serious discussion of other styles or performers. Other critics, whose writings support more varied styles, display a great deal of passion and erudition, though their engagement with or understanding of the music is not always apparent. As many of the commentators on jazz criticism have acknowledged, many of these individuals are first and foremost writers, capable of devising elaborate metaphors and choosing piquant adjectives, but few are adept at sustained argument. Any evaluation of critics, however, must acknowledge the editorial constraints they face, which determine what and how much they can write, the tone they can take, and how often their work appears. It can be difficult to present anything of substance in, say, a 250-word record review. Still, the growing body of literature on jazz criticism is peppered with laments about the absence of explicit criteria for hiring and evaluating critics (Baraka 1967b, 1990; Welburn 1986, 1987; Crouch 1990a; Gennari 1991, 2006; Gendron 1995). After a particularly scathing attack on Wynton Marsalis appeared in the *Village Voice,* the trumpeter pointedly and viciously raised similar questions about the critic Kevin Whitehead: "Who has this writer studied or played with, and what is the source of his authority other than poor editorial decisions?" (Marsalis 1994; see also Whitehead 1994).

These questions assume great importance when one realizes the degree to which well-placed critics might contribute to a musician's success. It is often difficult to determine whether a negative review or a less-than-stirring endorsement does harm to sales of a particular recording or to attendance at a performance. The effects of a positive review, however, are much easier to gauge. As of 3 January 1995, drummer Leon Parker was little known outside jazz circles. His engagement at Iridium, which began that evening and ran through 8 January, would hardly have attracted attention, but after a glowing review—proclaiming Parker's music to be "jazz of the future"—appeared in the *New York Times* on 5 January (Watrous 1995a), the remaining days of the engagement were sold out for each set.[35] Something nearly identical occurred with Kenny Garrett's appearance at Sweet Basil a few months later.

Jazz critics themselves have addressed the issue of their status and their importance, though with mixed results. In an article titled "Critical Analysis," Bret Primack (1994) surveyed the territory of jazz criticism. He interviewed a cross-section of New York–based critics—Bob Blumenthal, Gary Giddins, Ira Gitler, Peter Watrous, and Kevin Whitehead—to learn about their methods and their conceptions of the critic's role. Their answers, or Primack's presentation of them, were not enlightening. A sidebar to the article, supposedly written by a musician, however, is quite humorous and revealing. The anonymous writer asserts that critics assume a number of roles, including historian/professor, psychologist, producer, musician, alchemist, archaeologist, star maker, linguist, record collector, everyman, parent, and disseminator of agitprop. The unnamed musician provides examples of writing or writing styles that exemplify each role.

Still, one of the most eloquent statements on the role of jazz critics is an essay by Amiri Baraka (LeRoi Jones), "Jazz and the White Critic" (1967b). Baraka asserts that the problem with much criticism of jazz recordings and jazz performance is the result of largely white groups of critics failing to understand the African American culture that produced and nurtured the music.[36] Baraka asserts that rather than making an attempt to understand that culture, critics have adopted a strategy akin to that driving New Criticism in literature: "Usually the critic's commitment was first to his *appreciation* of the music rather than to his understanding of the attitude which produced it. This . . . meant that the potential critic of jazz had only to appreciate the music, or what he thought was the music, and that he did not need to understand or even be concerned with the attitudes that produced it, except perhaps as a purely sociological consideration" (Baraka 1967b, 13; cf. Floyd 1995, 234).[37] Of the critics whose acquaintance I made—among them Peter Watrous, Steve Futterman, Jim Macnie, Eugene V. Holley Jr., Tony Scherman, Howard Mandel, Stanley Crouch, Larry Blumenfeld, Ira Gitler, and Kevin Whitehead—many made serious attempts to grapple with musical, social, economic, and cultural issues in their writing. It was also apparent, however, that many came to the music as enthusiasts with a greater knowledge of literary theory or popular music styles than they had of jazz styles, history, and performance practice.[38]

Although there is more culturally sensitive criticism available today, there are still enough examples of uninformed jazz journalism to make many musicians and dedicated fans wary of print journalists. Joseph Hooper's profile (1995) of saxophonist Joe Lovano is one glaring example. In a manner similar to Gene Lees, Hooper asserted that the jazz world was biased against white musicians, many of whom were "forced" to play commercial music (like Kenny G) or avant-garde music (like John Zorn). Hooper claimed that Lovano is a great white hope for jazz, "a white man who has made it in a black man's world." For several weeks after the publication of Hooper's article, and particularly during the engagement at the Village Vanguard that the piece was supposed to promote, the article was mentioned by my acquaintances in hushed tones and always with incredulity. Lovano seemed particularly annoyed at having been used by a writer making contentious assertions. Hooper, though, is something of an anomaly. In general, the opinions of well-known critics are filtered through readers' level of agreement with their previous writings and opinions. Critical writing seems to be prized mostly for the factual information it presents: the background of a musician, the concept behind his or her latest releases or performances, and information about upcoming gigs or releases. One fan who discussed critics with me in September of 1994, Dave Pierce, observed that they frequently focus on unimportant issues that contribute to the star images of performers or that help them to project their own ideas about society and ideology onto the music (see also Lock 1988, 116). Musicians likewise were highly disparaging of critics but acknowledged that they served an important role in the functioning of the scene.

Other media, like radio and television, seem to be valued for many of the same reasons. While acknowledging both the work and alleged commercial compromises behind jazz radio stations' playlists, the musicians and dedicated fans with whom I talked continue listening to radio because it can expose them to or inform them about releases about which they may not otherwise have known. Moreover, radio and sometimes television (via broadcasts of documentaries or performances on PBS or cable outlets like Ovation) allow audience members to hear performances, interviews, announcements, and even retrospectives of musicians' work that can be extremely informative. The prospects for jazz on the radio, however, seemed to be in decline toward the end of the 1990s. Many of the public radio stations that had been mainstays of jazz programming found it increasingly to their advantage to air syndicated news or special interest programming in lieu of recordings in order to maintain the relatively affluent listenerships that keep them operational. That is, rather than being oriented toward to a potentially large and heterogeneous public, public radio stations constitute a "network founded by well-educated baby-boomers and targeted toward listeners with similar demographic and psychological profiles" (McCauley 2005, 116). In this scenario, jazz-related programming is often limited to the occasional record review, such as those done by Kevin Whitehead for *Fresh Air* or Tom Moon for *All Things Considered*.

In the end, critics and commentators and the media in which they present their work function on the scene as sources of information. In addition to announcements and evaluations of performances and recordings, they offer musicians potentially valuable exposure. Their role, however, is perhaps the least independent one: they are inextricably linked to the promotional apparatus of performance venues and the recording industry. Theirs is a position that is truly betwixt and between: their topics are largely determined by the decisions of club owners and the recording industry; some aspects of their work is guided by often invisible editors; and their writing is done for audiences largely unaware of the precariousness of their positions, the foundations of their knowledge, or the viability of their opinions.

PUTTING IT ALL TOGETHER

In discussing the role and function of each of the groups mentioned above, I have implicitly referred to their interactions with one another. As I noted at the beginning of this chapter, the scene does not function without the active participation of all of these groups at different times.

Musicians and audiences can have direct relationships with each other, but more often those relationships are mediated by performance venues, the recording industry, or the broadcast and print media. Musicians need and can potentially benefit from their interactions with all of the other groups and institutions in different ways. Audiences have direct contact with all of the other groups, which helps to shape their experiences on the scene. Educational institutions are important for training musicians who might become involved in the scene and facilitating the formation of alliances among them. Performance venues need musicians and audiences, but they also need the subsidies and publicity that come through the recording industry and the media, respectively. Likewise, the recording industry is dependent on each of the other groups, as well as record stores, to help it promote and sell recordings. And critics, as noted above, derive their subject matter from their interaction with other scene participants. Still, the derivative nature of their work does not erase the effect they have on the shaping and dissemination of knowledge.

Moreover, as the discussion of the makeup of the jazz audience illustrates, belonging to or working within one group or institution does not preclude belonging to or working within others. Many of the jazz audience members whom I identified during my fieldwork were connected to the scene in ways other than their interest in the music. They were often musicians, critics, or employees of record labels, publicity firms, or booking agents (see also McLeod 2001, 58). This overlapping of groups is manifest in other ways, too. The drummer Kenny Washington, for example, has maintained visible links with the media by being a disc jockey for WBGO-FM. Pianist James Williams devoted a considerable amount of his time to producing recordings by other musicians, arranging concerts through his production company, Finas Sound Productions, and directing the jazz studies program at William Paterson University. And saxophonist Steve Wilson and pianist Bruce Barth have both involved themselves in music education, teaching at William Paterson University and Long Island University's Brooklyn campus, respectively. Many critics and jazz writers have participated directly in the promotional apparatus of the recording industry by writing artist biographies and contributing liner notes for CD releases. Owners of performance venues have sometimes involved themselves in record promotion, as the releases of Knitting Factory Records, an arm of Michael Dorf's now-defunct Knitting Factory in Tribeca, illustrates.

All of this interactivity and the ability of various actors and agents to fill multiple roles reveal the scene to be a vibrant and constantly shifting entity. Decisions made by individuals in a number of realms mutually determine the publicly visible manifestations of the scene: Which musicians get gigs? Where do they play? With whom do they play? Who comes to their performances? Which musicians get recording contracts with major labels? Independent labels? How well are those records advertised and promoted? Which radio stations will program them and how often? Who listens to jazz radio? Who buys jazz recordings?

To answer any of these questions effectively requires some discussion of several groups on the scene. Guitarist Peter Bernstein spoke with me in July of 1994 about the difficulty of getting gigs in the New York area. He noted that younger musicians without major-label contracts (and sometimes even those who do have them) must have older, more established musicians featured on their gigs to attract audiences. For example, some jazz fans might not be interested in attending a performance by Peter Bernstein and Rob Bargad at Smalls, though they might be inclined to attend if drummer Jimmy Cobb 's name were featured in the announcement. Moreover, Bernstein asserted that a form of planned scarcity is necessary if one is to get a gig at a major venue like the Village Vanguard. Club owners, in order to ensure they fill their venues, prefer that a musician they book not have played any headlining gigs in New York City recently, perhaps within the previous four months. The reasoning is that if audience members haven't seen a musician in four to six months, they may be more inclined to come to hear him or her. Bernstein described the situation as a catch-22: if you want to get gigs, you cannot play too much and overexpose yourself, but if you want people to know who you are, you have to play. Musicians, audiences, and performance venues are directly implicated here, while the recording industry and the critical establishment are referred to more obliquely.

It is through such contingencies that the scene is partially constitutive of the meanings that one might derive from musical events, whether live or recorded. The experience of hearing and being able to hear music is mediated in a fashion similar to other experiences characteristic of Howard S. Becker's art worlds (1974, 1982). Networks of cooperation among different groups are essential for shaping what appears before the public. Those who are active participants in the scene perhaps have a wider context within which to assess the significance of each musical event, for the knowledge they bring to each performance or listening—a knowledge of the workings of the scene—is richer and more complex. Moreover, by participating on the scene, one comes into more frequent and stimulating contact with other individual scene participants. Through their interaction and communication, they help to transform individual understandings of jazz performance and musical events into contestable, shared cultural meanings.

By choosing the New York jazz scene as my unit of investigation, I am privileging a particular way of looking at jazz. Indeed, I have chosen as anchor points, agents and institutions that are themselves constantly in motion and redefining their relationships with one another. Even more, through focusing on such agents and institutions I am asserting that jazz is most fruitfully interpreted or analyzed when the analyst takes into account its production and consumption within an art world specifically known as the scene. In this sense, the musical events to be discussed in chapter 7 are processual in two ways. First, as I have shown here, they are part of an ongoing process in which meanings are created in part from the negotiation and interaction of individuals in a fluid network. Each event can be read through the processes that make it and similar events possible. Moreover, those events are crucial sites for the shaping and sharing of understandings of jazz performance. Those understandings, as articulated by musicians and other participants, are the subject of chapters 5 and 6.

PART THREE

Blowin' the Blues Away

CHAPTER 5

Toward a Blues Aesthetic

Symbolic birds, myth and ritual—what strange metaphors to
arise during the discussion of a book about a jazz musician!
And yet, who knows very much of what jazz is really about?
Or how shall we ever know until we are willing to confront
anything and everything which it sweeps across our path?

—Ralph Ellison, "On Bird, Bird-Watching, and Jazz"

Ralph Ellison makes the above comment (1964b, 224–25) in a review
of Robert Reisner's *Bird: The Legend of Charlie Parker* (1962). He feels
that Reisner—who recounts an apocryphal tale of how Parker got the
nickname "Bird" but does not explore the myriad implications of nick-
names and their signification of movement from given to achieved
status—has missed the opportunity to uncover something of Parker's
importance for those who gave to him and continued to use the nickname. In somewhat similar fashion, commentators on African American musics have frequently focused so narrowly on the surface features
of jazz performance that one barely glimpses in their work what else
might make the music meaningful. These analysts have, in effect, recounted stories without exploring the myriad ways of reading them and
their significance.

This chapter examines some of the meanings that emerge from jazz
performance based on statements by musicians regarding their approaches
to musical events and their interpretation and evaluation. Through identification of their common concerns, I propose that they have developed
and operate within the parameters of a set of normative and evaluative
criteria that I call a "blues aesthetic."[1] In defining that aesthetic, I explore its foundations in African American culture and other, parallel and
competing, discourses and aesthetic formations.

MUSICIANS' NORMATIVE VIEWS OF JAZZ
PERFORMANCE

In their normative statements about jazz performance and jazz audiences, the musicians interviewed for this study express a number of concerns that, taken cumulatively, express a considered vision of how one has to approach the varied facets of "musicking."[2] Those concerns can be characterized as the importance of having an individual voice; developing the ability to balance and play with a number of different musical parameters in performance; understanding the cultural foundations of the music; being able oneself to "bring something to the music"; creating music that is "open enough" to allow other musicians to bring something despite or because of what has been provided structurally or contextually; and being open for transcendence to "the next level" of performance, the spiritual level. All are important for the ability of a musician to communicate with listeners and other performers, individually and collectively. Below, I discuss those concerns and how each has been explained by the musicians consulted for this study.

Perhaps the chief concern of every musician I interviewed, whether formally or informally, is having an immediately distinguishable individual sound. The word *sound* refers not only to timbre but also to particular usages of harmonic, rhythmic, and textural resources in performance and composition. The way in which such individual sounds are achieved varies from instrument to instrument, and from musician to musician, but a number of variables, including both motivated and unmotivated decisions, enter into the process. For players of wind instruments, for example, the embouchure (the position of the mouth relative to the instrument), the type of mouthpiece, the manufacturer of the instrument, and the amount of air blown into it are among the factors that determine the timbre of an individual's sound. Players of string instruments such as the guitar write their sonic signatures through their techniques (plucking with fingers or plectra made of various materials), the size and type of strings they use, and the manufacturers and materials of their favorite guitars, as well as through their preferred amplifiers and settings for equalization and electronic effects (such as reverberation and chorus).

Players interested in achieving such distinctive sounds listen and practice diligently to determine what type of sound pleases them or expresses their particular attitude(s) toward music. Pianist Bruce Barth says that he is constantly absorbing ideas and techniques from the playing of other musicians. When he sits down to practice, however, he focuses on those ideas and techniques that seem "unique to him," that is, the ones that are most appealing to him, and he tries to "amplify them and develop them" (Barth 1994). Similarly, the saxophonists I interviewed tend to start their practice routines with "long tones," playing each note in a scale or in the instrument's range as long and as evenly as possible, paying attention to the way the sound exits the horn and the way the vibrations feel in their mouths.

Steve Wilson explains the importance of working on individual sound in discussing his teaching methods. He notes that many of his students come to him wanting to know how to play "the hippest stuff on the changes," that is, the most sophisticated material in terms of harmony and rhythm. He redirects their energies toward sound production, asking whether they could play a particular whole note in a tune the way alto saxophonist Johnny Hodges might have and hoping they will understand the skill required to produce such a sound:

> That's the litmus test. That's how you can identify Lester Young, Johnny Hodges, Coleman Hawkins, Sonny Rollins, Coltrane: *by one note*. Because they knew how to play a whole note. And, um, I remember being in college and hearing cats, some of the older cats, saying, you know, "Baby, a whole note is sure the hardest thing in the world to play." And for years I didn't understand that. Like, "Man, what are they talking about?!" And I understand that now, you know. If I can play one good note, that's it. And that's the way I try to approach my teaching. It's to really have your own sound, after all is said and done, after studying everybody. *Have your own identity,* you know. (Wilson 1995)

Or as saxophonist Antonio Hart suggests, "If cats want to be identified, they need [their own] identities" (Hart 1995).

Having an individual sound also includes the use that a player makes of other musical resources expressed through preferences for certain kinds of harmonies, harmonic substitutions, or voicings; regular use of certain melodic phrases (sometimes formulaically); methods of constructing a solo or writing a composition; and approaches to rhythm, texture, and interaction. A musician like Thelonious Monk, therefore, is recognizable not only for the way in which he produces each individual sound, but also for the way in which he chains those sounds together in performance or composition. Sam Newsome explains that playing in the quintet of trumpeter Terence Blanchard for three years was quite important in his own development because

> [Blanchard] kinda went against like the whole trend that was, I think, that was happening around New York [in the late 1980s and early 1990s], this

kind of "retrospective" approach to playing. 'Cause his whole thing was just like getting in, you know, getting in touch with yourself and just, uh, just trying to develop your *own personality* on the instrument. You know, still remaining true to the tradition, just as far as like keeping the, the, the swing element and the blues element in the playing, but not really, just not really taking everything so verbatim. 'Cause I always kinda looked at it as like, it's like I would treat, I try to treat music like a, as like I would treat a proverb. [Laughs.] You know, it's like you don't, you don't take it—if someone says "Don't put all of your eggs in one basket"—you don't take that literally. I mean, you kind of look at it that way musically, too. It's like if I hear someone play, like if I were to take Trane [John Coltrane], it's like if I just took, uh, the way, the *three-tonic* system of Trane, it's like I, I wouldn't, I wouldn't think of playing it the way he would play it.[3] It's like I would just use it as, um, as a *harmonic* device that he introduced . . . [I]t's up to the, it's up to the individual to *interpret* it any way that they want. (Newsome 1995)[4]

Newsome, like Barth in a previously cited comment, underscores the importance of taking whatever resources one gets from elsewhere and giving them a personal spin, an individual interpretation. He later amplifies his point and Wilson's previous one by asserting that one's sound should be consistent regardless of the tune serving as a vehicle for improvisation. Musicians without a distinctive sound tend to place the emphasis in the wrong place, having the attitude that "You know, if you play, I don't know, if you play 'Impressions,' [you should] play like Trane. And if you're playing a ballad, try to play like Ben Webster. And if you're playing 'Confirmation,' you know, try to play like Bird [Charlie Parker], rather than just have *one approach* which is you and just keep that" (Newsome 1995). Musicians who do not possess their own sound, who seemingly mimic the sound of other musicians, receive particularly harsh criticism and are sometimes referred to as "clones" who sound just like Miles Davis, John Coltrane, Herbie Hancock, Betty Carter, or other well-known musicians. The point of the criticism is not so much that one should be "innovative" or do something novel in terms of sound or approach, but that one should strive for something different and distinctive. In this regard, Bruce Barth emphasizes the importance of "*saying something* that's *original*. I'm not saying necessarily *ground-breaking* or *revolutionary,* but something that isn't just . . . like a, like a generic *rehashing* of things that you've heard before. Where you put that record on and you say, 'That sounds exactly like *this*. This piano player sounds like such-and-such a player. This tune sounds like such-and-such a tune,' you know" (Barth 1995).[5]

The ability to balance a number of different musical parameters in the course of performance follows from having an individual sound, for the possession of an identifiable musical persona is the product of having considered a number of approaches and synthesized them into a "concept." Steve Wilson praised alto saxophonist Kenny Garrett precisely for his ability to play well in and adapt to the demands of a variety of contexts—from his work in traveling shows like *Sophisticated Ladies* in the early 1980s to that in groups led by Freddie Hubbard, Woody Shaw, and Miles Davis. Garrett's concept, according to Wilson, works precisely because it balances a number of different elements and approaches, but it does so in a way that identifies their usage as "Kenny Garrett's."[6]

While a student at the Berklee College of Music, Sam Newsome learned about the need for balance from pianist Donald Brown. Brown told Newsome that most musicians know more harmony than they actually need for performing. According to Newsome, Brown asserted that

> "If you use *too much* [harmony], it's going to sound mechanical." 'Cause he, 'cause he always, he told me, he felt [there] wasn't enough *room* . . . if he wanted to be *musical* . . . to have too much harmony 'cause that doesn't leave much room for *melody* or, or dealing with rhythmic ideas. It doesn't leave room for, for maybe if you wanted to *develop* ideas, you know, that doesn't leave room for, for dealing with *blues,* the *blues aspect* of harmony. So I mean . . . there are so many *elements* that, that go into producing like a, a good, a good *solo,* that if you were to incorporate too much of one thing, it's, you know, it's gonna sound mechanical and unmusical. (Newsome 1995)

These musicians work on being balanced in their practice routines, which, depending upon their performance, recording, and touring schedules, might vary considerably. Because their time is limited—often to as little as a couple of hours per day and sometimes less—they frequently apply themselves to practical problems, focusing attention on the technical demands of their instruments, on improving their abilities to hear and respond to harmonies, substitutions, and chord scales, on playing well at different tempos, and on ways of developing melodic and rhythmic ideas. Sometimes these sessions involve listening to recordings of their own performances or going over difficulties they have encountered in performing. Joshua Redman says that his focus at such times is on "trying to learn tunes I don't know, play through the melodies, play them in different keys. As a general rule, I try to work on things that don't come naturally. The general concept is to stretch and grow" (Redman 1995a). Both Antonio Hart (1994) and Sam Newsome (1995) speak of having notebooks full of harmonic concepts that they have not fully incorporated into their playing, concepts that will require extensive practice to be internalized and effectively deployed in performance. Newsome, for example, has been interested in applying John Coltrane's three-tonic system to improvising over minor chords, while Hart, inspired by the music of Eric Dolphy, has been working out ways to apply "incorrect" harmonic substitutes and scales to harmonic progressions in improvisation—for example, superimposing a B major scale over an F dominant seventh chord.[7] Guitarist Peter Bernstein stressed the importance of using practice time to internalize standard forms and harmonic schemes in the jazz repertoire. But these specific materials and activities are only a part of practice routines, which vary depending on what musicians feel they have neglected, have failed to do well, or need to improve. Those lacunae are revealed when a player feels that elements of his individual style are not properly balanced.

In one of his previously cited statements, Newsome mentioned the "blues aspect of harmony" and partially defined traditional jazz playing with reference to "the blues" and rhythmic swing. In both respects, his comments are consistent with conversations I have had with other musicians and fans, most of whom considered developing the ability to play the blues or to play with blues feeling as essential skills for playing jazz. The integration and mastery of such skills is precisely what allows performers such as pianist Wynton Kelly, tenor saxophonist Hank Mobley, and guitarist Grant Green to be considered important figures in the music's history by knowledgeable players and listeners (Rosenthal 1992; Starks 1993, 149). Although historians rarely mention these musicians because they were not decidedly "innovative" in terms of their technique or harmonic conceptions, their playing is suffused with blues feeling via phrasing, rhythms, and pitch choices.[8] Pianist Bruce Barth, for example, took Wynton Kelly and Herbie Hancock as models for learning how to "comp," partially because of their occasional and compelling use of "blues licks" and melodic phrases in place of chords (Barth 1995). And, as Newsome asserted, playing with "blues feeling" is also an essential component in performance on tunes not using one of the variants of blues form. Indeed, in the field of rhythmic, harmonic, melodic, and timbre-based conceptions, the blues-based conception is of crucial importance to artists trying to make a connection with audiences by expressing a type of "soulfulness" (see Porter 1994–95, 92).

Joshua Redman credits his study of the playing of saxophonist Stanley Turrentine with having taught him about that soulfulness and its roots in the blues:

I think any kind of music has its own soul, and you can have, you know, you can play from the soul in any style of music. I mean, I think that *Pat Metheny* is a very soulful player. That['s one] definition of soul. There's another definition of soul which is more of a specific kind of, has more specific stylistic connotations, you know. A certain kind of emoting. Soulfulness which is associated with the blues, you know, the blues idiom and blues expression. And under that definition, Pat Metheny wouldn't, doesn't play with that, you know, that type of soul style . . . That's not pejorative. Whereas someone like Stanley Turrentine to me is exemplary of that. I mean, he is just an incredibly bluesy, soulful player . . . And, um, I think the thing I've gotten from him more than anything else is, you know, by listening to him I really learned a lot about playing the blues, and, and . . . that kind of "soul" style of tenor playing. Um, I've learned, I've learned a lot about, you know, how important the *strength* of your sound is, you know. Before you even worry about what notes, or what combination of notes, just the *power* you put into your sound and the *strength* of each attack, you know, and the way you play a note, whatever the note is. What you can do with that note, the kind of passion you can put into that note. Because, you know, if you broke down and ana– . . . , if you broke down Stanley Turrentine's improvisations and analyzed them, you know, from a harmonic standpoint, they wouldn't be what you would call particularly complex, you know. Even some of the combinations of notes that he plays, some of the licks that he plays, are in some ways very standard. I mean, you can get those combinations out of any, you know, book on be-bop. Bebop textbook. But the *way* in which he plays them, the way in which he phrases them, is *so unique* that there's no one who's, I mean, he has *such* an identifiable style. I can literally from two notes [snaps fingers]: [know that it's] Stanley Turrentine. (Redman 1995a)

Similarly, Peter Bernstein, reflecting on his experiences playing with saxophonist Lou Donaldson and organist Dr. Lonnie Smith, said:

It's not like a gig where it's like, you know, you kinda get all this difficult music, and reading all these shifting time signatures. It's not demanding in that way, but, man, you play a whole night of that . . . or a whole week of blues, and you're just like, "Man!" . . . You realize, like, you realize how much you can or can't get out of it. "Wow, this is hard, man!" You know, those tunes like "Midnight Creeper," just like a blues in C, you know, three-chord blues, you know . . . And that's the thing about playing with these guys also. It's like, what *not to play* . . . Like Lonnie, as harmonically advanced as he is in a lot of ways, he just lays it down . . . I mean, a lot of times it's *totally simple*. [There's] not anything complex about it, you know. And just really staying out of the way, and not trying to put in a bunch of stuff where it doesn't fit, you know. (Bernstein 1995a)

Blues-derived playing and expression, then, are not a function of harmonic or rhythmic complexity. Neither, however, are they merely a function of simplicity. Rather, they are concerned with the projection of strength and power, with laying down a groove, through the way in which one approaches whatever rhythmic, harmonic, or other sonic resources are being utilized.[9] Implicit in both statements is the assumption that other participants in a musical event can aurally identify such moments and effectively respond to and contribute to the engendered feeling.

In some ways, their assertions are borne out by the evaluative commentary of audience members at musical events. On numerous occasions I heard musicians, critics, and other participants disparage musicians whose playing was marked by an inability to play compellingly on blues-based compositions or with convincing blues feeling. The major criticism was that these players weren't "saying anything," that their playing was cold or mechanical. Peter Bernstein told me in July of 1994 that Donaldson refers to such musicians as "sad motherfuckers." Donaldson's critique positions blues feeling as a sine qua non of jazz performance. The balance that Donald Brown advocates, therefore, requires including blues feeling among the parameters to be balanced. The importance of blues feeling in the evaluations made by different participants on the jazz scene will be illustrated in chapter 6, where I note how often positive responses to performances come at those moments that are expressive via blues-derived performance practices.[10]

The necessity of having an individual sound, the notion of balance, and the importance of the blues are seen by some musicians as products of a larger African American musical or performative sensibility. Although none of the questions in my interview specifically addressed issues of race or culture, each African American musician brought those issues into the interviews at many points, and I infer the importance of African American sensibilities from non–African American musicians' frequent references to African American musics and musicians as centrally influential and inspirational.[11] Peter Bernstein, for example, cited as his early, nonjazz influences folk and rock musician Bob Dylan; rock and blues guitarists Jimi Hendrix and Eric Clapton; blues guitarists B.B. King and Freddie King; and the heavy rock group Led Zeppelin. With Bob Dylan as a notable exception, almost all of the musicians he named—African American or not—were heavily involved in playing blues and blues-derived musics in the early parts of their careers, if not throughout. In discussing his jazz influences, Bernstein named mostly African American musicians. His list included guitarists Wes Montgomery, Grant Green, Kenny Burrell, Joe Pass, John Abercrombie, and Pat Metheny; trumpeter Miles Davis; pianists Duke Ellington, Wynton Kelly, and Keith Jarrett; saxophonists John Coltrane, Cannonball Adderley, Wayne Shorter, and David Murray; and bassist Paul Chambers.[12]

Some scholars (e.g., Starks 1993; Meadows 1992) and musicians have argued that it is impossible to understand jazz without understanding African American culture. Similarly, younger musicians frequently cite a specific historical vision: they see African American musicians as those whose contributions have been picked up and studied most extensively by other musicians.[13] That particular vision, however, is not the one they see educational institutions promulgating. As Sam Newsome says,

> I feel a lot of times with the, when you institutionalize jazz, it takes it, in a way, it takes it from the culture. And lot of institutions don't like to deal with that. It's like I, I heard very little about jazz coming from the black culture when I was at, at Berklee . . . A lot of times you end up getting like a watered-down version of jazz, where it's like, you know, you're gonna talk some about, you know, they're like "Well, here's Louis Armstrong and *also Bix Beiderbecke*." And then it just goes, you know, it's like . . . "Here's [Charlie Parker]." Then, "Oh, okay. We also have, uh, *Lee Konitz and Paul Desmond*." You know, it's always you have, they have to always put that, put that other . . . perspective on it, which in a lot [of] cases isn't really that necessary. I mean, it's like these, all of those players, they, they could play, but if you just really want to deal with like the, the *definitive* sound and the people who, who made like the, the real contributions to jazz, you know, I think you, you have to give credit where it's due. (Newsome 1995)

In the formal interviews I conducted, issues of race and culture were most frequently mentioned in response to a question about the effectiveness of jazz education.[14] Musicians unanimously felt that jazz education was good for teaching technique and specific ways to use harmony, but they noted a gap between what could be taught in a conservatory setting and what one needed to know to play the music well (see also Ellison 1964e, 208–9).[15] Donald Harrison, Antonio Hart, Gregory Hutchinson, Sam Newsome, James Williams, and Steve Wilson all suggested that young musicians had to engage with African American culture and be apprenticed to master musicians—the majority of whom in their estimation are African American—to be effective performers of the music. Hart, for example, sought and was sought by older musicians upon his arrival in New York. He has performed extensively with Nat Adderley, Slide

Hampton, and Jimmy Heath. Those experiences, he believes, allowed him to tap "some of that spirit, some of that fire, of what the music is really about" (Hart 1995). Hutchinson feels that he has grown enormously as a musician through working with Betty Carter and Ray Brown, while Donald Harrison and James Williams say the same of their time with Art Blakey.[16] Even musicians from outside the United States who want to be good players on the New York scene—like the French pianist Jacky Terrasson—were and have been encouraged to work with seasoned African American performers like Betty Carter and Arthur Taylor in order to understand the concepts that underlie the technical demands of jazz performance.

In that sense, African Americans who have been socialized in communities that transmit values similar to those that have nurtured some of the most influential musicians have an advantage over others—including other African Americans—who have not. They conceivably have less distance to travel to tap into "what the music is really about."[17] Both Barth and Newsome expounded on this idea in describing different audience responses to jazz performance. Each of them related anecdotes comparing gigs in other countries with those in African American communities in the United States. Barth feels jazz has a certain "romantic appeal" for European (and some American) audiences. He contrasts the responses of Europeans to performances with those of African Americans in North Philadelphia:

> [Europeans] love the idea of jazz; they respect the tradition, that it's an American music, that it's a black music. And sometimes I feel that . . . especially like a younger audience in Europe, you won't necessarily have the kind of audience that knows the music the way [they do in Philadelphia]. Like you'll find, like you go to an audience, you play a club in Philly, and you'll . . . , there are a lot of people in the audience who knew McCoy [Tyner], you know. People who knew Lee Morgan and McCoy [and John Coltrane], when he lived there. Who know the music . . . who have just a very close, *personal* connection with the music. (Barth 1995)

More pointedly, Sam Newsome asserted in our interview:

> N: I think . . . a black person that's . . . , you know, familiar with the music can relate to something that comes from the black culture on a much deeper level than someone who doesn't. I mean, it's, um, I mean, even if it's someone that's [not familiar] maybe . . . they can hear like the *soulful* side of soloing. It's like, uh, I don't know, I think someone black can relate to *that* on a deeper level . . . than someone who doesn't, doesn't really come from the culture.

J: And, um, how can you tell?

N: They . . . respond in the right places. 'Cause I remember I did this thing in Japan, and it's like they would start clapping at the most bizarre places during a solo. It's like places that were not meant to excite them [laughing]. Whereas like the, the experiences I've had with black audiences, it's like, you know, it's like where you may peak your solo at a certain place, and it's like you're . . . exuding like a certain amount of emotions, and it's like you can feel like you're connected. Where with someone else, you . . . may *not* be able to, it's more . . . maybe more intellectual. *Not to say that other people can't connect spiritually,* but it's, I don't think, on the same . . . deeper level. (Newsome 1995)

Newsome here seems to be emphasizing certain forms of (learned) cultural knowledge that are deployed in responding to music, particularly those related to the soulfulness and blues feeling that Joshua Redman described previously. Although on the surface his comments may appear exclusionary, they are intended to draw attention to cultural conditioning rather than to skin color.

The cultural component of performing, along with having an individual identity and balancing a number of musical elements in performance, is linked to what Steve Wilson referred to as "bringing something to the music" (see also Floyd 1995, 140–41). He connects the depth and variety of one's non-musical experiences to that capacity when he explains that "the music is only what you bring to it, you know. And if your life condition is not . . . set, or if it, if it's not, if your life condition doesn't have a solid foundation, um, more often than not, your music won't" (Wilson 1995). He continues by noting that what made a musician like Duke Ellington so important was his connection to tradition and his understanding of African American culture:

I mean, let's take a look at tradition. What is tradition, you know? I mean, you cannot discard, uh, you cannot take out or pick and choose out of our experience what you want, you know. It's just like if you look at, if you look at the emancipation of black people in America, you can't, you can't, uh, say, "Okay, well I'll take Frederick Douglass, but I'll delete the Emancipation Proclamation," you know. That's all a part of our experience, too, you know. So, it's just . . . hey, man, that all comes into the music, you know. All of our experiences, music or any artistic endeavor or expression, you know, be it by word of mouth or painting or dance or whatever. All of it is there. And, and, uh, I think that that's what they were doing in the Harlem Renaissance, man . . . [T]hey were taking a look at all of our [African Americans'] experiences, and that's why Duke Ellington was such a, such a master, man. He took . . . all of our experiences and put 'em into his art form. (Wilson 1995)

Note here an apparent difference between Wilson's understanding of tradition and the one usually espoused by scholars. Whereas scholars have viewed traditions as selective constructions and "inventions" (Hobsbawm and Ranger 1983), Wilson seems to be contradicting them. He is saying, in effect, that one does not invent tradition; rather, it is already there and one must negotiate a relationship *to* it. Obviously, this view of tradition is still one that is constructed and invented, though his emphasis is on utilizing the whole corpus of materials in the cultural matrix rather than valorizing some and passing over others. Other musicians expressed similar sentiments, though all had trouble specifying how one's experiences in daily life might affect a musical event. The silence, however, is perhaps an indicator not of the illegitimacy of the concept, but of the difficulty of verbalizing experiential and musical concepts (Feld 1994b) that are deeply felt. Indeed, to the degree that musical events are multilayered experiences in and of themselves, they reciprocally influence and feed back into daily life in ways that the following discussion will reveal.

The complexity of "bringing something" as a metaphor was underscored near the end of my interview with Wilson. I routinely concluded sessions with an invitation for the interviewee to raise questions that had occurred to him or her during the course of the interview but had not been asked. Wilson pointedly asked what I, as a young African American listener, brought to the music. What emerged from that question was a lengthy discussion about modes of listening, musical preferences, performing experiences, and criteria for evaluating music.[18] I explained that I brought a set of experiences from listening to various forms of African American and African-derived musics beginning in my childhood, feeling the most contact with the work of musicians such as Stevie Wonder, Marvin Gaye, Al Green, Bobby Womack, and Bob Marley. In addition, I brought a deep understanding of Anglo-American rock and a detailed knowledge of jazz history and current jazz practice to each performance as well as a desire to *respond* to the kinds of interactions taking place in a performance or on a recording. In the ensuing dialogue, Wilson stressed the interconnectedness of forms of African American musics, the necessity of understanding tradition (see the previous quotation), and the importance of communicating with audiences. All of the other musicians felt as well that one had to bring something to the music to be able to communicate, to connect with audiences. The "something" that one brings to the music is the sum of his or her experiences—musical and non-musical—as well as his or her individuality, musical skill, taste, and ability to empathize with other musicians.

The necessity of bringing something to the music has implications as well for the way that jazz musicians structure their compositions and performances. By necessity, jazz's musical structures have to be somewhat "open." In addition to allowing room for improvisation, they have to be the kinds of vehicles that facilitate interaction among the participants in a musical event. Guitarist Peter Bernstein discussed the alternatives he considered in preparing for the recording session for his CD *Signs of Life:*

> With *jazz*, the thing that's been hard is to, like, 'cause really when you write a jazz kind of thing, it's really about letting people bring something to it. And that's what I learned, especially doing this last record, like, keeping the tunes so, you know, someone could just look at [them and play them], and you have to have enough of yourself in the tune, but you don't want to restrict the player, the individuality of the player from coming out. 'Cause that's when . . . when you get a good bass player [Christian McBride] and good drummer [Gregory Hutchinson], you know, it's not about telling them what to play, having them read eighteen pages of written music because . . . why have them? Why not have the guy from the, from the, you know, you know, Philharmonic, you know. I mean, it's like jazz is, is individual music. It's really about, you know, it's about egos and, like, making the egos work together, but you need the ego[s], you know. (Bernstein 1995a)

So while one of his tunes ("Minor Changes") may require that the musicians stick with preset harmonies and accents during the head, the structure on which they improvise, a minor blues progression, is a more open structure with only the key and tempo of the performance dictated.[19] The musicians are free, after the head, to play substitute harmonies and to blur the boundaries of the form (see Strunk 1988; Waters 1996).

The ways in which bandleaders interact with sidemen are equally subject to the requirement that there be a certain amount of space for each musician to make a contribution. When asked about the leadership styles of bandleaders with whom they had worked, each musician said that openness and adaptability were marks of great bandleaders. Steve Wilson noted that Miles Davis and Duke Ellington were great precisely because they "let the personalities shape the music" (Wilson 1995). About leading his own groups, Wilson says, "I have a concept about what I want to do, but I realize it's the personalities of the other players that are really going to bring it to fruition" (Wilson 1995). In a sense, then, such openness is a way of dealing with the materials at hand (structure, sound, skill, personalities, performing context) and fashioning them into viable and meaningful expression. They are also a direct outgrowth of the other factors discussed thus far. Flexible frameworks for improvisation and flexible leadership strategies have the potential to work well precisely because it is expected that each musician is knowledgeable and skillful enough to provide what is not explicitly arranged.

All of these criteria ultimately work in the service of reaching a state of transcendence, of getting to "the next level."[20] This next level has been described as being the "spiritual" level of the music, the level at which participants in the musical event are in a state akin to what psychologist Mihaly Csikszentmihalyi (1988) describes as "flow,"[21] or what others might refer to as trance or possession. In those situations performance seemingly takes place on its own. Musicians speak of their being outside of themselves, of being completely in tune with all that is going on around them musically, of instruments playing themselves. Although their descriptions of being in such a state can only approximate the experience, they are clear about what conditions are necessary for them to reach that level.

Steve Wilson notes that musicians must bring to a performance all that they can. In other words, each musician must come into each situation prepared to play, prepared to listen, and prepared to respond to other musicians and participants. Wilson describes the drummer Ralph Peterson, who was very much influenced by Art Blakey, as someone who puts all of his energy into making every performance—whether a live gig, a recording session, or even a rehearsal—the best it can be. For Peterson, the aim is putting the maximum into the music, knowing what he wants from it, and always pushing it to the edge, for that is the only way to get the maximum out of it, to tap into the music's spiritual side. Peter Bernstein learned from his study with guitarist Kevin Eubanks that one has to "be serious about music[, for e]very thing you play counts" (Bernstein 1995a). Bernstein explained that such a feeling could be applied equally to practice and performance. Part of reaching the spiritual level, then, is coming to each musical event prepared and ready to engage and be engaged by the process of performing with others.

Musicians feel that audiences are also responsible for whether the music reaches the next level. They, too, have to bring something to the performance. In addition to knowledge of the music's history and the work of individual performers, the audience must be willing to listen attentively and to respond to musical events, according to Wilson:

It's kinda like . . . in a sense going to church, you know, as they say, "You have to be ready to receive," you know . . . I don't even go to hear music if I'm not in the frame of mind to listen to it. I don't go just to be hanging, you know. If I'm really not in the frame of mind to go and support my peers and really listen to what they have to say musically, I don't go because that's a disservice to them. So, uh, when I do go to hang out, I really not only go to hang out for the social part, but for that too. And I think it should be the same for the audience. (Wilson 1995)

He continues by specifying the conditions necessary for musicians to get to the next level:

Once each musician can focus on the purpose at hand, and when you get the sense that each musician is focused on the purpose at hand, that will, uh, that will allow or facilitate that to happen, you know, that, that spiritual level to happen. I know particularly with [bassist] Buster [Smith]'s band, it was the use of space that everybody allowed, you know, and that, uh, you knew that you didn't have to, you weren't just *boxed in,* musically speaking, you know . . . Once you get the sense that you are allowed to use, um, your imagination and, um, to tune in with all of the other, uh, players, then *really* that sets the stage . . . for, for it to really, you know, to go to another level spiritually. And we had a few of those nights when it was just . . . , you know, it really went *beyond* what, you know, at least what I felt, um, [was] just a musical performance, you know . . . Because everyone has to be in tune. Yeah. Everyone has to be *subservient* to that.

And when a musician or group of musicians reaches that level, they sometimes make inexplicable strides in their playing, feel themselves carried by the flow of the music and transported by the sounds and activities constituting a musical event. They frequently find themselves unable to recall exactly what happened immediately after a performance. (It is also interesting to observe the spiritually tinged language employed by Wilson, particularly his references to "receiving" and "subservience.")

As an example of what happens in such moments, I include here an excerpt from my field notes that describes a performance by saxophonist Antonio Hart, pianist Benny Green, and bassist Ed Howard at the midnight set at Bradley's on the night of 4 September 1994:

During the second tune ["91st Miracle"], Hart . . . initiated some stimulating metric and rhythmic activity, most notably the superimposition of patterns in $\frac{3}{8}$ over a $\frac{4}{4}$ metric framework. He really got hot in this solo, getting lots of good, encouraging, sympathetic audience response. At one point, after playing some particularly intricate and long phrases that kept building in intensity, he stopped playing. What was most interesting about his stopping was that previously he had started to rock back and forth with the peaks and accents in his phrases. When he stopped playing, he continued to rock back and forth with the horn out of his mouth and with a look of intense concentration or absorption or pain or intensity (almost a pain-filled frown) on his face. After about eight seconds of rocking back and forth [without playing a note], he put the horn back into his mouth and resumed playing. I wonder what was running through his head at that moment. Did he have too much to say? Nothing to say? No way to say what he wanted to?

When I asked him about this performance in an interview in December, he said the following:

> I do that all the time, man. I, you know, I'm gone. When I'm playing, when the situation's right, I'm usually gone. I'm not even on earth anymore, you know. I'm really not here. So, um, a couple of . . . People tell me I do that all the time. I'll stomp my feet or I'll scream, you know. 'Cause I'm like in a trance, man. I'm, I'm not there. I remember doing stuff like that probably because [there's] something saying, "Stop. Breathe. Leave some space, leave some air." So um, that's what I do. And you, you pretty much hit it on the nose, man, I just . . . I didn't know what to do, so I just stopped and cleared my head and tried to get my thoughts back together and tr[ied] to come back and say something 'cause I am trying to talk. You know, I'm *trying* to. It doesn't always work, man . . .
>
> It's a blessing just to *play* music . . . It's just a blessing, and I try to take it that way. Every day, I try to think of it that way . . . It's not me that's playing. I'm just a tool that the music's coming through, the compositions are coming through, that's why when you see me going off and I'm rocking and shit, it's not me. At that particular point, I'm there, but I'm not there. The more spiritual I become—I've been laying low on that—but the more spiritual I become the further my music is gonna go. I know that already. (Hart 1994)

Not every transcendent moment is as intense as this one, nor is every response the same, but the connection between stimulating jazz performance and feelings that are best described as spiritual becomes more apparent through this example. Hart's mention of being a tool—along with Wilson's use of "receive" and "subservient"—suggests that at these and similar moments the individual's sense of self is temporarily suspended and he or she becomes part of something else. What happens at those moments is the core of what is meaningful about jazz performance for some performers and other knowledgeable participants. It is one of the major shared understandings of what jazz performance is supposed to be "about." Those shared understandings are constructed from engagement with performance and the importance in it of having an individual voice, balancing a number of musical and performative parameters, understanding the cultural foundations of the music, bringing

something to each performance, allowing other musicians and participants to bring something, and, in the end, being open to moving to the
next level.

On the basis of musicians' normative views of jazz performance,
from which one can infer ways of evaluating it as well, I want to posit
the existence of an integrating and encompassing aesthetic. Because of the
emphasis that musicians place on blues feeling, particularly as something that guides the use of other resources,[22] I use the term "blues aesthetic." The word "aesthetic" here denotes shared normative and evaluative criteria. It is also used as a label for a certain "iconicity of style." As
Steven Feld (1994a, 131–32) writes, when a style term (in musical performance, for example) becomes a "cross-modal homology" connecting
differing modes of interpersonal expression, its metaphoric force leads us
to view it as "naturally real, obvious, complete, and thorough." That is,
because of its versatility and applicability across modes it takes on a force
that makes it seemingly part of everything in the world. As a result, what
might be considered a metaphor—like the blues—becomes iconic, a symbol that stands for itself and is experienced "as feelingfully synonymous
from one domain or level of image and experience to another" (Feld
1994a, 132; see also Becker and Becker 1981).[23] At the same time, a blues
aesthetic may function in ways that Charles Sanders Peirce might describe as indexical (Turino 1999; Jackson 2000). That is, occurrences in a
single musical event may *point to* other experiences and thereby account
for the correspondences that make it seem natural. Surveying the comments of scholars and musicians makes it clear that blues-based performance, as a synonym for jazz performance, is metaphorically linked to
other realms of experience: it is an ethos that informs African American
visual art (Powell 1989b), literature (Baker 1984; Gates 1988), and daily
living (Ellison 1964a; Murray 1970, 1976; Small 1987a; Floyd 1995;
Wilson 1995) in addition to music. And in the popular imagination, blues
are associated with "realness," soulfulness, honesty, and sincerity.[24]

Other scholars have proposed the existence of a "black aesthetic,"
undergirded by analyses of African American art, literature, and music.
Their concept of blackness is, as the term indicates, intimately tied to
phenotypic and socially constructed notions of race. Many of their pronouncements started as description but quickly became programmatic,
connecting expression by visibly "black" artists and writers to a unique
essence possessed by all black people and dictating the kinds of expression that would qualify existing and future works as "black" (Fuller
1971; Welburn 1971; for critiques, see Baker 1984, 72–91; Jarab 1985).

More recent writers have sought to maintain the spirit that originally motivated work on the black aesthetic, choosing, however, to privilege culture, learning, and practice over race. They have focused on describing an "African American aesthetic" (Starks 1993), in some ways synonymous with a blues aesthetic (Andrews 1989; Powell 1989a, 1994; Baraka 1991 conflates the two).[25] Each of these writers, however, stops short of describing a blues aesthetic. Instead, they restrict their arguments to characteristics of the blues and what must precede the formulation of that aesthetic, such as consideration of the views of African American musicians as well as poets, novelists, and painters (see Starks 1993, 152).

A blues aesthetic, as such, is the sum of the reflective and normative assertions that musicians have made regarding processes of performance, interaction, and evaluation. In the simplest terms, it is constituted by (learned) practices derived from and continually fed by the interaction between African American musics and culture and others. It is not, however, racially based, nor is it "coded" in the genes of any group of individuals. Rather, it is learned through the engagement of individuals with those musics and cultures—to the degree that one can view them as separable entities—and through their close attention to the practices of African Americans and those in African American musics (see Wilson 1985, 1992).[26] Participants in musical events, using a blues aesthetic as a performative and evaluative framework (see Marshall 1982), place a premium on individual expression within established frames for performance (Hymes 1964; Bauman 1975; Bauman and Briggs 1990) and on equally patterned interaction with other performers and participants. Such events are oriented toward each performer "saying something" (Barth 1995; Monson 1996) about how to take the materials at hand (e.g., instruments, compositions, forms, harmony, venues, musicians, listeners) and spontaneously exploit their expressive potential. This aesthetic is another manifestation of what composer Olly Wilson has described as an African-derived "conceptual approach" to music making (Wilson 1974, 1992). Novelty is not among the primary concerns of the participant motivated by a blues aesthetic; creativity, distinctiveness, and interactivity are. These concerns manifest themselves in the ways in which performers sometimes reinforce and sometimes push against the frames that surround jazz performance.[27] Even more, a blues aesthetic is a statement of an egalitarian, enabling myth of jazz performance, a myth that says that any musician who understands and actualizes the normative criteria can be a good performer. The aesthetic is an underpinning for what musicians do when they perform and what some performing and non-performing participants call upon in evaluating performance.

What are the epistemological foundations of this aesthetic? And how is it transmitted or learned? According to the musicians I consulted, the aesthetic has its roots in African American culture and musics, particularly sacred ones.[28] Perhaps recognition of those connections is what enabled Sam Newsome to make some of the statements previously cited about African American audiences being able to relate to jazz on a deeper level. If one accepts his argument, one might assert that African American audiences understand the music in a deeper sense because they have more points of contact with its cultural valence, with notions such as soulfulness that are recognizable across the domains of speech, dress, and other African American forms of music, for example. Those perceived connections fuel Steve Wilson's previously cited comments about Duke Ellington's relation to tradition. Wilson noted that Ellington took all of "our"—that is, African Americans'—experiences and put them into his music. The crucial point, whether these assertions stand up to the empirical questioning of historians or analysts, is that some participants understand or believe, even if only in ways that are difficult to verbalize, that the connections between jazz and African American culture must be part of any understanding of the music. Thus understanding of or embeddedness within African American culture constitutes one potential source of or pathway toward understanding a blues aesthetic.

There are also suggestive analogues between jazz performance and performance in ecstatic African American religious worship, particularly in Pentecostal, Southern Baptist, and Church of God in Christ congregations. These analogues suggest that a blues aesthetic might have roots in the African American church. Steve Wilson's previously cited comments, which reference being "ready to receive," are one data point that pointed me in this direction. Also suggesting this connection are the statements of pianist James Williams, cited in chapter 2, as well as Antonio Hart's comments about spirituality enhancing his musical ability.

Even more suggestive are the similarities between the responses of participants at particularly moving musical events and the responses characteristic of African American religious worship. When saxophonist Stanley Turrentine, pianist Cedar Walton, bassist David Williams, and drummer Billy Higgins performed in Washington Square Park in September of 1994, they took a long time to establish a connection with the audience. At the point, five tunes into their set, when I started to feel that they were playing in a compelling fashion, with a groove that was in the pocket, and they began to elicit motor responses from audience members—hand clapping, foot tapping, and head shaking—I noticed another African American audience participant with his head lowered waving his right hand in the air. That response was one that I recognized from my experiences in church as a mild "shout," an affirmation signaling religious ecstasy (Lincoln and Mamiya 1990, 365). Likewise, singer Miles Griffith, at a performance by James Williams's Intensive Care Unit in February of 1995, responded to another musician's performance in a manner that was clearly analogous to response in ecstatic forms of African American worship: he fanned singer Roger Holland after a particularly moving cadenza, as though Holland, having "gotten happy" and "felt the spirit" while singing, needed cooling off. Moreover, there were a number of situations in which verbal responses such as "Preach!" and "Tell it!"—similar to those used to encourage a preacher—were used to encourage or express approval of what a particular performer was doing or had done (see, for example, Davis 1985). The importance of these kinds of responses is that they suggest a foundational link between African American religious and secular musics beyond musical style, that is, at the level of the conceptual system rather than the expressive system.

Perhaps the belief in cultural connections is what, in part, impels younger musicians to seek out older African American musicians. If we accept Antonio Hart's notion of getting the spirit of what the music is "really about," his work with elder African American musicians is an attempt to learn about the aesthetic directly and interactively. Moreover, elder musicians who have lived long lives as jazz performers and who have had extensive playing experience, particularly with now-departed legends, are seen as important sources of information, as true bearers of the tradition and its associated aesthetic. They pass on cautionary tales, apocryphal stories, meaningful anecdotes, and pieces of wisdom to younger musicians willing to listen.[29] Theirs is the firsthand oral history of jazz passed down seemingly without the mediation of publishers or editors. The knowledge one gets from these "masters" is often tacit rather than verbalized, particularly where performance is involved. Saxophonist Joshua Redman, for example, feels that much of what he learns from performing with older musicians is located on a "very general, intangible level":

It's not so much that I've learned *specific* things from specific musicians, um, because music to me is, um, you know, whatever you want to call it, an emotional or spiritual experience. It's about sharing a part of yourself, and not the intellectual part of yourself, but the, you know, your soul, the spiritual side of yourself, the creative part of your personality, with somebody else. [With] the other musicians, ultimately with the audience, but first with the other musicians . . . When I play with someone it's not like I walk [away] having better harmony, better rhythm, or something. I leave the experience having gotten to communicate with them and take a part of their self into me, you know, without it sounding too "new age" . . . You're basically trying to combine, you know, your individual emotional resources to kind of create this, this overall musical portrait which has meaning, and which will move people, which, which has emotional content . . . So in order to do that, I'm digging inside of myself. This person is digging inside of themselves. And we're taking what we've come up with and using it basically to create something. So basically what I'm saying is, you know, I'm, when I make music with someone, they're sharing a part of themselves with me, you know. In order . . . that's part of the process, in other words. *Especially* in jazz because you're creating at the spur of the moment. You know, it's improvisation. So you know, you can't fall back on a predetermined role or predetermined part you can play. You're right there. You have to be completely conscious of what the other person is saying musically. What's coming from them, you know . . . And when you play with great musicians, master musicians, it's like the little bit you take from them, the little bit that they shared with you, is so rich, so dense, there's so much depth to it because of their years and years of honing their craft and their years and years of life on this planet and, you know, the depth of their maturity as musicians and as human beings. Hopefully you internalize that and it makes you a deeper musician and a more mature person. (Redman 1995a)

Bernstein noted that his experiences playing with Jimmy Cobb and Lou Donaldson almost never involved receiving specific instructions about what or how to play. There are, however, many situations in which specific information about performance is communicated to or picked up by young musicians. Bruce Barth, for example, sometimes goes to clubs to observe piano players he admires, like Mulgrew Miller and Monty Alexander. He notices how they arrange their tunes and how they interact with other performers and with their audiences. Then, in the space between sets, he might sit down with them to ask specific questions about things he heard or saw them doing. Gregory Hutchinson recalled experiencing breakthroughs when he could see what drummers like Art Blakey and Arthur Taylor were physically doing that was not apparent to him from listening to recordings. Through performance interaction, observation, and verbal communication, then, musicians have another point of access to learning the aesthetic and transmitting it to others.

Two other potential sources of knowledge about jazz and a blues aesthetic are jazz recordings and writings about jazz. Like scholars, musicians learn much from listening to recordings (see Berliner 1994, 63–119). Each of the musicians whose home I visited for interviews had an extensive collection of recordings, jazz and otherwise, on compact disc, cassette, LP, and even reel-to-reel tape. They devoted significant amounts of time to choosing the music that would accompany the interviews.[30] There is a slight but significant difference between the way that musicians use recordings and the way that scholars do. Although each group to some degree sees recordings as documentation, what they see them as documenting differs. Scholars typically see recordings as a repository of jazz performance practices (see chapter 1). Their discussion tends to stop with the recording and its context, for their concern is with what is textualized and accessible to other scholars. Musicians, on the other hand, see recordings as learning tools that are more reliable than written sources produced by scholars and music publishers. When musicians want to learn a Duke Ellington tune, particularly since Ellington can no longer be consulted, they go to an Ellington recording rather than a "fake book" or published sheet music—with the tune's melody, chord symbols, and perhaps simple piano accompaniment—to get the "correct" harmonic progression, rhythms, and accents.[31] In those situations where the original performer continually reworked his or her own compositions, the curious musician may refer to several recordings. For those who are studying older recordings, however, the recording is only a starting point; it is a foundation for knowledge rather than the final authority. For although it may be analyzed and pored over for its characteristics and implications, it is generally raw material to be transposed, reharmonized, and altered. In other words, it is something that is learned primarily in order to be transformed, to be filtered through one's individual sound rather than repeated or strictly immortalized.

Non-performing scene participants sometimes use recordings in similar ways. As Lisa Michel's comments in cited in chapter 4 indicate, audience members, like musicians, learn a great deal about jazz performance from careful listening to recordings, such as repertoire, musicians' idiosyncrasies and individual approaches to improvisation, and different forms as well as modes of interaction. That knowledge is most useful in contextualizing and evaluating subsequently heard recordings or live performances. Those recordings contain the traces of musical history and tradition that they hear and expect to be transformed in performance. But, like Michel, audience members may also come to rely less on recordings as they engage more purposefully with live performances.

With regard to writings on jazz, the musicians evinced varying levels of knowledge about and respect for scholarly and critical writing. Joshua Redman mentioned Gunther Schuller's essay on Sonny Rollins (1958) during my interview with him, noting that Rollins's opinion of Schuller's article wasn't favorable. And many of the musicians seemed to be acquainted with the major histories of jazz and, as one might reasonably expect, were capable of naming the major jazz figures that would be mentioned in a college-level jazz history course. For the most part, however, when musicians' reading involved music at all, they tended to favor biographies of important musicians. Sam Newsome, for example, expressed great interest in biographies of John Coltrane written by Bill Cole (1993) and J.C. Thomas (1975). But as he recounted stories from those biographies in my interview with him, he sometimes questioned the anecdotes or contrasted them with those that he had heard from other musicians. In other words, published material is not considered the final authority, particularly when the words and ideas of other musicians who were there are available. The only book about jazz that was consistently recommended was, not surprisingly, one that is concerned more with the ethos of the music than with a strict historical narrative: Albert Murray's *Stomping the Blues* (1976). Pianist Eric Reed, in discussing writings about jazz with me in March of 1995, punctuated a discussion of books by Collier (1978) and Tirro (1977) with a question about whether I had read *the* book—a reference to Murray's work. In this sense, reading jazz history or criticism was not seen as a way to learn about a blues aesthetic unless it provided sustained and specific insight into how musicians negotiated performing and how they brought various aspects of themselves to the music.[32] The information gleaned from other musicians and from performers—that is, knowledge coming out of interactions on the scene—was the most trustworthy repository of knowledge.

It is also clear, however, that the blues aesthetic is not autonomous, even when it is seen as emerging from African American culture and performative practices. As many scholars writing about the origins and transformations of various ideas and discourses have shown (Foucault 1972, 1973; Bakhtin 1981; Williams 1977; Lipsitz 1990), there is no discourse that does not have significant and enduring ties to other discourses. In the case of a blues aesthetic, those links have a lot to do with what individual performers and audience members bring to the music and how their understandings leads to the emergence of a shared aesthetic. In short, they are an effect of the pathways (Finnegan 1989) that individual participants take to engaging with jazz performance. Musicians and audiences who espouse a blues aesthetic, by valorizing what individuals can bring to the music, allow for and expect interaction with other aesthetics and other musics. In this way the aesthetic contains the possibility of its dissolution. Other discourses may enter the discussion, but they must be shaped to the aims and practices privileged within the aesthetic.

Many of today's jazz scene participants are likely to have learned about jazz history and performance practice in institutional settings where other aesthetic frameworks are championed, as in college courses and conservatories. As Bruce Barth noted (see chapter 4), conservatories and their jazz programs function as substitutes for what were once vibrant scenes that fulfilled the function of educating young musicians (Reed 1979). In institutional settings, potential scene participants encounter Romantic discourses on art and genius, as well as criteria for assessing greatness (see Solis 2009). Those discourses and criteria seem almost natural in European and American culture. They are heavily concentrated in and promulgated by the "cultural systems" of conservatories (Kingsbury 1988; Nettl 1995) and colleges. The discourses surrounding Western concert music—its traditions, evolution, and universality—are implicitly evoked whenever one uses terms associated with it, for it has come to function as what linguists refer to as an unmarked category, a reference point for the discussion of other musics. When one speaks of any other form of music as "art," many individuals find themselves looking for the qualities that make it *artistic* in ways comparable to classical music. Though classical music's status as art is taken for granted, other musical traditions must, so to speak, demonstrate that they are through direct comparison to it.

A blues aesthetic functions as a related but alternate discourse on musical performance. Although it grows out of African American culture and the interaction between participants on the jazz scene, it also uses terms and concepts derived from the discourses on Western concert music. Jazz scene participants, like many other people, are aware of the ways in which the discourses surrounding classical music have historically been used by educators and critics to denigrate other musical styles, to deny their specificity and cultural significance. The musicians' knowledge of Western classical music, for example, encouraged by training at institutions like the New England Conservatory or the Berklee College of Music, surely contributes to a desire to see the music they perform recognized as being on par with classical music in terms of artistry and complexity. Indeed, their knowledge of and engagement with discourses on European art music help them strategically to call upon those same discourses to elevate jazz in the eyes of its detractors.[33] Moreover, they can strategically employ those same discourses to attract audiences whose understandings of music and strivings for social and cultural capital (Bourdieu 1984) lead them to evaluate and choose music based on its supposed artistic merit.

When musicians such as Donald Harrison describe jazz by analogy to classical music, therefore, they frequently do so with a specific intent that doesn't necessarily contradict the belief that blues aesthetic criteria are paramount in evaluating musical performance. Harrison ended a performance at Iridium in May of 1995 by thanking the audience for coming to hear his group and encouraging them to continue supporting "America's classical music" by buying recordings and attending live performances. The use of the label "America's classical music" can appeal to any number of social actors, regardless of racial, ethnic, or cultural background. Those who respond to it as a positive label constitute a self-selected group, perhaps allying themselves with an "American" version of classical music that is distinct from the European one. To the degree that musicians like Harrison believe that jazz is a music on par with Western classical music, they do not necessarily see as a corollary that the music must be analyzed or understood in the same way as classical music. At other times—as in Harrison's previously related anecdote about giving credit to the music's African American "creators and innovators"—they foreground the African Americanness of the music. The choice to describe jazz as American or African American, then, is frequently a strategic one. African American musicians, for example, might describe jazz as American when it is to their advantage, that is, when the definition includes the widest possible number of potential audience members or attracts potential listeners. Alternately, they might emphasize its African Americanness when a focus on its supposedly universal characteristics threatens to erase what they see as its cultural rootedness. Non–African Americans might likewise use the term "America's classical music" to escape the feeling that a term like "African American music" questions their participation in or erases their contributions to jazz (see also Monson 1996, 200–203).

Like some of their classical counterparts, however, either group can describe jazz in non-technical, non-academic terms without mentioning (African American) culture for other strategic reasons. In such situations, they are often arguing for separating jazz from an overly cold and analytical paradigm that seems concerned only with harmony, melody, rhythm, and other notatable aspects of performance. In that case, they are moving closer to a classical notion of "transcendence." Joshua Redman's liner notes from his 1994 recording *MoodSwing* are instructive here:

> Jazz is music. And great jazz, like all great music, attains it value not through intellectual complexity, but through emotional expressivity. True, jazz is a particularly intricate, refined, and rigorous art form. Jazz musicians must amass a vast body of idiomatic knowledge and cultivate an acute artistic imagination if they wish to become accomplished creative improvisers. Moreover, a familiarity with jazz history and theory will undoubtedly enhance a listener's appreciation of the actual aesthetics. Yes, jazz *is* intelligent music. Nevertheless, extensive as they might seem, the intellectual aspects of jazz are ultimately only means to its emotional ends. Technique, theory, and analysis are not, and should never be considered, ends in themselves.
>
> Jazz is not about flat fives or sharp nines, or metric subdivisions, or substitute chord changes. Jazz is about feeling, communication, honesty, and soul. Jazz is not supposed to boggle the mind. Jazz is meant to enrich the spirit. (Redman 1994b)

All of the key words are there: "all great music," "refined," and "art." Redman takes great pains to indicate the ways in which those descriptors apply to jazz, even as he wants to distinguish their use as applied to jazz rather than classical music. Classical music aficionados may make similar claims about the disservice analysis does to music, but Redman's assertions proceed differently from those that see the musical experience as communicative or expressive in and of itself (see Kivy 1990). His attempt to deemphasize the intellectualism of musical response foregrounds notions of communication, soulfulness, and expressivity. But those terms must be understood in light of their connection with a blues aesthetic and the way in which notions like soulfulness and communication are configured within it. Redman *learned* about that soulfulness from listening to Stanley Turrentine (as well as Stevie Wonder, Otis Redding, and Aretha Franklin) and from working with master musicians.

The foundations of a blues aesthetic are found in various domains of activity: in the interaction between African American musical practices, in African American religious worship, and in other aspects of African American culture and the corresponding traditions of other groups.

Musicians and other scene participants become acquainted with the aesthetic through their engagement with and understanding of African American musics and African American culture as well their interactions with parallel and competing discourses. Through verbal and performative communication, record listening, and reading, participants tap into and shape different aspects of this aesthetic, learning how to make, interpret, and respond to the sounds and other stimuli in musical events.

CHAPTER 6

Jazz Performance as Ritualized Activity

The scene and a blues aesthetic are two related means of framing musical events as jazz and as performance. Although the scene—space and place through time—constitutes both a setting for and snapshot of jazz performance, the criteria of a blues aesthetic provide participants a way to negotiate the resultant spatio-temporal formation. Other forms of music or performance might be framed or understood via their positioning in other scenes and/or via the normative and evaluative criteria of other aesthetics. Within a jazz scene and working within a blues aesthetic, the emphasis placed by musicians on "taking it to another level," their many mentions of spirituality, and participants' church-derived responses to jazz performance together suggest a view of jazz musical events as *ritualized* performances.

To describe these events as ritualized is different from describing them as ritual, a category of activity anthropologists and scholars of comparative religion and literature have long seen as important in structuring human experience (e.g., Van Gennep 1960; Kluckhohn 1942; Eliade 1959; Turner 1969; Asad 1983; Comaroff 1985; Smith 1987; Combs-Schilling 1989; Seremetakis 1991; Bell 1992).[1] In addition to being used to explain society and religion, insights from the study of ritual have figured in other scholars' work on African-derived musics, including jazz (Marks 1974; Burnim 1985, 1988; Leonard 1987; Small 1987a; Salamone 1988). In each case the meanings of the term *ritual* have been subject to debate with a limited set of views tending to dominate, both within and beyond the academy. In one such grouping, commentators have tightly circumscribed the concept such that "definitions of ritual . . . have tended to share a presupposition about their object . . . [Ritual has been] indigenously represented as 'ancient' and unchanging. [connected] to 'tradition,' the sacred, to structures that have generally been represented in stasis" (Kelly and Kaplan 1990, 120). In this view, rituals are essentially conservative and devoted to maintaining a status quo or (re)establishing social and/or cosmic equilibrium. Those performing rituals, then, follow relatively rigid scripts from which deviations might be dangerous. It is precisely in this sense that many everyday speakers equally attach the word to activities that carry great social significance and to others that call for formulaic adherence to a more or less predetermined sequence of events.

In another grouping, that former set of views has been challenged in anthropological theory since the late 1970s, particularly on the grounds that not all rituals are seasonal, calendrical, or concerned with healing or social integration, for example. Just as researchers studying identity and ethnicity have come to see those concepts as plastic and negotiable—concerned more with policing boundaries than with specifying content (Barth 1969)—so too have anthropologists come to view ritual more dynamically. Some see it as possessing varying degrees of and responses to formalization (Irvine 1979; Schieffelin 1985; Kelly and Kaplan 1990) and as characterized less by rote repetition than by performative negotiations with structure that are enunciative, that rely upon multiple media, and that have indexical relationships to—that is, that point toward—other aspects of social life (Tambiah 1979, 119).[2]

Whether one sees ritual as conservative or performative, common threads regarding its role in individual and social transformation and its power to organize experience still emerge in the literature, threads that might have value for research on musics and musicians. Comaroff (1985), for example, sees the efficacy of ritual in its ability to play "most directly upon the signifying capacity of symbols, using them as the means through which to grasp, condense, and act upon qualities otherwise diffused in the social and material world" (78). African Zionists in South Africa, she notes, "construct rituals so as to reform the world in the image they have created, to reestablish a dynamic correspondence between the self and the structures that contain it" (198). In this case, ritual escapes the connotation it has, for some, with meaningless routine. That is, ritual not only informs the interactions that one might have with the surrounding world, but it also provides a means through which one might intervene directly in that world to change its structures or, at least, one's relation to them. Similarly, in her book *Sacred Performances: Islam, Sexuality, and Sacrifice* (1989), M. E. Combs-Schilling stresses ritual's usefulness for combining images or ideas metaphorically such that participants must search for "their points of likeness and opposition" (248). Critically, this use of metaphor does not allow for free association; rather, it "demands imagination and creativity and yet . . . is highly constraining in the kinds of understandings it allows to be built, for it defines the parameters of comparison" (248), linking present actors with the past and other ritual practitioners. Ritual at once facilitates the perception of meaning and constrains the operations whereby one might come to apprehend it. In the process, ritually constructed meanings become iconic representations,[3] "truths" that are not easily destroyed: "Ritual's fullness, independence, and capacity to orchestrate experience [enable] it to build definitions that impact upon all others. . . . Other definitions and experiences exist, definitions that can be quite oppositional to the ones that are ritually built. . . . Yet, when effective, the ritual definitions come to dominate, for they are experienced as essential definitions—definitions in purest form. Their cultural worth enables them to overshadow all others" (Combs-Schilling 1989, 253). Issues of selfhood and cultural identity thus find perhaps their strongest articulations in rituals understood in this sense, for such events provide definitions that not only extend into daily life but help to determine its very fabric.

As novel and as flexible as these formulations are, they share with their predecessors, in Catherine Bell's estimation, a certain conceptual slipperiness. In each of them ritual is a delimited, cross-culturally identifiable entity that can intervene in the world as though it possessed (human) agency. That is, even as they distinguish between ritual activities and their everyday counterparts, these writers do so in ways that might diverge significantly from practitioners' understandings of what they are doing. The category of ritual, in other words, is a frame that analysts *impose* upon the phenomena they have observed. As a result, the concept often seems to slip "out of the analyst's hand and into the data he or she is trying to interpret" (Bell 1992, 13), with most discussions of ritual reducing it to "a type of critical juncture wherein some pair of opposing social or cultural forces comes together" and/or seeing it as a form action distinct from "conceptual aspects of religion, such as beliefs, symbols, and myths" (16, 19). For such analysts, then, ritual as concept and event is a symbolic staging ground for a confrontation, where actions in the moment crystallize or work through preexisting, more fundamental cultural categories. Moreover, that analytic separation cf action and thought reappears in different guises in writings on ritual, first where scholars describe ritual as the "functional or structural mechanism" that integrates thought and action (20), and then where they use it distinguish between ritual participants, who act, and those observing them, who think: "In ritual activity, conceptions and dispositions are fused for the participants, [a joining] which yields meaning. Meaning for the outside theorist comes differently: insofar as he or she can perceive in ritual the true basis of its meaningfulness for the ritual actors—that is, its fusion of conceptual and dispositional categories—then the theorist can go beyond mere thoughts about activity to grasp the meaningfulness of the ritual" (28). Thus, Bell asserts, a method of analysis comes to justify the existence and work of a researcher at the same time that it is deployed to illuminate what the researcher studies.

For those scholars wanting to bypass self-serving circularity, Bell recommends shifting attention away from a bounded concept of ritual—and defining characteristics like formalization and routinization—and toward *processes of ritualization*. For her, the latter encompass "culturally specific strategies for setting some activities off from others, for creating and privileging a qualitative distinction between the 'sacred' and the 'profane,' and for ascribing such distinctions to realities thought to transcend the powers of human actors" (1992, 7–8, 74). Through focusing on the strategies whereby social actors demarcate and ascribe significance to specific kinds of actions, analysts might avoid having always to gesture toward (and endlessly modify) "container" definitions (Lakoff 1987, 271–73) of ritual, concentrating instead on the locally specific inflections of those actions and their relations with other ensembles of cultural activity.

A focus on processes of ritualization, however, advances a broader aim. In addition to distinguishing some activities from others, the "implicit dynamic" of such processes, their purpose, is "the production of a 'ritualized body' [social or individual] . . . invested with a 'sense' of ritual" (98). Following Pierre Bourdieu, she continues, "This sense is not a matter of self-conscious knowledge of any explicit rules cf ritual but is an implicit 'cultivated disposition'" (98). Such dispositions develop over time, as social agents engage repeatedly with the practices that characterize ritualized activities, incorporating them into their personal and collective repertoires of postures, behaviors, and orientations. Once they have cultivated such dispositions, these agents—whether they are, for examples, performers who know how to improvise creatively or non-performers who are capable of distinguishing creative improvisation from its more prosaic counterparts—have potentially developed the ability to "deploy schemes of ritualization in order to . . . shift or nuance . . . other, non-ritualized situations to render them more coherent with the values of the ritualizing schemes" (108). Or, more clearly, processes of ritualization are one of the means through which social agents learn how to "[manipulate] the meaning of things by manipulating their relationships" (110), whether those things are the symbols and (hierarchical) relationships that are ritually defined or similar entities in the non-ritualized world. The production of such agents leads, finally, to the development of what, again following Bourdieu, she calls ritual mastery, "the ability—not equally shared, desired, or recognized—to (1) take and remake schemes from the shared culture that can strategically nuance, privilege, or transform, (2) deploy them in the formulation of a privileged ritual experience, which in turn (3) impresses them in a new form upon agents able to deploy them in a variety of circumstances beyond the circumference of the rite itself" (116).

In this light, one way of understanding why certain performers and influential musicians are celebrated is to add to assessments of their instrumental virtuosity (or vocal dexterity) consideration of how their participation in musical events resonates with the world outside them, how they negotiate the internal dynamics of ritualized events, and, crucially, how their work helps to create a sense of ritual mastery in other event participants. Indeed, Steve Wilson's praise for Duke Ellington in the previous chapter is an alternative, less academic statement of this proposition: "That's why Duke Ellington was such a, such a master, man. He took . . . all of our experiences and put 'em into his art form" (Wilson 1995). That is, ritualized agents can *hear* in Ellington's work not only the traces of the cultures that nurtured him but also his way of working through and re-presenting that culture for the benefit of ritualized performers and listeners.[4]

For those participating in ritualized activities, then, there are always a number of conditioning elements: the prior social and cultural schemas that allow an event to register as ritualized; the oppositions, definitions, strategies, and orientations created and experienced in those activities; and the culturally contingent strategies for making ritualized schemas useful outside specially defined contexts. Those contexts suggest that ritualized activities do something different from traditionally conceived rituals, described by analysts as "transmitting shared beliefs, instilling a dominant ideology as an internal subjectivity, or even providing participants with the concepts to think with" (Bell 1992, 221). Unlike rituals conceived thus, ritualized practices are neither secondary nor reflective. They are, as a number of social theorists might put it, structured and structuring and therefore best understood as constitutive of rather than supplemental to social life.

Bell's descriptions of ritualization have numerous points of contact with the way Paul Connerton understands the creation, transmission, and transformation of social memory, the accumulated, interconnected narrative accounts through which social groups derive and represent their identities to themselves and others (1989, 21, 38–39).[5] For him rites are central elements in the creation and transmission of social memory, and they are, moreover, not merely expressive, strictly formal, nor efficacious only within the spheres that contain them (44). Rather than being scrims obscuring, or proxies for, something prior or more fundamental, rites constitute one means for their participants to *do things* via their performances and the enunciative force of their actions (59). Indeed, especially in the case of commemorative national rituals, he argues against the possibility of such activities functioning as some sort of eternal return—a temporary journey into mythic or even historic time. He writes, "Under the conditions of modernity the celebration of recurrence can never be anything more than a compensatory strategy, because the very principle of modernity itself denies the idea of life as a structure of celebrated recurrence." Under such circumstances, something else has to be happening, for "capital accumulation, the ceaseless expansion of the commodity form through the market, requires the constant revolutionising of production, the ceaseless transformation of the innovative into the obsolescent. The clothes people wear, the machines they operate, the workers who service the machines, the neighbourhoods they live in—all are constructed today to be dismantled tomorrow, so that they can be replaced or recycled" (64). He argues that instead we should understand (commemorative) rites as a "collective variant . . . of personal memory, that is to say a way of making sense of the past as a kind of collective autobiography" (70).

Such rites achieve persuasive power, become intelligible and extensible, through the ways in which their participants habituate themselves to and through them via bodily practices, of which Connerton delineates two overlapping varieties: incorporating and inscribing. In the former category, he includes "messages that a sender or senders impart by means of their own current bodily activity, the transmission occurring only during the time that their bodies are present to sustain that particular activity" (72), for example, handshakes, words spoken in person, gestures, or even bodily posture. In the latter category presence is less important since the practices so classed "require that we do something that traps and holds information [for retrieval] long after the human organism has stopped informing" (73), for example, writing, photography, and audio recording. Connerton acknowledges that his practice categories are not mutually exclusive, for it is hard to imagine inscription practices without incorporating ones. After all, writing is still a set of physical actions and, under certain circumstances, one's examination of someone else's penmanship might reveal a docile, disciplined body (or its opposite) in ways similar to what observations of posture might show. Both incorporating and inscribing practices find frequent expression in habitual action, understood both as an "affective disposition" and as a "cluster of features collected together to form a practice: an activity which is acquired in the sense that it is influenced by previous activity; which is ready for overt manifestation; and which remains operative in some subdued way even when it is not the obviously dominant activity" (94). Thus construed, habit becomes something more than symbolic repetition evacuated of meaning: "Habit is a knowledge and a remembering in the hands and the body; and in the cultivation of habit it is our body which 'understands'" (95). In this view, *incorporating practices* become crucially important for any understanding of social memory— distinguished from textualized historical memory—because of two of their most salient features: "They do not exist 'objectively,' independent of their being performed. And they are acquired in such a way as not to require explicit reflection on their performance" (102). Those two features, in turn, help us to understand the great power of practices of the body and even ritualized activities, for they together "contain a measure of insurance against the process of cumulative questioning entailed in all discursive practices," by their being lodged in the bodies and actions of people rather than in texts or other static forms. That is, ritualized activities and the ritualized bodies they create are effective more because of what they do than because of what they reflect, express, or comment upon.

Both Bell's and Connerton's ideas provide useful and flexible means for approaching musical performances and understanding their embeddedness within and influence upon other social and cultural phenomena. Against scholarship where writers might slavishly try to match each aspect of jazz performance to preexisting analytic categories (e.g., Leonard 1987), their frameworks bracket the question of whether performance is or is not ritual. They encourage researchers to focus instead on what sets performances apart from other activities, musical or otherwise, and the means through which participants in performance events both become habituated to them—as performers and listeners—and see them as related to and capable of modifying schemas operating outside a given event or set of events.

More precisely, a focus on ritualization affords the scholar of jazz a way to integrate the flux and mutability of the scene with the attitudes toward performance, participation, and evaluation that achieve iconicity and indexicality in blues-based performance. Ritualized activity becomes a heuristic for simultaneously navigating the structure provided by the scene and musical style and negotiating it via blues aesthetic criteria— at once enabling the interpretation of meaning while constraining its possible forms. Although several scholars have proposed that African American musical forms, including jazz, are ritualistic or ritualized,[6] and though each of them states the purpose of such musics differently, they agree that their focus is stomping the blues and giving participants metaphoric "equipment for living," different ways of understanding and intervening in the world around them. Understanding the ritualized nature of performance, particularly as it emerges from the statements and actions of scene participants, allows one to see more clearly that, *in addition* to its function as entertainment, jazz has socially expressive and transformative potential (see also Burnim 1985, 160).

Christopher Small's commonsense notion of ritual (1987b; see also Small 1987a, 1998) provides a point of departure for detailed discussion of the ways in which ritualized activities set musical performances apart from their everyday counterparts. In describing the "ritualistic" aspects of Western concert music performance, Small explicitly details the following: (1) that performance takes place in a space specifically set aside for that purpose; (2) that the space is constructed in such a way as to focus attention on the performers; (3) that there are workers charged with maintaining and ensuring the sacredness of the space; (4) that there are conventions regarding the dress of performers and other participants; and (5) that there are strict behavioral expectations for both performers and participants (1987b, 8–11). He goes on to note that "most concerts consist mainly of a limited number of works which get played over and over again, with minute variations in interpretation, and that audiences become extremely skilled in perceiving these variations and comparing them" (13–14). Although Small's argument relies on a static, container-like definition of ritual rather than on processes of ritualization, his list of criteria nonetheless illustrates the ways in which classical music concerts might be distinct from both everyday life and other kinds of performances that take place in similar venues or employ similar means of demarcation.

Jazz as performed in bars and nightclubs, at festivals, and in concert halls shares many of the previously mentioned characteristics: there are spaces in New York City that are (temporarily) set aside for jazz performance, both legally (in terms of zoning laws) and functionally (in terms of what venue owners do in sanctioned spaces). The performers are central in those spaces, often being the reason why non-performers are present. The layout of many venues, as noted in chapter 4, focuses the attention of other participants on performers, who typically occupy an area raised above floor level. To varying degrees, these spaces are maintained for the presentation of music with images of jazz musicians, instruments, and other memorabilia adorning the walls and sound systems amplifying and projecting the sound(s) of the performers. Owners and managers make more or less committed efforts to maintain performance spaces, keeping pianos in tune and even improving or modifying the appearance of a space over time.[7] There are, moreover, conventionalized though variable expectations regarding the dress and behavior of both performers and other participants. The "quiet policies" of various venues seem intended, for example, not to prohibit all verbal activity, only that which is not in response to the music. Shouts of encouragement are prohibited only when their excessiveness interferes with the ability of others to hear or see what the performers are doing (Racy 1991, 15–16). Finally, there is a more or less unvarying repertoire of compositions known as "standards" that will often be performed or that can serve as models or springboards for new compositions (Monson 1991; Jackson 1992). All of these elements and behaviors link jazz performance in such venues to the ritualized activity described by Small. On a muted level, recording studios, to the degree that they serve as venues for jazz performance, share status with other locales as ritualized spaces.

Whereas Small is attentive to details of context, Frank Salamone (1988) focuses on the negotiation of structure within ritualized performances, treating jazz as a sacred form that musical event participants create and renew through ritualized acts. Like Small, he pays considerable attention to the conventions that make jazz performance similar to repeated ritual activity. He sees agreements about solo order, chord progressions, and other musical matters as part of the repeated ritual of performance. And, like Neil Leonard (1987; see also Faulkner and Becker 2009), he recognizes (and perhaps overstates) the degree to which conventions of song form and interaction make possible "spontaneous performance": "Only when a musician thoroughly understands musical structure is exceptional improvisation possible. The individual's seemingly featured status, therefore, is based only on the strength of the group's internal cohesiveness" (Salamone 1988, 96). In that sense, the openness of musical structure discussed by Peter Bernstein and Steve Wilson functions as an "enabler" (Jackson 1992) or frame that both allows interactions to take place and helps to make them comprehensible. Although each individual must say something, each has to do so in a way that other performers and event participants can either reconcile with previous experience or use to modify their understandings of what is possible and/or permissible.

Within scene- and blues aesthetic–based musical events, there is a specific governing structure, a sequence of events nested within varying frames, that helps to define performances as ritualized acts distinct from everyday life and from other performances. There are, of course, variations depending on whether the performance takes place "live" in front of an audience or in a recording studio before a more limited set of participants (just as no wedding or funeral is exactly the same as any other). In either event, musicians must come into a space having prepared themselves through rehearsals specifically geared toward that event or through cumulative preparation and study from their engagement with musical performance over time. They must also bring a willingness to listen to and interact with other performers and participants. Non-performers are also expected to come to the performance with specific kinds of knowledge of how performance normatively proceeds and how to listen to and evaluate performance as it is occurring. As Steve Wilson puts it, all must be "ready to receive." When listeners come with other expectations or alternate ways of apprehending the event's position vis-à-vis other activities—evident in their insistence on holding (loud) conversations or on conducting informal meetings—a critical mass of other participants, musicians, or even management can censure them through polite requests for silence or less polite calls for their immediate departure.[8]

Similarly, at recording sessions observers are required to be quiet and unobtrusive, literally speaking only when addressed by someone with a more central role in the recording process.

The contours of the ritualized structure of jazz performance can be sketched by reference to a musical event in a nightclub. Its beginning is framed by the venue's lights being dimmed and/or by the introduction of the performers. Depending on their personal preferences, the performers or the bandleader may further frame the performance by addressing the audience with talk about the occasion or the tunes they are going to play. If the order of tunes has not been set prior to the performers' entrance into the performance space, the leader might quickly communicate verbally or musically to the other musicians what tune will be played, perhaps in the process indicating the key, dynamics, and other information. The leader then indicates the tempo through visual and aural means, with motions such as finger snapping or foot tapping combined with sotto voce counting. This framing of the performance is extremely important. Although a particular tune might be played at any of a number of tempos, finding one that will ensure that the musicians fall into a groove—or at least don't grow fatigued from playing too long at fast or slow extremes—is one of many skills that a bandleader has to inculcate through her or his body. For that reason, the leader may stomp or snap several pulses before cuing the band to start. Once the tune has begun (and this scheme applies for recording sessions as well), a group will tend to follow a scheme used by small jazz groups since at least since the mid-1940s. The progression of events is generally similar to that presented in figure 1. The scheme presented is merely a template: although the all-lowercase or italicized items are often omitted, any of the others might also be removed or modified.

The head consists of all the musical material prior to the beginning or after the end of improvised solos.[9] At the beginning of a tune it might be referred to as the " head-in." Correspondingly, it would be the "head-out" at the end, though the term "out-chorus" is used more frequently. The head might include a prearranged introduction or even an improvised one. In some cases the material for the introduction comes from a commonly played coda or from the statement of the theme, particularly the last portion of a sectional form—for example, the final A of an AABA form, the C of an ABAC form, or the last four measures of a twelve-bar blues progression. Likewise, an introduction might consist of a vamp on a two- or four-measure harmonic progression. (Some bandleaders, like saxophonist Lou Donaldson, frequently dispensed with this aspect of

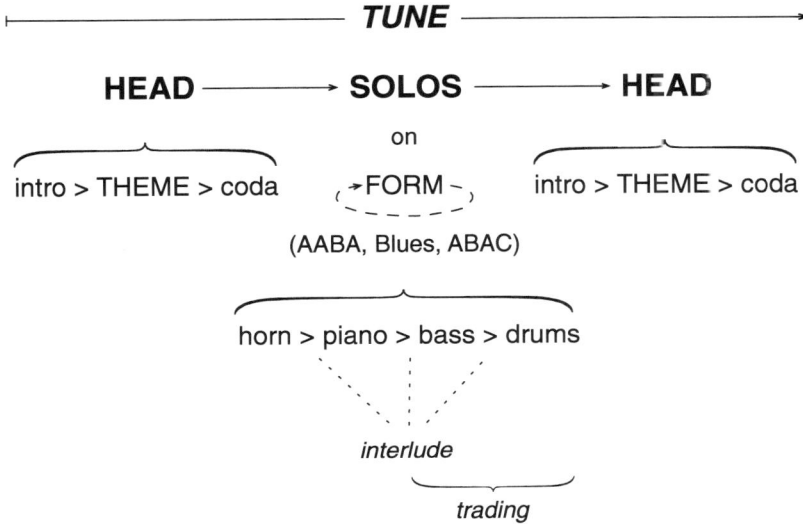

FIGURE 1. Typical progression of events in a tune.

framing, simply starting to play and expecting the other members of his ensemble—like organist Dr. Lonnie Smith, guitarist Peter Bernstein, and drummer Fukushi Tainaka—to know the tune and to infer tempo and key from what and how he played.) The statement of the theme follows the introduction (or begins the tune when an introduction has been omitted). This portion of the head most clearly allows other participants in the musical event (or record listeners) to identify a tune if it is one already known to them. Otherwise, it provides them the opportunity to hear and grasp the form of and contours of an unfamiliar composition.

Forms are harmonic/metric/rhythmic structures that serve as a basis for improvisation. Sections within them are generally four, eight, or sixteen measures in length. Designations such as "AABA" or "blues" denote the organization of a particular form. An AABA form, for example, has two sections at its beginning and one at its end that are of equal lengths and have (nearly) identical harmonic progressions or modal configurations. The B section of such a form generally modulates to a contrasting tonal area or through a series of contrasting areas that eventually lead back to the A section. George and Ira Gershwin's "I Got Rhythm" is a frequently used AABA example, in which each section, in practice, is eight measures in length.[10] A blues form is typically twelve measures in length, though there are numerous variants, as Koch (1982) outlines. Short forms (like the blues or sixteen-bar songs of various kinds) or those that are unconventional tend to be played twice during the head (perhaps to aid in their being fixed in performers' and listeners' ears), while longer forms are rarely played more than once. Indeed, although all these forms may seem structurally simple, they can contain enormous variety in terms of harmonic, melodic, rhythmic, and textural activity. From measure to measure and from section to section, there may be changes of feel, meter, or any other musical parameter.[11] In composing and improvising on tunes, jazz musicians often treat forms in a highly elastic manner, taking well-known tunes or forms and extending or truncating sections, using unconventional meters and the like to make the listening and performing experience more challenging. In some cases the statement of the theme is so intricate that the performers choose a less complicated form for solos.[12]

For participants, recognizing and understanding form is essential to comprehending the musical event. Visual/spatial metaphors (some derived from written notation) help them to describe some portions of the form. The top of a form or of a section, for example, is its beginning. Listeners and performers frequently describe B sections in AABA tunes as "bridges" or "channels" because they connect A sections to one other. Performers who frequently lose their way in a form are harshly criticized, for understanding and being able to perform effectively on a number of forms is a basic skill, the development of which perhaps precedes the comparable one that allows a musician to improvise expressively and idiomatically—that is, far beyond the threshold of competence and closer to the realm of ritual mastery.[13]

Once the statement of the theme is complete, the performers may move into the next frame—solos on the form—or delay its arrival with transitional material or a coda. As with the introduction, such material may be pre-composed or improvised—in the latter case, for example, via a passage based on a vamp. In some cases the material for the coda and the introduction may be identical. The head-in and head-out/out-chorus, in any event, frame the group improvisational activity of the solo sections in the same way that verbal introductions and tempo setting frame the performance of a tune.

The harmonies, feels, textures, meter, and tempo of the form generally furnish the given material with which performers work during the solo sections of the performance and function as aural markers for listeners (Tirro 1967; Byrnside 1975; Kernfeld 1995).[14] Each cycle through the form is referred to as a chorus. As figure 1 indicates, the order of solos generally proceeds from the solos of "horns" (brass and reed instruments), to those of chording instruments (e.g., piano, organ, and guitar), and then to bass and drums. Individual ensembles or bandleaders may modify that order from tune to tune for contrast, omitting bass and drum solos, for example, or changing the order of solo slots. Composed interludes or improvised vamps may occasionally fill the space between individual solos or function as backgrounds on solos in progress.[15]

In some cases a leader or a group of soloists may "trade eights" or "fours" with one another or with the drummer (in lieu of or prior to a drum solo). In that case, each performer solos for the specified number of measures, generally completing a phrase on the first beat of the measure *after* the designated grouping, and is followed by the next performer, who observes the same procedure. In trading fours with a drummer, for example, a saxophonist will solo for four measures accompanied by the entire ensemble (including the drummer), finishing his or her first section of trading on the first beat of the fifth measure. The drummer will begin a four-measure solo passage at that same moment and, on the first beat of the ninth measure, will resume an accompanying role as the saxophonist begins soloing again. This procedure continues until a visual, verbal, or musical cue from the bandleader near the end of a chorus signals that the drummer will take an extended solo on the form or that the ensemble should start moving toward the head-out/out-chorus.[16] Trading passages often generates considerable excitement, particularly when performers turn them into competition (to discover, for example, which musician can play the fastest or most registrally extreme phrases) or when they manipulate the terms of the trading process (starting by trading eights, cutting down to fours, then twos, single measures, half measures, and finally beats, for example).

When the solos are finished, the leader of the group cues the band to play the head again. Introductory materials from the head-in may be reused to signal the head's return, or the band may simply play the theme statement without introductory material and then use what was the introduction as a coda. In some cases, the final statement of the theme is followed by more solos (on a vamp) or a cadenza played by the leader of the group. When the tune is done, and typically before the last sounds have decayed, the performers may frame the end of the performance by slightly bowing their heads and acknowledging audience applause. In a studio setting, the performers maintain silence for several seconds, until the recording engineer or producer informs them that the tape, or its digital equivalent, has stopped rolling.

This scheme characterizes the playing on most tunes in a nightclub set, in a concert hall, or on a festival stage. It also comprises a series of acts that register primarily via sight, sound, and experience and whose function is to demarcate events in time: separating the musical event from what precedes and follows it, distinguishing preset materials from those improvised by a group in real time; confirming or delaying event participants' recognition of known songs or forms; and reinforcing or modifying conventions regarding solo order, for example. When one tune ends, the performers begin framing the next tune, agreeing to follow a preset arrangement or to depart from it, perhaps taking time to introduce the band members to the audience, to acknowledge other musicians or important people in the audience, to remind listeners about currently available recordings of theirs, or to announce the previous tune(s) and/or the next one(s). Afterward, the leader again sets the tempo and the performers enter the tune frame. The pre- and post-tune framing differs in the context of rehearsals or recording sessions, but what happens within the tune frame is typically the same, with the important exception that performers are more likely to stop a tune in a rehearsal or in a recording session if they are not satisfied with it.

A typical nightclub set ends after four or five tunes. The performers leave one temporal frame. If there is another set to be played that evening, they may remain within a spatial frame and may invite nonperforming participants to attend later sets. The performers might also seek ways to relax and dissipate the energy amassed during the previous set and to prepare themselves for the next one through conversation with other participants, concentration, or practice (see also Berliner 1994, 453). Or they may remove themselves from the venue, only to reenter the spatial frame before the next set begins. If they have finished an evening's final set, the performers or venue personnel invite the other participants to come again for an engagement later in the week. And if the performers have finished the last set of a weeklong engagement, then they leave that frame as well. Venue personnel focus their energies on informing other participants of other engagements. Likewise, in a recording session or rehearsal, a studio or an apartment might be the spatial frame within which musical performance takes place.

These different frames, graphically represented in figure 2,[17] are different areas in which participants in musical events can creatively manipulate and respond to the materials at their disposal. These frames also furnish the differing arenas into which all participants are expected to bring something. The participants adapt themselves to the perfor-

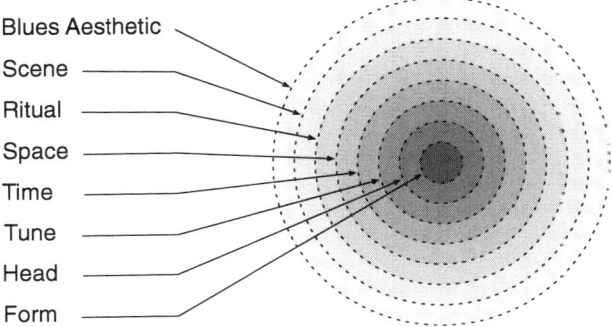

FIGURE 2. Frames around jazz performance.

mance space, taking into account the vibe—the "general atmosphere" (Berliner 1994, 449)—of a particular venue, studio, or rehearsal space. Whether performing or listening, they adjust themselves to the temporal demands placed upon them by the space within which the event occurs, such as the set length, engagement length, and allotted studio time. Once those adjustments are made—and they are all subject to renegotiation—the performers enter the frames in which they most specifically grapple with the performative and evaluative criteria of a blues aesthetic. Here they find creative ways to play the head of a tune, through the way they introduce it, the ways in which they play the materials presented to them as the head of a tune (harmonies, rhythms, melodies, timbres, dynamics), and the ways in which they adhere to or obscure the form. Likewise, in the solo passages, each performer ideally plays with all the musical parameters that make up a composition and its form. This process is, again, one of setting up distinctions, of highlighting the similarities and differences between ritualized settings and their more quotidian counterparts. It is, as well, a process that creates ritualized social agents, attuned to the particularities of jazz performance events as well as their relationships with other kinds of events.

When performers successfully synthesize and work with all of the materials of a performance (space, time, tune, form, other performers, and other participants)—when they exhibit ritual mastery—that is when a performance is most likely to proceed to the next level. Performers and other participants then experience sensations or a series of feelings that they describe, like Antonio Hart, as being literally "out of this world." Every element of a performance seems to fit, and each individual appears to be making a contribution to what is occurring. Some of the feelings associated with possession or ecstasy lead to an apparent nullification of time outside the performance and of space outside the venue. In the process, a musical event is said to be "swinging," "burning," or "on," or described with a similar phrase that indicates positive motion, activity, and good feeling (compare with Monson 1990, 35).

The responses of participants attending such events are variable and sometimes virtually indistinguishable from those that might accompany stirring sermons in African American Baptist and Pentecostal churches or ecstatic portions of African-derived spiritual practices more broadly (Pitts 1988). At a performance by trumpeter Nicholas Payton, pianist Mulgrew Miller, bassist Peter Washington, and drummer Lewis Nash at the Village Vanguard in March 1995, for example, the shared nature of response to impressive musical performance was foregrounded by silent, visually perceived actions. In the middle of the tune "Maria's Melody," Washington and Nash played an intense groove over which Miller soloed—playing riff-based figures alternating with long, intricate single-line passages with his right hand. One of my table companions, Bess Weatherman, was moving her head up and down in time, entrained to the groove in the same way that I was. As the interaction between the rhythm section members intensified, I looked across the room and made eye contact with Sharon Blynn, who opened her mouth as if silently to say, "Wow," cocked her head in the direction of the stage, and looked back at me in awe. I nodded my assent, smiled, and turned my own gaze back toward the stage.

In some cases participants clearly verbalize their responses and spur the performers on to greater heights. One might assert that when performers have "said something" to non-performing participants, sometimes those non-performers feel the need to say something in response (see Burnim and Maultsby 1987, 132–33), thus distinguishing extraordinary events from ordinary ones. A striking example that highlights the degree to which blues-inflected performance can generate positive audience response comes from a performance by pianist James Williams, singer Kevin Mahogany, and bassist Curtis Lundy at Bradley's in October of 1994. Near the end of one of the evening's sets, the musicians performed the song "Since I Fell for You." Some of the participants seated at the bar were urging Mahogany on as he sang at the beginning of the tune. They shouted encouragement to him at every bluesy turn of phrase and every embellishment of the tune's standard melody, and someone shouted, "Go on, Kevin! Sing the blues!" right before the word "blues" came up in the lyrics. Perhaps in response, but definitely on cue,

Mahogany caressed the word by descending pentatonically from the initial pitch on that syllable. He also mirrored the pitch descent by gradually decreasing dynamics. One might argue that in this case the musical performance was a truly participatory and dialogic event, with both performers and non-performing participants contributing to and influencing its emergent shape.

Jazz performers ideally take the materials at their disposal—both what is provided to them and what they bring—and attempt to "say something" with them, to become one with each other and with other participants in the musical event (Jackson 1992). A blues aesthetic might be said to provide a series of schemata that shape the way they approach those materials, and the materials themselves—framed by space, time, tune, and form—are part of ritualized performances. The scene and an aesthetic describe the conditions that allow the participants in the musical event to go to the next level, to remove themselves temporarily from all concerns beyond those of the performance, and to give them metaphoric tools for understanding and intervening in the world differently once a performance has ended. Each musician who shows him- or herself capable of responding creatively, distinctively, and interactively at the same time shows other musicians and participants ways of seeing what is possible within the structures of musical performance and the varied structures individuals negotiate in their daily lives.

It is in this sense that jazz performance can be seen as a ritualized form of social action with the potential to affect the daily lives of those who listen to and perform it. It does not merely reflect the events and circumstances that frame it (see Williams 1977, 95–100). Rather, within those frames, musical items or other sound terms (Meyer 1955)—phrases, rhythms, voicings, approaches, compositions, and techniques—become signs, iconically and indexically linked via the shared interpretive moves of performers and other participants with other performances, other performers, and others musics. They are not so much signs *of* something prior, but signs that might have demonstrable *connections to* something. That is, they mobilize events, actions, and understandings external but related to a performance for resignification, in the process remaking the ritualized activity and producing ritualized social agents and social bodies. Meanings emerge from the linkages and oppositions between juxtaposed musical sounds and their interpretations by listeners. As listeners engage with what musicians are doing in the moment-to-moment flow of performance, they connect what they are hearing and seeing in the present with what they have heard and seen in the past and might encounter or do in the future. For some of them, the recognition of how performers creatively negotiate with one another as well as with time, place, tune, and form can provide an opening to seeing their own lives as more fluid.

Moreover, each musical item and its creative use become a way for event participants to connect with some of the most deeply held values of African Americans, and those sympathetic to them, toward performance, toward living, and toward who they are as people, values that ideally stress active acceptance of individual variation and group cooperation in the service of survival (see the introduction of Gwaltney 1993; see also Roberts 1989). It is not merely a music of resistance—a term closely associated with social action: it is a music of survival as well for those, regardless of racial, cultural, or ethnic background, who understand the ways in which various conventions are or can be manipulated in performance. Jazz performance therefore assumes a synecdochic relationship to African American culture: one brings to the musical event those ideals that should motivate daily living—as in music, so in life. As Joshua Redman noted, when younger musicians play with older ones they hope that they will internalize something of the older musicians' spirit and wisdom in order to become not only better performers, but also better people. That is, through observing and imitating and emulating their practices, their postures, their ways of being—in short, through incorporating their practices in and beyond ritualized settings—younger musicians not only come to understand the schemata that inform jazz performance, they also learn how to manipulate those various schemata to other ends.

CHAPTER 7

In the Studio and on Stage

The framings discussed in the previous chapters foreground the importance of attending to the details of a specific musical event via its nesting in successive frames—a scene, a blues aesthetic, ritual, space, time, tune, and form.[1] They emphasize, as well, relating that single event to others and noting how each event is constituted by references and responses to others displaced in time and space. Building on those ideas, I shift the focus here to the ways that the work of different actors and institutions shapes musical events in recording studios or clubs. For recordings, I will indicate whether the released version of a tune comes from a single take or is a composite of two or more, and for both recordings and live performances, information from my field notes about other performances by the musicians or groups in question will inform the analysis, particularly when there are discernible patterns of interaction that recur from event to event. Moreover, I will analyze the statements made by the musicians about the performance contexts and their approaches to performance where available and relevant.

In the process I will examine how performers manipulate "statistical parameters" of musical performance, those that Elliott (1987) argues are difficult to quantify and/or notate: timbre, dynamics, density, intensity, and feel. *Density* refers to both the number of sonic events occurring per unit of time and the number of discrete sonic elements present at a given moment. *Intensity* is a function of combinations of kinds of timbre, dynamics, register, density, the perceptibility of meter, and the manner in which those combinations produce expectation or ambiguity. A high level of intensity, then, might result from high density and dynamics, "noisy" instrumental timbres of indeterminate pitch content, and registrally extreme playing by a featured performer or group. Intense moments might likewise be the result of "metric dissonance" (Krebs 1987), disagreement between the established metric framework, on one hand, and the grouping of accents in the playing of one or more members of a group, on the other. Alternatively, intense playing can be characterized by opposite extremes, for example, low density and dynamics combined with metric regularity—particularly when contrasted with louder, denser passages. Those possibilities, of course, don't foreclose other readings or perceptions of intensity.

More specifically these analyses examine performers' interactions and negotiation of forms, feels, and harmonic/modal and metric structures in the course of improvisation. *Forms* are harmonic and metric structures that provide raw materials for the rhythmic, melodic, and harmonic parameters of improvisation: the phrasing of improvised solos and accompaniment patterns alternately reinforces or obscures it. Strong cadences and phrasing whose peaks and accents agree with major structural points, for example, typically reinforce form, while the use of harmonically ambiguous progressions or substitute chords at cadences, for example, can obscure major structural points (Bastien and Hostager 1991). A *feel* is a distinct rhythmic, accentual, and/or textural pattern whose character arises from sedimented practices. In performance, different feels can be applied to entire compositions or specific sections within them, and each of the many named feels (for example, Latin, bossa, samba, ballad, two-beat, and swing) carries expectations about how rhythm section members (piano, bass, and drums, in particular) are supposed to interact. A feel is, as a result, not reducible to a characteristic rhythm; rather it is a composite emerging from the combination of a number of musical elements (Dudley 1996). Indeed, some feels are associated with prominent bandleaders or groups: one can therefore speak of a "Sam Jones–Louis Hayes feel"[2] or "Art Blakey feel," in the process indexing a number of sonic parameters.

The *harmonic* or *modal structure* of a tune is the sequence of harmonies (chords) or modes (scales) that govern the pitch selections of improvising soloists and accompanying musicians. In the course of performance, individual musicians may stick to the prescribed harmonies or may replace them with a number of substitutes. Given a twelve-bar blues progression like the one in figure 3, one might either directly and literally

F7	B♭7	F7	F7
B♭7	B♭7	F7	Amin7 D7
Gmin7	C7	F7	Gmin7 C7

FIGURE 3. Twelve-bar blues in F.

produce those harmonies, add tensions or extensions to them, or replace them with other harmonies. One might, for example, substitute a G♭7 chord for the G minor 7–C7 progression in measure twelve. Likewise, a recurrent, AABA modal structure—from Miles Davis's "So What"—uses two eight-measure units in D Dorian followed by eight measures a half step up in E♭ and an additional eight measures in D. Such a structure, however, does not preclude musicians' using pitches, like G♯/A♭, which are not strictly part of the D Dorian, for instance.

The *metric patterning* of a tune refers to regular groupings of pulses. Although most tunes have pulses grouped in fours—that is, every fourth beat receives greater stress than the others—many others feature different groupings or have regularly shifting ones. One way in which performers manipulate metric patterning is by playing phrases whose accentual patterning is different from that established by the metric framework. Changes in accentual patterning might also result from displacement of metric accents (consistently playing accents before or after their expected positions); changing the number of beats in the metric pattern while retaining the basic pulse (playing phrases that appear to coincide with five-beat groupings in $\frac{4}{4}$ time, for example); by changing the basic pulse (from ♩ to ♩., for example); or layering several different pulses.

Additionally, these analyses consider the proxemic and kinesthetic dimensions of musical events, relating the varied participants to one another in space. They explore the ways in which non-performing participants respond (or do not respond) to the interactions of musicians and the ways in which their responses contribute to the overall texture of a musical event. Because so many aspects of performance being considered here would require unwieldy modifications to be represented in Western staff notation, I have elected not to employ transcriptions. By presenting each performance discussed as a narrative incorporating various performative and contextual parameters, I am privileging the social in musical events, in hopes that that strategy allows me better to preserve their dynamism.

The three studio and three nightclub musical events discussed here took place in New York City during my fieldwork. The studio events, partially available on commercially released recordings, are by James Williams and ICU (Williams and ICU 1996), the Steve Wilson Quartet (Wilson 1996), and the Peter Bernstein Quartet (Bernstein 1995b). One of the nightclub events, featuring the Joshua Redman Quartet, comes from a performance at the Village Vanguard that was recorded and released in part on compact disc (Redman 1995b). The other nightclub events feature unrecorded performances by the Kenny Barron Quartet at the Village Vanguard and Mulgrew Miller's group Wingspan at Sweet Basil—both from a single night in September of 1994.

I include both live and studio performances here to highlight the similarities and differences between each performance setting and to present a view of musical events that shows how, through differential framing, a club or a studio becomes a performance venue with a particular set of constraints and relationships to the scene and an aesthetic. The non-performing "audience" for a recording session is a more highly specialized and homogeneous group than the one that comes to live performances in clubs or concert halls. It therefore might have a highly interactive relationship with the performers, but a relationship that is of a different order from a nightclub audience. By contrast, the forms of interaction that characterize live performances might be out of place in a recording studio. Indeed, the variable composition of live audiences, in terms of their experience, knowledge, and expectations of jazz performance, is something that performers have to consider (see Becker 1982; Berliner 1994) and that can substantially affect a musical event.

Although many previous researchers have used commercially released recordings to study performance interaction (e.g., Rinzler 1988; Monson 1991, 1994; Berliner 1994), their work is not always explicit regarding the role participant observation might have played in their analyses. For all of the commercial releases discussed at length in this chapter, I was a participant observer at the recording sessions. Because of this, my analysis of them is informed not only by the sounds made accessible by recording, but also by knowledge of the interactive contexts and constraints of recording as well as the long-term interactions of the performers. In other words, my analysis is the result of knowledge not only of sound, but also of a musical event that was recorded and the frames surrounding it.

IN THE STUDIO I: JAMES WILLIAMS AND ICU

After meeting me at a performance by pianist Mulgrew Miller's Wingspan in September of 1994 (to be discussed below), pianist James Williams invited me to a recording session he was producing for a Memphis pianist named Charles Thomas, which featured Ron Carter and Billy Higgins.[3] It was at this recording session, the first I attended during fieldwork, that I was shown an effective model for how a recording session might be run. Williams was highly organized and, as a musician himself, was keenly attuned to the various parameters of what he was recording, including the pianist's harmonic choices and the group's ability to maintain a strict tempo. He made numerous suggestions to the performers but left the final decisions to them. His choices were an enactment of the blues aesthetic ideal of bringing something into a situation—in this case, his understanding of jazz performance practice—while allowing others to do so as well, even when he was not performing.

This level of sensitivity to context was characteristic of Williams's playing as well. When I saw him sitting in with Miller's Wingspan group in September 1994, playing with singer Kevin Mahogany and bassist Curtis Lundy at Bradley's in October, or doing a duo-piano set at Bradley's with Donald Brown in December, he showed himself to be a supportive and attentive performer. His playing seemed to enhance each musical setting. He picked up and modified the phrases and figures played by other musicians and transformed them in his own solos. As a member of the seasoned "lost generation," he has also developed a sense of when to push other performers and when to leave them space.[4]

The way that Williams ran his own recording session at the Power Station on Thursday and Friday, 8 and 9 December 1994, therefore, was not surprising to me.[5] Nor were the different frameworks for performance that he brought to the session. Williams was producing this session independently and ran the session quite fluidly, recording tunes quickly and communicating to the other musicians what he wanted. He later shopped the master tape around to various labels, finally releasing the recording, *Truth, Justice and the Blues,* on Evidence in the spring of 1996.

A number of scene-based interactions enabled the recording session to work in the way it did. The musicians on the session were ones who had become known to Williams in a number of different settings since he began his career in jazz. Saxophonist Billy Pierce and bassist John Lockwood, for example, Williams met during his years teaching at the Berklee College of Music in Boston. Saxophonist Steve Wilson and singers Miles

Griffith and Roger Holland became acquainted with Williams in New York City. His relationships to the various observers of the recording session (Javon Jackson, Mulgrew Miller, Bruce Barth, and me) were also intricate and tangled: some were linked to him by their participation as performers, some were former members of his group, others were alumni of Art Blakey's Jazz Messengers, and some were from his home state of Tennessee. In other words, the participants in the recording session—performers, engineers, and observers—came to it through their engagement with Williams's pathways to musical performance and the scene via alliances formed in educational institutions, performance venues, and contexts of recording.

Upon arriving at the Power Station, I first noted the layout of the studio and the relative position of the musicians with respect to each other and the control room. The session took place in Studio A, a fairly large wood-paneled room with several isolation booths.[6] Across the studio drummer Yoron Israel was in a booth slightly to the left (viewed from the control room). In a booth to the right were James Williams and bassist John Lockwood. Lockwood stood behind a series of baffles that would prevent the piano's sound from bleeding into the microphone in front of his bass. In the center of the studio proper, facing toward the isolation booths and away from the control room, were saxophonists Steve Wilson and Billy Pierce. Not easily visible from the control room were Miles Griffith and Roger Holland, who were inside an isolation booth whose windows faced only into the studio, to the right of the control room. Their isolation booth was the only area of the studio that one could enter directly from the control room. The relative positioning of each musician is indicated in figure 4.

When I arrived at the studio, they were in the midst of recording "You're My Alter Ego," an updating of Williams's 1984 composition "Alter Ego," with lyrics written by Pamela Baskin-Watson.[7] When Williams was satisfied with the take, they moved on to the next tune, "A Certain Attitude." The recording of that tune was illustrative of the kinds of negotiation that take place in the studio. Wilson was going to be playing soprano saxophone rather than alto saxophone. The recording engineer, Jim Anderson, therefore had to go into the studio to reposition Wilson's microphone and then return to the control room to adjust the volume and reverberation levels. As Anderson, back in the control room, manipulated the faders on the mixing console, Wilson, wearing headphones, played through different portions of the tune from the sheet music on a stand in front of him and offered his desiderata to Anderson

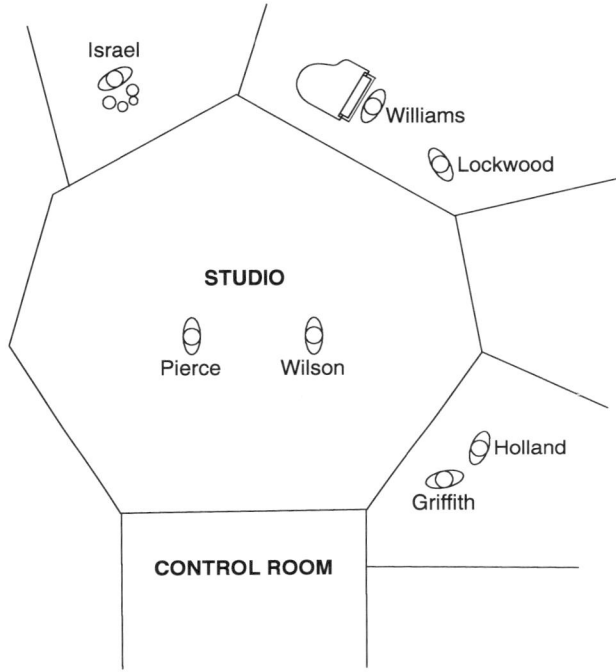

FIGURE 4. Arrangement of musicians power station.

regarding equalization and effects in his headphone mix. Once the levels were set, Wilson worked through the tune more assiduously while Williams offered suggestions on phrasing and dynamics and answered Wilson's questions. During this time John Lockwood was practicing bass patterns for the tune's harmonic progression.

Before they started the first take of the tune, Williams discussed the solo order with the other musicians, indicating that each soloist—Griffith, Wilson, and Williams—would be limited to one chorus since the tune had a long form. He also reminded Griffith and Holland that they were to do arranged backgrounds behind the instrumental solos. From the control room, the first completed take sounded good to me. Williams, however, was not satisfied with it. He said, "That didn't groove. Maybe we should do another one . . . slower. And one chorus seems to be going too fast. Maybe we should do two[-chorus solos], even though . . ." He then asked Jim Anderson, "How long was that?" Anderson replied, "5:24." Williams continued, "That'll put us close to eight minutes, but that's okay." Miles Griffith then suggested that in order to shorten the take perhaps he might do only one chorus while Wilson and Williams did two each. Williams agreed, and soon they started a second take.

Griffith's solo on this take consisted of straight bebop-style scat singing and a number of odd vocalizations and sound effects. They were so bizarre and unexpected that those of us observing from the control room—Anderson, Anderson's assistant, and I, along with new arrivals Pierre Chambers and Don Sickler—were laughing uncontrollably during Griffith's entire chorus.[8] Williams was smiling and shaking his head as he played as well as watched and listened to Griffith. The conversation between Sickler and Anderson indicated that they felt that the groove that Williams thought missing from the first take was present in this second one. Williams, however, was still not completely pleased with the take and suggested that inserts be done for two portions of the tune. None of us in the control room, when polled by Williams, thought the errors he perceived were significant enough to warrant inserts or rerecording. Williams, of course, had the final say, deciding to leave one portion as it was and to rerecord the other.[9] After a second attempt at the insert, he was satisfied enough with the tune to move on.

The foregoing highlights the kinds of framing, interaction, and negotiation that characterize the recording of a tune in a recording session. There are, as is the case with live performances, negotiations regarding solo order and length, phrasing, and tempo, among other things. Discussions of these issues frame the beginning of each take, and after a take is complete, these same issues or others may be discussed to frame additional ones. Concurrently, there are conversations taking place about individual sound and how that sound is to be captured and processed. Moreover, those individuals observing the recording session from the control room are not always passive listeners. Instead, they can be additional sets of ears whose judgments help the musicians to evaluate a performance and to improve subsequent takes. The criteria used for evaluation are those described by a blues aesthetic: individual sound, balance, blues feeling, bringing something to the music, letting others bring something, and taking it to the next level.

Similar kinds of negotiation characterized the next tune they recorded, "Just a Feeling." Afterward, Anderson had to reposition the microphones again, this time for Billy Pierce, who was going to play on "For Old Times' Sake." The momentum of the session was slightly interrupted after that tune, for Anderson had to change tape reels. Williams suggested that everyone take a break while Anderson prepared for the next tune. The social aspects of the recording session were foregrounded during this break, during which Bruce Barth, Mark Gross, and Javon Jackson arrived to observe the session.[10] Barth and I discussed arranging work that he was doing for a Japanese singer, while Gross and Jackson talked about a performance they had just heard at the Blue Note, featuring saxophonist Joe Henderson, guitarist John Scofield, and drummer Adam Nussbaum. They were particularly critical of Nussbaum's playing, which they felt was too loud and overshadowed Joe Henderson's playing.[11] Barth and I then discussed his own upcoming gigs as well as some of the difficulties associated with keeping a group together when there's little work. When I told him of my intention to see the Terence Blanchard Quartet the next night, he and I discussed the games of musical chairs that were taking place in the bands of other musicians. He informed me that Blanchard's bassist, Chris Thomas, would be leaving, but he wasn't sure whose band Thomas would be joining.[12]

By the time the group started preparing to record "J's Rhythm Song," therefore, they had already recorded several tunes and established patterns of interaction and negotiation with each other and with their observers that would make the session run more smoothly. They had also taken a break, during which they ate and discussed the recording session and various other issues—confirming and celebrating their knowledge of the scene and the varied and changing aspects of life on it. After the break and right before "J's Rhythm Song," they recorded "Self-Esteem." By that time they seemed warmed up and fairly relaxed.[13]

"J's Rhythm Song" is difficult to characterize in terms of form. It began with a rubato drum introduction improvised by Yoron Israel. His introduction was followed by a sixteen-measure, two-part contrapuntal figure played by Williams on the piano (the two parts are distinguishable by register). This passage was then repeated twice and arranged differently with each repetition. The first repetition was for Lockwood and Wilson, while the second was for Holland and Griffith's voices, with the first member of each pair playing the lower line and the second the upper one, respectively. Williams followed these three statements with a rubato, harmonically meandering piano interlude. Israel entered again on drums after this interlude and established the metric framework that would support the duet between Pierce and Wilson. The full ensemble did a sendoff for the duet, which was accompanied only by bass and drums. Another piano interlude followed the saxophone duet. Lockwood then took a solo with sparse accompaniment from Israel. Another piano interlude followed, this one ending with a vamp that introduced a repeating eight-measure riff, featuring the full ensemble. Over this repeated pattern, Miles Griffith took another "out" vocal solo.[14] The contrapuntal figure that opened the composition returned at this point, played in turn by Williams, Lockwood and Wilson, and Griffith and Holland. The composition ended after the vocal repetition of the figure.

In what is largely a heterogeneous form, Williams left space for the other musicians to bring something to the recording, but he also served as a guide. His piano interludes set the stage for each of the changes, from solo to solo or section to section. The duet between Pierce and Wilson was perhaps the most interesting portion of the event. I will restrict my analysis of this tune to this portion, for it highlights the ways in which the scene and a blues aesthetic frame and enable interaction in a musical event.

At the recording session, as well as during repeated listening to the recording after its release, I had been unable to discern a single form guiding the improvised duet between Pierce and Wilson. (A phone conversation with Williams on 4 April 1997 confirmed that there was no specified formal or tonal design for the duet.) Instead, their duet and Lockwood and Israel's accompaniment proceeded on the basis of careful listening and responsive playing by the musicians, with each being open to what the others were bringing to the music. Their ability to respond to one another was facilitated by the collective playing experiences of Lockwood, Pierce, and Israel (regular members of ICU) and forms of visual communication. In addition to listening carefully, for example, Israel and Lockwood kept their eyes focused on Pierce and Wilson throughout the duet. At times, though, they expectantly looked at one another, particularly at points with marked changes in density and/or intensity. The microphone placement for Pierce and Wilson also facilitated their visual communication, for they performed the duet facing each other, negotiating its progress through aural and visual means.

The duet passage hovers around a D tonal center and proceeds at a tempo of ♩~296. In dictating little of what Wilson and Pierce were to do, Williams provided them with an extremely open situation that would allow them as well as Israel and Lockwood to bring something to the performance. In addition, Williams reduced the possibility that they would be able to rely heavily on their usual responses to chord progressions or modal frameworks.

Wilson and Pierce started their duet by playing short overlapping phrases, almost in call-and-response fashion. They continued for twenty-seven measures, gradually lengthening their phrases and increasing the density of their "dialogue." The accompaniment by Pierce and Israel left them a great deal of space, for Israel devoted most of his energy to keeping time, playing variants of a standard tap on his drum kit's ride cymbal, while Lockwood played a walking bass line. They delineated the phrases played by the saxophonists by accenting hits on the drum kit (Israel) and anticipating the first beat of a measure by beginning on the previous upbeat and sustaining a pitch (Lockwood).

Pierce and Wilson then played short imitative phrases for four measures before starting again to lengthen their melodic lines, which allowed them to overlap more and more until the lines were being performed simultaneously. Israel's drumming became more insistent as Pierce and Williams's lines grew less distinguishable. Wilson and Pierce were intently focused on each other during this portion of the duet, visually as well as aurally negotiating the performance. After approximately twenty measures of increasing overlap, a perhaps unexpected moment of synchrony appeared. Afterward their phrases lengthened and became more dense. Lockwood and Israel increased the density and intensity of their accompaniment, particularly by emphasizing off-beats and implying a pulse change from ♩ to ♩.. In addition, Israel played an almost unceasing string of rolls on the tom-toms and snare of the drum kit, while Lockwood further intensified his playing by frequently and abruptly shifting registers, going from low to high or vice versa.

Wilson and Pierce continued to play simultaneously, with neither seeming to attempt to phrase in response to the other. Each attempted instead to develop melodic lines and remain registrally distinct, leaving space for what the other was bringing to the performance. Each seemed as well to be manipulating and transforming short pitch cells during this portion of the duet.[15] After thirty-two measures during which Wilson and Pierce seemed to be playing completely different phrases, they played contrapuntally for four measures. Afterward, Pierce played a sustained G. Wilson, treating Pierce's sustained pitch as a call, played a figure that led into his own sustained pitch, an F. Pierce responded, repeating Wilson's lead-in figure and sustaining an F as well. The density of their playing and the accompaniment increased seven measures after this moment of imitation: Lockwood played more static, metrically ambiguous pitches; Israel played more off-beat accents, making extensive use of his crash cymbal; and both Pierce and Wilson began to emphasize "harsher" timbres obtained by overblowing and false fingering.[16] Repetitive phrases that rendered the meter more ambiguous followed, played by Wilson and Pierce.

TABLE 2   STRUCTURAL DIAGRAM: SAXOPHONE DUET ON "J'S RHYTHM SONG"

A (approx. 27 mm.)	Short imitative phrases by Pierce (P) and Wilson (W) gradually grow longer and less distinct; standard accompaniment by Lockwood (L) and Israel (I).
B (approx. 4 mm.)	Short imitative phrases by P and W.
C (approx. 20 mm.)	Phrases gradually lengthen again; L and I increase level of intensity.
D (approx. 2 mm.)	Moment of synchrony for P and W.
E (approx. 32 mm.)	P and W play simultaneously; lines less responsive to each other. L and I increase metric ambiguity.
F (approx. 11 mm.)	P and W play contrapuntally, building to sustained pitches. L and I increase density, dynamics, playing of off-beat accents.
G (approx. 70 mm.)	P and W reach high level of density and intensity; reinforced by metric and harmonic ambiguity of accompaniment.
H (approx. 30 mm.)	Intensity drops when P plays phrase; W repeats; P repeats; density and intensity build again. L and I continue to obscure meter and feeling of form.

The density and intensity continued to increase for nearly seventy measures until Pierce started to repeat a phrase. Wilson responded by filling in the spaces left by Pierce's rests and sustained pitches, and then began playing a pattern that interlocked with Pierce's—eliminating any space and making the texture denser. Israel provided consistent off-beat accents on the crash cymbal at this point as well. Lockwood's bass rhythms and pitches reinforced the ambiguity created by Israel's off-beat accents. Both Pierce and Wilson moved toward high-pitched "screams" that overlapped and led to descending cadential figures that closed their duet.

Those of us observing from the control room watched in interested silence. I was fascinated by what the musicians were playing but was growing frustrated because I could not figure out the form. It would have been interesting to have Gross and Jackson's "take" on the take, but they left before I could engage them in conversation.

The structure of the interaction during the duet has been summarized in tabular fashion (see table 2). Without an explicit form or structure on which to base improvisation, Wilson, Pierce, Lockwood, and Israel created an ad hoc structure built around the alternation of short phrases and reinforcement of meter (beginning of A, B, D, beginning of F, beginning of H) with longer, less distinct phrases and rising density and intensity (C, E, F, G, latter portion of H). The musicians started with meager resources in terms of form or harmonic or modal structure, yet through listening intently to each other they created something that sounded quite magical. Those of us watching the performance from the control room were observing two observers, Wilson and Pierce, who were looking at each other as they performed this duet. Their visual cues were just as important as the aural ones in helping them to negotiate what was a difficult assignment. Wilson clearly described that difficulty when I interviewed him two months later. I asked him about the difference between the first and second takes of the tune. He answered,

> W: Well, the first take. I think both of us felt that we didn't know what we were supposed to do or what James wanted. We just said, "Well, let's just try this thing and see what happens," you know. And, uh, we were kinda flying by the seat of our pants, you know, 'cause it was like, "Well, we're not sure where to start it, where to end it, [in] what direction does he [want us] to take it. Does he want us to get really involved with this, or just kind of, sort of, you know, sort of be nice with it?" or you know . . . Um, so I think we both felt a little tentative, you know, about, uh, the direction of what we were doing. And I think we had a better idea of how to edit ourselves on the second take.

> J: And what chan . . . what changed to get you to that point, or what'd you realize in the first take or between takes that . . . ?

> W: Well, think of just, uh, as I can recall, just having a general direction, a road map, if you will, of where, of the chain of events in the tune [for example, how the rest of the tune would proceed]. So, when you know that, you kinda know how far you can take your particular statement or where to take it. Because if you let it peak too soon, then the rest of the tune's not going to have anywhere to go. So you realize what your place is and your purpose is in the particular, um, movement of a piece. And I think both Billy and I felt that, um, we knew where the tune was going, and we had a sense of what we both wanted to do, of what each of us wanted to do, in the dialogue, you know. And as I recall, I think James said he wanted the first, he liked the first take better.

> J: Yeah, and that seemed strange to me 'cause I didn't like the first take.

> W: Yeah, well it's funny 'cause when I've gone back and listened to some takes of my own material, sometimes the first takes work better because you *don't* approach it with any preconception, and it gets to the essence of what you want to hear or what the composer wants to hear. So, a lot of times the first takes work better, you know, for that reason . . . So that was really fascinating, you know. Um, 'cause I remember Billy and I both scratching our heads going, *"I don't know!!"* [Laughs.]

Wilson's description helps to explain why there were several minor climaxes in the first take, the one released on the recording. Each buildup of density and intensity had the potential to make them "peak too soon" and thereby render the rest of the performance pale in comparison. Indeed, after reaching their most prominent climax near the end of H, they immediately moved away from trying to sustain such a high level of intensity. Their closing cadential figure and Lockwood's bass solo provided a welcome release of the energy amassed in their duet.[17] Moreover, Wilson emphasized the processual nature of performance, not by referring to sections that one might see on a score or lead sheet, but by referring to motion: a direction, a chain of events. The negotiation of the duet was part of a process: he and Pierce needed to have an idea of "where [they were] going" before they could proceed more effectively. Williams, in the end, chose the first take because of what he saw as its more interactive, adventurous feel.

In an obvious sense, the recorded version of this duet is an example of performers taking materials—materials that some might consider forbidding because of their lack of specificity—and doing something creative with them. More significantly, even in a performance without a specified form, the four musicians found ways to blur any emergent ideas that listeners might have about formal frames by increasing the density and intensity and playing off-beat accents to frustrate a sense of regular meter or measure groupings. Although one might gather from engagement with the sound captured on the recording some sense of the differing levels on which the performance unfolds, fuller understanding requires an examination of not only the sounds but also the proxemic, interactive, and constraining factors that helped to generate it. Each musician brought to the event an understanding of form and interaction in jazz performance, his own individual sound, and the willingness to interact with other performers. At both their moments of synchrony and great intensity, they were moving to the next level, on one hand through cooperation, and on the other by maintaining and frustrating a sense of the groove and an implicit metric and modal framework.

The musicians came to the session and shaped their interactions based on their participation in the scene and their understanding of the criteria of a blues aesthetic. And, as the statements of various observers and Wilson's commentary, cited above, show, those criteria were not taken for granted. Rather, they were actively employed and negotiated, not only by the performers but also by the other participants in the musical event, even when there was no explicit structure to guide the performance.

IN THE STUDIO 2: THE STEVE WILSON QUARTET

On 10 December, two days after recording the duet with Billy Pierce described in the previous section, Steve Wilson spent six hours in RPM Sound Studios near New York University making his third recording for the Dutch label Criss Cross.[18] I had seen Wilson perform previously on several occasions, generally in groups led by or featuring drummer Leon Parker and pianist Bruce Barth. Regardless of the leader for a given engagement, the group generally consisted of Wilson, Parker, Barth, and bassist Larry Grenadier.[19] The level of empathy and interaction among these musicians, honed through the time they had spent playing with each other, made each of their performances engaging. In fact, in our conversation at James Williams's recording session, Bruce Barth had told me that Parker, Grenadier, and Wilson were his preferred group because the four of them worked so well together.

An edited excerpt from my field notes from 27 October 1994, when these four musicians performed at Bradley's, gives an indication of how they generally interacted in performance:[20]

> The fourth tune started with Parker on the drums . . . It was a barely recognizable version of "In the Still of the Night." I found out later that it was Barth's arrangement.[21] Barth took the first solo. At the end of each chorus there was an added passage with a pulse half as fast as the one that characterized the rest of the arrangement . . . The group effectively created rhythmic/ metric contrast by launching into a heavy swing after each half-time passage. Parker and Barth interacted with each other extensively during this tune, particularly by playing games with rhythmic patterns and meter, like superimposing patterns in three over the duple metric framework. Parker was even more on fire during Wilson's solo which followed. Wilson, perhaps spurred on by Parker, turned in his most impressive solo of the evening. He even surprised me by quoting from . . . "Seven Come Eleven" in his solo.[22] Parker took the next solo, his first of the evening. He played the first couple of choruses entirely on the cymbals while maintaining a heartbeat-like sound on the bass drum. The rhythm was intense and steady. He accented different eighth notes in the steady pattern to provide variety and emphasis at certain points. He seemed to have the shadings of dynamics well in hand as well. A woodblock-like sound I'd heard him playing earlier in the evening was back as well. I listened to it harder than I did the first time and decided that it had more of the sound of the side of a drum than it did a woodblock. At the end of Parker's solo, an audience member yelled "Bravo!"

This short excerpt shows how familiar these musicians were with one other's styles. Each of them brought to the event a knowledge of what the other musicians might do and a willingness to listen and respond to what they did. Each of them, as well, brought the memory of their collective and individual performances in other venues and their individual approaches to performance. All of those performative actions were conditioned by their long-term social interaction on the New York scene. And because the size of Bradley's made it impossible for the musicians not to be in close proximity or in sight of one another, Parker and Barth were able to add visual depth to their interactions, a depth that other event participants could observe. Likewise, their interplay, and particularly Parker's display of skill, was remarkable enough to elicit enthusiastic verbal response from audience members.

During one of the breaks on Friday, 9 December, the second night of James Williams's recording session, I had noticed Wilson writing intently on a large piece of manuscript paper. He was writing portions of his arrangement of "Perdido." From what I could see of one of the melodic lines in the arrangement, what he was writing was similar in complexity to a Charlie Parker solo because of the dexterity and rhythmic facility it would require of a performer, even at a moderate tempo. I was also curious because what he was writing wasn't a lead sheet; rather, it looked like an extended pre-composed solo. I already knew and had interviewed Bruce Barth (who was at Williams's session as an observer), but I did not know Wilson very well. Barth had informed me of Wilson's upcoming recording session and provisionally invited me to observe, telling me that I needed Wilson's permission. On the strength of Barth's recommendation, Wilson agreed.

When I arrived at RPM Sound Studios shortly after 2 PM on 10 December, I noted that the studio was physically smaller than the rooms I had seen at the Power Station and Sound on Sound.[23] There was one isolation booth visible from where I was sitting. It was on the far left side of the room, slightly elevated above floor level. It was also in a corner, a position that made it possible for someone inside to see every other person in the studio as well as anyone in the control room. Wilson was inside this booth. There was another isolation booth that I could not directly see in which Larry Grenadier was positioned. It was visible to everyone inside the studio, but not to the people in the control room, except via reflections in the control room glass. Likewise, it was the only recording position that couldn't be accessed from the studio proper; one entered it, instead, from a door in the same hallway that led into the studio. Inside the main room, Barth was positioned near the back. The piano

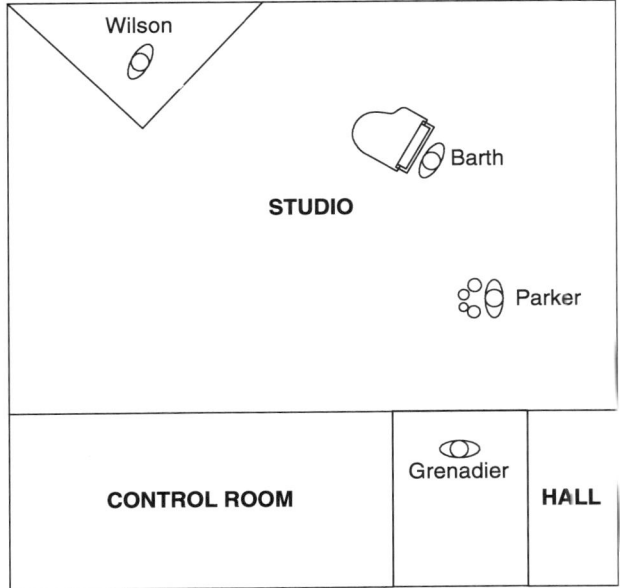

FIGURE 5. Arrangement of musicians, RPM Sound Studios, ᴄo.

was behind a series of baffles and covered with various quilt-like materials to keep its sound from bleeding into the room. Closer to the control
room and almost directly in between Barth and Grenadier was Leon
Parker on drums. I was seated in the control room with Max Bolleman,
the recording engineer, and Gerry Teekens, the head of Criss Cross.

The studio setup (see figure 5), as in the Williams and ICU example,
facilitated and encouraged visual communication among the musicians
in the course of recording. The first tune I heard the musicians rehearse
was Parker's "Belief." In the third chorus of Wilson's solo on the only
recorded take, Barth and Parker hooked up on a supportive passage
leading up to the fifth bar of a blues form.[24] They looked at each other
immediately afterward and smiled. In the next tune they recorded, "Everything Must Change," Wilson foregrounded aspects of visual communication by informing the other musicians that he would cue a return to
tempo after a fermata: "There's a hold before the coda; there's a fermata.
If you guys watch me, I'll bring you in. Keep it in tempo the first time
[through the form]. Hold the chord, the F minor seven[th chord], the
second time." In the third take of this tune, Parker used an intriguing

visual/aural gesture to end the tune: he waved the brushes with which he had played the tune back and forth rapidly under one of the ambient drum microphones as the other instruments' sounds decayed. The result, onomatopoeically, sounded like "whishing" or "swooshing." In response, Teekens, Bolleman, and I exchanged glances and smiled at one another. At the same time I noticed Barth looking at Parker while smiling and shaking his head. He then looked at those of us in the control room and continued shaking his head. This recognition of the inventiveness of a particular performative action helped to confirm for all participants that we were engaged with the performance and that we perhaps shared some ways of evaluating it. It also signaled that we were operating within similar conventions of response: recognition, followed by smiles and seeking confirmation of our response in the eyes and actions of other participants. Our responses were silent because of the constraints of recording. No words were to be uttered until Bolleman made it clear that tape was no longer rolling.

"Perdido" was the sixth tune recorded during the session, after two untitled tunes by Barth, Wilson's "Wish You Were Here," Parker's "Belief," and Bernard Ighner's "Everything Must Change."[25] The Wilson quartet played "Perdido" in B♭ at a tempo of ♩~302. The tune has a thirty-two-bar AABA form centered strongly on the tonic in each A section (Sher 1991, 287).[26] The contrasting B section is a variant of the III–VI–II–V bridge from George and Ira Gershwin's "I Got Rhythm." The released version of the recording can be considered a full processual performance only up to the last eight measures of Parker's solo. Afterward, we hear inserted into that performance a retake of Parker's last eight solo measures, a rapid unison passage for saxophone and piano and the "Perdido" melody—played only once. The following edited field note excerpt describes the recording of the tune in general terms, after the solo order (Wilson, Barth, Parker), length (six choruses each for Wilson and Barth, one for Parker), and tempo had been determined:

> The arrangement started with a rapid unison passage to be played by Wilson and Barth. Parker and Grenadier spent a couple of minutes working on one part of the arrangement that had [half-note triplets being played in the A sections]. Parker counted off a second attempt at negotiating that part of the arrangement after he and Grenadier failed at their first attempt. He started counting in Spanish, rather than English, and made everyone laugh. They did better when he counted that part off again [in English].

They then attempted their first take. After the saxophone-piano intro and a bass-drum duet, Wilson entered soloing over the form. Barth laid out for Wilson's first chorus.[27] After they did the intro again, Barth took his solo. He and Wilson then played their unison passage again, followed by a drum interlude. After [Parker's interlude], the group finally played the "normal" melody of the tune and took it out. As soon as the tape stopped rolling, Wilson asked, "Can we burn that?" All of the other musicians agreed that the take had been pretty dismal. Grenadier was especially disappointed. Barth looked a little tired. It was apparent that they hadn't had a break since starting the session. Parker asked whether they wanted to keep the drum interlude that preceded the head-out. Wilson replied, "Yeah, after that soli we [he and Barth] need a break before we go back to the head."

Then they started rolling tape on the second take. Barth and Wilson started off with the intro. Parker and Grenadier again entered with their interlude. This was the passage that had the metric changes. Each time they moved to the triplet feel, Grenadier [visually] cued the change. Parker, in turn, cued the return to the original meter. They both looked at each other intently while doing this passage. (I couldn't directly see Grenadier from where I was, but I could see his reflection in the angled panes separating the control room from the studio.) After their interlude, Wilson started his solo. Barth came in after Wilson's third chorus, playing sparse melodic figures and occasional chords. Wilson played an obviously cadential figure at the end of his sixth chorus to communicate that he had finished his solo. The intro followed, and Barth took his solo. Parker played a solo after Barth's and before the rapid unison passage. He then played another interlude before the head out. The opening figure ended the song, following two statements of the head.

They wanted to do an insert at the top of the soli. Parker did eight measures of his solo to set up the soli. Barth missed the start of the head on this insert and Wilson flubbed the second phrase. They decided to take a break and come back to the tune and the inserts after the break. (field notes, 11 December 1994)

Note here the negotiation characterizing the talk between songs and takes. As with the Williams example, there was discussion of specific compositional and interactive elements. Even cursory examination of them reveals the degree to which there were concerns other than the purely artistic motivating the arrangement of a tune, such as the practicality of following one passage with another. And again, aspects of visual communication were foregrounded, particularly where difficult passages were concerned. A tabular representation of the series of events in the tune is presented in table 3.

On one level, this recording has a direct relationship with at least one previously released version of the tune. Recognizing such a relationship

TABLE 3   PROGRESSION OF EVENTS IN "PERDIDO"

Intro	19 bars (cf. Ellington 1963)
Interlude 1	AABA, ♩ triplets on A sections, swing on B section
Wilson chorus 1	32 bars, AABA
Wilson chorus 2	32 bars, AABA
Wilson chorus 3	32 bars, AABA
Wilson chorus 4	32 bars, AABA
Wilson chorus 5	32 bars, AABA
Wilson chorus 6	32 bars, AABA
Intro 2	Same as intro 1
Interlude 2/Barth chorus 1	Same as interlude 1
Barth chorus 2	32 bars, AABA
Barth chorus 3	32 bars, AABA
Barth chorus 4	32 bars, AABA
Barth chorus 5	32 bars, AABA
Barth chorus 6	32 bars, AABA
Interlude 3/Parker chorus 1	
Wilson/Barth soli	Cf. Ellington 1963
Drum interlude	
Head	Statement of melody
Intro 3/coda	

foregrounds the importance of the shared knowledge of performance practice and the music's history that each person brings to the music. The introduction of Wilson's arrangement was a blues-scale–based pattern played by him and Barth that cycled up in fourths and grew louder dynamically phrase by phrase. Supporting rhythmic and tonal gestures were played by Grenadier and Parker: the former played a figure that emphasized the pitch F descending to B♭ to establish the tonality, while the latter emphasized the main rhythm with clicks on the snare drum rim (on the second and fourth beats of each measure) and cymbal crashes that coincided with Grenadier's bass notes.[28] Wilson's acknowledged source for the opening melodic figure he played with Barth is a 1963 recording by the Duke Ellington Orchestra of the same tune.[29] Wilson's use of the passage was different from Ellington's. Whereas the earlier recording uses it only twice—to separate solos from each other— Wilson slightly lengthened the ending, gave it a different climax, and made it a lead-in to the half-note triplet duet for bass and drums. This extended passage—the Ellington figure and the bass-drum duet—opened the recording, separated solos, and functioned as a coda to the song. What was peripheral or incidental in Ellington's recording became more central in Wilson's: it was part of what held the performance together and differentiated it from performances framed by a head containing a melody associated with the tune. Indeed, as the description from my field notes indicates, the melody of "Perdido" was not heard until the end of the tune.[30]

There is one more parallel with the Ellington recording. The difficult portion of the arrangement I saw Wilson writing out at Williams's recording session was the passage after the third interlude that he and Barth had to rerecord. Further examination of the Ellington recording reveals that what Wilson and Barth recorded is half of a duet that Ellington's arrangement provided for Paul Gonsalves and Jimmy Hamilton, both playing tenor saxophone and at a tempo ($\downarrow \sim 241$) slower than Barth and Wilson's.[31] In his arrangement, Wilson brought his knowledge of Ellington's recorded legacy into what he did. He referred to the previous recording but took the borrowed material in a different direction, giving it a personal stamp by rearranging it.

Wilson started the first chorus of his solo with short phrases, leaving lots of space between each note, but it grew more lyrical as he proceeded through each eight-measure segment. Parker played fills at the end of each eight-measure section, varying the element(s) of the drum kit he used: the snare drum for A1, the rim of the snare and his crash cymbal for A2, the tom-toms for the B section (bridge), and the bass drum, tom-toms, and cymbals for A3. In that way he balanced the use of the different elements of his drum kit, helped to delineate the sections of the form, and supported the changes in Wilson's approach to those same sections. The sound of his time-keeping tap on the cymbal was notable as well: it had a sharp attack and a rapid decay, sounding like the hybrid metallic/glassy sound produced by striking the edge of a cymbal.[32] Grenadier performed his bass duties by outlining the harmonies, but he also listened, as is evident in his note choices in the last eight measures when he imitated Wilson's manipulation of a melodic cell. As Wilson's solo proceeded, his phrases grew longer and less distinct from each other.

In his second chorus, Wilson manipulated a particular melodic cell throughout. It consisted of three pitches: B♭, G, and F. He transposed those pitches, altered their rhythmic patterning, and interpolated other pitches at various points. Whether or not it registered at the time, those of us listening first heard a phrase that definitively used the cell at the end of A1. It functioned as a call to which Parker responded on the drums. One might almost have predicted Parker's musical responses to and proddings of Wilson by noting the number of times he turned his gaze toward the saxophonist. It seemed as though aural response or pushing required visual confirmation. Those same moments elicited smiles and nods from Bolleman, Teekens, and me. Wilson then treated a figure sequentially in A2. His playing in the bridge was more lyrical and ended with the three-note cell played twice. Parker again answered Wilson's call with a roll on the tom-toms. A3 showed Wilson again manipulating a melodic figure. The Parker fill at the end of that section set up a climatic high, held note by Wilson that spilled into the next chorus.

At the top of the third chorus we heard a response to that high, held note. The excitement it generated continued, with a fill from Parker, into the fifth measure of the chorus (A1). Grenadier dramatically moved into the upper register of the bass in these measures. Teekens, Bolleman, and I were glancing at each other briefly during these interactions, almost as if to say, "Did you hear/see that?" An especially rewarding moment was the final release of the intensity built up by the climactic note with Parker's fill ending in the fifth measure. Almost anticipating it, each of us in the control room, on the edges of our seats, relaxed after that final accent. In A2 Wilson repeated a figure, playing it three times. The repetition sounded like an invitation to respond, which Parker did after the second iteration. In the B section Parker played irregular off-beat accents on the snare drum and crash cymbal that intensified the sense of forward motion and helped to distinguish the bridge from the A sections of the tune. The last eight measures of this chorus (A3) again found Wilson manipulating short melodic figures like the three-note cell.

The fourth chorus started with a four-measure phrase played by Wilson. The silence before his next phrase was filled by the entrance of Bruce Barth on piano, whose playing momentarily recalled Thelonious Monk's recording of "Friday the Thirteenth."[33] Wilson then played a series of short phrases whose spaces Barth filled with sparse melodic figures of his own. Wilson's playing in A2 consisted of longer, more lyrical and virtuosic playing than in his first three choruses. Although Leon Parker limited himself to keeping time at this stage, perhaps cautiously assessing what Barth might do, Grenadier began an ascent to the bass's high register in A1, culminating with the arrival of the bridge. Barth continued playing harmonically ambiguous supporting figures behind Wilson, and Parker demarcated the end of the bridge with a fill. In A3, Wilson played a riff-like figure (which would return as a cadential figure in the last measures of the sixth chorus to signal the solo's end).

Wilson played one short melodic figure that marked the end of the chorus, which was not accentuated by Parker, Barth, or Grenadier.

Movement into the fifth chorus was somewhat hazy, not because the musicians deliberately obscured it, but because they chose not to demarcate it. Wilson's phrasing in the first eight measures (A1) sounded like a continuation of the figure he played at the end of the fourth chorus. Combined with Barth's metrically unstable chords in these measures, this strategy momentarily clouded my understanding of the form. Barth and Parker dispelled the ambiguity at the end of A1, Parker by playing a fill and Barth by playing a clear cadential pattern. The placement of Barth's chords was more regular in A2 and reinforced Wilson's descending treatment of a melodic figure. Barth's well-placed chord at the beginning of the eighth measure clearly prepared the move to a D dominant sonority at the beginning of the bridge. Wilson repeated a one-measure riff for the first four measures of the bridge, creating a sense of regularity and forward momentum. Barth and Parker clearly highlighted the end of the bridge with harmonic and rhythmic fills.

In the last eight measures (A3), something remarkable, although not unusual for these four performers, happened. As the example from the group's performance at Bradley's, cited earlier, indicated, I was continually fascinated by the way these four musicians played with meter, improvising patterns that seemed to upset the metric flow. Eventually, however, in the midst of such play and upon arrival at structurally important areas in the form, they would confirm the original time feel. While Wilson's riff and Parker and Barth's fills helped to reinforce my sense of the metric framework in the bridge, Barth set up a pattern of off-beat accents in the A3—on the "and" of each beat. Parker responded to and reinforced Barth's pattern. By contradicting the meter and my (our?) expectations of its accentual patterning, these off-beat accents created considerable tension, particularly when Barth started alternating low and high register chords and making the low-register chords sound like upbeats. The result was sonically dense, intense, and ambiguous. The tension was released only at the top of Wilson's sixth chorus.[34]

Teekens, Bolleman, and I again seemed to be on the edge of our seats during this passage. I was unconsciously leaning forward, and the posture of both Bolleman and Teekens suggested they were tense and expectant. All of us relaxed at the beginning of Wilson's sixth chorus, when the original metric framework again assumed dominance. Wilson, for his part, blurred the distinction between the fifth and sixth choruses by again playing a figure at the end of a chorus, his three-note cell, which he developed at the beginning of the next.

While Wilson worked over this figure in the sixth chorus's A1, Parker helped to reestablish a regular meter and sense of form by playing time-keeping figures and accenting the end of the eight-measure unit with a fill. Barth laid out for the first sixteen measures of this chorus. At the beginning of A2, Wilson played what sounded like another call to which no one responded.[35] Barth and Grenadier highlighted the arrival of the bridge with denser accompaniment, Parker via a fill and Grenadier with repeated figures on the bass. Wilson played a lower-pitched version of the one-measure riff from his fifth chorus in the bridge of this last chorus. Barth reentered during the bridge. With all the musicians knowing that this was Wilson's last chorus, they emphasized the end of the bridge and the beginning of the last A section, Barth with two accented chords and Parker with a roll on the tom-toms and the striking of his crash cymbal. The rifflike fragment played in the last eight measures of the fourth chorus returned as a two-measure riff that Wilson played and repeated twice with slight modifications to end his solo. Barth and Parker added responsive punctuation to Wilson's statement of the riff.

Whereas the musicians playing "J's Rhythm Song" were forced to create an ad hoc form on a more or less stable metric and modal framework, the musicians here had an explicit one. A metric and harmonic scheme provided a template for Wilson's arrangement and the improvisation of each musician. Moreover, the interactive sensitivity they developed in frequent performances and recordings with each other as scene participants was brought to the recording as well. Their performance during Wilson's solo alternately reinforced and obscured the harmonic and metric framework. Likewise, the arrangement acknowledged the role of history in a musical event: the history of recordings of the tune "Perdido," the history of group's collective performance (particularly interactions between Wilson and Parker and between Barth and Parker), and even the localized developments occurring in a single performance (Wilson's calls and Parker's responses, Wilson's processes of motivic repetition and variation).

Engagement with a blues aesthetic's criteria of performance and evaluation and the framing provided by the scene helps us to understand these varied levels of interaction. That is, by examining the interactive nature of the event, what the musicians brought to it, and the ways in which participants in the event responded, as well as by examining the harmonic, rhythmic, and melodic parameters, we might come to an understanding of the ways the scene and an aesthetic inform performance and its evaluation. The musicians' place on the scene and understanding of the aesthetic informed and enabled their ability to interact with one another and to perform effectively in the recording studio. Through previous experiences, they understood the constraints of recording and overcame some of their difficulty through discussion and visualized negotiation in performance. They engaged the aesthetic by alternately reinforcing and obscuring the structural and harmonic frames, taking previously existing material and making it their own, and bringing different aspects of their individual performative sensibilities into the performance context. They also foregrounded making a connection with each other through musical response, before- and after-take verbal commentary, and visual communication.

Teekens, Bolleman, and I responded similarly to the way in which the musicians interacted and dealt with different aspects of the performance. Our emergent understanding of the event was apparent in our glances at each other in response to remarkable aspects of the performance. Moreover, our individual understandings of what these musicians brought to the performance, not only in terms of their pathways or individual style but in terms of their past interactions with each other, enhanced our moment-to-moment understanding of the tune as it was being recorded. The performance I'd seen at Bradley's in October was fresh in my mind. Teekens and Bolleman had heard them before on their different visits to New York and had seen and heard them individually on other Criss Cross recording dates. Likewise, the ways in which the musicians took the materials at hand—blues aesthetic criteria, scene-based interaction, the temporal and spatial constraints of recording, and the form of the tune—placed them firmly within a ritualized frame that allowed, albeit in recorded form, for the possibility of each participant deriving aesthetic equipment for living from listening and participating. Teekens hinted that he liked recording these musicians because they "give him something," they play with fire and energy. In contrast, he observed, "A lot of the older ones [recording for Criss Cross] come just to collect their money."[36] As this example and the previous one show, the constraints of recording do little to encourage real-time interactive communication among performers and other participants, restricting most verbal and visual interaction between performers and other participants to the spaces between tunes. They do, however, engender—in the moment of recording—responses similar to those that accompany live performance. Moreover, they allow for an interactive form of communication between musicians and other observers in the space between takes.

IN THE STUDIO 3: THE PETER BERNSTEIN QUARTET

I first became acquainted with Peter Bernstein when I was conducting fieldwork for my master's thesis (Jackson 1992). He was also one of the first musicians with whom I made contact upon beginning this project. I met Gregory Hutchinson in early 1993 in connection with further research on the role of age and education in the formation of small jazz groups (Jackson 1993a, 1993b). I had also seen bassist Christian McBride and pianist Brad Mehldau performing in various settings, especially with Joshua Redman. I went to this recording session, therefore, well acquainted with their performance styles.

These musicians recorded "Will You Still Be Mine?" on Saturday, 17 December 1994, at RPM Sound Studios in New York City, a week to the day after Wilson's quartet recorded "Perdido." The studio setup was approximately the same as that for Wilson's session (see figure 6): McBride was in the isolation booth where Grenadier had been positioned; Hutchinson's drums occupied the space that Parker's had; and the piano, now played by Mehldau, was still near the back of the studio. The major difference was that Bernstein's amplifier was in the isolation booth, while he was seated in the studio, facing Hutchinson.

Although these four musicians had never played together as a unit before this date, each had had numerous interactions with some of the others. Bernstein and Mehldau had frequently performed together in various New York clubs since meeting at the New School in the late 1980s, and they had also played in a group led by drummer Jimmy Cobb. In addition, Mehldau and McBride had spent more than eighteen months playing together in the Joshua Redman Quartet. Hutchinson had joined the two of them in Redman's group for a short tour in September of 1994 and also during the latter portion of Redman's performance at Town Hall in New York City on 2 December 1994—fifteen days before this recording session. Hutchinson and McBride had also worked together under various circumstances, most notably during the sessions for Joe Henderson's celebrated 1992 recording, *Lush Life: The Music of Billy Strayhorn*.[37]

Formally, "Will You Still Be Mine?" is a fifty-six-bar AABA tune frequently done in E♭ (Sher 1991, 425–26).[38] Each A section is sixteen

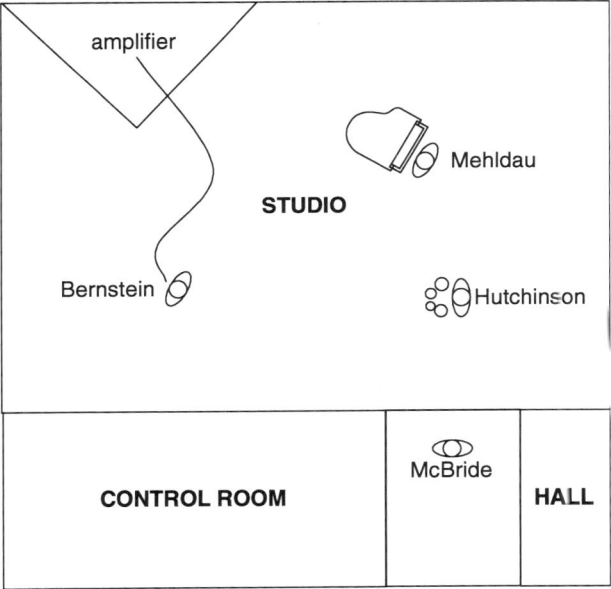

FIGURE 6. Arrangement of musicians, RPM Sound Studios, 17.

measures in length, and the B section is eight. Bernstein chose to play the tune in D rather than E♭ because he liked the sympathetic ringing produced by the open strings of his guitar in standard tuning (personal communication, 23 September 1995). There had been a brief rehearsal on Friday, 16 December, during which the musicians learned the music for five original tunes by Bernstein. In keeping with common practice, the musicians didn't rehearse the four standards for the date, including "Will You Still Be Mine?" On Saturday, therefore, after recording four other tunes ("Nobody Else But Me," "Jet Stream," "Blues to Bulgaria," and "Jive Coffee"), taking a break, and recording another ("Minor Changes"), the musicians started a run-through of "Will You Still Be Mine?" without having played it together before.[39] There was also a degree of tension at the recording session. Bernstein, Hutchinson, and McBride were annoyed with Mehldau, who disappeared during what was supposed to be a five-minute break and delayed their being able to proceed with the session.[40]

They chose a blisteringly fast tempo, greater than $\quarternote = 360$, for the run-through. One of Bernstein's friends, organist Sam Yahel, who was observing the session along with Max Bolleman, Gerry Teekens, and me, predicted, "If they do the first take at that tempo, they'll do another one slower." I was unable to hear all of the in-studio conversation when the musicians were discussing the basic outline for the tune and the solo order. I did note, however, they would play an eight-measure introduction followed by the statement of the theme with a send-off. Bernstein would solo first and take three choruses. He would be followed by Mehldau and Hutchinson, each of whom would also solo for three choruses.

The following edited field note excerpt describes the process of recording this tune in general terms:

> Hutchinson started playing the head of the tune with brushes. Bernstein stood up and shook his head, stopping the tune during the bridge. He said that the tempo was too fast. Apparently, Yahel was right. In the booth they decided to erase this first attempt at doing the tune completely because there was too much before-tune talk on the tape.
> The second take started with an eight-measure intro. The head came next, followed by a three-chorus solo by Bernstein. Mehldau's solo was next. He was playing his ass off. His lines were long and intricate, harmonically rich and challenging, rhythmically varied, swinging like hell. Hutchinson soloed next. After his solo, they played the head-out. The take was so good that, when it was done, Teekens yelled, "Shit!!" [And] Hutchinson said from the studio, "That was a burner!" Mehldau, however, wanted to do another take. Bernstein overruled him, saying that they would redo only the head-out because he had himself missed the first bar of the head. Hutchinson would play the last four measures of his solo as a lead-in to the head. After they did the insert, though, Bernstein wasn't happy with it and wanted to do it once more so that he could "phrase the melody better." He tried taking more liberties with the melody's rhythm's and contours. It didn't come off too well. The third attempt at an insert was more conservative on Peter's part [but was the one they kept]. (field notes, 17 December 1994)

Since the released version truncates and edits Hutchinson's solo by combining different takes, my discussion is limited to the second-take performance preceding the drum solo.

Bernstein had chosen a tempo greater than ♩ = 360 for the first take. For the second, he settled on a slightly more relaxed tempo of approximately ♩ = 334. After an eight-measure introduction based on measures 13 and 14 of A1, the musicians started playing the head. While Bernstein played the melody, accompanied by Mehldau's chords and filler phrases, Hutchinson and McBride articulated a two-beat feel, emphasizing the first and third beats of each measure. Hutchinson's use of wire brushes rather than sticks helped them to maintain a low dynamic level.

In A3 of the head, Hutchinson changed the accentual patterning. Instead of playing the first four measures of this section with a two-beat feel (as eight half notes), he played four dotted half notes plus two halves (♩♩|♩♩|♩♩|♩♩|♩♩|♩♩). The resultant pattern made what would have been four measures of $\frac{4}{4}$ sound like four measures of $\frac{3}{4}$ plus one measure of $\frac{4}{4}$. Although playing triple patterns in a duple texture, maintaining the same pulse, is not uncommon in jazz performance,[41] Hutchinson heightened the effect of this device by repeating it three times, up to the tag.[42] For Bernstein's and other solos, the musicians switched to a swing feel, with McBride typically playing a four-notes-to-the-bar walking line.

Bernstein started his solo with a repeated pitch that emphasized triple-pulse groupings (as Hutchinson had in A3 of the head). Bernstein's phrases were mostly short and coincided with the four- and eight-measure groupings of the written tune. Mehldau's comping and Hutchinson's drumming were supportively conventional, as was McBride's bass playing, though the latter distinguished the second eight measures of A1 from the first eight by ascending to the bass's high register. He descended for the beginning of A2, only to ascend again in the second eight measures. Bernstein's phrases were longer but still corresponded mostly to the structural breakpoints dictated by the form. Hutchinson played a fill that, along with Mehldau's comping, set up the beginning of the B section. Here Mehldau began playing the triple figure that both Hutchinson and Bernstein had previously played. Bernstein's phrasing was noticeably more lyrical and ended with a phrase that carried him into A3. There he played shorter phrases; Mehldau treated them as calls to which he responded. In the last eight measures Bernstein started a phrase that went over the barline, culminating in the next chorus. Simultaneously, in the last two measures Hutchinson played a fill that emphasized, again, triple groupings.

At the top of the second chorus, Mehldau joined Hutchinson just as he was abandoning the triple pattern. Mehldau continued it briefly as a chordal riff. In A2, Bernstein varied a few short melodic ideas, but he seemed tentative about what to do with them. Starting at the ninth measure, he again incorporated the triple-time superimposition into his solo with a repeated pitch that he approached chromatically from below three times. McBride ascended to the bass's highest register, building to the bridge. In these same measures, Bernstein started a figure whose completion, like the one at the end of A3 in the first chorus, would take it over the barline separating A2 from B. Mehldau and Hutchinson hooked up with him on the triple superimposition at the beginning of the B section. This was a moment that engendered response from those of us in the control room. Having heard various iterations of the triple-beat superimposition by various members of the ensemble, it was pleasurable to hear three of them accenting it together. While smiling at the hookup, I observed similar responses from Yahel, Bolleman, and Teekens. Hutchinson's accentuation here recalled his playing during the head. In the final sixteen measures of this chorus (A3), Bernstein began with a rising figure that he treated as a call for his own response. In the last eight, he again started a phrase whose completion would not come before the beginning of the next chorus.

In the third chorus, Bernstein began again with a triple pattern, emphasizing a repeated pitch, and Mehldau supplied a chordal answer. Bernstein's lines were growing longer, as could be heard in the continuation after his opening notes. He completed the second eight measures with a two-note fragment. Varying that fragment allowed him to phrase over the barline into A2. He continued manipulating that two-note figure for the first eight measures of A2. In the second eight, he used the triple rhythmic motive once more, this time with double-stops. Hutchinson's playing started growing denser as he added to his brushwork hits on the cymbals and the bass drum. McBride's registral changes became more prominent in A3, where he began playing in the high register— repeating a figure—descended momentarily to the lower register, then ascended once more. Bernstein's line in the first half of A3 comprised the entire eight measures. In the last four measures, before the tag ending his solo, Bernstein played a concluding figure.

The most dramatic shift—in texture, dynamics, and tempo—came at the end of Bernstein's solo and the beginning of Mehldau's. When Bernstein dropped out, he essentially left behind a well-rehearsed trio. Their interaction in the three choruses that followed pulled everyone in the control room—Bolleman, Teekens, Yahel, and me—into the performance, leaving us mesmerized. Hutchinson played the first six measures of the tag with brushes. Then, over the next six beats, which passed in little more than one second, he put away the brushes, retrieved his sticks, and played a two-beat fill that continued into Mehldau's first solo chorus. Hutchinson's attacks with the sticks were dramatically louder than those with the brushes, further lending a sense of urgency to the beginning of Mehldau's solo. The louder attacks registered as a signal to me and the other observers that something different was occurring, that the level of intensity might be rising. Moreover, perhaps in his haste to get the sticks in his hands and to begin playing, Hutchinson reinforced the sense of urgency and intensity by rushing his two-beat figure, following it with slightly out-of-phase half-note triplets in the first two measures of A1 of Mehldau's first solo chorus.[43]

Hutchinson's fill continued through the first four measures of A1, culminating with a rim shot on beat three of the sixth measure. In the second four measures of A3, Mehldau utilized the repeated-note triple-meter pattern that Bernstein used frequently during the previous solo. In measures 9–16 of this section, Mehldau played a five-note figure and repeated it twice before again using the repeated notes he played in measures 4–8. At the beginning of A2, Mehldau paraphrased the tune's melody. He followed the paraphrase with a figure that ascended to an unstable pitch. In answering his own ascent, beginning on the third beat of measure 8, he played an off-beat phrase whose accents suggested a grouping of six (rather than four). Having heard this particular melodic pattern in Mehldau's playing before, McBride and Hutchinson adjusted their accents to highlight what the former was doing.[44] The trio played four measures of this modified metric accentuation. The last ten beats of the section were used to renegotiate a $\frac{4}{4}$ meter. This moment of pushing against the metric framework garnered smiles and nods from the control room participants. The meter seemed reestablished by measures 15–16, where Hutchinson played a fill, an over-the-barline release, that started in those last two measures, continued into the bridge, and culminated with a snare hit on beat four of the second measure of B. It cemented for me the feeling that they were back in four. Mehldau's playing in the last measures of the bridge consisted of a four-note motive that he continued developing into the second measure of A3. In doing so, he made the boundaries of the form seem more obscure with relation to his phrase rhythms. In the next two choruses, his obscuring of the line between the bridge and A3 would be even more pronounced.

Mehldau started his second chorus by repeating a three-note melodic cell for emphasis; Hutchinson marked the beginning of this chorus with a snare drum hit on the "and" of beat three in the second measure. Mc-Bride ascended to the high register in the fifth measure and descended in the second eight. Mehldau's playing here was highly virtuosic, eliciting incredulous head shaking from those of us in the control room. At the top of A2, Mehldau played his own call-and-response figure, answering a single-line call with chords. McBride again ascended. In the B section, Mehldau played a repeated figure in measures 1–4, and one of McBride's unstopped strings was buzzing in measure 3. Beginning in the fifth measure, Mehldau played an off-beat phrase that went against the prevailing feel of four and whose patterning obscured the end of bridge, without a resolution coming until he played a melodic paraphrase in the fifth measure of A3. The response in the control room to Mehldau's playing and interaction with Hutchinson and McBride was more head shaking, astonished looks, and scarcely audible exhalations of air (like the ones that would accompany the utterance of "Whew!"). Hutchinson's fill leading to a cymbal crash/kick drum hit on the "and" of beat four of measure 8—a move that typically acts as a section marker—combined with Mehldau's over-the-barline phrasing, made it seem as though the bridge comprised sixteen measures. It also functioned for me to mark forcefully where one, the first beat of a measure, was. He reinforced my interpretation by again playing a snare hit on the "and" of beat three in measure 11.

In the first four measures of the third chorus, Mehldau varied a one-measure melodic cell; he played an "answering phrase" in octaves in measures 5–8. Hutchinson started to play accents on the cymbals more frequently, increasing the density and intensity of the texture. In measures 9–12, Mehldau repeated another one-measure cell four times, displacing it rhythmically with each repetition, and again played an answer. In section A2, Mehldau started with a repeated phrase that sounded as though it might have come from a baroque composition for the keyboard. Eventually, Hutchinson and McBride emphasized the repetitions with a triple overlay. McBride played a pedal point, heightening tension for a release that came in the B section. Here Mehldau played another of his signature patterns, a repeated figure played in the upper register with his right hand contrasted with a slower improvised melody played with the left. His repetition of the figure again obscured the transition from the bridge to A3. He managed a concluding four-measure phrase before the beginning of the tag that marked the beginning of Hutchinson's solo.

In this event, one again sees the value of close attention to interactions beyond those that one might hear in a recording. The degree to which Bernstein, Hutchinson, and Mehldau made use of the triple pattern first played by Hutchinson carried them through four choruses of solos. After noting the points at which those types of phrases occurred, the musicians hooked up at later, analogous structural points, most clearly at the beginning of the bridge in Bernstein's second chorus. Likewise, past interactions between Mehldau, McBride, and Hutchinson conditioned the way they became more rhythmically and metrically adventurous during Mehldau's solo. In the end, they made the $16 + 16 + 8 + 16$ structure into an apparent $16 + 16 + 16 + 8$. Mehldau's frequent use of a pattern in six was part of his individual sound, one he brought to the recording and to which McBride and Hutchinson, having recognized it, responded.

Their reactions when the take was complete, as well as those from inside the control room, made it clear that they indeed "took it to the next level" and created a feeling of flow by manipulating dynamic levels, changing textures, temporarily superimposing other metric frameworks, utilizing off-beat phrasing, and obscuring important section markers in the tune's form. Moreover, they did each of these things within the context of criteria described by a blues aesthetic and informed by their interactions on the scene. Each brought something to the recording, showed themselves to be adept at manipulating a variety of musical parameters in the process of performing, and were open and responsive to each other in playing. They took the materials at hand—the recording studio, form, key, and tempo, for example—and did something creative with them.

Additionally, the correspondence between studio and control room response during and especially after the take perhaps confirms the degree to which criteria for determining a good performance were shared among the performing and non-performing participants in that studio session. The moments at which the musicians pushed against the structural framework, hooked up with each other, or returned to or confirmed the framework drew other participants into the performance. Implicit in the moment-to-moment evaluation of the proceedings were comparisons to other performances, featuring not only these musicians but many others.

ON STAGE 1: THE JOSHUA REDMAN QUARTET AT THE VILLAGE VANGUARD

A live performance presents a number of interesting contrasts with one taking place in a studio and being recorded. Apart from the fact that musicians in a live setting generally continue playing if they make mistakes, there is a different pattern of interaction between them and other participants in such musical events. The audience for a live performance is likely to be much more heterogeneous than one in a recording studio, comprising fans and spectators, both purposeful supporters of jazz and more casual consumers (see DeVeaux 1995). Moreover, although live performers might note the response of an audience to a performance more immediately than their counterparts in the studio, they frequently do so with less certainty about the meaning of that response. As Sam Newsome observed in chapter 5, an audience might be audibly responsive but make themselves heard at what seem, to some musicians, to be the wrong times.

At the beginning of 1995, saxophonist Joshua Redman started working with a partially new ensemble.[45] While drummer Brian Blade remained from the quartet's previous incarnation, he and Redman were joined by Peter Martin on piano and Christopher Thomas on bass. Redman's choice of these particular musicians was strategic: he knew of their previous experiences playing together and with Brian Blade. Both Thomas and Martin had worked with singer Betty Carter. Thomas and Blade had worked with pianist Ellis Marsalis in New Orleans, and the two of them, along with Martin, had made a recording in 1992 with trumpeter Nicholas Payton and saxophonist Wessell Anderson.[46] As a rhythm section, consisting of piano, bass, and drums, they had some knowledge of each other's playing from their experience making that recording. They did not, however, possess knowledge of each other's playing in the context of Redman's group or his compositions.

Wanting to develop a "group sound," particularly because a live recording date was approaching (see below), all four musicians decided to devote time to intensive rehearsal. Joshua Redman explained,

> I never called an independent rehearsal with [the old] band. With this new band, they were all in New Orleans [during January of 1995]. So, I didn't know they were going to do this, but they got together and learned all the music. Brian taught Chris and Peter all the music. So I didn't really need to, but we rehearsed one day before we left for Japan [for a two-week tour in February]. And then two or three separate rehearsals while we were in Japan. Which was really strange because I've never done that before. And it wasn't because we needed it. Although, at this point, the book has become so large, that what they have to tackle is much greater than what, you know, Chris, Kevin, and Greg had to tackle in the beginning. There's no song that I've stopped playing. But the repertoire's five times as big.[47]

> The reason I called the rehearsal was because I was trying to develop a *real* group sound . . . sooner. Because I'd been working with a group that had developed a strong sound over a long period of time, I wanted to rush that with the new band. I wanted to get . . . to where we really felt comfortable playing, as if we'd been together longer than just a week. I'd also written five or six new pieces that I was trying to work up. (Redman 1995a)

In those rehearsals, Redman says, the band members focused on different ways of approaching the tunes. He emphasized collective work, each musician giving according to his capacities and instrumental role, with considerable guidance from him regarding harmonic and rhythmic structures, tempos, appropriate grooves, bass parts, piano voicings, and hits.[48] Redman acknowledged and was pleased by the fact that his control could go only so far: "It's *jazz*. So, you know, most of it is improvised. So, I mean, in that sense, once we get to the blowing [i.e., solo] section, you know, and I say what kind of groove I want them to blow on, then, you know, we're all composing, and that's what jazz is about" (Redman 1995a).

Because Redman had been the subject of much writing in the popular press (e.g., Keegan 1994) and because of the fall 1994 release of his recording *MoodSwing,* considerable excitement within and beyond the jazz scene preceded his weeklong engagement at the Village Vanguard in March of 1995. Moreover, the excitement around this gig was surely affected by the extensive publicity given to Redman's concert at Town Hall the previous December. Prior to the concert, Peter Watrous had written a lengthy piece—with the provocative question "Is Josh Redman a New Archetype?" supplied by another party as the headline—for the Sunday *New York Times* (Watrous 1994b). The concert was later reviewed favorably by Watrous, whose only criticism was that Redman perhaps spent too much time playing to the audience: "Mr. Redman has often written and spoken about his quest to make jazz more accessible, and he did it in [the tune] 'Headin' Home.' . . . It had the guest artist—trumpeter Roy Hargrove—and Mr. Redman spouting as many rhythm-and-blues phrases as they had in their vocabulary. It was disconcerting. . . . Circumstances can create hacks; it's not so pleasant to see the better minds of a generation choosing the route themselves, and being given standing ovations for their trouble" (Watrous 1994d, 16).

In my interview with him in early March, Redman expressed annoyance at that example of Watrous's critical writing. He said that it bothered him when critics posited a connection between enthusiastic audience response and lack of seriousness on the part of the performer(s): "In general I have a big problem with critics who just assume that because something appeals to an audience or because something is 'popular,' then by nature it is less serious or has less integrity. That, that's bullshit." Redman continued, with interjections from me,

> *R:* But a lot of critics assume [a musician is less serious], you know, [especially when] you see a situation . . . where, you know, where it's an *obvious* thing that, you know, something that the crowd can really get into. And immediately they say, "Oh," you know, "they were playing down to the crowd," . . . which really upsets me. There *is* something that is true: that is the *more that you perform, the more you realize* that there are *certain* things that people have a tendency to respond to.
>
> *J:* High notes . . . ?
>
> *R:* Yeah.
>
> *J:* Repetition . . . ?
>
> *R:* Right. Exactly. And I think, there's nothing *wrong*, I mean, the fact that people respond to those things, there's absolutely nothing . . . that doesn't make there anything wrong with doing those things. Um, the problem arises is that . . . the more . . . as musicians begin to realize that certain types of things, certain techniques elicit certain kinds of audience responses . . . sometimes they begin, sometimes they can start to do those things *purely* for the sake of audience response. And if they begin to do that too much, then it can, you know, it can come at the expense of the seriousness of their music or at the expense of them really saying what they want to say, you know . . . I've seen musicians, and I've done it too, you know . . . There have been times that I've, you know, that I have gotten into things and because of the nature of the atmosphere, because of interaction with the audience, I've done things and maybe, maybe, you know, repeated a figure, you know, five, ten too many times . . . Five more times than was necessary for me to communicate what I trying to communicate because on some level . . . I realized that that would, you know, bring people into the music . . . Sometimes I'll look back on it and sometimes I've been very, very upset with myself, you know . . . and sometimes I haven't. [I think] maybe I made a slight sacrifice in terms of not being *100 percent* genuine . . . in saying exactly what I had to say, but what I gained from that sacrifice was a certain bond with the audience which carried over . . . Sometimes you can establish a bond, and once you've established that bond, you know, then that gives you, in a certain way, the *license* or the *freedom* to do . . . , you know, they trust you more . . . As much as I love Peter Watrous, in the review that he wrote of the Town Hall show, there was a point at which, you know, he said, um, I think, if

I'm right, you know, "Joshua Redman has written and spoken about his quest to make jazz more accessible." *That's wrong.* And that, to me, that is the same thing, you know, that's someone doing what you were talking about,[49] you know, because I've never written about that or spoken about the need to make the *music* more accessible.

J: It, it just struck me as funny when I heard things like that, too, because I always . . . When I did a couple of lectures last fall at a couple of schools here in New York about, about jazz. I would start the lecture off with the little anecdote [from your liner notes] about non–jazz fans saying to you, "Jazz is weird and too intellectual . . ." And I would get all these knowing glances from everybody in the room.[50] And then I would spend the next hour, hour and a half, telling them why that perception was at least misguided . . .

R: It's very tempting for people to read into what I've said this idea about making the music more accessible because it allows them, it's easier if you read *that* into it, then you can dismiss it by saying, "Oh, this is just someone who's talking, who wants to compromise the integrity of the music." I don't want to *change* the *music* at all, you know. (Redman 1995a)

Rather, he argued, his concern is to change the way in which people approach and listen to the music. He wanted to counter the public pronouncements of critics and historians whose emphasis on the "seriousness" and "intellectual" aspects of jazz, he felt, were intimidating to young or novice audiences, creating a barrier to engagement. Moreover, the intellectual and technical focus, he asserted, might distract them from another purpose of jazz performance: communication.

When I arrived at the Village Vanguard with Peter Watrous on the night of 21 March, therefore, there were a number of factors that might have made the event unusual. It was going to be a live recording situation rather than a typical nightclub gig. Redman was going to be playing with a new ensemble that had never played in New York City as a unit. In addition, barely three weeks after my interview with him and little more than three months after the Town Hall review, he was perhaps still mildly annoyed by Watrous's assertion that he had sacrificed the seriousness of his music to play to the audience. And Redman's patterns of interaction with different audiences were complicated by his growing celebrity, particularly among young audiences who weren't regular participants on the New York jazz scene or those in other cities (Watrous 1995b). Indeed, Redman had already expressed ambivalence about how he had reacted to and interacted with such audiences in the past.

Watrous and I passed the large mobile recording unit on Seventh Avenue South slightly after midnight before descending the staircase into the venue and stepping over thick black cabling.[51] The second set was already in progress, and there was only standing room in the club. Many audience participants were crowded right up to the edge of the stage area, close enough to tug on the hem of Redman's pants as he played. Had Watrous not been on the guest list to review the show, it is unlikely that we would have gained admission. As a result, we were obliged to stand for the duration of the set. Standing in a high-traffic area of the club, neither of us was in a good position to take notes on the performance. Before settling into positions near the wall on the left side of the venue, we asked Lorraine Gordon, the owner of the Village Vanguard, how much of the set we had missed. She informed us that the performers were nearing the end of the first tune.

The response after that first selection was almost deafening. During the next tune, "Herbs and Roots,"[52] it became clear that in attendance was an overwhelmingly young and enthusiastic audience, one responding to the event in ways different from those we typically expected.[53] The first indication that this might have been the case came during the tune's head. It started with a repeated four-measure figure played by Martin, Thomas, and Blade. Redman started playing the melody shortly afterward over an altered twenty-four-bar blues framework with harmonic touches—where the IV chord in a blues would come—borrowed from his tune "Headin' Home" as well as, perhaps, the Prince composition "Vicki Waiting."[54] As soon as he finished his first run through the melody, he received an enthusiastic verbal response from the audience in the form of whoops and "yeahs." Although Redman's playing on the head was surely energetic, neither Watrous nor I felt it merited so enthusiastic a response. After all, the convention for regular participants on the scene was not to applaud until after the first solo was complete. Only under rare circumstances did applause accompany or follow the playing of a tune's melody.[55]

Likewise, as the performance of the tune progressed, the younger audience members seemed to respond primarily to Redman's playing of high notes, squeals, and repeated phrases, precisely the kinds of "obvious" devices that he and I had discussed in February. Watrous remarked to me that the other audience members seemed as though they were attending a sporting event rather than a live jazz performance.[56] To be fair, however, I must note that they responded as well to Peter Martin's virtuosic playing and his intensive interaction with Thomas and Blade, particularly following the resolution of temporary moves away from the established metric framework. Indeed, Thomas was so impressed with what he heard Martin playing at these same moments that he frequently nodded his head, smiling, pursed his lips, or pulled his chin back to signal approval.

After "Herbs and Roots" ended, Redman thanked the audience for its enthusiasm and responsiveness. He proceeded to make a joke about the first sets on Tuesday nights in New York jazz clubs, saying, "We're going to kick back and relax and really play in the second set, now that the industry people are gone." He also explained, for anyone who did not already know, that they were making a live recording for his next release on Warner Brothers Records. I wondered then whether the enthusiastic responses might have been attempts to make the recording sound more lively or, more cynically, the result of individual participants attempting to ensure that they'd hear themselves on the released recording. On the next tune, "Wait No Longer," it also became apparent that the band had actually started to develop its group sound, for they executed changes in feel, texture, and rhythmic patterning in a way that also garnered positive response from the entire audience and each other. They also demonstrated a firm grasp of the use of dynamic shadings.

An understanding of the Joshua Redman Quartet's position on the scene and the patterns of interaction between them and the audience makes an examination of the next tune, the group's performance of "My One and Only Love," quite fascinating. During that tune, the third one after our arrival, Watrous and I again wondered aloud whether our fellow participants were bringing to the event normative and evaluative criteria quite different from those that we were. "My One and Only Love" was one of only two tunes not composed by Redman or a member of his group that appeared in the set.[57] It is a ballad with a thirty-two-bar AABA form that they played at a tempo of $\quarternote < 53$.

Peter Martin started the tune with a gospel-tinged introduction. Afterward, he, Thomas, and Blade (who was playing with brushes) articulated a two-beat feel. When Redman entered playing the melody with a "breathy" timbre that recalled the characteristic sounds of tenor saxophonists from the 1930s and 1940s, instead of nodding or smiling in recognition or offering sotto voce "yeahs," as Watrous and I expected, the younger participants near the edge of the stage proceeded to "ooh" and "aahh," sounding almost as though they were witnessing an extraordinary spectacle. Like Watrous in December, I felt disconcerted, not because of Redman's playing but because of what seemed a strangely adulatory response. And the issue for me was not merely that the response seemed disproportionate or extravagant, but also that I was unable to determine what was triggering such a collective enthusiasm. The audience participants were apparently framing their responses to the moment-to-moment flow of the event via a different set of evaluative criteria, one perhaps more suited to rock concerts or performances of singers. And although I was not able to talk to Redman at length after the show, because I deferred to a long line of autograph seekers vying for his attention, my guess was that he might have been a bit disconcerted as well. What I inferred as Redman's discomfort, though, was simply a result of what he and I had discussed three weeks previously.

In the second eight measures of his solo, Redman played a vocalized phrase in the altissimo register of the saxophone, which he followed with a long, sequentially descending phrase. Supporting him, Martin and Thomas played chromatically descending chords and single pitches, respectively. Redman closed his descending phrase with a low honk on the saxophone, followed by more high-register vocalized "squealing." The younger audience participants responded immediately and enthusiastically to Redman's honk and playing in the upper register. Perhaps feeling a bit self-conscious about getting such a response from a high note, Redman, who had been playing with his eyes either closed or downcast, seemed at that moment to look directly at Watrous, back at the crowd, and then again at Watrous. I guessed that he was wondering whether Watrous would again accuse him of playing to the crowd; alternatively, he might have been playing a game with the critic.[58]

When Martin started his solo after Redman's first chorus, it also became apparent that Redman was responding to some aspects of the performance differently from the younger members of the audience (but similarly to Watrous and me). Martin began by playing short phrases and using an approach and voicings that recalled the playing of pianist Bill Evans. In the second A section, Martin played even more varied and compelling lines, seemingly without any response from the audience. In the first four measures of the B section, he offered a series of phrases alternating repeated, blues-inflected pitches and virtuosic runs that culminated in an unexpected low-register blues-scale phrase. I shook my head and smiled at this point, looking to Watrous, who also seemed pleased with Martin's playing. Redman responded positively as well, audibly saying "Ah!" (around the 6:42 mark on the released recording). In the next four measures Martin's phrasing was more rapid and virtuosic. He treated a short figure sequentially, gradually ascending toward the high register. There was a momentary descent, followed by an ascent nearly to the top of the piano's range. Martin followed it with repeated high-register notes, a descent with a brief pause after a melodic reference to Thelonious Monk's "52nd Street Theme," and a continuation of the descent to the extreme low register of the piano. While Watrous and I nodded knowingly after the reference to the Monk composition, the wider crowd's response came only when Martin hit his registrally extreme bass pitches. Watrous and I then heard a verbal audience response and light applause. In addition, many audience members were shaking their heads as if to say, "Wow!"

Redman returned after Martin's improvisation on the final A section of the form, beginning at the bridge instead of the first A, and continued playing with the ensemble until the seventh measure of the final A section, where he started a cadenza consisting of successive iterations and alterations of a long melodic figure. Afterward, he played the eight measures of the A section, replacing many of the "standard" pitches with squeaks, honks, squeals, or octave displacements. At the end of the tune, the loud and long response of the younger members of the audience again seemed to be proceeding along lines different from those of the regular scene participants I had observed. Their enthusiasm seemed extravagant to me, Watrous, and singer Maria De Angelis, who by then had joined us.

On one level, the preceding example indicates the degree to which what can be brought into a performance by musicians is not limited to the conventionally "musical." Although on different tunes the rhythm section members in particular revealed a growing empathy with each other—via their ability to collectively manipulate feels, textures, metric frames, and dynamics—there were also pertinent non-musical issues. This example also shows how disparate musical events on the scene might affect and find their way into subsequent events. Redman's memory of his Town Hall performance and dislike for one of Watrous's essays seemed to me implicated in his response to *his audience's* response to his playing. One is tempted to say that he almost "broke" from the performance frame when he looked at Watrous to gauge or problematize the critic's evaluation.

On another level, though, this example speaks to the degree to which not every participant in a musical event draws on the same normative and evaluative criteria in responding to it. The celebrity Redman enjoyed from the numerous feature articles written about him and the success of his Town Hall concert helped to garner a large audience for him. This audience was responding to the musical event with gestures, Watrous might say, that were more suited to a sporting event or another kind of musical performance. Although I was admittedly disturbed by what I felt was the extravagance and quality of their reactions, two related concerns kept me from being more critical. First, various musicians had stressed to me the importance of being open to what different individuals brought to a performance. I could take comfort in the fact that these other audience members were listening and actively participating in the musical event, even if they were responding to it differently. In other words, they were *there* and were supporting the music and musicians. Second, their reactions were indicative of something that should have been obvious to me: that a blues aesthetic as normative and evaluative framework was not the only one that might be deployed at a jazz performance. Whatever authority the tendencies grouped under that rubric might have, it nonetheless continues to be challenged by what participants bring to musical events. The productive tension that can arise between it and alternate or competing aesthetics/discourses has the potential to transform (or obliterate) it for new listeners.

ON STAGE 2 AND 3: KENNY BARRON AT THE VILLAGE VANGUARD AND MULGREW MILLER AND WINGSPAN AT SWEET BASIL

A very different kind audience response characterized the interaction at a performance by Mulgrew Miller's group Wingspan on 22 September 1994. Miller is certainly a well-known figure on the jazz scene. In addition to performing extensively on recordings and in live engagements with other musicians—including trumpeters Freddie Hubbard and Woody Shaw, saxophonist Joe Lovano, drummer Tony Williams, and singer Cassandra Wilson—Miller had been leading several ensembles of his own, recording some of them for Orrin Keepnews's Landmark label. Wingspan was one of these ensembles, characterized chiefly by its instrumentation—piano, alto saxophone, vibraphone, bass and drums—and its repertoire.[59]

Miller, however, is not well known beyond the jazz scene. Unlike Redman in the previous example, he had not been the subject of major feature articles in the *New York Times,* nor had he received extensive promotion, even though at the time of this performance he was signed to a major label, Novus, a subsidiary of BMG (which also had Antonio Hart, Roy Hargrove, Carmen McRae, Steve Coleman, and John Pizzarelli under contract at the time). It is possible, therefore, to see his audience as more oriented toward the jazz scene than Redman's was at the Village Vanguard. In other words, more of Miller's audience would have been drawn by their interest in and knowledge of Miller's music rather than by his youthful celebrity. Their responses to the ongoing flow of the musical event and their interactions with the musicians were indicative of their closer relationship to mainstream jazz performance and blues aesthetic criteria.

I arrived at Sweet Basil with Mark Tucker around 8:45 PM to see the group. Tucker had spoken with me about Antonio Hart and was interested in hearing both him and Miller in a live setting. We learned upon arrival that the 9 PM set was sold out. Tucker and I decided, therefore, to go to the Village Vanguard to hear the first set of an engagement by pianist Kenny Barron with bassist Buster Williams, drummer Ben Riley, and a guest, alto saxophonist Jesse Davis. Afterward we would return to Sweet Basil for the 11 PM set.[60]

Both Tucker and I found the set by Barron's group competent but unremarkable. Tucker at one point described the set as being "somnambulistic."[61] The tunes were well played but never really moved to the next level. Williams and Riley were playing feels that mildly swung but engendered little inclination for me to tap my feet or dance. I didn't marvel at the level of swing, nor did I notice any beyond-the-ordinary or greater-than competent level of interaction among the musicians. It seemed as though they were merely playing another gig. It did not seem that they were risking, exploring, or reaching for something different or distinctive: there weren't any moments of surprise, or any interesting or uncommon harmonic choices. The low level of interaction between Barron, Williams, and Riley was particularly disappointing because they form one of the most legendary jazz trios. One might recall that their recording *Green Chimneys* was one of the "blessed" records mentioned to me by Leon Parker and discussed in chapter 1. Reflecting upon the performance later, I saw it as confirmation that even the best musicians can have off nights. They seemed to be giving very little to the audience. Similarly, though, they were receiving very little from it. As we walked back to Sweet Basil afterward, Tucker and I wondered whether it might have a been a "chicken and egg" situation, whether their performance might have been different or more inspiring in front of a livelier audience.

Upon returning to Sweet Basil, Tucker and I were led to a table right next to the stage area. I talked to Antonio Hart briefly. After he left to prepare for the set's beginning, Tucker and I discussed the other musicians and their backgrounds. Hart and I had been friends since the summer of 1993, and I had seen him performing in several different contexts. I knew vibraphonist Steve Nelson's playing primarily from Miller's recording *Hand in Hand* and was enamored of his work.[62] He was going to be featured on a couple of tunes at an upcoming Antonio Hart recording session. I knew the drummer, Tony Reedus, from separate recordings by alto saxophonists Kenny Garrett and Vincent Herring. The only musician whose playing I wasn't familiar with was Richie Goods, the bassist. Goods and Reedus, however, were regular members of Miller's trio, having toured and recently recorded with him.[63]

They started the set with "Return Trip" from *Hand in Hand*. Immediately Tucker and I felt the energy that seemed lacking at Barron's performance. Nelson took the first solo, during which striking differences came to the fore. Nelson seemed to be moving out, taking charge, trying different phrasings, playing very dissonant, "out"-sounding phrases alongside more conventional ones. Moreover, it was apparent that the other members of the band were listening and responding to him. Miller smiled at several of Nelson's phrases, and Reedus supported the solo by responding to Nelson's melodic and dynamic peaks, accenting his repeated phrases, and constantly changing the level of intensity and rhythmic density. Hart's solo was next. The band lowered its dynamic levels and intensity at the beginning of the solo. Goods, for example, who had been playing in the high register of the bass at the end of Nelson's solo, played the beginning of Hart's solo in the lowest register. Likewise, Reedus decreased the density of his playing, concentrating mostly on a cymbal pattern, giving very few prods after the cymbal crash and bass-drum bombs that coincided with the end of Nelson's solo and the beginning of Hart's. Hart's solo was energetic and compelling. The form was apparently guiding his solo, but he was consistently phrasing over the barlines and reached a dramatic peak right before his solo's end. Again, the level of intensity dropped as Miller's solo started. The leader's note choices and harmonic substitutions were refreshing after the set by Kenny Barron. In his third chorus, Miller started playing a series of chromatically shifting quartal chords. In order not to clash too strictly with that texture, Goods started playing a pedal point on the bass. At what first seemed like an abrupt ending to his solo, Miller raised and dropped his hands very quickly. Had I not noticed that he was holding up four fingers on each hand, I might have thought that he was being flashy. In fact, he was communicating to Nelson and Hart that the three of them would trade eights with Tony Reedus. When the first tune ended, Tucker and I discussed the level of positive energy and interplay already evident in this set, particularly compared to what we had just heard and witnessed at the Vanguard. The only complaint that either of us had was that sitting next to Tony Reedus was less than ideal. Our ears were ringing from the volume of his playing at intense moments.

The second tune, "Come Rain or Come Shine," opened with a piano introduction. Nelson again took the first solo. The groove was slower and less urgent than the one on "Return Trip" but no less compelling. In his third chorus, Nelson played a few high-register phrases, which led into repetitions of pitches with lower, half-step grace notes for a very bluesy sound. These repetitions, as one might expect from the Redman example cited previously, received positive verbal responses from the audience. The inventiveness and integration of those repetitions into the flow of his solo, however, kept us from seeing them merely as devices to inspire audience response.

Hart followed, starting his solo with a "breathy" timbre, sounding more like a tenor than an alto saxophonist. As Hart's solo progressed, Goods and Reedus treated the groove more flexibly: Goods was keeping time, but with several embellishments and deviations from his metronomic, time-keeping role; and Reedus added timbral variations, using different cymbals for ride patterns as he moved from one chorus to the next. Hart started building toward the peak of his solo in the fourth chorus, and he reached it in the fifth, where he played intricate eight-measure phrases alternating with flurries of isolated pitches and arpeggios. He ended his solo with a sequential pattern. Miller supported and pushed Hart by playing challenging background riffs. Scanning the audience at this point, I noted many other participants smiling and nodding in astonishment and apparent approval.

At the beginning of the next solo, Miller's, Reedus immediately switched ride cymbals to accommodate the different timbre and softer volume of the piano. A couple of particularly "down-home," bluesy-sounding phrases played by Miller received enthusiastic verbal audience response in the first sixteen measures of the solo. Miller clearly started to build toward a peak in the second chorus of his solo. As the third chorus began, Reedus again changed ride cymbals, while Goods moved from playing in the bass's high register to playing in the middle. Miller started this chorus with a loud chordal passage. Reedus started to drop more bombs here, not having to be as concerned about dynamically overwhelming the piano. Moreover, he made very effective use of accents on the snare drum and his crash cymbal. Miller started the fourth chorus with an "out" melodic figure that seemed to clash with the harmonic progression, but he resolved it prominently at the next cadence. Midway through the chorus he returned to playing chordal material in a "locked-hands" style that recalled pianist Red Garland's playing on Miles Davis recordings from the mid-1950s.[64] Reedus switched to brushes as Goods's bass solo started. Miller supported Goods with occasional richly embellished chords. After Goods's solo, Hart played the melody in the restatement of the head while Nelson provided an obbligato.

Miller then stood to introduce the band, announce the names of the tunes, and inform the audience that it was Tony Reedus's birthday. Leaning away from the microphone, he told the musicians the name of the next tune, perhaps to give them a chance to find their parts. He then pointed out several jazz celebrities who were in the audience: pianists James Williams and Renee Rosnes, bassist Charnett Moffett, and drummer Billy Drummond. He also introduced bassist Dave Holland, who, having departed before Miller's introductions started, was not present to acknowledge the applause.

At this point in the set, several aspects of the interaction among the members of the ensemble were worth noting. It seemed that blues aesthetic criteria were being called upon by the performers as well as the audience members in various forms. There was a high level of interaction and support among the members of the ensemble: all of them were listening and responding to the others, being open to what their bandmates were bringing to the music. In the process, each of them was deploying the varied resources of his instrument, actively balancing and coordinating them with the other performers by changing dynamics, density, and levels of intensity. Their negotiation of these parameters was especially clear in the transitions from one solo to the next. By lowering the level of intensity for each one, they helped each soloist to begin on terms different from those of the preceding one. In this respect, Miller, Goods, and Reedus, moreover, could call upon their sustained interactions from touring and recording together to shape their performance styles to meet the context. Nelson and Hart both had some familiarity with Miller's music and playing, Nelson through his playing on *Wingspan* and Hart through study of that recording.[65]

Moreover, aspects of visual and verbal communication among participants were foregrounded in various ways. The most salient was Miller's communication to the band that he, Nelson, and Hart would trade eight-measure passages on "Return Trip." Likewise, Miller visually responded to compelling aspects of Nelson's solo by smiling. Non-performing participants also highlighted their engagement with the flow of the musical event by responding to aspects of the performance both verbally and visually. In particular, their immediate response to Miller's use of blue tonality in "Come Rain or Come Shine" seemed to be an indicator of the value they placed upon that kind of playing, even in tunes not formally based on blues progressions. Lastly, Miller's acknowledgment of the presence of other musicians indicated his knowledge of and respect for other performers on the scene. He, of course, had to recognize them visually in order to note their presence, and by doing so he made clear his embeddedness in a scene where the names of those individuals were meaningful.

"One's Own Room," from *Wingspan*, was the next tune that the band played. It started as a feature for Goods. During his opening solo he quoted from not only the playing but also the style of Charles Mingus by playing phrases that the latter might have played had he been the bassist on this gig. Likewise, Goods played some strummed passages, one of which sounded melodically like the theme from the 1970s film *Love Story*. A few audience members laughed at the presumed reference. When the rest of the ensemble entered playing the tune's melody and form, Hart was playing soprano saxophone; Reedus was playing with brushes rather than sticks; and Goods was playing an ostinato. Miller took the first solo. At times he played dissonant pitches and clusters that caused me to wince, but he always resolved them in refreshing ways. Following a drum cue played by Reedus, the band increased the tempo slightly, while the rhythmic density of the accompaniment increased markedly. Goods seemed to be stretching, contracting, varying, and manipulating the ostinato. The texture definitely seemed as though it were heading out, far out. The metronomic pulse seemed to be getting lost or at least harder to locate in the thicket of activity. Reedus switched to drum rods for more timbrally complex, slightly louder attacks. Miller verbally cued Nelson, who was standing next to the stage, to return for his solo.

In a perhaps tongue-in-cheek manner, Nelson turned the vibrato controls on his vibraphone to their maximum setting for a "spacey"-sounding effect, presumably to join the out voyage upon which the rest of the band had already embarked. This portion of his solo and of the accompaniment seemed completely free from the form articulated at the beginning of the tune and throughout Miller's solo. Then, without warning, the form returned. Reedus switched to his crash cymbal and started articulating a clear and regular pulse. Nelson again started playing repetitive figures. Miller supported him with complementary riffs based on tone clusters. Hart followed Nelson, starting his solo with sustained tones and phrases reminiscent of John Coltrane's "The Father, Son, and the Holy Ghost."[66] His opening lowered the intensity level, focusing attention on his solo as distinct from, rather than as a continuation of, Nelson's. Hart soon started playing more angular lines, with wide, disjunct leaps. Miller accompanied him by playing descending arpeggios at low volume. By the fourth chorus, Hart's melodic lines were becoming more conjunct and lyrical. I suspected he might again play disjunct, out lines, because the density of the accompaniment started to increase at this point. Paradoxically, Reedus, while increasing density, *decreased* dynamics by switching back to brushes. Afterward, Hart confirmed my expectations by starting to screech and squeak. When it seemed that he was about to abandon playing discrete pitches altogether, he lowered his head and played one long, sustained pitch, perhaps using circular breathing. He slowly decreased the pitch's volume—so slowly, in fact, that many of us in the audience were not certain when it passed out of audibility. We, therefore, did not applaud the end of his solo. I was waiting for the visual confirmation that would come when he raised his head, which he did not do until Miller, with an exaggerated cadence, cued the band to play the head-out. In the song's coda, Hart again assumed solo duties, at one point quoting "Papa Was a Rollin' Stone."[67] Reedus and I exchanged smiles after hearing Hart's quotation.

After another tune, the set ended. I then introduced Tucker to Hart. Hart told Tucker of his desire to return to school to study composition. Both Tucker and I complimented Hart on his playing during the set. He responded that our praise was premature, explaining that Miller's music was very difficult to play. When we asked him why, he responded that Miller's music was harmonically and structurally quite open: "You can't play bebop style on these tunes." Hart soon walked off to talk to some of the other musicians in attendance. Tucker and I talked for a few minutes about how impressed we both were with the performance, especially in comparison to what we had heard at the Vanguard right before. Tucker left soon afterward.

The performance on "One's Own Room" highlights additional aspects of the interactions that take place between performers and other participants in a musical event. Goods brought to and displayed in his opening feature his knowledge of the styles of other influential bass players as well as, perhaps, references to popular culture phenomena. Nelson's manipulation of the vibrato controls on his vibraphone might have been a timbral commentary on the shape and texture of the tune when he started his solo. Additionally, it might been an attempt to fit more clearly into the flow of the musical event. And Hart's solo, particularly its ending, revealed the degree to which visual cues, even when the form of a tune is apparent, were integral to the ways in and times at which audiences respond to musical events. When the aural information that would have definitively marked the end of his solo was unclear, we in the audience looked for a physical change in his posture. When that cue did not materialize, there was effectively no response. Lastly, Hart's playing on the coda brought another kind of referentiality to the performance. By quoting a hit song by the Temptations, he made a connection with any participants who recognized the reference, particularly those with any knowledge of African American popular musics from the 1970s. In addition, he made it possible for those who possessed such knowledge to feel a connection with each other as well, as evinced by my exchange of smiles with Reedus.

I stayed for the third set, during which the band played more material from *Wingspan*. After it ended, I talked more with James Williams about jazz education and how, as a Tennessee native, I had made my way to New York to study. I discussed similar issues with Reedus, talked with Hart and saxophonist Gary Bartz about audio and notation software for Macintosh computers, ate a piece of Reedus's birthday cake, and discussed romantic relationships with Hart and Goods. Through these and many other conversations, which lasted for nearly ninety minutes after the last note decayed, I understood again the degree to which connections made during a musical event can extend beyond that event, opening different avenues for communication about music and any of a number of other issues. In other words, shared experience can reinforce group awareness, making those who have simultaneously participated in a particular performance, for example, feel part of the same thing.

CHAPTER 8

Conclusion

The events analyzed in chapter 7 could be viewed exclusively in terms of the musical parameters preserved on a compact disc and capable of being transcribed into Western notation. Presenting a performance thus transcribed might privilege and perhaps encourage the analysis of the sounds in terms similar to those for Western concert music (see Seeger 1958, 186). Such analysis, although perhaps making one more aware of the rhythmic, melodic, and harmonic parameters of the musical event, would omit the kinds of interactions taking place prior to, within, and after the event that are equally constitutive of and contributory to its impact.

The meanings of jazz performance, however, have just as much to do with kinesic and proxemic factors in performance, with the roles of race/culture and memory/history in shaping musical performance, and with the importance of the scene and a blues aesthetic. In that sense, it is more accurate to see jazz's primary meanings as contextual, as process-oriented rather than the product-oriented. No musical sounds are meaningful outside the varied cultural, spatial, and temporal contexts that name and specify the forms that meanings can take. In those contexts, the understandings of event participants, resulting from their individual and collective interpretive moves and made evident through musical, visual, and verbal communication, allow the performances to become meaningful and powerful for them.

"What this music is really about," as the musicians and some scholars have stated, is making connections (see, e.g., Stanyek 2004). In that sense, there are three discernible but interrelated registers of meaning in jazz performance, three distinct ways in which performers might make connections with other participants in a musical event. In what we might term the most common register, participants see themselves as engaged in culturally important activity, thus reinforcing self-identified cultural or group identities. It is here that discourses about jazz performance as "art," "America's classical music," or as "African American music" are of the most importance. Performing, listening to, or otherwise supporting jazz becomes partially an act of patronage and preservation. Bruce Barth's description of European audiences' respect for jazz and their understanding of it as an American music and a black music resonates most profoundly in this register of shared understanding. Likewise, many of the analyses of jazz by previous scholars could be said to be motivated by this understanding of jazz's nature and role in American and world cultures. As I observed previously, however, this kind of understanding requires the least engagement with the scene or a blues aesthetic. It is the register in which extrinsic discourses hold considerably more sway in the evaluation of a musical event.

The second register is accessible through one's greater degree of engagement with the scene and a greater understanding of a blues aesthetic. It is in this register that, in addition to being considered a culturally important activity, a ritualized musical event is a potentially transcendent experience. Here, participants attribute meaning to or derive it from a musical event through engagement with the ways in which performers negotiate the frames around jazz performance, through the ways in which they play with its ritualized structures and constraints. One here interprets a musical event by attending to musical sound and performer-performer and performer-audience interaction in addition to the history of the music, the scene, and individual performers, seeing all of these items as means to an end, as ingredients, if you will, in an improvised recipe. In other words, participants ideally understand the music through their knowledge of the scene and an aesthetic, and by deploying that knowledge participants might take the music, or follow it, to the next level.

In the third register, understanding a musical event as both culturally important and potentially transcendent, participants see an event as a metaphoric expression of a way to negotiate living, as a form of aesthetic "equipment for living." Engagement with the scene and an aesthetic, with the ritualized nature of performance, becomes a way of relating to the social world. Jazz, in this register, can be likened to a "lifestyle."

Antonio Hart says that he learned this aspect of meaning from older musicians:

> What I've learned from all those cats, man, is to love music. And to take it very seriously, but to have fun at the same time. That's it. Music is a lifestyle. Jazz is a lifestyle. It's a very serious music, a very intense music that you have to really love, and you can only get to a certain level, a high level, transcending the technique and all that stuff, you can only get to that spiritual element when you really love it and you devote your life to it, you know. It takes a long time to get to that. And all the people that I've played with, for the most part, have transcended to that next level. The masters . . . (Hart 1995)[1]

Their attention to individual sound, to mastering a number of performative parameters, to what is brought to the music, to what others bring to it, and to going to the next level reveal that the music, for them, implicates all three registers: cultural importance, transcendent experience, and daily living. As Redman says, the point is not to boggle the mind but to enrich the spirit, to make a connection with the varied participants in an event. As such, being able to categorize and describe the interactions of a performance as I have attempted to do here is subordinate to going through the process and actively participating in the event: being able to recognize the kinds of interactions, to understand the kinds of negotiations taking place, and to see them as the transcendence of the circumstances or frames that enclose performative activity.

The interaction between Pierce, Wilson, Lockwood, and Israel on "J's Rhythm Song" shows how in situations of extremely high ambiguity, attention to one's surroundings and a willingness to lead as well as to follow can produce astonishing results. By bringing their own sensibilities into the performance but being open to those of other musicians, the performers created something distinctive. They did so, however, in the context of a recording session, through verbal and visual communication with each other and other participants, and through negotiations with musical structure and their respective performing histories. The leader of the session, Williams, deserves a great deal of credit, for his choice of musicians, the setting, and the improvisational framework fostered a situation that demanded such work from the four musicians discussed. One might reasonably connect the musical negotiations here to the kinds of improvisation within ambiguous situations one faces in daily life.

Likewise, Wilson's recording of "Perdido" is an example of a different way of negotiating a performing situation and, by extension, daily living. Indeed, it brings to life Ralph Ellison's comments about each improvisation expressing one's identity as an individual, a member of a collectivity, and a link in the chain of tradition: "True jazz is an art of individual assertion within and against the group. Each true jazz moment . . . springs from a contest in which each artist challenges all the rest; each solo flight, or improvisation, represents . . . a definition of his identity: as individual, as member of a collectivity and as a link in the chain of tradition. Thus because jazz finds its very life in an endless improvisation on traditional materials, the jazzman must lose his identity even as he finds it" (Ellison 1964d, 234). Each performer brings a set of skills and musical preferences to the recording. Moreover, each partakes of a collective history and understanding shaped through accumulated mutual interactions. Additionally, links to the history of the music are encoded not just in terms of performance practice but in explicit references to previously recorded material by the Duke Ellington Orchestra. In a manner different from the interactions on "J's Rhythm Song," this recording shows the performers taking the materials at hand—space, time, tune, and form—and doing something creative and engaging with them, through rearranging structural elements and listening intently as they perform, allowing themselves to play over the barlines, to play with metric patterns and timbral shadings, and to send out expressive, well-placed calls that, in turn, receive similarly well-placed responses. The exemplary way in which the musicians perform and interact here recalls Feld's emphasis on the importance of "social experience, background, skill, desire and necessity" in discerning musical meaning (1994b, 84). One might fruitfully see those factors as essential qualities not only in the interpretation of meaning but also in the processes of performing and interacting: performance, process, and meaning are inextricably linked. And those same factors, deployed in different contexts, might be seen as important aspects of the ways in which individuals negotiate daily life.

In the Bernstein Quartet's performance of "Will You Still Be Mine?" interaction proceeds on multiple levels. In addition to the localized calls and responses, there is also a triple-pulse figure being taken up by each of the performers, being used as an element in their improvisations as well as an invitation to hook up. As in the Wilson example, the previous interactions of the performers with each other condition the event as well. Mehldau, McBride, and Hutchinson achieve a level of empathy and interactivity possible perhaps only because of their prior association with each other. The ways in which they obscure the form of the tune, particularly through blurring the distinction between the B and A3 sections in the second and third choruses of Mehldau's solo, effectively changing the form of the tune, are indicative of that level of empathy.

This example speaks to the way in which performative transformation of structure and form can metaphorically open space for transformative negotiations with the structures that surround our daily activities.

The Joshua Redman Quartet's performance of "Herbs and Roots," "Wait No Longer," and especially "My One and Only Love" also illustrate the degree to which what is brought to a performance can have a profound impact on its progress. This group did not have the same kind of collective history that the others did, but in a relatively short period of time they were able to develop, through hard work and their own individual skills, the ability to play well and interactively as a unit. In particular, Martin, Thomas, and Blade revealed that they could play effectively with the different parameters of a tune, dramatically departing from and returning to the metric framework, responding interactively and supportively to each other and to Redman. As an observer at their performance I also noticed how impressed they were with each other (for example, when Thomas at one point pulled back his chin to approvingly acknowledge that Martin was playing something "different" that was not, as Bruce Barth would say, "a generic rehashing" of something that had gone before). Moreover, the response of the youthful, presumably less knowledgeable audience revealed the kinds of clashes that might occur when different aesthetic frameworks are used to evaluate musical performance. Redman in particular seemed at once pleased with and troubled by the audience's response: glad for their enthusiasm, but cognizant of how a critic like Watrous might interpret his role in generating it.

The comparison of sets by Kenny Barron's quartet and Mulgrew Miller's Wingspan is instructive as well about the interlocked roles of scene-based interaction founded on a blues aesthetic and the negotiation of musical performance. Whereas the Barron performance failed to make an impact on at least two of the non-performing participants, the Miller performance was immediately and noticeably different. The musicians performing with Miller were interacting positively and sympathetically with one another and the audience, expressing their enjoyment in the process of performing. They brought into the performance frame their varied and previous interactions on the scene and their understanding of jazz performance, as well as a knowledge of an engagement with other musical styles. They seemed focused on making connections with each other as well as with the audience through their negotiation of the formal, timbral, harmonic, and dynamic aspects of the performance. And, in some ways, that connection extended beyond the actual sounds of the musical event.

Performances like these become engaging through close listening and observation on a participant's part. Through interpreting the varied aspects of the flow of a musical event; relating them to previous events, to other aspects of the same performance, and to different aspects of the setting; and seeking (and finding) confirmation of resultant interpretations with other participants, individuals engaged with a musical event develop sometimes shared understandings of what is significant or compelling in it. Without being able to characterize or classify, for example, the precise form, if any, manipulated in "J's Rhythm Song," or the varied interactions taking place in "Perdido," "Will You Still Be Mine?," "My One and Only Love," or "One's Own Room," it might still be possible for participants to recognize them as exemplary, culturally important, and potentially transcendent performances. Each of them takes on these meanings through their connections to other events, in other times and places, and their ability to be compared (positively) with them. The sense of awe such performances generated in listeners and performers alike has the potential to become transformative through performance's capacities to draw actively engaged participants into its flows. Once inside those flows, it becomes possible for them to see new ways of understanding, manipulating, and mastering the materials, situations, and constraints presented to them in performance and daily life. Redman speaks of this possibility, noting the potential for performing with other musicians to make one a better, "more mature" musician and person. Antonio Hart speaks of jazz as a way of living, a view that has parallels in one of the chapter headings of Berliner's *Thinking in Jazz* (1994). And at least in part, these attitudes might be seen as a product of jazz's connection to African American religious traditions and patterns of response in addition to their relationships to other traditions and patterns. Those who come to the musical event "ready to receive" derive a form of spiritual nourishment from their engagement with performance.

Meaning in jazz performance, as noted in chapters 5 and 6, is constructed primarily via (engagement with) performance and the shared understandings of participants in the scene, the criteria of a blues aesthetic, and the musical events all of them frame. That those understandings are shared is evident in the ways in which performers surprise each other with fresh responses to sometimes overfamiliar situations. Their commonalities are stressed as well by the pleasant moments of hookup or synchrony between performers and between them and other participants. The Redman example, alongside the anecdotes related by Bruce Barth and Sam Newsome in chapter 5, adds another dimension. It is possible for the non-performing participants to bring a different set of evaluative criteria to a musical event. They can share understandings of performance that diverge wildly from those of the musicians or more regular scene participants. A musical event can, obviously, be meaningful to non-regulars, but the connections they have to the performance are necessarily of a different order than those of long-term participants. They conceivably have fewer points of contact with the concepts and interactions that motivate and contribute to the musical event. Although they may relate to high notes, repetition, or "soulfulness," they might also miss references to other events or performers. But with continued engagement, they may come to understand as well as to modify or replace the aesthetic.

Meaning in jazz performance is constructed through the process of participants connecting events, contexts, and procedures—musical and otherwise—to each other. It results, as well, from the intermusical and metaphoric transferences made by performers and other participants in active processes of listening and performance. Neither completely internal nor freely and wildly external, these meanings are conditioned by culture, history, context, and interaction. What jazz is about is showing each individual willing to listen, to participate, and/or to perform how to proceed from situations where one is mastered by externalities to situations where one can bring something to those externalities and transform his or her relation to them. One scene participant whom I frequently saw at musical events explained, as we discussed an upcoming performance by the Kenny Garrett Quartet, that hearing and understanding the way Garrett interacted with the musicians in his ensemble and negotiated and manipulated the different parameters of a performance always reinvigorated and inspired her. She saw an analogy between her understanding of his ability to play with and within the frames that surround his performance and her ability to negotiate the frames that constitute her daily life. In an alteration of the phrase's intent, one might say that jazz has helped her to see life as a series of "regulated improvisations" (Bourdieu 1977, 78) that she must confront creatively. Although individuals may not radically alter those structures or situations in confronting them, they hopefully find ways to exist more comfortably within those constraints. If not, there's always the next chorus.

Several different concerns and issues were the focus of the previous chapters: the meaning of the term "jazz"; scholarly motivations toward and approaches to its study and analysis; the utility of ethnomusicological methods in such investigation; the relative valences of terms like race, culture, history, and memory; the nature of the socially constructed world known as the "scene"; the normative and evaluative criteria knowledgeable participants draw on in performing and evaluating performance; and the implications of the foregoing for the analysis of performance. These concerns and issues were initially a product of my interest in and curiosity about jazz performance. In seeking information about jazz in both popular and scholarly writing, however, I was continually reminded that my questions were different from those of many previous writers and researchers. Consequently, my personal interest became a scholarly one, particularly as deeper investigation revealed a gap between the scholarly record and the experiential accounts of musicians and other jazz scene participants with whom I came into contact.

Numerous meanings have been attributed to jazz in the past, and many more, I'm certain, will be in the future. Although one might be able to make a case for its being pure, direct emotional expression or protest against injustice and oppression, such attributions limit the scope and compass of jazz performance as knowledgeable scene participants understand it. The foregoing should make clear, however, that some scholarly analysts have missed or not been concerned with one of the major findings of this project: jazz performance is not, and cannot, simply be about itself. Through a blues aesthetic and ritualized performances, some of the shared viewpoints and strategies developed by African Americans for the negotiation of daily living engender a musical counterpart that feeds back into them. By stressing individual contributions, collective cooperation, and ways of negotiating structure, jazz performers and their performances metaphorically open a space for seeing life differently. No single performance or even group of performances ultimately can escape the contexts that frame them, but the purpose of ritualized practice is to engage those conditions repeatedly and creatively.

In the same way that we might understand musical styles as changing over time, it is to be expected that the contours of the scene and criteria of a blues aesthetic may change as well. The possibility and inevitability of such change suggest that there might be alterations in the way that the meanings of jazz performance are interpreted.[2] Particularly as new musicians and audiences bring to the music different ideas about musical performance, as successive generations of musicians become "masters," and as the configuration of the scene changes, the levels of meaning and shared understanding discussed here may give way to others. And such change, of course, is a not a novel function of this historical moment. It has been characteristic of the music from its earliest and haziest beginnings.

In perhaps twenty years, the majority of musicians performing jazz, those who will then be considered masters, will have come to the music through conservatory education rather than the apprenticeship system that primarily trained today's masters. Moreover, many of them will have had much more acquaintance with various styles of post-1960 popular music than with jazz in their formative years. Their audiences, likewise, will be more likely to have learned of jazz through college courses and after similar degrees of engagement with and understanding of rock, funk, hip-hop, reggae, salsa, merengue, and any of a number of other kinds of music. One might only guess what kind of impact such shifts will have.

Moreover, as educational institutions, performance venues, and the recording industry adjust to larger changes in the cultural and economic climate of the United States and the world, our understandings of jazz may undergo a "paradigm shift" (Kuhn 1996). Indeed, after reaching a ten-year peak in 1991, jazz record sales have steadily fallen, perhaps indicating a decline in the number of consumers interested in purchasing jazz recordings. More accurately, though, the sales decline may be a function of the increasing specialization of the jazz audience. On one hand, this audience includes the connoisseurs and aficionados who might tap into jazz's three varied registers of meaning. On the other, this audience is becoming increasingly restricted to those individuals with the cultural and educational capital to learn about jazz in college courses (or suburban high school music programs), to attend performances in nightclubs and concert halls, and to support the few remaining public radio affiliate stations that are its only "free" outlet.

Richard B. Woodward's observations (2001) suggest that the major record labels, if they remain in the business of recording jazz, will have to find different strategies to make it worth their investment. With most of them in the 1990s having switched to a style of portfolio management, the future of jazz on major labels appears dim. As of early 2001, Atlantic Records had eliminated its jazz program altogether; RCA released all of its jazz artists save Dave Douglas from their contracts and turned administration of his recordings over to its popular music division; and Columbia Records fired its jazz staff and released most of its artists, including Wynton Marsalis, from their contracts, choosing to focus more attention on artists whose connections to paradigmatic jazz performance (Richard Bona and Angelique Kidjo, for example) is more tangential. In subsequent years, Warner Brothers eliminated its jazz division as well, with its two most successful artists, Brad Mehldau and

Joshua Redman, later being signed by Nonesuch. Only Blue Note and Verve remain healthy, buoyed in part by the success of singers such as Cassandra Wilson, Norah Jones, Jamie Cullum, and Diana Krall and in part by the signing of artists with more tangential connections to jazz, such as Al Green and Van Morrison. Even independent entities like Concord Records and Mack Avenue maintain financial stability by signing artists across genres rather than focusing strictly on conventional jazz performers. Again, one can only speculate on how the scene and the aesthetic will be affected by these events and responses. As time progresses, however, attention to the relationships between the agents and institutions constituting the scene and to the interactions between the various discourses shaping a blues aesthetic will remain the most fruitful means of tracking jazz's transformation. As another ethnomusicologist might say, such attention would keep the researcher focused on the ways in which jazz continues to be historically constructed, socially maintained, and individually created and experienced (Rice 1987).

Such investigation, suggested implicitly and explicitly in the work of a number of recent scholars, has implications for the ways in which we study all forms of music. The concept of a scene, for example, is another way of construing the meaning of "context." But as a contextual frame, the scene does not merely provide background for the "real" action taking place in the foreground. It has an interactive relationship to that foreground: it constitutes and is dialectically constituted by it (Jameson 1971, 10–11). The scene, therefore, is not a static context (though one might reasonably question whether any context is static). Indeed, following the autumn of 2008, the point at which the neoliberal policies that emerged in the late 1970s (Harvey 2005) led, by some accounts, to a crisis of global proportions, the kinds of policies that have made urban areas increasingly inhospitable for jazz performers and venue owners during those same years may now have to be reexamined. Whether municipalities' recovery strategies result in more "bloody legislation" of the kind that prevailed in New York City beginning in the 1970s (Sites 2003) is an open question. Likewise, a blues aesthetic is not a fixed and immutable normative and evaluative framework. In its expression by musicians, it is open, allowing for and expecting interaction with other discourses, with whatever is brought to it and might shape or be shaped by it.

The broader implications of that brief catalog of possible changes suggest ways of dealing with how musics take on meaning in specific places at specific times. In many cases, some scholars of Western concert music, despite their having developed more expansive outlooks in the last few decades, still see context as something that helps to explain the music itself rather than as something inseparable from it. More studies along the lines of Henry Kingsbury's *Music, Talent, and Performance* (1988) and Georgina Born's *Rationalizing Culture* (1995) would illuminate the ways in which composers and performers of and audiences for Western concert music come to understand the meanings of that music and the ways in which those understandings are transmitted, negotiated, and transformed. Those two books reveal the degree to which "high" art's meanings, contexts, and discourses cannot themselves be taken for granted. It would be refreshing as well to have more studies that integrated ethnographic insights on the construction of classical music scenes and aesthetic frameworks into understandings of its meanings rather than the score- and work-centric studies that continue to characterize much published research. The same is true for research on various popular musics.

In any event, our understandings of jazz or any of a number of other musics can only be enhanced by exploring them through attention to musical events, their contexts, and the concepts that inform their performance, evaluation, and interpretation. Through such examination and exploration of music, we may come to a better understanding of how different social actors construct and negotiate meaning in music, how they can find that it so powerfully speaks to them and articulates a sense of who they are. In the end, one hopes, we may come closer to understanding what the music is really about.

Glossary

ARTIST BIOGRAPHY a short informational sheet or group of sheets sent by record labels or publicity firms to critics, radio stations, and other media outlets to publicize a new recording or a particular musician.

ARTISTS AND REPERTOIRE (also A&R) the division of a record company focused on signing musicians and supervising their recordings.

BACKGROUND a rifflike ensemble figure that functions as an accompaniment for a solo or a portion thereof.

BASS DRUM the lowest-pitched drum in a drum kit, played with the right foot by means of a foot pedal.

BEHIND (the beat) indicates attacks that come rhythmically a fraction of a second after a perceived metronomic pulse.

BLEEDING a situation in which a sound, in a recording studio, is picked up by a microphone intended to capture other, isolated sounds.

BLOW to take a solo; to play behind/with a soloist as if one were taking a solo.

BOTTOM the last section or measures of a tune's form.

BREAK a section, generally in the final measures of a form, in which all instrumentalists, save a soloist, cease playing for a specified number of measures. The other performers rejoin the soloist at the location in the form where they would have been had they *not* ceased playing.

BREAKPOINT a point in a form that marks the separation of sections or choruses from each other.

BRIDGE the section of a tune's form that presents a contrasting key area, sometimes with changes in texture, tempo, and/or feel, usually eight measures in length or some multiple thereof. In an AABA form, the bridge would be the B section.

BUILD to move gradually toward a climax. Building can be done in a variety of ways, none of which are mutually exclusive, such as decreasing the amount of space, increasing volume, thickening texture, or increasing density.

CAT musician; more generally, a scene participant.

CHANGES harmonic progression for a given tune.

CHANNEL see *bridge.*

CHORUS (1) one cycle through a tune's form.

CHORUS (2) audio effect produced by splitting an electronic or digital audio signal into two streams, detuning and slightly delaying one before recombining it with the unaltered stream.

COMP to provide rhythmic/harmonic/textural accompaniment.

CONCEPT the general principle undergirding a particular recording or group of compositions by a given musician. It can also refer to an individual's approach to performing.

CRASH CYMBAL a usually large cymbal in drum kit, named onomatopoeically for the loud "crashing" sound it makes when struck with force. It is usually struck for emphasis.

DENSITY the number of sounding events occurring per unit time; the number of sounding events occurring in a given moment.

DOUBLE BOOK to agree to do multiple engagements or recording sessions occurring simultaneously, e.g., to agree to play two gigs on a certain day, both of which begin at 9 PM.

DOUBLE-STOP on a stringed instrument, the act of playing two pitches simultaneously.

EFFECTS electronic devices for altering sound, such as reverb and chorus.

EMBOUCHURE for brass and wind instruments, the positioning of the mouth, lips, tongue, and/or teeth with respect to an instrument's mouthpiece.

FEEL the rhythmic/accentual/textural patterning of or approach to playing a tune or section thereof based on conventional understanding. Several different feels exist; among the most common named ones are Latin, bossa, samba, ballad, two-beat, and swing, each of which carries with it expectations about how rhythm section members (piano, bass, and drums, in particular) are supposed to play. Indeed, some feels are named for particularly distinctive players, especially drummers: Art Blakey, Elvin Jones, Roy Haynes.

FLOW the general sensation or perception of continuous forward motion or drive generated in a musical performance, analogous to swing, but more inclusive, engendered by rhythmic, harmonic, dynamic, and textural means. References to "getting into the flow," like stepping into a river, are frequent. Also, to create and maintain such a sensation or perception.

FORM the harmonic/textural/rhythmic structure that is the basis for improvisation. Forms generally consist of a specific number of measures divided into sections that are usually multiples of four or eight measures in length. Frequently used forms are twelve, sixteen, and thirty-two bars in length. Ones based on variants of the twelve-bar blues and on the structures of popular standards ("I Got Rhythm," "Cherokee") are used often as well. (See also *intro, bridge, tag, vamp.*)

FREE denotes situations in which musicians perform without a pre-established agreement regarding harmony, meter, tempo, or other musical parameters.

FREE BOP denotes styles of performance that partake of both the procedures and practices of "free jazz" as well as bebop-derived jazz styles.

HANG to be present at live performances, at recording sessions, and in other places where musicians and other scene participants gather. In its noun form, the term denotes a particular kind of hanging or hanging in a particular place, e.g., the 2 AM set at Bradley's can be considered a "late hang."

HEAD the portion of a tune consisting, usually, of the complete statement of the form and attendant melodies along with intros, vamps, and sendoffs, i.e., the portion of a tune that precedes the first solo statement. When played at the beginning of a tune, it can be referred to as the head-in; correspondingly, at the end of tune it is the head-out or, more frequently, the out-chorus. In some cases the entire form will be played more than once during the head.

HI-HAT a set of cymbals with their concave sides facing each other. They may be struck or opened and closed by means of a foot pedal. When open they do not touch each other; when closed, one rests atop the other.

HIT note or chord in the head of a tune that members of a performing ensemble are to accentuate, either by increasing volume, changing timbre, or some other means; to start a set or performance.

HOOK UP describes what happens when two or more ensemble members achieve a level of synchrony that creates or contributes to flow; also, a situation in which ensemble members come together spontaneously in playing a riff or accentual pattern. It also refers to a successful, i.e., swinging or flowing, bass player and drummer combination, i.e., a "Sam Jones–Louis Hayes hookup."

IN THE POCKET describes a particular rhythmic feel that is behind the beat and perceived as relaxed.

INSERT at a recording session, a section or group of measures recorded to be mixed into an otherwise complete take to eliminate mistakes.

INTRO an introductory figure or section that precedes the top of a tune's form, usually omitted during solos; can be used as an interlude between solos.

KEEPING TIME when a drummer plays standard patterns, particularly on the hi-hat and ride cymbal, that unambiguously delineate a tune's metric framework. The pattern ♩, ♪♪, ♩, ♪♪, played on the ride cymbal, is the most common time-keeping pattern.

LAY BACK to play behind the beat.

LAY OUT when a particular musician, generally a pianist, chooses or is instructed not to play at time when he or she would typically be fulfilling an accompanimental role. Pianists often lay out to give soloists greater freedom in their choice of pitches.

LINER NOTES prose or poetry, in addition to recording and legal information and song listings, included with the packaging of a commercially released recording. Usually such notes are written by a critic, a record producer, or a musician, particularly the one who leads the group on a given recording.

LOCK UP to hook up.

LOOSE indicates a noticeable degree of rhythmic asynchronization; can be used evaluatively to indicate relaxed (positive) or sloppy (negative) performance.

MIXING the process of arranging and otherwise manipulating the tracks captured on tape after a recording session. Dynamic levels as well as effects and stereo positioning are decided upon at this stage. This is the last stage prior to the making of a master for mass reproduction.

ON TOP OF (the beat) indicates attacks that come rhythmically a fraction of a second before a perceived metronomic pulse.

OUT ways of manipulating musical or performative parameters that go far beyond conventional or idiomatic practice; can also be applied to unconventional behavior or situations.

OUT-CHORUS see *head.*

PLAY OVER BARLINES to play phrases or figures whose beginnings or endings do not coincide with the beginnings or endings of structural units, i.e., whose beginnings or endings come in places that are structurally unexpected.

QUIET POLICY policy instituted in many New York City performance venues that requires that patrons restrict their conversation in order not to interfere with the ability of other patrons to hear the music.

QUOTE to play a melodic, rhythmic, or textural fragment clearly recognizable to knowledgeable listeners as coming from another (pre-existing) source, either another tune or the work of another musician.

REGISTER a segment of an instrument's range. Generally, reference is made to an instrument's low, middle, and high registers.

REVERB an electronic or digital effect that makes a sound signal seem as though it is coming from a large room, concert hall, or some other space by giving it a resonance associated with sounds produced in such spaces.

RIDE CYMBAL the portion of drum kit on which the drummer "keeps time." More resonant than the crash cymbal and used for subtler accents, this cymbal sometimes has holes with loosely placed rivets in them to add a buzzing sound when struck, in which case they are called "sizzle cymbals."

RIFF a rhythmically propulsive harmonic or melodic figure that is often repeated (and altered accordingly) over changing harmonies. It can also be played as a background figure. In verb form, it denotes playing such a melodic or harmonic figure.

RUN-THROUGH the act of playing the head of a tune in its entirety prior to recording it to ensure that all members of an ensemble understand what they are to play, when, and how.

SCENE the socially constructed world within which jazz performance occurs and is enabled. It is an interlocking network whose nodes are musicians, audiences, educational institutions, performance venues, the recording industry, and print, radio, and television media.

SEND-OFF a rifflike ensemble passage that functions as an introductory figure for a solo.

SEQUENCING the ordering of tunes on a commercially released recording.

SET one of several performances in a night club. Each evening of an engagement consists of two to three sets averaging from forty-five to sixty minutes.

SIGN a musician or group's entering an exclusive contractual agreement with a record label.

SOUND a musician's characteristic timbre or approach to dealing with harmony, melody, rhythm, or other musical parameters in performance.

SPACE refers to the density in overall texture or in the work of a specific member of a performing ensemble. It sometimes refers to levels of harmonic complexity or ambiguity (e.g., whether a musician plays ambiguous chord voicings), which determines, for example, whether a particular pianist leaves space for a soloist to explore. One might say of a pianist that "He leaves a lot of space for me to work in."

STRAIGHT-AHEAD denotes jazz styles that operate primarily within the conventions of bebop and bop-derived harmonic, rhythmic, compositional, and improvisational practices. Improvisations are generally based on forms with established metric and harmonic (or modal) frameworks.

SUBSTITUTION a chord or harmony that can be used in place of another chord or harmony without changing the basic function and direction of a harmonic progression.

TAG a repeated cadential figure that usually follows or extends the head-out and allows for additional improvising at the end of a tune.

TAKE IT DOWN the opposite of build. Frequently, an ensemble will decrease levels of density and volume, thin out texture, and increase the amount of space in the transition from one solo to another.

TAKE one complete or partially complete (because aborted) recording of a tune during a recording session.

TAP a drummer's characteristic way of playing the ride cymbal and its associated time-keeping rhythms.

TIGHT indicates a high degree of rhythmic synchronization; the opposite of loose. Its evaluative use is always positive.

TOP the first measure of a tune's form or the first measure of a section.

TRADE to alternate passages featuring different ensemble members in fixed units, usually four or eight measures, e.g., "to trade fours." In trading fours, however, a soloist always ends his or her phrases on the first beat of a fifth measure.

TUNE a composition, or a composition as performed by an ensemble, with a distinct identity.

VAMP repeated rhythmic/harmonic figure, generally two to four measures in length and based on limited harmonic material, that can serve as interlude material or as introductory material. Also, to play a vamp, or to improvise a vamp as an introductory or closing figure.

VIBE short for "vibration"; atmosphere or mood. Also, as a transitive verb it denotes projecting ill will toward someone else or acting in a manner that makes such an interpretation possible, for example, "I thought he was vibing me."

VOICING a particular arrangement of pitches in a particular harmony. For example, one might voice a D-minor seventh chord, from lowest to highest pitch, in the following two ways: D–C–F–A or D–A–C–F. Numerous other voicings are also possible.

WALKING BASS a pattern where a (usually low-pitched) instrument plays primarily quarter notes and plays a different pitch on each quarter beat.

Appendix: Excerpt from an Interview with Steve Wilson

2 March 1995

Wilson: I guess just, um, as a, as a listener, what do you, when you go to hear music, when you go to hear a jazz performance, what are you . . . do you bring anything to the performance? Do you . . . What, what do you bring to the performance?

Jackson: What I bring in is, um—I was talking to Bruce [Barth] about this before, um—like when I was, when I was in school, when I was coming up, you know, I was listening to a lot of funk and a lot of soul, um, a lot British rock music, um, at least in the early part of the '80s 'cause, you know, I was born like, I was born in 1969. And so, I had all those things, and I was playing in bands and stuff like that, playing guitar. Um, and I didn't start listening to jazz until I was about fifteen or sixteen. My grandfather brought me Charlie Parker, Charlie Christian, Thelonious Monk, you know. So I started getting into those things then. And, like all throughout college, you know, I was trying to learn how to play and do all this other stuff, so I bring to it basically, like, um, you know, having a bunch of favorite records, a lot of favorite performers, um, you know, like all those '50s Miles Davis recordings, '60s Miles Davis recordings, John Coltrane, um, um, and then, you know, Horace Silver, Art Blakey, um, *a lot* of listening to Duke Ellington and Count Basie. And so basically knowing the history of the music and knowing a lot of performers and also knowing people who are active now.

So when I come to a performance, I'm listening to . . . First I'm listening for like the heads for the compositions. If it's material I don't know, originals, you know, just listening for the way the compositions are put together, you know. So like when I saw Stephen Scott the other night, he was playing some really heavy compositions, you know. And I dug the fact that he had all these compositions with like all these metric changes, tempo changes, you know, and this other stuff that *worked*. You know, it didn't sound, you know, it didn't sound, um, like "Okay, well, because I can do this, let me do this," you know. So that's the first thing I listen for.

And then after that, um, when, um, you know, when the solos start, um, you know, what kinds of note choices are being made, you know, by the person who's soloing? What's the bass player doing? What's the drummer doing? So basically, what's the whole band situation? I don't know whether every listener comes in with that. But what I'm really li . . . I'm listening most of the time for like, you know, for the *groove*, for the interaction between the musicians, um, and, and for the *shape* of a solo. So that like, um, you know, where does it go? Um, you know, a lot of people start off with short phrases, you know. You know, you start off with short phrases, and you, you sort of play around with them, and then, you know, things get, you know, they get more lyrical, you start to peak, you know, and like the band increases intensity and response, and you know, so that's the kind of stuff that I listen for to see whether it happens.

And if that doesn't happen, then, you know, what does? And why does it work? Or why doesn't it work?

W: Do you ever get the same, um, the same *feelings* from some of these performances that you would get, say, from, um, some of the other types of music that you would listen to? You know, like some of the old funk stuff, you know, or some other kind of . . . In other words, are you moved in the same way?

J: Yeah, actually that's, that's a really good question because, um, this, um, a friend of mine called me yesterday 'cause she's been listening to, um, to the, to 98.7 Kiss[-FM] a lot lately . . .

W: So have I.

J: Yeah, and they're playing all the old stuff on there. And she said, you know, she said, "I heard this song," said it was a live song . . . she didn't listen to a lot of radio when she was coming up. So like all these songs I know from coming up, she, you know, had never really heard before. And she said, um, "I heard this song with this man singing about like breaking up with some woman, and, you know, it just sounds like he really means it, and he wants her to come back." And I'm like, "Well, how does the song go?" And, um, she says, you know, "It's something about some kind of lover, or, you know, and somebody being far away." And I said, "All right. Hold on a second." So I go and get this Marvin Gaye CD and put the song "Distant Lover" on and ask her if that's the song.[1] And she said, you know, "Yeah, that's it! That's it!" And so, um, so that, I told, you know, whenever I start playing that stuff and she's around, or, you know, I'm talking to her, she always just starts laughing at me 'cause I get so excited about it. 'Cause I'm like, you know, "Well, you got to remember that this song is about this. And listen to the groove, and listen to this, and listen to that."

So, I mean, I think that basically there're all different kinds of grooves, but there're all different kinds of music that touch me in different ways. So, I get things from listening to Marvin Gaye, from listening to Al Green, from listening to Bob Marley, you know, from listening to Stevie Wonder, you know. I mean, you know.

W: Absolutely.

J: So, you know, I try to take everything in, and I, you know, come to, come to whatever I'm listening to, knowing, you know, knowing the history of whatever I'm coming to.

W: Yeah. Exactly, yeah. 'Cause, it's funny because I remember, um, um—and it could have been more of a preconception on my part—some of the, you know, well, it's funny because you don't find a lot of jazz musicians in general (maybe a little more so now in my generation) but you don't find a lot of jazz musicians that talk about a lot of other music, you know. Or at least I didn't, you know, prior to meeting some of the guys in my generation that I know. And, uh, I think—well, one thing I was gonna say was about Kenny Garrett, was, I think, in my opinion (and, uh, uh, this can be argued, I guess, one way or another), but in my opinion, Kenny Garrett is the most important musician of our generation. Because he's, um, really the first cat that's tying together all the traditions of black music, you know, in, within his, uh, sound and compass, you know. Um, I mean, I know Steve Coleman 'n' 'em have done a thing, you know, with M-BASE and, you know, doing the odd-meter funk thing, and I know they know tunes and all of that, you know, so that's been important, too. But I think if I were to choose any one individual . . . I mean, because, man, when Kenny plays *one note*—and we're back to this one note again—when he plays one note, you can hear [Johnny] Hodges, you can hear Maceo [Parker], you can hear Grover [Washington Jr.], you can hear Bird [Charlie Parker], I mean, of course . . . *in one note.* And he can play *one long note,* and you can hear all of that in his sound, you know. I mean, more, more than that, you, you hear Kenny Garrett, obviously and most importantly, but you can hear the progression and the history and how it got to . . . where he is. You can hear that in one note. And then when he starts playing all these other things, you know, I've heard Kenny, man, in, you know, in a lot of different contexts, you know, with Miles, his stuff, you know, Woody Shaw, Freddie Hubbard, Art Blakey, um, [snapping fingers and trying to remember], shoot, um, a Bobby Lyle record that's, that's been out for a little while, which is like some funk stuff, the last Al Jarreau record, and he always sounds like him, first of all. I mean, that's most important. He's like Wayne Shorter or Sonny Rollins, you know.

But, um, but, you know, I think it's really important now, in this day and age, that, especially us as young African Americans and African American musicians and artists, that we begin to, to tie this, to continue the continuum. You hear the whole continuum, you know, and that's what it should be. That's what the music should be, you know. Not just like, "Well, um, I'm gonna take the hippest stuff of this era and expound on that." I mean, that's all right, too, but, man, music, it didn't get to that . . . by that selective process. It's been a whole continuum, man, you know. From the time that, from the time that the drum left Africa, that was the start of the process. And I think that, you know, if we can keep that vision, you know . . .

J: Yeah, 'cause I mean, I think, I think stuff like that, I mean, that kind of vision is really important 'cause you realize that, like, like even, especially . . . I think that the early '70s, early or mid-'70s were such an important time . . .

W: Absolutely.

J: . . . because there were so many people—Stevie Wonder, included or maybe as a prime person, but even Maurice White—Earth, Wind, and Fire—you know all these people who are trying to, who are really trying to take in the whole compass of black music . . . and put that together, you know.

W: Yeah that's right. That's right. It's like, um, our, you know, we're talking about Marvin and we're probably both big Marvin fans, I remember telling a friend a couple of weeks ago, "Man," I said, "you should check out some of the stuff Marvin did for Motown when he was singing just tunes, standards," you know. He was like "What?!" I was like, "Yeah, Marvin wanted to be like Nat King Cole, you know. That was his thing, that was his dream, you know." As a matter of fact, I keep saying I'm gonna get that boxed set, you know, 'cause it's got all that stuff on there, you know. But I've seen like video of him singing that stuff, and, man, he is killing! Uh, uh, what's-his-name that sings "Little Green Apples," O.C. . . . . O.C. . . . .

J: "Smith"?

W: O.C. Smith.[2] 'Cause Kenny Washington played O.C. singing with some big band, Basie or somebody, and he was like, *shh,* in there, man! And that was the great thing about all of those, all of our musicians and artists, I think up until the '80s, somewhere we lost it. But, um, or with this next generation coming up (and I know that's a whole 'nother issue) but all of those people, man, were listening, you know, they were taking in everything, you know, and I think one thing that has changed with this generation, and, uh, for me, there's still a vacuum in terms of like the great vocalists and singers. Because I think that, uh, my own personal opinion is . . . one primary reason is that, uh, we aren't seeing these singers come through the church, you know. Like most of our singers, our great singers, always got their foundation in the church. Always.

So, um, and I think the other thing is that we've kind of let technology outsmart us in a way. That we've kinda lost control of it because I think it was wonderful in the '70s with, uh, like all the people you're talking about—Stevie [Wonder], George Duke, Maurice [White]—one of the wonderful things they did was to incorporate the synthesized sounds. But now when this technology took off, and people found out they didn't have to leave the house to make music, shh! I think that was the beginning of the downfall of R&B, you know. Because, uh, everybody stopped getting together, you know. Everybody stopped gathering together, either at church or on the corner or in the garage. And everybody started saying, "Check me out," you know. And, um, that's really sad, man. I don't think we've recovered from that. That's why I'm so glad Kiss is back on the air, man, 'cause you hear that music, man, and you hear the same *organic process* that you hear in jazz and classical music: people coming together, you know. This other stuff, you know, I really cannot get with it, man. I've given it a shot. I tune into videos from time to time [to] try to keep up with what's going on. I still, I do like Earth, Wind, and Fire's last record, *Millennium,*[3] I love that record. It took, took a while for it to hit . . .

J: Yeah, 'cause I still haven't gotten it yet, and I listened to it a couple of times, and you know, I was like, "Well, maybe . . ."

W: Yeah, it's not quite what we're used to. You don't get the same feeling, definitely. But there's a couple, there's a few tunes on there that are . . . slammin'. But, um, that to me is the key, man. You know, I just have not seen this thing on the R&B level, this same type of process. I mean, I know people talk about Boyz II Men all the time, and they're good. They're good, you know. I can't call myself a big fan, and in all fairness I haven't gone out and bought their records and checked 'em out. But I, I've heard them a few times. And I'm saying "Okay, okay. But, you know, give me the Spinners. Give me the Temptations." Because, you know, these cats, they could sing a cappella and not only sing root, third, and fifth, but they were singing sevenths and ninths, you know. And I saw the Spinners on Johnny Carson one time, man. These cats did "Route 66" a cappella; it was out of sight, man! Oh, my goodness! And you just don't get that same, I don't get that same feeling from, from, you know. Take 6, I love.

J: Yeah, I love Take 6. But I mean, I even think that like their records have become more and more produced as time has gone on. 'Cause I love that first record. The first record, to me, is the best one still. And it's gotten more slick as time, you know, has gone on. I mean, who's the other guy? I got into this argument with my brother when I went home for Christmas. We were riding around in the car listening to the radio and, um, and, uh, one of those guys from Jodeci redid Bobby Womack's song "If You Think You're Lonely Now."[4]

W: Aw, yeah, yeah, yeah.

J: And I was telling my brother how much I hated that, you know. And he said, "Man, you know, it's good. He's singing the song well." I'm like "Naw, man, he's just yellin' and screamin'!"

W: Right, right.

J: You know?

W: Right, yeah. It's just like the difference between Teddy Pendergrass and, uh, what's his name that was making a little run here? From the group . . . Uh, Johnny Gill, you know. I mean, you know, you listen to Pendergrass, man. Pendergrass. Now Pendergrass got his thing from Marvin Junior from the Dells, you know. And it was always within the context of cats that could *sing!* You know, that could really sing, could really hear, you know, and not just like go for house, you know. So, that's the difference, you know. So, like when you talk about that, yeah, I can relate. The same difference, man. Bobby Womack was there with . . . there with all those cats from Chicago, you know, coming up. So I mean, his thing is sincere, and it's original. Still. He still has the same voice. Absolutely, man. So, yeah, well that, that really answers a lot of stuff because, you know, sometimes I just wonder . . . I, I, and maybe you do, too. Specifically, and it's gotten to the point where, quite honestly, you know, I'm surprised, yet, um, enthused when I see young brothers and sisters come out to see jazz music, live music. 'Cause normally the only time you see 'em, it's somebody like yourself or another musician or if, if, uh, Branford or Wynton

[Marsalis] are playing at the Vanguard, then they come from *all over* the place, or if it's free at Grant's Tomb, then they just come out of holes in the ground, you know, and just like "Yeah!" you know. I mean, hell, you could put Kenny G down at the Vanguard, and I bet you the place would be 80 percent brothers and sisters.

J: Or when George Howard was down at the Blue Note a few weeks ago, I'm sure the place was packed. I didn't even go by there.

W: Yeah, you know what I mean? So, um, and, and not so much to bring Kenny G and George into it because they do what they do, you know, I mean, you know, whether we're with it or not is, is, you know, irrelevant, but, uh, I mean, it just . . . And I, and I often wonder, too, man, where, now how did they get to this point? 'Cause it's, it's more than just like "Man, I'm just glad to see them here," you know. "Yeah, they must be . . . They got into this thing some kind of way. I don't know how they got here, but I'm glad they're here," you know. Same kind of deal.

J: Yeah, 'cause I know one thing that's kind of encouraging to me, um, and I know that, I know some critics who are, uh, who would be put off by this, but I remember I was really encouraged when I went to see Roy [Hargrove], Roy playing down at the Vanguard back in maybe January of "94, must have been January of '94 'cause that was right around the time they were recording the *Tenors of Our Times* record, and, um, Sunday night, last set, um, and I don't think anybody came up to sit in, but, um, they were just, you know, they burned out. They were burned out from playing the whole week, and, um, Roy counts off the next tune. And Greg [Hutchinson] starts playing this funk, this funky thing on the drums. And I'm like "That sounds really familiar!" And then when I, I realized what it was right before Roy and, um, Ron Blake came in with the horn parts. They were playing "Knee Deep."[5]

W: Oh, um . . .

J: The Parliament-Funkadelic . . .

W: Yeah, yeah, yeah!

J: They were playing "Knee Deep," and, you know, it was cool to me that like, you know, after this, this set of like standards, you know, and all this other stuff, that they were playing that, but they were playing it with the same level of seriousness that they tried to approach everything else.

W: Right, exactly, yeah. I think, uh, we will probably see more of that. I know, um, I mean, I'm trying to bring some of that into my music, and . . .

J: Yeah, like recording "Everything Must Change" on your . . .[6]

W: Yeah, exactly, 'cause I've had eyes to do, to do that for a while, to bring all of these elements in. I mean, this is how I always thought about, when I get the opportunity to finally get a band together and when I get a chance to tour or something, I want to, like I want to use, uh, like Monte Croft. Monte and I talk about this because Monte covers a lot of territory. And, um, I would really like a band that could do both of that, both, both things. I shouldn't even say both things. I mean, just to tie that continuum together 'cause I think there's a way for it to be done. Definitely. So, uh, and you're hearing a few more musicians that kinda, they, they're giving out inklings of it here and there, you know. Granted it hasn't gone like the route of M-BASE where they've taken their thing and just sort of gone a whole different direction, you know, and it's really in your face. I dig that, too. I think we need that, you know. But, um, you know, I just, again I want to find a way of like, uh . . . Like when Kenny [Garrett] recorded "Someday We'll All Be Free,"[7] you know, the, uh, Donny Hathaway thing, you know. So, uh, I think we're gonna see a little bit more of that, you know, I think. And it's high time, you know. It's definitely. This is definitely time. I think that's got to happen with this generation of musicians, or that continuum could get lost.

J: Yeah, 'cause I, I remember when I first started, once I really started getting into the music—and remember this is mid-'80s, right—so I get a lot of this classic stuff, um, but I'm trying to figure out, "Well, what's happening now? What's going on now?" So the obvious first things I get are like Wynton's records. Like I got *Black Codes*.[8] *Black Codes* is still one of my favorite records.

W: That was his best record in my opinion.

J: But, um, one thing that was bad about that was that I started reading Stanley Crouch's liner notes and believing everything he said in there. 'Cause I hadn't, I hadn't read that much. And so, when I started off, I had this very narrow vision, you know. Like "Okay, well yeah. You gotta focus. You gotta be true to the tradition, and," you know, "you gotta like throw, you gotta cast everything else off," you know. And, you know, and after a while I realized that's a dead end.

W: Yeah, right. I mean, let's take a look at tradition. What is tradition, you know? I mean, you cannot discard, uh, you cannot take out or pick and choose out of our experience what you want, you know. It's just like if you look at, if you look at emancipation of black people in America, you can't, you can't, uh, say, "Okay, well I'll take Frederick Douglass, but I'll delete the Emancipation Proclamation," you know. That's all a part of our experience, too, you know. So, it's just . . . hey, man, that all comes into the music, you know. All of our experiences, music or any artistic endeavor or expression, you know, be it by word of mouth or painting or dance or whatever. All of it is there. And, and, uh, I think that that's what they were doing in the Harlem Renaissance, man. Was they were taking a look at all of our experiences, and that's why Duke Ellington was such a, such a master, man. He took . . . all of our experiences and put 'em into his art form, you know, so . . .

J: Yeah, you know if you get a chance, I want . . . I should probably stop the tape from, I forgot the tape was still running, um, if you get the chance, you should talk to Tony Hart about some of this stuff. 'Cause I mean whenever we, whenever the two of us sit down to talk, we talk about basically the same kind of stuff, about a lot of the same kind of stuff.

W: Yeah, we talked a little bit about that. Yeah, yeah, Tony, Tony, he's another brother, man, that's like, you know, who's got that vision. Yeah, definitely, absolutely.

J: Yeah, as a matter of fact, let me, I'm going to go ahead and stop the tape.

Notes

CHAPTER I

1. In fact, one Johnston & Murphy advertisement stretches reality somewhat by depicting pianist Eric Reed holding a tenor saxophone along with three other musicians seated on the stairs leading to the basement of the Village Vanguard. See *GQ*, October 2000, 57.

2. House Congressional Resolution 57, proposed by John Conyers Jr. on 3 March 1987 and passed by the House of Representatives and the United States Senate on 23 September and 4 December 1987, respectively. One could also track the increased interest in jazz shown by the various localities and corporations that have begun to sponsor jazz festivals, particularly during the summer months. For a discussion of jazz as America's classical music, see Sales (1984) as well as the statements of pianist and educator Billy Taylor (Clarke 1982).

3. Those same audiences are less interested in other publicly supported art activities. According to the National Endowment for the Arts' 2008 *Survey of Public Participation in the Arts*, between 1982 and 2008, live audiences for classical music, ballet, non-musical theater, and jazz "have aged faster than the general adult population" of the United States. "Even among the most educated, adults are participating less than in previous years" (Williams and Keen 2009, iii).

4. Some of the essays in Ted Gioia's award-winning book present that precise view of jazz as an "imperfect art" (1988); and while Gunther Schuller's writing on jazz (1958, 1968, 1989) has served to unlock some of its mysteries for many who might have ignored the music, his work suffers from a similarly misguided emphasis. See also Walser (1997).

5. In the mid-1970s Greil Marcus (1975) was making similar claims about the work of (at least some) rock musicians. See Mazullo (1997) for further discussion.

6. WQCD switched to an adult rock format on 6 February 2008. WBGO continues to operate as a straight-ahead jazz station.

7. The first five terms refer to those musical styles that are consistent with common practices of jazz musicians from the 1920s to the 1960s—particularly those of musicians who based their improvisations on chordal or modal frameworks. "Free bop," on the other hand, indicates those styles that partake of those common practices and approaches to improvisation as well as some of the approaches pioneered by performers associated with "free" or "action" jazz in the 1960s and 1970s. There are situations, however, in which the term "traditional" applies more specifically to styles that precede the 1950s—particularly New Orleans–style jazz. For the origin of the term "mainstream," see Tucker (1999, 231–33).

8. Many of the musicians who play primarily in "free" styles, such as saxophonists Charles Gayle and David S. Ware or pianist Matthew Shipp, are not part of the straight-ahead jazz scene, precisely because they play in different venues and for audiences that have different conventional expectations about how musical events are to proceed (see Freeman 2001 for one account of those expectations in the 1990s). Likewise, smooth jazz musicians, such as saxophonists Kenny G and George Howard, and musicians whose work is marketed primarily to the audiences for classic Broadway shows, such as Michael Feinstein, are not generally performing participants in the straight-ahead scene.

9. Multiple LP set Savoy 5500 and multiple compact disc set Riverside RCD 022-2, respectively.

10. See Goehr (1992) for an exploration of the regulative function of the work concept in some forms of musical research.

11. Similar arguments have been advanced by Tirro (1974, 305), Clark (1985, 34), and Griffin (1985, 112). For scholars doing research on subjects who are no longer living, Schuller's claim has some validity. But when many of the performers, as well as others who were acquainted with them, are still living, a recording is not the only data available to the researcher.

12. It is clear from Hodeir and Schuller's comments that neither distinguishes between scores as "prescriptive" sets of instructions for realizing musical sound and recordings as "descriptive" accounts of performances (Seeger 1958). For discussions of the problems of transcription, see List (1963, 1974), Jairazbhoy (1977), Nettl (1983), and DeVeaux (1988, 126).

13. In early acoustic jazz recordings remastered for reissue, William Tallmadge, for example, has shown how recording and rerecording processes could distort the sounds they were supposed to capture. He explains that "in many instances distortion of pitch, tempo, and tone quality of an original performance has occurred because of a malfunction of the original recording equipment or of the equipment used to remaster the original 78 rpm discs. Distortion may also have occurred because the producers in charge of remastering previously issued recordings have assumed that 78 rpm was the correct recording and playback speed" (Tallmadge 1979, 61). He observes that several issues of a single recorded tune might sound as if they are in different keys because of inconsistencies in recording or remastering speeds. Such difficulties cannot be attributed solely to the lack of standardization in the era of acoustic recording,

for, as Barry Kernfeld notes in an appendix to "Two Coltranes," "[While 1950s] jazz is typically free from problems of accurate pitch identification that plague transcribers of early jazz: out-of-tune instruments and faulty recording or remastering equipment . . . apparently Columbia engineers speeded up the master of Davis's March 2, 1959, session to fit three long cuts on one side of the *Kind of Blue* album. 'So What' is one-quarter-step sharp (A = *ca.* 451), and the resultant pitch ambiguity led to transcriptions of Davis's solo in D [Dorian], by James Patrick and William Drabkin, and in E-flat by André Asriel. . . . [A]ll the subsequent recordings of 'So What' support [the interpretation of the solo being in D Dorian]" (Kernfeld 1983, 62). Those errors were repeated in the 1987 reissue of the recording and were corrected only in a late 1992 reissue by Sony/Columbia, although a different explanation for the speed differences is offered there (see Orgill 1993). Moreover, I wonder whether generations of listeners might have responded to Miles Davis's *Kind of Blue* were it not for the subtle echo added to the recording to enhance the natural reverberations in the 30th Street Studios. See Kahn (2000, 101–2) and Buskin (2010, 84–86) for a description of the process.

14. In some cases these choices are foregrounded on recordings that specify the recording equipment used to make them. The notes to several Columbia/ CBS recordings by Branford Marsalis contain a statement similar to the one found on *Renaissance* (LP, Columbia FC 40711, recorded 31 December 1986, New York, New York, and 25–28 January 1987, Los Angeles, California): "To obtain a more *wood* sound from the bass, this album was recorded without usage of the 'Dreaded bass direct.' " In other words, the recording engineer placed a microphone in front of the bass to capture the resonance from its sound chamber and the sound of the room instead of physically attaching a contact microphone or an electronic pickup to the instrument's surface and running the output, via direct injection, into a mixing console.

15. In surveying late 1990s writing on rock, Philip Auslander (1998) raises similar questions about the fidelity of rock recordings to what he sees as perhaps more primary live performances.

16. See also Rudolph (1996). Note that even Levinson has to acknowledge the use of editing even in the golden age he evokes. While some recordists might argue whether there is, in fact, an *optimal* location for microphone placement, many others, like the proprietors of Mapleshade Records, continue searching for more transparent recording means by using "minimum miking and minimum-length cabling" as well as eschewing the use of a "mixing board, filtering, compression, equalization, noise reduction, multitracking or overdubbing" (quotes taken from the liner notes for John Hicks, *Trio Plus Strings* (CD, Mapleshade 05532, recorded 23, 24, and 27 September 1997).

17. These three sessions were released as *Thelonious Monk Plays Duke Ellington* CD, Original Jazz Classics OJCCD-024-2 [originally released as Riverside RLP 201], recorded 21 and 27 July 1955, Hackensack, New Jersey); *The Unique Thelonious Monk* (CD, Original Jazz Classics OJCCD-064-2 [originally released as Riverside RLP 209], recorded 17 March and 3 April 1956, Hackensack, New Jersey); and *Brilliant Corners* (CD, Original Jazz Classics OJCCD-026-2 [originally released as Riverside RLP 226], recorded December 1956, New York, New York), respectively.

234 I Notes to pages 10–13

18. All references to interviews will be designated parenthetically with the name of the interview subject and the year of the interview. The dates of all interviews can be found in the list of references.

19. They make these comments in the liner notes for *The Duke's Men: Small Groups, Volume 1* CD, Columbia/Legacy C2K 46995) and for *Charlie Parker: The Complete Savoy Studio Sessions* (multiple LP set, Savoy 5500), respectively.

20. In a December 1985 interview conducted by Ted Fox, Alfred Lion of Blue Note observes that Blue Note's 1950s recordings were superior to those produced by Prestige and Riverside, both of which used the same engineer, Rudy Van Gelder, for their sessions. One major factor was Lion's allowing and even encouraging musicians to listen to playbacks and to record alternate takes, even if it became necessary for him to pay them overtime (Fox 1986, 111).

21. Thelonious Monk's recording of the tune "Brilliant Corners" in 1956 is perhaps the ur-example of a recording that foregrounds these issues (see note 17, above). Orrin Keepnews describes the recording of the tune at length in his memoirs (1988, 131–32). In summary, he writes that Monk and the members of his ensemble were unable, in an extremely difficult evening of recording, to produce a satisfactory complete take. The released version of the recording is spliced together from several takes. Keepnews's inexperience with tape splicing and editing is painfully audible at a few points in the recording.

22. Joshua Redman, *Spirit of the Moment: Live at the Village Vanguard* (CD set, Warner Brothers 9 45923-2, recorded 21–26 March 1995, New York, New York); Joe Lovano, *Quartets: Live at the Village Vanguard* (CD set, Blue Note CDP 29125 2-1, recorded 12 March 1994 and 20 and 22 January 1995, New York, New York). Redman's first evening of recording will be discussed in chapter 7.

23. Roy Hargrove's 1993 live quintet recording *Of Kindred Souls* (CD, Novus 63154-2, recorded in unspecified locations), for example, contains on its jacket the indication that it was "Mixed, Sequenced, and Mastered" in New York, New York, postrecording, and that five individuals were involved in the final mixing of the album prior to its being mastered in 1993. There is little reason to believe that live recordings such as Hargrove's would not be recorded on multiple tracks to facilitate the process of adjusting individual balances in the final mix.

24. In *Orality and Literacy*, Walter Ong (1982, 43–44) notes that literacy encourages analytical procedures that distance a researcher from the contexts that produced a particular object. He asserts that writing fosters "abstractions that disengage knowledge from the arena where human beings struggle with one another. It separates the knower from the known. By keeping knowledge embedded in the human lifeworld, orality situates knowledge within a context of struggle." By extension, one might say that recording and transcription foster similar abstractions.

25. Stephen Blum has written forcefully that " wherever we turn, we can find skilled performers engaged in the exercise of their musical knowledge. It is difficult to avoid the impression that analysts of music often fail to recognize much of the guidance that is readily available to us" (1992, 213). Even those researchers focusing on more strictly historical topics, or musicians no longer

living, might benefit from the wide-ranging approach of cultural historians such as William Kenney, who see context not merely as explanatory but as constitutive (1993, 171).

26. Eric Porter's *What Is This Thing Called Jazz? African American Musicians as Artists, Critics, and Activists* (2002) takes such work a step further.

27. Like those for musical sound, the approaches that scholars have taken in discussing musical meaning are varied but can be grouped according to four basic orientations: psychological, philosophical, semiotic, and ethnomusicological. The meanings attributed to music from the first three of these viewpoints derive almost exclusively from its notated and notatable parameters (see Davies 1994). In the first group, the exemplary work is still Leonard Meyer's *Emotion and Meaning in Music* (1956), whose focus on "embodied meaning" and whose claims regarding the universality of his model have been questioned by other researchers (see Keil 1994; Elliott 1987). A clear, if controversial, philosophical approach to musical meaning can be found in Peter Kivy's *Music Alone* (1990). Because the subject of semiotics is "meaning," claims for its nearly universal applicability are frequently advanced (Agawu 1991, 10), and, arguably, the two most influential attempts to apply semiotics to music are studies by Coker (1972) and Nattiez (1990). Criticisms and modifications of Nattiez's work can be found in the writing of Boilès (1982) and Dunsby (1983). A more recent, and less universalist, application of semiotic theory appears in the work of Thomas Turino (1999, 2008). To varying degrees, each of these analytical frames depends on the existence of what George Lipsitz calls the "maximally competent listener," the individual who, through neutral formal analysis, can reveal the myriad meanings in a musical work, even those concealed from other makers and consumers of music (Lipsitz 1990, 101). An ethnomusicological approach, by contrast, is concerned more with music's social and cultural meanings. Such meanings emerge not only from the music but also from the "principles and procedures that are actualized in performance" and from the ways that skilled performers and other culturally informed participants contribute to it (Blum 1992, 191–95). Although one could hardly claim neutrality for anthropological and ethnomusicological approaches (see Clifford and Marcus 1986; Gourlay 1978), such studies do examine emic meanings alongside etic ones. That is, the meanings discovered via these procedures are not so much products of the skillful application of terminology as they are, ideally, the fluid products of an active, interpretive process.

28. Locational moves place the event in a field of like and unlike events; categorical moves may more specifically characterize the kind of event taking place. Associational moves relate the event to or draw analogies between it and other kinds of verbal, musical, or visual imagery, while reflective moves relate the event to past experiences. Evaluative moves concern interpretations of the effectiveness or value of the event. Feld poses no specific hierarchy among or order in which one might make these moves.

29. In only one instance did I use a method other than an in-person approach (in this case, a telephone call) to establish contact with a previously unknown musician. In general, I felt that such approaches might be too impersonal and would result in a rejection or a number of reasons given why that individual

236 | Notes to pages 17–21

could not participate in my study. Meeting musicians in the context of musical events, particularly when other scene participants known to me were present, made it possible for individuals to see that I, too, was connected and part of the scene. In the single instance in which I deviated from that procedure, despite the recommendation of another musician and several attempts to explain my project in more detail, a rejection is exactly what I got.

30. Although I can only guess why some musicians did not agree to become part of the study, in some cases I was given explicit reasons. Saxophonist Jimmy Heath informed me that he was working on his own autobiography, only recently published (Heath and McLaren 2010), and thought my interviewing him might undercut what he was doing. Some older musicians were being interviewed as part of an oral history project being conducted by the Smithsonian Institution and were generously compensated for their time. My resources did not allow me to offer them anything nearly equivalent. Female musicians might have resisted getting involved with the project for fear that I would make them ancillary to the main narrative, seeing them as representative only of "women in jazz" (see Tucker 2004). Alternatively, they might simply have regarded me with the same kind of suspicion they applied to other men who approached them in nightclubs. I chose not to pursue certain other musicians either because they performed in the city infrequently or lived far from New York (such as drummer Terri Lyne Carrington, based in Los Angeles), or because I learned firsthand or through others about the difficulty dealing with them, either because of their temperament or drug or alcohol problems.

31. I became acquainted with this term through Peter Watrous. The Kenny Barron Trio's *Green Chimneys* (CD, Criss Cross Criss 1008, recorded 9 July 1983 and 31 December 1987) was one such record recommended to me by Leon Parker. Bruce Barth's praise for James Williams's *Alter Ego* (CD, Sunnyside SSC 1007CD, recorded 19–20 July 1984) also led me to find that record. Antonio Hart made me aware of how great a recording McCoy Tyner's *Tender Moments* (CD, Blue Note CDP 7 84275 2, recorded 1 December 1967) was. Something about each of these recordings made them special—compositionally, interactively, improvisationally, or some combination of those possibilities.

32. For a time, the bartender at Bradley's seemed quite fond of playing Oliver Nelson's *Blues and the Abstract Truth* (CD, Impulse! IMPD-154, recorded 23 February 1961, Englewood Cliffs, New Jersey) immediately following the last set.

33. Steve Wilson and I, for example, had a brief discussion about our mutual admiration for the 1970s rock group Steely Dan prior to the beginning of my interview with him (1995). The discussion was spurred by my noticing a solo recording by band member Donald Fagen (*Kamakiriad*, CD, Reprise 9 45230-2, 1993) on Wilson's coffee table when I entered his apartment. Indeed, many of the interviews were preceded by talk about music—either current jazz releases or current popular music. Joshua Redman and I discussed, for example, the rock bands Soundgarden and Portishead prior to our conversation on 27 February 1995.

34. In the process it quickly became apparent to me why so many features on musicians in the popular press tended to repeat the same anecdotes over and

over. Either the reporters were reading each other's work, or they were all taking the same "human interest" anecdotes from artist biographies. In fact, as I found myself with many record reviews to write on deadlines, I relied heavily on artist biographies to add contextual information to essays about unfamiliar musicians.

CHAPTER 2

1. Indeed, many conservative politicians in the United States have used such logic in interpreting Martin Luther King Jr.'s 1963 plea that people be judged by "the content of their character rather than the color of their skin" to support policies that eliminate consideration of race in hiring, education, or the awarding of government contracts. In a different sense, Walter Benn Michaels (1998) has argued that seeing race as a construction is not significantly different from seeing it as real.

2. For overviews of writings on and conceptualizations of race (academic, legal, and otherwise), see Omi and Winant (1994) and Crenshaw et al. (1995). Where culture is concerned, works that are part of the "turn to practice" have been particularly influential in shifting the emphasis from culture as inventory to cultural as practical activity (Sahlins 1976; Bourdieu 1977). For a cogent overview of practice theory and its importance in anthropology, see Ortner (1984). The work of Lila Abu-Lughod (1991), Christoph Brumann (1999), and Ulf Hannerz (1992) explores in more depth the culture concept's utility. Joseph Roach's *Cities of the Dead* offers an implicit but sustained meditation on the pitfalls of using racial and cultural categories uncritically over time through examining performance in a "circum-Atlantic" world (1996).

3. For Geertz's understanding of culture and his means of reading it, see his essay "Thick Description: Toward an Interpretive Theory of Culture" (1973). Critiques of the categories of race and culture would be incomplete without an examination of literature that explores the nature of categories themselves. Exemplary in this regard is George Lakoff's *Women, Fire, and Dangerous Things: What Categories Reveal about the Mind* (1987). For an illuminating discussion of the history of the uses of the word "culture," see the opening chapters of Raymond Williams's *Marxism and Literature* (1977).

4. One might argue, additionally, that archives privilege *textualized* sources, which emerge from a limited swath of the much wider range of activities that constitute everyday life.

5. A recent flashpoint for the intersection of such issues was Ken Burns's equally praised and condemned documentary *Jazz,* which aired on PBS stations in January and February of 2001. For an assortment of contemporary responses to it from musicians, club owners, scholars, and critics, see the Arts and Leisure section of the *New York Times* from 7 January of that year (Bayles et al. 2001). Steven F. Pond (2003) charts the wider reception of the documentary, incorporating less "official" forms of discourse.

6. All references in the text are to the revised edition published in 1983. In addition to Williams, one might recognize the importance of former Oxford University Press editor Sheldon Meyer, who pushed through Williams's work as

well as that of Gunther Schuller and Francis Davis during his years working for the press. For an assessment of Meyer's impact on writing on jazz and other forms of American music, see Giddins (1997). Moreover, the formulation of a "jazz tradition" in the 1970s and since emerged from the process of "main-streaming" Mark Tucker (1999) has described.

7. In this regard, it will be interesting to see the effect that changes to the set, now titled *Jazz: The Smithsonian Anthology,* will have on future jazz history courses. In its more contemporary, perhaps less comprehensive, form it faces competition from *Ken Burns' Jazz: The Story of America's Music* (5 CD set, Columbia/Legacy 61432, 2000), released in conjunction with the 2001 documentary *Jazz.*

8. For an examination of the history of jazz criticism and the roles and backgrounds of these individuals, see Gennari (1991, 2006) and Gabbard (1995). Although many have read Schuller's work as excellent works of musicology, they might better be described as criticism written by someone with considerable musical knowledge but little reflexive concern for the degree to which his own background affects his approach to his subject matter.

9. Arthur Blythe, *In the Tradition* (LP, Columbia JC 36300, 1979). Saxophonist Anthony Braxton also made two albums with the same title a few years earlier. For a discussion of his different motivations, see Radano (1993, 1, 183, 196) and Lock (1988, 136–37).

10. There are a number of notable exceptions to this characterization, among them saxophonist Anthony Braxton, who was signed to an unprecedented and highly publicized contract with Arista Records early in the decade. For more information, see Radano (1993). On the downtown "loft" scene, see Lewis (2008, 330–36, 349–53). A good sampling of music from that period comes from the 1977 five-LP live series *Wallflowers* (Douglas/Casablanca 7045, 7046, 7047, 7048, and 7049; reissued in 2009 as a three-CD set, Douglas AD10), recorded at Sam Rivers's Studio Rivbea.

11. For a list of other contemporaneous projects partaking of the same spirit, see Francis Davis's discussion in *In the Moment* (1986, 194). Keith Negus and Michael Pickering (2004) offer a sustained meditation on the relational nature of creativity vis-à-vis experience, convention, tradition, genius, and other, often taken-for-granted concepts.

12. Blythe's thinking resonated outside instrumental jazz performance. It inspired, among other things, a fiery poetry and jazz collaboration between poet Amiri Baraka, saxophonist David Murray, and drummer Steve McCall. For a discussion and analysis of the genesis of the poem, its recording, and the tradition-creating strategies of the musicians and the poet, see Jackson (2004).

13. Stuart Nicholson describes "neo-conservatism" in terms of similar approaches to performance: "Effectively, these young neo-classicists looked to role models who had defined bop and hard-bop from around 1948 to the mid-'60s. . . . But with so many musicians supporting the same sources of stylistic inspiration, similarity in concept and execution was inevitable. . . . Consequently individuality became less important than shared values of craftsmanship—technique, familiarity with the harmonic and rhythmic conventions of the music, an orthodox tone and precise articulation" (1990, 252). During the same decade,

however, nonclassicists were also signed by major recording labels. Among them were Sun Ra, Don Cherry, Don Pullen, Steve Lacy, the World Saxophone Quartet, and John Zorn.

14. Lara Pellegrinelli (2000) has argued more compellingly that Lincoln Center's policies aggressively maintain the *masculinist* ethos of the jazz tradition, particularly since no women are regular members of the ensemble and none have been considered for inclusion.

15. The terms of this debate recall those in Ira Gitler's criticism of Abbey Lincoln and Max Roach (Gitler 1962a, 1962b; cf. Monson 1995) as well as those in Nat Hentoff's discussion of "Crow Jim" or antiwhite discrimination (1961b, chapter 4). Interestingly, no musicians in any of these writings were accused of being sexist or homophobic for having no women or gay musicians in their ensembles. Discussions of other racial groups, such as Native or Asian Americans, were also conspicuously absent.

16. Charley Gerard expresses a similar viewpoint, though less dramatically, in the first chapter of *Jazz in Black and White* (1998). Teachout's article, in particular, generated a lively response in the letters section of the January 1996 issue of *Commentary* ("Race & Jazz" 1996, 13–21).

17. Indeed, some readers of the *New York Times,* writing in response to an article (Sudhalter 1999a) promoting *Lost Chords,* made the same observation. See "Letters" (1999).

18. There has been an extensive amount of contentious writing about Jazz at Lincoln Center's policies and programs. A sampling of relevant articles from my fieldwork period includes Giddins (1993), Whitehead (1994), Marsalis (1994), Woodward (1994), and Piazza (1997, 156–70). More recent critiques appear in works by Gray (2005, 32–51) and Gennari (2006, 339–71).

19. *Meritocracy* and *reverse racism* appear on page 53 and *politically correct* on page 51 of Teachout (1995). Richard Delgado's discussion of the dismissiveness of white "imperial scholars" toward the critical work of feminists and nonwhite legal scholars (1995) makes a compelling argument similar to the one I'm presenting. I thank Martha S. Jones for alerting me to that correspondence.

20. See the introduction to Crenshaw et al. (1995) for the ways in which critical race theorists responded to a similar crisis in legal studies. Without devaluing the work of individuals like Martin Luther King Jr., the authors assert that 1960s legal gains were easily co-opted, largely because the principles on which they were based—while designed to appeal to white liberals—did not fundamentally challenge an overarching American belief in meritocracy or the criteria for assessing merit. Likewise, see Ingrid Monson's work (1995) as well as Ramsey (1999, 2001) for discussion of white writers' ideas about and relationships to jazz and African American musics.

21. Rudinow (1994), in fact, argues that the ahistorical nature of such criteria renders them invalid. It seems, however, that he is missing a crucial point: that such aesthetic criteria don't necessarily prescribe the forms in which they have to be realized. The rhetorical question in his title—can white men really sing the blues?—may indeed be the wrong one. It might be more fruitful to ask what kinds of things performers need to know and what kinds of processual understandings they might need to possess to be "good" blues

players. The questions are perhaps not as tidy, but the answers might be more illuminating.

22. For one expression of this modernist position, see Gioia (1988); a useful critique of Gioia's position and related ones has been presented by Johnson (1993). The modernist focus emphasizes jazz's status as "art" and its expansive "Americanness" rather than its seemingly less expansive *African-Americanness* (see Starks 1993).

23. For a critical review of jazz pedagogical materials, see Witmer and Robbins (1988).

24. Discussions of the development of formalized jazz education, beginning with the establishment of what would later become the Berklee College of Music in Boston in 1945 and the dance band program at the North Texas State University in 1946, can be found in Dobbins (1988), Helland (1995), Joyner (1997), and Roach (1998). For a discussion of jazz bands at historically black colleges and universities, see Goodrich (2001). Equally useful for understanding how jazz musicians learned their craft—and the importance of notated music in learning processes—is David Chevan's dissertation "Written Music in Early Jazz" (1997).

25. The first use of this term to describe young musicians was perhaps in the liner notes to the LP *The Young Lions* (Vee-Jay 3013, recorded 25 April 1960), which featured members of Art Blakey's Jazz Messengers and the Modern Jazz Two + 3, collectively including Lee Morgan, Frank Strozier, Wayne Shorter, Bobby Timmons, and Bob Cranshaw. In the liner notes for that release, Julian "Cannonball" Adderley cites Irwin Shaw's war novel, also titled *The Young Lions* (1948), for the way its protagonists navigated situations that called for varying degrees of conformity. Adderley argues that rather than pursuing projects formulated by unnamed traditionalists—"who unofficially feel that the music introduced to us by Parker, Gillespie and Monk has not been fully developed"—or avant-gardists—who "feel that music is reactionary unless something 'different' is either suggested or produced stylistically"—these young musicians are producing individual work that will not conform to direction. Invoking that spirit more than two decades later, Nesuhi Ertegun and Bruce Lundvall enlisted Michael Gibbs to organize a "young lions" concert for the 1982 Kool Jazz Festival. As Lundvall recalled in the liner notes for the resultant live recording *The Young Lions* (Elektra Musician 60196, recorded 30 June 1982, New York, New York), he wanted "young players and composers who had a real knowledge of their musical roots and who were also developing their own distinctive voices on their instruments" regardless of their stylistic or ideological leanings. Likewise, Leonard Feather indicated in his notes for the LP that the criteria for determining who was *young* were flexible, as performers then in their forties, such as Hamiet Bluiett, were included alongside those in their twenties and thirties, such as Anthony Davis, James Newton, Wynton Marsalis, Kevin Eubanks, and Bobby McFerrin. By the late 1980s, however, the term "young lions" lost its association with individuality and nonconformity and became an almost generic journalistic and marketing term for younger, and often black, musicians.

26. Originally published in 1953.

27. A similar criticism might be made of the use of Bach chorales to teach students Western harmonic theory. Although those pieces are an excellent primer on the rules of voice leading and harmonic progression, they do not provide a good foundation for students learning the more difficult procedures involved in creating compelling melodies or dealing with harmonies that change less often. For a more extensive discussion of these issues in a jazz context, see Ake (2002, 112–45).

28. Though Allison would be described by most people as of primarily European ancestry, his upbringing in the Mississippi Delta connected him to African American musics and culture, particularly a blues sensibility.

29. All of these pianists are African American.

30. He was not clear whether he learned the song through Ike and Tina Turner, Creedence Clearwater Revival, or both.

31. Polymeter needs further explication. If one sees it as the "clashing of rhythmic accents or the creation of cross-rhythms," then it, too, is characteristic of African American music (Wilson 1974, 6–7). He brings in the example of secondary rag in ragtime to emphasize the point. Wilson makes a useful distinction between polyrhythm and syncopation: "If the foreground rhythm (i.e., basic metrical pulse) is not displaced or is displaced only momentarily, the result will be syncopation . . . , but if the foreground rhythm is displaced . . . or a lesser rhythmic level is displaced over a long time span, the effect of polyrhythm will occur" (9). See Krebs (1987) and Hasty (1997) for a more extensive discussion of syncopation, polymeter, and concepts of metric consonance and dissonance.

CHAPTER 3

1. Those scholars who have considered the world that jazz musicians make and inhabit have focused abstractly on changing human relationships, approached via the concept of a "jazz community," either taking space for granted or omitting consideration of it altogether. In the earliest writings the jazz community was composed of "deviants" whose departure from norms was couched in terms of the sociological and psychological theories of the 1940s and 1950s (Berger 1947; Becker 1951; Esman 1951; Cameron 1954; Margolis 1954; Merriam and Mack 1960; Stebbins 1966, 1968). As scholars actively developed the concept through the end of the 1960s, what was once a focus on jazz as an occupational subculture became a meditation on and ranking of agents and institutions.

2. Although musicians and other scene participants use the words *community* and *scene* interchangeably, I am privileging the latter precisely because of its unique use among participants in such groups. That is, it does not carry the connotations that the word *community* does among scholars.

3. Compare Shank's concept of a signifying community with Jean Comaroff's understanding of "signifying practice" (Comaroff 1985, 6): "the process through which persons, acting upon an external environment, construct themselves as social beings."

4. For more on the importance of radio in the promulgation of early jazz, see Douglas (1999, 83–99).

5. For a chronicle of the legal struggle, see Chevigny (1991, 64–67) and Cohen (1993).

6. Of course, New York City was not alone in having jazz radio stations that had difficulty cultivating audiences and therefore promoting the work of musicians. Charles Mitchell, a former music director at WRVR, asserted as much in an article published shortly after the station went off the air (1980).

7. Giovannoni's consultation and results are not without controversy, as Tom McCourt's work (1999) indicates.

8. See, for example, Frith (1987), Finnegan (1989, 329), Lipsitz (1990, 34), Waterman (1990), Gilroy (1991a, 211–17), and Stokes (1994).

CHAPTER 4

1. My observations during fieldwork indicated that the union is peripheral in the lives of jazz musicians. Perhaps one salient indicator of the union's irrelevance is that, of all of the issues musicians and other scene participants raised in conversation and interviews, it was never one of them. And membership in the union does not seem to be a prerequisite for musicians to be booked into various venues or to record for some independent labels. See Roberts (2002, 26–29) for a discussion of the way that independent label production undercuts the benefits musicians might derive from union membership. Indeed, today the union seems to have relevance only when musicians recording for major labels go into the recording studio. Then care has to be taken that the union rules regarding wages, hours of recording, and breaks, for example, are observed.

2. The remaining boroughs, the Bronx and Staten Island, are probably less favored because living in either one greatly increases the amount of time one spends on trains or in taxis going to and from gigs that largely take place in Lower Manhattan. Indeed, it is easier to get to Manhattan from some areas in New Jersey than it is from Staten Island, particularly when one drives.

3. Systems Two is located at 117 Ditmas Avenue in Brooklyn. Sheila's, also in Brooklyn at 271 Adelphi Street, was a supper club that served as a jam session site in the 1980s and early 1990s. The status of some the borough's neighborhoods as "musicians' neighborhoods" was brought clearly into focus by the numerous excursions I made into Brooklyn for interviews and recording sessions. There were many occasions on which merely taking a walk or a subway ride from one place to another in Brooklyn would result in my meeting musicians, seemingly at random.

4. The designation "Memphis pianists" includes musicians who got much of their early musical training in Memphis, Tennessee, such as Harold Mabern, Chris Thomas, James Williams, and Mulgrew Miller. The New School crowd includes those who were associated with the jazz program at the New School for Social Research in the late 1980s, such as Jesse Davis, Larry Goldings, Christopher Hollyday, Brad Mehldau, and, more tangentially, Peter Bernstein and Leon Parker (neither of whom was enrolled in the school's program). The Jones brothers are pianist Hank, drummer Elvin, and the late arranger and flügelhornist Thad. The Smalls scene denotes the activities centered around the club Smalls in Greenwich Village.

5. In contrast, Redman's bassists and drummers have been almost exclusively African American, although he has used the white bassist Larry Grenadier as a substitute on occasion. He defends his choices by asserting that African American bassists and drummers are more likely to have had musical experiences—listening to and playing funk, rhythm and blues, and soul in addition to jazz—that help them to play the kinds of grooves he wants.

6. Such reasoned explanations, of course, do not eliminate the presence of racial ideology as a significant issue. Points similar to those regarding race could be made regarding the role of female jazz musicians. The cumulative effects of historic discrimination against women and the tendency of men to form alliances with other men, not necessarily with the specific intent of excluding women, can lead to the appearance of rampant sexism in the jazz world (see Jackson 1993c; Watrous 1994e). What is important, then, is interrogating the processes by which those appearances come into being.

7. Gilroy's arguments in that regard owe a large debt to the first edition of *Racial Formation in the United States* (Omi and Winant 1994).

8. In the summer of 1995 Newsome made the soprano saxophone his primary instrument.

9. In Carter's case, I wrote the artist biography to accompany the release of his second recording for Atlantic, *Conversin' with the Elders* (CD, Atlantic 82908-2, recorded 2 October 1995 and 30 January and 5 February 1996, New York, New York). I was also the off-camera interviewer for a videocassette that constituted the electronic press kit (EPK) used to promote the recording. For Gordon and Westray I also wrote an artist biography and contributed liner notes for their recording *Bone Structure* (CD, Atlantic 82936-2, recorded January 1996, New Orleans, Louisiana).

10. Verve, however, had great success in the 1990s with older musicians, particularly singers. Musicians who enjoyed renewed popularity, partially via their association with the label, include saxophonist Joe Henderson and singers Betty Carter, Shirley Horn, and Abbey Lincoln. They have also signed other senior musicians to shorter-term contracts, including organist Jimmy Smith and pianists Kenny Barron and Hank Jones. Likewise, Elektra/Musician's signings and releases in the previous decade were remarkably varied, as evidenced on the samplers *The Musicians Guide, Volume 1* (E1–60043, 1982) and *Musicians Guide, Vol. 2* (E1–60136, 1982) as well as the "supergroup" recordings *Echoes of an Era* and *The Griffith Park Collection*, whose personnel were Chaka Khan, Freddie Hubbard, Joe Henderson, Chick Corea, Stanley Clarke, and Lenny White. Those four releases introduced a roster that, in addition to the musicians already named, included Red Rodney, Ira Sullivan, John McLaughlin, Lee Ritenour, Freddie Hubbard, Material, Eric Gale, David Sancious, Bobby McFerrin, Billy Cobham's Glass Menagerie, Mose Allison, Dexter Gordon, and Woody Shaw.

11. One such musician whom I interviewed told me that his annual income, derived entirely from his touring as a sideman and doing recording sessions, was roughly $55,000 to $60,000 in 1994.

12. As of 1 February 2004. Information taken from Local 802, American Federation of Musicians' information sheet "Phonograph Scales Summary." A

session is defined as "three (3) hours during which not more than fifteen (15) minutes of finished product may be recorded." The sheet also details various stipulations regarding amounts to be paid into a pension fund, additional monies for musicians who play more than one instrument at a session, and various overtime and premium rates. Curiously, a representative from Local 802 told me in a 1996 phone conversation that such information was not public *after* it had been provided to me by a recording industry contact. The same union representative informed me that its constitution and bylaws were not public record.

13. The numerous appearances by the mysterious trumpeter "E. Dankworth" on recordings by Marcus Roberts and Eric Reed in the 1990s might be attributed to the desire of Wynton Marsalis, who has used the name Dankworth as a pseudonym, to save them costs or avoid contractual difficulties.

14. This assertion might be used to support an interpretation of jazz as having a particular appeal to African Americans whose approaches to and preferences with regard to music making are more in keeping with those of many of the musicians, though other explanations might be equally compelling.

15. As a result of WQCD's rapid growth in popularity in 1994 and 1995 and its claim to be a jazz radio station, WBGO changed its on-air slogan to "Real Jazz, All the Time" in 1995. If nothing else, the claims that both stations have made show how contested the term is and reveal that a certain level of prestige (and perhaps ratings) might accrue to the station that can most effectively market itself to a potential "jazz" audience.

16. WBGO Audience and Demographics, http://wbgo.org/sponsorship/demographics.asp, accessed 23 November 2004. The presentation of the categories, particularly "not black or Hispanic," seems to indicate that the station is attempting to foreground the African American and Latino portions of its audience.

17. Note also that the major jazz towns that Barth describes were cities with large African American populations that supported jazz performers and performance venues, particularly many of the small bars that Reed discusses.

18. Such a criticism, of course, is not unique to jazz musicians or even Western musical traditions, as Kingsbury (1988) and Brinner (1995) note.

19. Lovano, however, maintains that his father was his most important and best teacher.

20. Each Music Minus One recording contains a number of different tunes played by a rhythm section so that an individual learning to improvise can play along with a competent rhythm section without having physical access to one. A lead sheet is a form of notation that includes, at a minimum, a melody and symbols denoting the attendant harmonies. In some cases they also include suggestions for tempo, feel, accents, and accompaniment patterns. Chuck Sher's series of "real books" (1988, 1991, 1995) and "fake books" more generally are collections of lead sheets.

21. Among the things that young musicians learn when apprenticed to more experienced ones are where to get haircuts on the road and how to keep their bills current, manage money, and negotiate salaries and contracts. A humorous

take on these issues can be found Rafi Zabor's novel *The Bear Comes Home* (1997).

22. There are obvious parallels with the migration of blues clubs to Chicago's North Side, which is discussed by Grazian (2003). For a discussion of St. Nick's Pub and some history of uptown jazz performance venues, see Gossett (1996). St. Nick's Pub, along with the Lenox Lounge, was part of a tourism- and gentrification-led reinvigoration of Harlem at the beginning of the twenty-first century (Hoffman 2003).

23. The six clubs were the Cooler, Dan Shaku, Metronome, Downstairs at the Metropolis Cafe, the Down Beat, and Iridium. Iridium and the Cooler were still operational in 1995, though only Iridium (now in a new location near Times Square to capitalize on the revitalization of that area under Rudy Giuliani) is still in business. Metronome later reopened with different management. Other venues that closed just prior to or during the period of my research were Condon's, Indigo Blues, Fortune Garden Pavilion, and Yardbird Suite. Smalls, which also opened in 1994, has weathered several crises, closing and reopening at least twice since the late 1990s.

24. For a discussion of contemporary big-band performance in New York, see Stewart (2007). Some of the musicians consulted for this study were participants in many such ensembles.

25. Bradley's and Smalls were unique with regard to scheduling. Bradley's featured three sets every night of the week starting at 10 PM, midnight, and 2 AM. Smalls featured a varying number of sets but always had a jam session starting at roughly 2 AM and lasting until 8 AM or until the last musicians left.

26. One performer informed me that he had learned from an older musician how important it was to record one's own compositions rather than a series of standards. He would receive publishing royalties for each copy of his recording sold if he had composed his own music; otherwise, the estates of George Gershwin, Thelonious Monk, or other composers would simply grow richer. More than other musicians, he was also adamant that his recording sessions leave no alternate takes or otherwise unreleased material that his label might use to profit from his work after it terminated his contract.

27. Many producers and recording engineers have studios with which they have had good experiences or in which they prefer working. Freelance engineer Jim Anderson, pianist and producer James Williams, Warner Brothers producer Matt Pierson, and Warner Brothers engineer James Farber seemed to prefer recording at Avatar (formerly the Power Station); BMG/RCA engineer James Nichols used Sound on Sound; Criss Cross's Gerry Teekens and Max Bolleman have used RPM Studios frequently; and a number of sessions for other labels have been done at East Side Sound, Sear Sound, and Systems Two.

28. Personal communication with Christopher Thomas, bassist in Blanchard's band, 8 December 1994.

29. According to Bruce Barth and Sam Newsome, trumpeter Terence Blanchard regularly requested that studio engineers place the microphones in a manner that replicated his band's usual positioning for live performances (see also Buskin 2010, 86, 88).

30. The artists take care to play the insert at approximately the same tempo as they played the full take, and thus it is common for the artists to hear playback leading up to the portion where they are to do the insert. If the tempo of the insert is not exactly the same but reasonably close, it can be digitally time-stretched or -compressed during mixing and editing.

31. As far back as 1990 officials at Sony/Columbia maintained that the success of Wynton Marsalis was largely due to their promotion and marketing of him and the "reams of press clips" generated by his publicist, Marilyn Laverty of Shore Fire Media (Sancton 1990).

32. This is compared to 27.5 percent for rock, 24.7 percent for rhythm and blues, 23.6 percent for country, 12.1 percent for rap music, and 7.8 percent for classical. These percentages are based on the number of records sold in the United States between 1 January and 21 May 1995. Note that the jazz figures are gross figures, including any music that a retail outlet might classify as jazz. There has been controversy over SoundScan's sampling practices because its sales figures are drawn largely from department stores and other outlets that carry limited, conservative selections of recordings (see Goldberg 1991 for more information). The year-end figures for 2001, compiled for the Recording Industry Association of America, paint a bleaker picture, with jazz recordings constituting only 3.4 percent of all record sales. Other categories had the following shares of the market: rock, 24.4 percent; country, 10.5 percent; rhythm and blues/urban, 10.6 percent; pop, 12.1 percent; rap/hip-hop, 11.4 percent; religious, 6.7 percent; and classical, 3.2 percent. The margin of error in the RIAA figures, compiled by Peter Hart Research, is ±1.8 percent.

33. Personal communication, Yves Beauvais, Atlantic Records, 22 October 1996.

34. In the 1990s pianists Brad Mehldau and Kevin Hays and drummer Brian Blade were signed to major-label contracts in part based on the celebrity they gained from being members of Joshua Redman's groups. The same was true for a number of Wynton Marsalis sidemen who signed contracts with Atlantic, Novus, MoJazz, and Columbia during the decade. The fame that musicians in earlier eras, like Ella Fitzgerald, Wayne Shorter, and Cannonball Adderley, garnered by playing with better-established leaders also led to recording and performing opportunities.

35. Such was the level of excitement that, after I was already inside the club on the evening of 7 January, I learned that two patrons had been removed for fighting over positions in line for the second set.

36. Kembrew McLeod (2001) makes similar observations about the backgrounds of rock critics, while Keith Negus (1992, 1999) argues that white, middle-class status (or the adoption of such an outlook) is almost a prerequisite for work in the recording industry.

37. One of the major concerns of New Criticism is "close reading." Paramount importance is attached to reading and analyzing the "words on the page" rather than the contexts and circumstances that shaped them. It is a decidedly formalist way of looking at literature, one that sees reality as contained within an artwork. No further study of context, therefore, is necessary. For a concise discussion of New Criticism, see Terry Eagleton, *Literary Theory: An*

Introduction (1983, 43–53). For a discussion of New Criticism's relation to jazz criticism, see Gennari (1991, 476–85).

38. Mark Mazullo (1997) makes similar observations regarding celebrated rock writer Greil Marcus's training in American studies at the University of California, Berkeley, in the mid-1960s.

CHAPTER 5

1. I am not the first to use this term, though my usage is somewhat different from that proposed by previous scholars.

2. I borrow this term from Christopher Small (1987a, 50), who laments the lack of a single verb in English to denote the act of making music: "*Music is not primarily a thing or a collection of things, but an activity in which we engage.* One might say that it is not properly a noun at all, but a verb. . . . I define the word to include not only performing and composing . . . but also listening and even dancing to music; all those involved in any way in a musical performance can be thought of as musicking." Small's understanding of musicking is quite similar to that revealed in Charles Seeger's writings. Seeger thought of music, among other things, as a culturally conditioned "communicatory medium" (1961, 77) that was not well served by the classificatory analytical schemes associated with speech and language (1960, 225). Marcia Herndon (1974, 246) extends Seeger's concern by asking whether music scholars should "speech" about music or "music" about it (see also Seeger 1977, 183–84).

3. Coltrane's three-tonic system, reportedly influenced by his practicing with Nicolas Slonimsky's *Thesaurus of Scales and Melodic Patterns* (1947), was a system that allowed the substitution of pitches with a tonal center a major third away from a goal chord's root in improvisation or composition. Approaching a G-major seventh chord via an A-minor seventh and a D dominant seventh chord, for example, one might use pitches from a Mixolydian scale starting on G. In the three-tonic system, Mixolydian scales starting on E♭ and B, with chromatic alterations, might be interpolated. This system is employed most famously on "Giant Steps" on *Giant Steps* (CD, Atlantic 1311-2, recorded 4 May 1959). See Porter (1998, 145–53).

4. One way in which Blanchard forced his musicians to break old habits was by writing compositions relying heavily on nonfunctional tonal progressions, particularly using the sonority of the minor-seventh chord with a flattened sixth. With C as root, the pitches contained in a closed-position voicing of the chord would be C–E♭–G–A♭–B♭.

5. Barth's statement has interesting correspondences with the ideas developed in Mikhail Bakhtin's essay "Discourse in the Novel." The meaning of a particular word or utterance, for him, is neither fixed nor created anew but intimately tied to previous meanings and emerging from the social and material circumstances of its use: "The word in language is half someone else's. It becomes 'one's own' only when the speaker populates it with his own intention, his own accent, when he appropriates the word, adapting it to his own semantic and expressive intention. Prior to this moment of appropriation, the word . . . exists in other people's mouths, in other people's contexts, serving other people's intentions: it is

from there that one must take the word, and make it one's own" (1981, 293–94). The emphasis, as for Barth and Newsome, is not on novelty or revolutionary usage but on making the word (sound) "one's own" through its deployment in specific contexts and with specific, personal intentions. Similar sentiments have been expressed by Arthur Blythe, as I noted in chapter 2.

6. See Wilson's discussion of Garrett's work in the Appendix.

7. The substitution is "incorrect" because the E♮ in the B major scale creates a clash with E♭, the seventh of the F dominant chord. In jazz harmonic theory, analysts describe chord extensions or embellishments that create minor ninth (or augmented octave) intervals with respect to lower-voiced chord tones as sounding unpleasant. The one "permissible" minor ninth interval is one measured from the root of a dominant chord.

8. William Tallmadge (1984) and Eric Weisethaunet (2001) discuss the definitions and applicability of the terms "blue note" and "blue tonality," particularly as they relate to harmonic progressions, whether categorized as "blues progressions" or not. In short, "blue tonality" is characterized by specific kinds of pitch play in varied harmonic contexts. A blue note on a C dominant seventh chord, such as the pitch E♭, might not be a blue note in another harmonic context, such as over an F dominant seventh chord (where E♭ is an essential pitch in the sonority's definition).

9. This line of argument has continuity with Gates's understanding of "signifyin(g)": one does not signify *something,* one signifies *in some way.*

10. The centrality of the blues is also confirmed by the staggering number of compositions based on its eight-, twelve-, or sixteen-bar forms. For a discussion of those forms and their various transformations, see Koch (1982). DeVeaux (1997, 345–47) observes that some bebop players initially found the blues antithetical to their progressive aims.

11. One might only speculate about the degree to which my being African American encouraged musicians to raise or made them feel comfortable raising such issues. In some situations, however, the centrality of race and/or culture goes unaddressed when the researcher and the interviewee are not African American (see Monson 1990, 38–39).

12. Burrell, Pass, Abercrombie, Metheny, and Jarrett are those on the list who are not African American. Wynton Kelly (1931–71) was black and born in Jamaica. His family moved to New York when he was four years old.

13. For example, musicians such as Louis Armstrong, Duke Ellington, Count Basie, Coleman Hawkins, Art Tatum, Lester Young, Billie Holiday, Charlie Parker, Dizzy Gillespie, Bud Powell, Miles Davis, Art Blakey, Horace Silver, Sonny Rollins, John Coltrane, McCoy Tyner, Elvin Jones, Freddie Hubbard, Wayne Shorter, Herbie Hancock, Tony Williams, Woody Shaw, Kenny Garrett, and Mulgrew Miller are more frequently cited as influential by musicians than are non–African American musicians such as Bix Beiderbecke, Lennie Tristano, Red Rodney, Gil Evans, Bill Evans, Phil Woods, Scott LaFaro, Chick Corea, Keith Jarrett, Dave Holland, Joe Zawinul, or Michael Brecker. Those in the latter group are most often cited by European American musicians. I am not suggesting that the influence of these non–African American musicians is not as important as that of African Americans. Based on what many musicians and

audience members say, however, it would seem that the music's paradigmatic tradition bearers have been African American and that the reason for their early and continued influence might be located in the connections between musical performance and wider African American cultural practices. This argument is often misinterpreted by non–African Americans—and some African Americans—as one for the existence of a racial essence that all African Americans possess and that non–African Americans will never have, experience, or understand. To my mind, the most informed presenters of a cultural viewpoint locate it in the degree to which one *learns* to understand different facets of African American culture and their relationship to and emergence in musical performance. For a discussion of these issues and their relation to Pierre Bourdieu's adaptation of Marcel Mauss's notion of *habitus* (Bourdieu 1977), see Monson (1990).

14. Antonio Hart saw as problematic the segregation of different groups of musicians at the Berklee College of Music in Boston in the late 1980s, observing that racial and cultural differences mapped onto stylistic ones. Sam Newsome confirmed he came to the same conclusion when he was at Berklee a few years prior to Hart's arrival. Newsome asserted that the majority of white—European and European American—students were interested in musicians like Gary Burton, while many of the African American musicians were interested in learning "how to swing."

15. Benjamin Brinner's informants (1995) make similar arguments regarding conservatory training of gamelan musicians.

16. So pervasive is Blakey's influence that a number of musicians who had played with him spent nearly an hour discussing his wisdom and his foibles during and after a break during the second evening of recording for James Williams's CD *Truth, Justice, and the Blues* (field notes, 12 December 1994). It was also clear in this instance that more aspects of African American culture than the musical might be important to the sensibility of (male) jazz musicians, for other topics of conversation included James Brown's music (sparked by news of his arrest on a domestic violence charge), Mike Tyson's imminent release from prison and his future prospects, and the relative merits of boxers Lennox Lewis, Michael Moorer, and George Foreman. For more writing on the importance of boxing in African American culture, see Early (1992), Wright (1992), and Hare (1992).

17. Again, compare with Monson (1990, 37).

18. This exchange is excerpted from the larger interview, which appears in the appendix. Compare the topics of our discussion with Feld's concern with the importance of "social experience, background, skill, desire and necessity" in discerning musical meaning (Feld 1994b, 84).

19. Herbie Hancock's composition "Eye of the Hurricane" (*Maiden Voyage*, CD, Blue Note CDP 46339, recorded 17 May 1965) is a similar but more complicated example. Hancock's tune has a difficult head with abrupt metric and harmonic shifts, but the form for solos is blues in F minor. Bernstein continued discussing compositional openness by likening jazz to team sports: "Being a leader, I think, is like being a coach of a basketball team. You have to coach the team you have. You can't say, 'Well, you know, I'm Pat Riley [the coach of the

New York Knicks at the time]. I used to coach the [Los Angeles] Lakers. So you be [Earvin] 'Magic' Johnson, and you be Kareem [Abdul-Jabbar, both former Lakers].' That's not gonna work, you know. You have to say, 'I don't have Magic and Kareem. This is who I have. So this is how we're going to build . . .' That's a team. Jazz is a team thing" (Bernstein 1995a). Peter Watrous (1995b), in a separate instance, has been critical of comparisons or convergences between jazz and sports.

20. Note that this next level is not so much a transcendence of place or circumstance as a form of communion in which participants share aspects of their identities and understandings in the context of musical performance. In other words, it is less a form of escape than it is a form of deep involvement. In this sense, it is different from the notion of transcendence as applied to music in the Western art tradition. In the latter scenario, transcendence has precisely to do with music's surviving or taking on meaning outside the context of performance, when it becomes timeless and universal. In the former instance, it is akin to religious or spiritual ecstasy. This does not mean, however, that jazz scene participants don't sometimes speak of jazz in terms of transcendence in the classical sense. I argue below that sometimes such usages are strategic.

21. Those who are experiencing flow do not perceive or recognize the passage of time or other items that normally register in consciousness. Moments of flow are most likely to occur when the challenge of a particular activity and the skills possessed by an individual are nearly matched. When the challenge outweighs one's skill, anxiety about one's skill is the result. When one's skills exceed what is required by a certain challenge, then boredom is highly likely.

22. Scholars writing about African American musics have often seen the blues as musical form and/or as ethos as pivotal to an understanding of all African American musics. Samuel A. Floyd Jr., for example, writes that "since the blues appears to be basic to most of forms of black music, and since it seems to be the most prominent factor in maintaining continuity between most of them, we might think of it as the Urtrope of the tradition" (Floyd 1995, 79), while literary critic Houston A. Baker Jr. (1984, 4) sees it as the "always already" in African American music making.

23. In his discussion of Chicano rock-and-roll bands in Los Angeles, George Lipsitz (1990, 152–53) makes similar points about cross-modal homologies.

24. See Keil (1991, 164–90) for the way in which the blues functions as a locus of realness, honesty, and sincerity across modalities. Recently James Lincoln Collier has questioned the degree to which jazz can be considered an African American music (1993, 183–224). In a fashion typical of his other writings, Collier confuses and conflates several unrelated issues, particularly by citing the involvement of non–African Americans in jazz as performers and listeners as evidence refuting its African Americanness. One wonders whether the involvement of Americans in the teaching and performance of Verdi's operas makes his works less "Italian." For criticism of Collier's writing and presentation skills, see Carner (1991) and Craddock-Willis (1995), respectively.

25. Powell's writing about a blues aesthetic was first published in conjunction with a traveling exhibition called "The Blues Aesthetic," for which he served as curator. His essay in the catalog accompanying the exhibit proposes

ways of finding commonalities in the styles of modernist African American visual artists using the blues as a lens. That his theorization is an attempt to avoid the racial determinism of previous writers is evidenced by his seeing the blues as a "point of view that one might inherit, as well as choose to embrace" and his avoiding the term "Afro-American aesthetic" because its racial connotations might overshadow its cultural focus (1989b, 20–21). In this essay and a later one (Powell 1994), he sees the blues as a thoroughly modernist twentieth-century manifestation of African American culture. It is clear from his exposition, however, that his primary concern and expertise lie with visual art and that his aim is to use an implicitly self-evident, music-derived blues aesthetic as a way of reading or interpreting visual art. As a result, it would seem somewhat circular to use his blues aesthetic—formulated from a limited understanding of music and intended to elucidate aspects of visual art—to read and explain music. An alternative approach would be to formulate a blues aesthetic from engagement with music and musicians to read and interpret other blues-based musics. This line of reasoning follows from Clifford Geertz's argument that "Art and the equipment to grasp it are made in the same shop" (1983, 118). And it is precisely this line of argument that makes me skeptical of works that attempt too strictly to apply Henry Louis Gates Jr.'s understanding of "signifyin(g)" (1988) to the analysis of African American music. Although there are numerous suggestive correspondences between African American music and literature, those correspondences alone do not make a convincing case for applying his theory to the analysis of African American music. That is, they do not make a case for applying a theory, derived partially from music and intended for the analysis of writing, to the analysis of music. Indeed, one can understand musical signification without making the journey through literary signifying, a journey that might cause one to misapply concepts and oppositions germane to speech to music (Seeger 1960; 1969, 233; 1977, 181).

26. Indeed, I prefer "blues aesthetic" to "African American aesthetic" because the term "African American" has a tendency to be equated with biological and ideological constructions of race, even though its meaning has more to do with cultural practice.

27. This argument has some continuity with studies of hegemony and resistance that note that any act that resists hegemony also serves in some ways to reinforce it. Likewise, there is a suggestive relationship to Pierre Bourdieu's notion of *habitus,* defined as "a system of lasting, transposable dispositions which, integrating past experiences, functions at every moment as a *matrix of perceptions, appreciations, and actions,* and makes possible the achievement of infinitely diversified tasks" (1977, 82–83).

28. See Burnim (1985, 1988), Burnim and Maultsby (1987), and Harris (1992) for more discussion of the relationships between African American secular and religious musics.

29. Sometimes, however, older musicians "signify" on their younger counterparts' willingness to take their words as wisdom. In December of 1994 saxophonist Billy Pierce recounted a story about Art Blakey in Rome. Blakey was pointing out various landmarks, such as the Coliseum, and noting the skill displayed by the (ancient) Romans in constructing them. Pierce and other band

members were somewhat impressed with Blakey's knowledge until he pointed out a gas station and said, with no apparent irony, "The Romans built that!"

30. Gregory Hutchinson played a series of tunes by Dizzy Gillespie recorded in the 1950s for Verve Records, while Antonio Hart played an Earth, Wind, and Fire "greatest hits" collection as well as Cannonball Adderley recordings I had never heard that made me reassess the late saxophonist's career. Peter Bernstein and I frequently turned talk away from the interview to react to the Sonny Stitt recordings that were being played on a WKCR broadcast.

31. Publishers frequently mislabel half-diminished seventh chords as minor sixth chords, so that a D half-diminished seventh chord is labeled an F minor sixth chord. Each chord consists of the same set of pitches, but they have different functions. The former has a dominant function, while the latter typically has a minor tonic function. For more information on the history of fake books, see Kernfeld (2006).

32. Indeed, reading most frequently seemed configured as an opportunity to escape from music rather than to be engaged further with it. Joshua Redman and Peter Watrous discussed the relative merits of Thomas Pynchon's novels at the Village Vanguard one evening, for example, and Sam Newsome and I discussed Toni Morrison's writing during my interview with him.

33. As narrow as many of the musicians I interviewed (and I) find Wynton Marsalis's comments about jazz, it is precisely out of this context that his comments proceed. See Pareles (1996) for a discussion of Marsalis's use of the institutional power of Lincoln Center to increase the profile of jazz in American society.

CHAPTER 6

1. Van Gennep's book was originally published in 1908 as *Les rites de passage*.

2. Victor Turner's work in some ways straddles these perspectives: "In order to live, to breathe, and to generate novelty, human beings have had to create—by structural means—spaces and times in the calendar or, in the cultural cycles of their most cherished groups[,] which cannot be captured in the classificatory nets of their quotidian routinized spheres of action. These liminal areas of time and space—rituals, carnivals, dramas, and latterly films—are open to *the play of thought, feeling, and will*; in them are generated new models, often fantastic, some of which may have sufficient power and plausibility to replace eventually the force-backed political and jural models that control the centers of society's ongoing life" (1969, vii; emphasis added). Turner's emphasis on the performative aspects of ritual became more pronounced in his later years, when he came to view ritual as dramaturgical and to focus on the theatrical aspects of daily life (e.g., in 1974b, 1974a, 1982).

3. For Combs-Schilling, an icon "is an enduring physical representation of truth in which the specifics of physical form are crucial to the meaning constructed" (1989, 168). Icons, so conceived, allow for metaphoric associations to be made between physical entities and deeply held beliefs. Note the correspon-

dence between her invocation of iconicity and Steven Feld's mentioned in the previous chapter.

4. To be sure, Ellington's work might well appeal to those listeners with other "metacultural" outlooks (Urban 2001), other interpretive schemas, though the uses to which his work might be put and the kinds of beings it might help to create will, of course, be different.

5. The narratives that are the basis of social memory, as such, differ from those supporting historical reconstruction in that they are part of an interconnected social world rather than the seemingly detached evaluation of evidence (Connerton 1989, 14–21). See chapter 2 for further discussion of the distinctions between history and memory and the role that power plays in valorizing the former.

6. See, for example, Ellison (1964a, 256–57), Keil (1991, 164), Murray (1970, 58; 1976, 17), Levine (1977, 234–37), Leonard (1987, 23, 53–55, 61–64, 71–75), Small (1987a, 70, 302), Salamone (1988), and Floyd (1995, 140–41).

7. These concerns, of course, are also directly linked to the ability of performance venues to remain viable as businesses. During my period of fieldwork and shortly thereafter, extensive renovations were undertaken at the Blue Note and Iridium. Lorraine Gordon also proudly told Peter Watrous and me in the summer of 1995 that the Village Vanguard had purchased a new piano with the advice and blessing of pianist Tommy Flanagan. The profit motive, however, might be considered less important in light of the recurring joke among journalists and scene participants that one shouldn't open a jazz club if one wants to make money.

8. The responses to such requests are highly variable. Some individuals claim a "right" to do whatever they want because they are "paying customers." The disdain reserved for such audience members is similar to that engendered by European tourists who visited Harlem churches in the 1990s and sometimes disrupted services, for example by taking photographs at times and in ways that regular parishioners deemed disrespectful. See Lii (1995), Bruni (1996), and Gomes (1996).

9. In typical usage, the term *head* simply refers to a tune's melody and harmonic progression, which form the basis for improvisation. I am using the term in a more inclusive sense here to distinguish between "head" and "form." At performances and in recording sessions, musicians would frequently refer to solos "on the form," but never to solos "on the head." For that reason, I construe "head" and "form" to be distinct entities, the former including the latter in most cases. For situations where the head does not include the form, see note 12, below.

10. Actually, the last A section in Gershwin's tune is ten (eight plus two) measures in length, but jazz musicians frequently use only the first eight. Gershwin's tune is so well known that, in the same way that one can say "blues in F minor," count off a tempo, and have other musicians play along, one can also say "rhythm changes in F"—indicating the harmonic progression from the Gershwin tune and a key—and get a similar result. Not all AABA compositions consist of sections eight measures in length. Jerome Kern and Dorothy Fields's

"The Way You Look Tonight" is a form with sixteen-measure A and B units, while "Will You Still Be Mine?" by Matt Dennis and Tom Adair has sixteen-measure A sections and an eight-measure B section.

11. "Feel" refers to the rhythmic/accentual/textural patterning of or approach to playing a tune or section thereof based on conventional understanding. Among the most common named ones are Latin, bossa, samba, ballad, two-beat, and swing, each of which carries with it expectations about how rhythm section members (piano, bass, and drums, in particular) are supposed to play.

12. Herbie Hancock's previously cited "Eye of the Hurricane" is a good example. Wynton Marsalis's "J-Mood" (*J-Mood*, CD, Columbia CK 40308, recorded 17–20 December 1985, New York, New York), like "Eye of the Hurricane," features several changes of meter and tonal center in the head. The form for the solos is a blues progression. David Sánchez's composition "Ebony" (1994, *The Departure*, CD, Columbia CK 57848, recorded 23–24 November and 7 December 1993, New York, New York) is a thirty-two-bar form divided into eight-, six-, eight-, and ten-bar sections, respectively. There are also marked changes of feel, as when the ensemble switches to a Latin feel in the second eight-bar section. The feel changes are maintained for all solos.

13. For example, in an AABA tune one plays three A sections in succession between each B section. Some performers unwittingly drop one of the A sections from time to time. The resultant harmonic and rhythmic clashes can be embarrassing for the performer and other participants in the musical event. Ingrid Monson's discussion of mistakes in the "time cycle" in a performance of "Bass-ment Blues" is instructive here (1991, 245–52). Gregory Hutchinson notes that failure to understand form can lead to conflicts in bands: "I used to [get upset], man . . . [when] cats [would] start messin' up the form, I'd be like, 'Aww, man! Shhhhhhhhhit! Not *again!* Don't you know this tune by *now?!*' " (Hutchinson 1994).

14. In a sense, the term *solo* is misleading, for multiple performers are improvising during the "solo" sections of a performance. The term *feature* might be more appropriate.

15. Under different circumstances, composed interludes might be called "sendoffs" or "shout choruses."

16. See Jackson (1992) for more discussion of communication and cueing.

17. By nesting the scene frame within the blues aesthetic frame, I am leaving open the possibility of examining other African American music scenes through the prism of a blues aesthetic.

CHAPTER 7

1. Interestingly, these frames are the same ones that Kenneth Burke suggests help to determine the nature of any dramatic action. His concern in analyzing action is to attend to action, actor, purpose, agency, and scene. For an explanation of those terms and their use in analysis, see Burke (1969) and O'Meally (1994, 245–46).

2. Monson's related understanding of grooves (1996) is largely, though not exclusively, devoted to rhythmic propulsion. The notion of "feel" presented here

is distinct from groove through its deployment. Although in some cases the two are interchangeable, "feel" is typically used, with qualifiers, in very specific contexts, such as in the example of the Sam Jones–Louis Hayes feel, to refer to a complex encompassing both rhythmic propulsion and other statistical elements of performance. Jones and Hayes were the bassist and drummer, respectively, who played with Cannonball Adderley's quintet throughout the 1960s.

3. The resulting disc was issued in 1996 as Charles Thomas, *The Finishing Touch* (CD, Space Time 9602, recorded 27–29 September 1994, New York, New York).

4. The "lost generation" is an appellation for those musicians too old to be considered young lions (and thus aggressively pursued by record companies), but too young to be signed by the same labels as "legends." Masland (1990) discusses a number of musicians in their thirties and forties who fall in that group, including pianist Mulgrew Miller and saxophonist Bobby Watson. Williams preferred the term "young veterans" to "lost generation."

5. Now known as Avatar, the Power Station was located at 441 West 53rd Street in Manhattan.

6. A room that I am certain is Studio A can be seen in a short promotional video that forms the electronic press kit (EPK) produced for the Joshua Redman Quartet's *MoodSwing* (1994a). Although one might be tempted to view this video as indicative of what happens in the studio, it perhaps reveals only how musicians are positioned relative to one another. The lighting and Redman's playing to the camera in the EPK make it quite clear that this video is not indicative of what performers actually do in the recording studio. A panoramic view of Studio A at Avatar Studios (the new name of the Power Station) can be seen at www.avatarstudios.net/rooms/studio_a.html (accessed 24 November 2007).

7. The first recorded version of the tune can be found on *Alter Ego* (CD, Sunnyside SSC 1007D, recorded 19–20 July 1984, New York, New York). The tune has become something of a modern standard, widely performed and recorded by other artists, including Donald Byrd.

8. Sickler is a trumpeter and arranger who was employed primarily by Verve Records during my fieldwork, and Chambers is the son of the celebrated jazz bassist Paul Chambers.

9. In the end, Williams decided not to include this tune on the final release of the recording.

10. Javon Jackson is a tenor saxophonist who recorded a series of well-received albums for Blue Note in the 1990s. Mark Gross is an alto saxophonist who, at the time of this session, was a member of the Mercer Ellington orchestra.

11. Based on their account, one might say that Nussbaum's use of dynamics was unbalanced with the other aspects of his sound, or that, by playing too loudly, he failed to be open to what Henderson was bringing to the music.

12. Talking to Thomas the following night, I learned that he would be joining Joshua Redman's quartet as a replacement for Christian McBride, who would be launching a solo career. In addition, pianist Brad Mehldau was departing Redman's group and would be replaced by Peter Martin, who at the time was the

pianist in the Roy Hargrove Quintet. Subsequently, Hargrove spent the greater part of 1995 trying to find a steady replacement for Martin, who had himself replaced Marc Cary. Cary had departed from Hargrove's band to play with Abbey Lincoln.

13. The level of relaxation might also have been a result of the band's having rehearsed for the session on the previous Saturday, 3 December. The atmosphere at the session was so jovial and loose that singer Miles Griffith was improvising words to "Just a Feeling" about James Williams growing old and losing his hair when they ran through the tune before recording it.

14. The term *out* has many levels of meaning. In all cases, it signifies something that goes beyond conventional expectations. When an improviser, for example, chooses pitches whose relationship to the prevailing harmony is distant and perhaps extremely dissonant, his pitch choices can be described as being "out." Likewise, when a singer such as Griffith interlards what most would expect to be a scat solo with various nonverbal and humorous vocal sounds, approximating the growling of an animal, hysterical laughter, yelling, and the calling of chickens, his singing is said to be "out." The varied meanings of the term are frequently invoked in discussions of "avant-garde" jazz performance. Eric Dolphy's recording *Out to Lunch* (CD, Blue CDP 7 46524 2, recorded 25 February 1964, Englewood Cliffs, New Jersey) and David Such's book *Avant-garde Jazz Musicians: Performing "Out There"* (1993) are pertinent here. The tune "Lunch Time Again" on Antonio Hart's *It's All Good* is a sonic homage to the Dolphy recording.

15. Some of Wilson's cells, in fact, would be manipulated by him in the same way two days later at his own recording session. See the analysis of "Perdido" by the Steve Wilson Quartet below.

16. Overblowing is a technique by which players of wind instruments produce partials above a fundamental pitch instead of the pitch itself, akin to producing harmonics on string instruments. In doing so, an instrumentalist expands the effective range of an instrument, and, when the technique is combined with adjustments to embouchure, it can lead to different shadings of timbre. False fingering is a technique by which players of wind instruments, like the saxophone, alter the instrument's vibrating air column by stopping other holes that don't alter a given pitch. What is altered, however, is the timbre of the note produced. See the entries on overblowing and false fingering in the *New Grove Dictionary of Jazz* (New York: Macmillan, 1988).

17. In some ways this performance is an example of what Ingrid Monson has described as a process of "musical intensification," proceeding on rhythmic and melodic planes simultaneously (1991, 234–62). The kind of intensification occurring here includes those planes as well as parameters such as timbre, texture, and density.

18. RPM Sound Studios is located at 12 East 12th Street, Suite 11, in Manhattan. For information about the history of Criss Cross and its importance for the current jazz scene, see Stein (1993) and Watrous (1996b).

19. For Barth's record dates the group would be augmented by trumpeter Scott Wendholt.

20. Bradley's was a small venue with a policy of booking piano-based groups of three or fewer musicians, thereby encouraging intimate interplay between the musicians and interaction with their audiences. On some occasions, such as this one, quartets performed. Interestingly, the preference for small groups was not originally an artistic decision. Rather, it was a result of New York City's cabaret laws (see Chevigny 1991, 82).

21. I later learned that this was a modified version of the arrangement that appears on Barth's (then unreleased) recording *Morning Call* (CD, Enja 8084–2, recorded 28–29 July 1994, New York, New York).

22. "Seven Come Eleven" was composed by Benny Goodman and Charlie Christian.

23. Antonio Hart's *It's All Good*, a portion of whose sessions I observed, was recorded at Sound on Sound, located at 322 West 45th Street in Manhattan.

24. Among other things, "hooking up" refers to ensemble members coming together, often spontaneously, in playing a riff or accentual pattern. See the glossary for further definitions.

25. Barth's tunes were titled "Up and Down" and "By the Window" for the record's release in 1996. "Everything Must Change" was a popular song among rhythm and blues, jazz, and gospel performers in the 1970s. A few of the many recordings that featured the tune include Randy Crawford, *Everything Must Change* (LP, Warner Brothers BS 2975, released 1976); George Benson, *In Flight* (LP, Warner Brothers, BSK 2983, released 1977); Morgana King, *Everything Must Change* (LP, Muse MR 5190, recorded 8 August 1978, New York, New York); and the Milt Jackson Big 4, *At the Montreux Jazz Festival, 1975* (LP, Pablo 2310–753, recorded 17 July 1975, Montreux, Switzerland).

26. For the purpose of clarity, the sections in an AABA form will be referred to as A_1, A_2, B, and A_3, respectively.

27. To "lay out" means not to play.

28. Parker played the first few cymbal crashes on his ride cymbal, but he soon switched to his crash cymbal for more emphasis.

29. Duke Ellington, *The Great Paris Concert* (CD, Atlantic 304–2, recorded 1, 2, and 23 February 1963, Paris, France).

30. There are other tunes that use this kind of organization, that is, where one does not hear the melody of the tune until the end. One that immediately comes to mind is John Coltrane's "Countdown" on *Giant Steps* (CD, Atlantic 1311–2, recorded 4 May 1959).

31. There is another version of this duet passage in the recording of "Perdido" on Ellington's *Ellington Uptown* (CD, Columbia CK 40836, recorded 1 July 1952, New York, New York). This earlier recording indicates that the intricate bebop-style playing of the duet—complete with melodic references to Charlie Parker's compositions—might have been a function of Ellington's rearranging one of his standby numbers to accommodate younger, bebop-oriented members of his orchestra, such as Clark Terry, and his audience.

32. Here I am speaking of Parker's cymbal sound more from hearing him in live settings than I am on recordings. In fact, on recordings made by different engineers, that aspect of Parker's playing always comes through. The same

sound is clearly evident on his debut Sony release *Belief* (CD, Columbia CK 67457, recorded 1995, Waterford, Connecticut, and New York, New York). I became more keenly aware of his cymbal playing after he urged me to listen to drummer Ben Riley's playing with pianist Kenny Barron.

33. From Thelonious Monk and Sonny Rollins, *Thelonious Monk and Sonny Rollins* (CD, Original Jazz Classics OJCCD-059-2, recorded 13 November 1953). I thank Mark Tucker for pointing out the reference. The Monk tune's title is a playful commentary on 13 November having been a Friday.

34. An excerpt from Barth's recording of "In the Still of the Night" (*Morning Call*, CD, Enja 8084-2, recorded 28–29 July 1994, New York, New York) provides an example of these same musicians doing something quite similar at an earlier time. As on Wilson's recording, a more or less regular pattern of pulses (starting at approximately 1:23) is contradicted by what Barth and Parker play while Grenadier maintains the pulse in the background. Instead of displacing the metric accent in this example, however, they change the basic pulse, from a quarter note to a dotted eighth. Near the end of this passage Barth even begins playing off-beat accents within this new pattern.

35. Perhaps Parker, who had responded to each other call, assumed that Barth might reenter at that moment.

36. There are many ways of reading Teekens's statement as well as the behavior he attributes to older musicians. It may well be that the small amount of money Teekens pays older musicians may not be incentive enough for them to put their best into a recording. One might speculate that whatever else a recording session may be at other times, for older musicians recording for Criss Cross, a session is just a job.

37. CD, Verve 614-511-779-2, recorded 3, 6, and 8 September 1991, Englewood Cliffs, New Jersey. Interestingly, after Mehldau and McBride had left Redman and moved on to other groups, in 1996 Bernstein began touring and recording with Redman.

38. The Sher lead sheet presents the tune as an AABA form. Most recorded versions of the tune use a simplified AABA form. Bernstein had previously recorded this tune in E♭ with organist Larry Goldings and drummer Bill Stewart on Goldings's compact disc *Light Blue* (CD, Minor Music 801026, recorded September 1992, New York, New York). Another version of this tune, also in E♭, appears on George Benson's *The New Boss Guitar of George Benson* (CD, Prestige OJCCD-461-2, recorded 1 and 14 May 1964, New York, New York). In each recording of the tune on which Bernstein performs, he plays the third phrase of the A sections transposed down an octave from the version on Sher's lead sheet and the one played by George Benson.

39. Many musicians choose not to rehearse standards prior to recording sessions or live performances unless the leader of the date has written new or strikingly difficult arrangements of them, as when saxophonist Steve Wilson adapted Duke Ellington's arrangement of "Perdido." Because every musician is supposed to be familiar with the melodies, forms, and harmonic progressions of standards, rehearsal seems unnecessary.

40. At the time, Mehldau's drug problems were common knowledge to individuals on the scene but not to the general public. After leaving Redman's band

at the end of 1994 and going through a rehabilitation program, Mehldau discussed his prior problems with an interviewer for *Hot House* (Kalbacher 1997). Whether one can attribute it to being clean or not, Mehldau's playing did change markedly from the beginning of 1995 to 1997, becoming less frenetic and more subtle. Or, as he put it, "There's a little more restraint now. I'm playing with a little more taste" (quoted in Kalbacher 1997, 18).

41. The playing of "secondary ragtime" (superimpositions of passages based on groupings of three eighth notes in common time; see Wilson 1974, 7–9) is an early example of this practice. Another example can be found in Louis Armstrong's vocal improvisation on "Hotter Than That" (CD, *The Hot Fives and Sevens, Volume II*, Columbia CK 44422, recorded 13 December 1927, Chicago, Illinois).

42. The tag, in this case, is the same as the introduction. The last two measures, however, are treated as a break, to be played only by the next soloist.

43. In "rushing" the figure, that is, Hutchinson played it slightly faster than the established tempo required.

44. Mehldau's playing on Joshua Redman's *MoodSwing* contains this particular figure at least once in each composition where he takes a solo.

45. See note 12, above.

46. Payton, Anderson, Martin, Thomas, Blade, *New Orleans Collective* (CD, Evidence ECD 22105–2, recorded 28 December 1992, New Orleans, Louisiana).

47. Christian McBride, pianist Kevin Hays, and drummer Gregory Hutchinson comprised the main group for Redman's first recording, *Joshua Redman* (CD, Warner Brothers 9 45242–2, recorded 27 May, 4 June, and 15 September 1992, New York, New York). The word "book" refers to the group's repertoire of jazz standards and original tunes.

48. "Hits" are the notes or chords in the head of a tune that members of an ensemble are to accentuate, through increasing volume, changing timbre, or some other means.

49. That is, inferring from Redman's comments (that jazz, like all great music, was about expression) that he wants the music to be more accessible. Interestingly, Redman's recall of what Watrous wrote is nearly exact: only one word is missing.

50. A similar set of experiences led Branford Marsalis to title his 1990 album *Crazy People Music* (CD, Columbia 46072), a phrase taken from a friend who asked why he didn't focus more on accessible melodic playing (personal communication, November 1990).

51. Watrous and I arrived so late, shortly after midnight (and thus technically on 22 March), because we had observed a long set by Al Grey at the Blue Note before walking to the Village Vanguard.

52. Comparison of my notes with a hearing of *Spirit of the Moment* (Redman 1995b) indicates that, of the tunes I heard on 21 March, "Herbs and Roots," "Count Me Out," and "My One and Only Love" from the second set were all included on the released recording.

53. These younger audience members appeared to be, like me at the time, in their twenties, though if their attire was a reliable indicator, most of them were considerably more gainfully employed than the typical graduate student.

54. Redman's "Headin' Home" can be found on *MoodSwing* (CD, Warner Brothers 9 45643–2, recorded 8–10 March 1994, New York, New York).

Prince's "Vicki Waiting" comes from his soundtrack for the film *Batman* (CD, Warner Brothers 9 25936-2, recorded 1989, Chanhasset, Minnesota). At several points during my interviews with him, Redman expressed admiration for the music of Prince. To see where the IV chord in a twelve-bar blues progression occurs, refer to figure 3. The B♭7 chord is the IV chord.

55. When singers perform jazz standards or popular songs, however, applause frequently follows the opening figures of a tune, particularly once the audience recognizes a lyrical or melodic phrase. For recorded evidence, listen to Randy Crawford's live version of "Everything Must Change" (discographical information in note 25, above).

56. He formally addressed those issues in an essay in April (Watrous 1995b).

57. "My One and Only Love" was composed by Guy Wood and Robert Mellin. One of the most celebrated recordings of the tune can be found on *Johnny Hartman and John Coltrane* (CD, Impulse! GRD-157, recorded 7 March 1963, Englewood Cliffs, New Jersey). The other non-original tune was Sonny Rollins's "East Broadway Run Down."

58. I thank Mark Tucker for suggesting the second interpretation here.

59. Much of the ensemble's repertoire can be found on the recording *Wingspan* (CD, Landmark LCD-1515-2, recorded 11 May 1987, New York, New York). The difficulties of keeping a group together over a long period of time made it impossible for Miller to maintain the same ensemble from 1987 up to 1994 or even from then into 1995. Two of the musicians from the recording session, bassist Charnett Moffett and alto saxophonist Kenny Garrett, were replaced for this live engagement by Richie Goods and Antonio Hart, respectively. Performances in 1995 by Wingspan saw drummer Tony Reedus replaced by Karriem Riggins and Antonio Hart replaced by Steve Wilson.

60. When we arrived at the Village Vanguard it was close to being sold out, primarily because of the Panasonic Village Jazz Festival, which had been taking place for three days.

61. Peter Watrous used the same term to describe a performance by Eddie Harris, Stanley Turrentine, and others at the Panasonic Village Jazz Festival in Washington Square Park on 19 September (Watrous 1994a). Interestingly, Watrous left the performance right before the group started to make the connection with audience members discussed near the end of chapter 5.

62. CD, Novus 63153-2, recorded 16 and 18 December 1992, New York, New York.

63. Mulgrew Miller, *With Our Own Eyes* (CD, Novus 63171-2, recorded 21–22 December 1993, Brooklyn, New York).

64. The unsigned "Locked hands" entry in the 1988 edition of the *New Grove Dictionary of Jazz* describes the technique well: "A type of chord voicing for piano in which block chords in close position are played in the right hand and the left hand doubles the melody at the lower octave."

65. Hart, during my interview with him as well as in conversation, professed admiration for saxophonist Kenny Garrett's playing. He explained that while he was a student at Berklee he frequently spoke with Garrett by phone and at-

tempted to purchase every recording featuring him. *Wingspan* was a highly valued item in his collection of recordings featuring Garrett.

66. John Coltrane, *Meditations* (CD, Impulse MCAD-39139, recorded November 1965). Although the place of recording is not indicated on the compact disc, Rudy Van Gelder's role as engineer makes his studio in Englewood Cliffs, New Jersey, a likely location.

67. A soul song by Norman Whitfield and Barrett Strong, from the Temptations' recording *All Directions* (LP, Motown 5417, released 1972).

CHAPTER 8

1. Hart's comments recall those by pianist McCoy Tyner that gave Valerie Wilmer's *As Serious As Your Life* (1980, 258) its title: "The general public, I feel, are swayed by a lot of different things. They're persuaded by a lot of different elements around musicians without really understanding what music is supposed to mean. It's a personal thing[;] it has a lot of meaning to it. Music's not a plaything—it's *as serious as your life.*"

2. Those meanings can be articulated differently on different local scenes. Future investigation will perhaps reveal the ways in which those articulations are distinct from those characteristic of New York City.

APPENDIX

1. From Marvin Gaye, *Let's Get It On* (LP, Tamla T329, 1973).

2. "Little Green Apples" was a hit for Smith in 1968.

3. CD, Warner Brothers 45274-2, 1993.

4. The Bobby Womack version of the tune comes from Bobby Womack, *The Poet* (CD, Razor and Tie RE 2029, 1993), which was originally released in 1981. The Jodeci version comes from the soundtrack for the film *Jason's Lyric* (CD, Polygram 314 522 915 4, 1994).

5. "(Not Just) Knee Deep" can be found on Funkadelic's *Uncle Jam Wants You* (LP, Warner Brothers BSK 3209, 1979).

6. Other recordings featuring "Everything Must Change" include Randy Crawford, *Everything Must Change* (LP, Warner Brothers BS 2975, recorded 1976); Johnny Lytle, *Everything Must Change* (LP, Muse Records, 1978); George Benson, *In Flight* (LP, Warner Bros, BSK 2983, 1977); Morgana King, *Everything Must Change* (LP, Muse MR 5190, recorded 8 August 1978, New York, New York); and Milt Jackson Big 4, *At the Montreux Jazz Festival, 1975* (LP, Pablo 2310-753, recorded 17 July 1975, Montreux, Switzerland).

7. Hathaway's version of the tune can be found on *Extension of a Man* (CD, Rhino R2 71520 [originally issued as Atco 7029], recorded September 1972–April 1973, New York, New York, and Chicago, Illinois). Garrett's version can be heard on *African Exchange Student* (CD, Atlantic 782156-2, recorded on unspecified dates in New York, New York).

8. Wynton Marsalis, *Black Codes (From the Underground)* (CD, Columbia CK 40009, recorded 7–11 and 14 January 1985, New York, New York).

References

Abu-Lughod, Lila. 1991. "Writing Against Culture." In *Recapturing Anthropology: Working in the Present,* edited by Richard G. Fox, 137–62. Santa Fe: School of American Research Press.

Agawu, V. Kofi. 1991. *Playing with Signs: A Semiotic Interpretation of Classic Music.* Princeton, NJ: Princeton University Press.

Ake, David. 2002. *Jazz Cultures.* Berkeley: University of California Press.

Anderson, Iain. 2002. "Jazz Outside the Marketplace: Free Improvisation and Non-Profit Sponsorship of the Arts, 1965–1980." *American Music* 20(2): 131–67.

Andrews, Dwight D. 1989. "From Black to Blues." In *The Blues Aesthetic: Black Culture and Modernism,* edited by Richard J. Powell, 37–41. Washington, DC: Washington Project for the Arts.

Appadurai, Arjun. 1981. "The Past as a Scarce Resource." *Man* 16: 201–19.

Asad, Talal. 1983. "Notes on Body Pain and Truth in Medieval Christian Ritual." *Economy and Society* 12: 287–327.

Atkins, E. Taylor. 2001. *Blue Nippon: Authenticating Jazz in Japan.* Durham, NC: Duke University Press.

———, ed. 2003. *Jazz Planet.* Jackson: University Press of Mississippi.

Atkinson, Connie Zeanah. 1997. "Whose New Orleans? Music's Place in the Packaging of New Orleans for Tourism." In *Tourists and Tourism: Identifying with People and Places,* edited by Simone Abram, Jacqueline Waldren, and Donald V.L. Maclean, 91–106. Oxford: Berg.

Auslander, Philip. 1998. "Seeing Is Believing: Live Performance and the Discourse of Authenticity in Rock Culture." *Literature and Psychology* 44(4): 1–26.

Baker, Houston A., Jr. 1984. *Blues, Ideology, and Afro-American Literature: A Vernacular Theory.* Chicago: University of Chicago Press.

Bakhtin, M.M. 1981. *The Dialogic Imagination: Four Essays.* Edited by Michael Holquist. Austin: University of Texas Press.

Balliett, Whitney. 1977. "Jazz: New York Notes." *New Yorker,* 6 June, 120–29.

Baraka, Amiri (LeRoi Jones). 1963. *Blues People: Negro Music in White America.* New York: Morrow.

———. 1967a. *Black Music.* New York: Quill.

———. 1967b. "Jazz and the White Critic." In *Black Music,* 11–20. New York: Quill.

———. 1990. "Jazz Criticism and Its Effect on the Art Form." In *New Perspectives on Jazz,* edited by David Baker, 55–70. Washington, DC: Smithsonian Institution Press.

———. 1991. "The 'Blues Aesthetic' and the 'Black Aesthetic': Aesthetics as the Continuing Political History of a Culture." *Black Music Research Journal* 11(2): 101–9.

Barth, Bruce. 1994. Interview by author, New York, NY. 16 November.

———. 1995. Interview by author, New York, NY. 22 February.

Barth, Fredrik. 1969. "Introduction." In *Ethnic Groups and Boundaries: The Social Organization of Culture Difference,* edited by Fredrik Barth, 9–38. Boston: Little, Brown and Co.

———. 1978. "Scale and Network in Urban Western Society." In *Scale and Social Organization,* edited by Fredrik Barth, 163–83. New York: Columbia University Press.

Bastien, David T., and Todd J. Hostager. 1991. "Jazz as Social Structure, Process, and Outcome." In *Jazz in Mind: Essays on the History and Meanings of Jazz,* edited by Reginald T. Buckner and Steven Weiland, 148–65. Detroit, MI: Wayne State University Press.

Bauman, Richard. 1975. "Verbal Art as Performance." *American Anthropologist* 77: 290–311.

Bauman, Richard, and Charles L. Briggs. 1990. "Poetics and Performance as Critical Perspectives on Language and Social Life." *Annual Review of Anthropology* 19: 59–88.

Bayles, Martha, et al. 2001. "Watching 'Jazz' for Its High Notes and Low." *New York Times,* 7 January, Sec. 2: 33, 40.

Becker, Howard S. 1951. "The Professional Dance Musician and His Audience." *American Journal of Sociology* 57: 136–44.

———. 1974. "Art as Collective Action." *American Sociological Review* 39: 767–76.

———. 1982. *Art Worlds.* Berkeley: University of California Press.

Becker, Judith, and Alton Becker. 1981. "A Musical Icon: Power and Meaning in Javanese Gamelan Music." In *The Sign in Music and Literature,* edited by Wendy Steiner, 203–15. Austin: University of Texas Press.

Béhague, Gerard, ed. 1984. *Performance Practice: Ethnomusicological Perspectives.* Westport, CT: Greenwood Press.

Bell, Catherine. 1992. *Ritual Theory, Ritual Practice.* New York: Oxford University Press.

Benadon, Fernando. 2006. "Slicing the Beat: Jazz Eighth-Notes as Expressive Microrhythm." *Ethnomusicology* 50(1): 73–98.

Bender, Thomas. 1982. *Community and Social Change in America.* Baltimore, MD: Johns Hopkins University Press.

Berger, Morroe. 1947. "Jazz: Resistance to the Diffusion of a Culture Pattern." *Journal of Negro History* 32 (October): 461–94.

Berliner, Paul F. 1994. *Thinking in Jazz: The Infinite Art of Improvisation.* Chicago: University of Chicago Press.

Bernstein, Peter. 1995a. Interview by author, New York, NY. 31 January.

———. 1995b. *Signs of Life.* Criss Cross 1095. Recorded 17 December 1994. New York, NY.

Björn, Lars, and Jim Gallert. 2001. *Before Motown: A History of Jazz in Detroit, 1920–60.* Ann Arbor: University of Michigan Press.

Blank, Uel. 1996. "Tourism in United States Cities." In *Tourism in Major Cities,* edited by Christopher M. Law, 206–32. London: International Thomson Business Press.

Block, Steven. 1990. "Pitch-Class Transformations in Free Jazz." *Music Theory Spectrum* 12(2): 181–202.

———. 1993. "Organized Sound: Pitch-Class Relations in the Music of Ornette Coleman." *Annual Review of Jazz Studies* 6: 229–52.

Blum, Stephen. 1992. "Analysis of Musical Style." In *Ethnomusicology: An Introduction,* edited by Helen Myers, 165–218. New York: W.W. Norton.

Blumenfeld, Larry. 1994. "New Kids on the Block." *Down Beat,* October, 10–11.

Blumenthal, Bob. 1980. "Arthur Blythe: Refreshing Traditions." *Down Beat,* April, 25–26, 64.

Bohlman, Philip V. 1999. "Ontologies of Music." In *Rethinking Music,* edited by Nicholas Cook and Mark Everist, 17–34. Oxford: Oxford University Press.

Boilès, Charles L. 1982. "Processes of Musical Semiosis." *Yearbook for Traditional Music* 14: 24–44.

Borgo, David. 2005. *Sync or Swarm: Improvising Music in a Complex Age.* New York: Continuum.

Born, Georgina. 1995. *Rationalizing Culture: IRCAM, Boulez, and the Institutionalization of the Avant-Garde.* Berkeley: University of California Press.

Bourdieu, Pierre. 1977. *Outline of a Theory of Practice.* Cambridge: Cambridge University Press.

———. 1984. *Distinction: A Social Critique of the Judgement of Taste.* Cambridge, MA: Harvard University Press.

Briggs, Charles L. 1986. *Learning How to Ask: A Sociolinguistic Appraisal of the Role of the Interview in Social Science Research.* Cambridge: Cambridge University Press.

Brinner, Benjamin. 1995. *Knowing Music, Making Music: Javanese Gamelan and the Theory of Music Competence and Interaction.* Chicago: University of Chicago Press.

Brothers, Thomas. 1994. "Solo and Cycle in African-American Jazz." *Musical Quarterly* 78: 479–509.

Brumann, Christoph. 1999. "Writing for Culture: Why a Successful Concept Should Not Be Discarded." *Current Anthropology* 40 supplement: S1–S13.

Bruni, Frank. 1996. "Drawn to Gospel, if Not Gospels, Foreigners Arrive by Busload." *New York Times,* 24 November, Sec. 1: 37.

Burke, Kenneth. 1969. *A Grammar of Motives.* Berkeley: University of California Press.

Burnim, Mellonee V. 1985. "The Black Gospel Music Tradition: A Complex of Ideology, Aesthetic, and Behavior." In *More Than Dancing: Essays on Afro-American Music and Musicians,* edited by Irene V. Jackson, 147–67. Westport, CT: Greenwood Press.

———. 1988. "Functional Dimensions of Gospel Music Performance." *Western Journal of Black Studies* 12(2): 112–21.

Burnim, Mellonee V., and Portia Maultsby. 1987. "From Backwoods to City Streets: The Afro-American Musical Journey." In *Expressively Black: The Cultural Basis of Ethnic Identity,* edited by Geneva Gay and Willie L. Baber, 109–36. New York: Praeger.

Buskin, Richard. 2010. "Classic Tracks: Miles Davis 'Round Midnight.' " *Sound on Sound,* April, 82–84, 86, 88–89.

Butterfield, Matthew W. 2000. "Jazz Analysis and the Production of Community: A Situational Perspective." Ph.D. diss., University of Pennsylvania.

———. 2006. "The Power of Anacrusis: Engendered Feeling in Groove-Based Musics." *Music Theory Online* 12(4). http://mtosmt.org/issues/mto.06.12.4/mto.06.12.4.butterfield.html.

———. 2010. "Variant Timekeeping Patterns and Their Effects in Jazz Drumming." *Music Theory Online* 16(4). http://mtosmt.org/issues/mto.10.16.4/mto.10.16.4.butterfield.html.

Byrnside, Ronald. 1975. "The Performer as Creator: Jazz Improvisation." In *Contemporary Music and Music Cultures,* edited by Bruno Nettl, Charles Hamm, and Ronald Brynside, 233–51. Englewood Cliffs, NJ: Prentice-Hall.

Cameron, William Bruce. 1954. "Sociological Notes on the Jam Session." *Social Forces* 33: 174–82.

Carner, Gary. 1991. "The Agony and the Agony: James Lincoln Collier's Jazz Writing." *Annual Review of Jazz Studies* 5: 81–89.

Cavicchi, Daniel. 1998. *Tramps Like Us: Music and Meaning among Springsteen Fans.* New York: Oxford University Press.

Certeau, Michel de. 1984. *The Practice of Everyday Life.* Berkeley: University of California Press.

Charters, Samuel B., and Leonard Kunstadt. 1962. *Jazz: A History of the New York Scene.* Garden City, NY: Doubleday.

Chevan, David. 1997. "Written Music in Early Jazz." Ph.D. diss., City University of New York.

Chevigny, Paul. 1991. *Gigs: Jazz and the Cabaret Laws in New York City.* New York: Routledge.

Clark, Anita. 1985. "Transcription in Jazz: Pedagogical Applications." *Jazz Research Papers* 5: 34–44.

Clarke, Catherine K. 1982. "Conversation with . . . William ('Billy') Taylor: The Jazz-Mobile Man." *Black Perspective in Music* 10(2): 179–88.

Clifford, James, and George E. Marcus, eds. 1986. *Writing Culture: The Poetics and Politics of Ethnography.* Berkeley: University of California Press.

Cohen, Harvey G. 2010. *Duke Ellington's America*. Chicago: University of Chicago Press.

Cohen, Maxwell T. 1993. *The Police Discord*. Metuchen, NJ: Scarecrow Press.

Cohen, Sara. 1991. *Rock Culture in Liverpool: Popular Music in the Making*. New York: Oxford University Press.

———. 1999. "Scenes." In *Key Terms in Popular Music and Culture,* edited by Bruce Horner and Thomas Swiss, 239–50. London: Blackwell.

Coker, Wilson. 1972. *Music and Meaning: A Theoretical Introduction to Musical Aesthetics*. New York: Free Press.

Cole, Bill. 1993. *John Coltrane*. New York: Da Capo.

Collier, James Lincoln. 1978. *The Making of Jazz: A Comprehensive History*. Boston: Houghton Mifflin.

———. 1987. *Duke Ellington*. New York: Oxford University Press.

———. 1993. *Jazz: The American Theme Song*. New York: Oxford University Press.

Comaroff, Jean. 1985. *Body of Power, Spirit of Resistance: The Culture and History of South African People*. Chicago: University of Chicago Press.

Combs-Schilling, M.E. 1989. *Sacred Performances: Islam, Sexuality, and Sacrifice*. New York: Columbia University Press.

Connerton, Paul. 1989. *How Societies Remember*. Cambridge: Cambridge University Press.

Corbett, John. 1995. "The Sorry-Assed State of Jazz Radio." *Down Beat,* June, 30–35.

Craddock-Willis, Andre. 1995. "Jazz People: Wynton Marsalis vs. James Lincoln Collier." *Transition* 5(1): 140–78.

Crenshaw, Kimberlé, et al., eds. 1995. *Critical Race Theory: The Key Writings that Formed the Movement*. New York: New Press.

Crouch, Stanley. 1987. "Wynton Marsalis: 1987." *Down Beat,* November, 16–19, 57.

———. 1990a. "Jazz Criticism and Its Effect on the Art Form." In *New Perspectives on Jazz,* edited by David N. Baker, 71–87. Washington, DC: Smithsonian Institution Press.

———. 1990b. "Play the Right Thing." *New Republic* (12 February): 30–37.

Csikszentmihalyi, Mihaly. 1988. "The Flow Experience and Its Significance for Human Psychology." In *Optimal Experience: Psychological Studies of Flow in Consciousness,* edited by Mihaly Csikszentmihalyi and Isabella Selega Csikszentmihalyi, 15–35. Cambridge: Cambridge University Press.

Daley, Dan. 1997. "New York Studios: All Quiet on the Eastern Front." *Mix,* October, 66–76.

Davies, Stephen. 1994. *Musical Meaning and Expression*. Ithaca, NY: Cornell University Press.

Davis, Francis. 1986. *In the Moment: Jazz in the 1980s*. New York: Oxford University Press.

———. 2002. "In the Macho World of Jazz, Don't Ask, Don't Tell." *New York Times,* 1 September, Sec. 1: 19, 21.

Davis, Gerald R. 1985. *I Got the Word in Me and I Can Sing It, You Know*. Philadelphia: University of Pennsylvania Press.

Davis, Miles, and Quincy Troupe. 1989. *Miles: The Autobiography.* New York: Simon and Schuster.

Delgado, Richard. 1995. "'The Imperial Scholar' Revisited: How to Marginalize Outsider Writing, Ten Years Later." In *Critical Race Theory: The Cutting Edge,* edited by Richard Delgado, 401–8. Philadelphia: Temple University Press.

DeNora, Tia. 2000. *Music in Everyday Life.* Cambridge: Cambridge University Press.

Deutsche, Rosalyn, and Cara Gendel Ryan. 1984. "The Fine Art of Gentrification." *October* 31: 91–111.

DeVeaux, Scott. 1988. "Bebop and the Recording Industry: The 1942 AFM Recording Ban Reconsidered." *Journal of the American Musicological Society* 61: 126–65.

———. 1991. "Constructing the Jazz Tradition: Jazz Historiography." *Black American Literature Forum* 25: 525–60.

———. 1995. *Jazz in America: Who's Listening.* Carson, CA: National Endowment for the Arts/Seven Locks Press.

———. 1997. *The Birth of Bebop: A Social and Musical History.* Berkeley: University of California Press.

DiMartino, Dave. 1991. "The Majors: Jazz Gains Momentum as Lions, Young and Old, Come on Strong in Drive for Even More Success." *Billboard,* 6 July, J6, J10–12.

Dobbins, Bill. 1988. "Jazz and Academia: Street Music in the Ivory Tower." *Bulletin of the Council for Research in Music Education* 96: 30–41.

Douglas, Susan J. 1999. *Listening In: Radio and the American Imagination.* New York: Times Books.

Dudley, Shannon. 1996. "Judging 'By the Beat': Calypso versus Soca." *Ethnomusicology* 40: 269–98.

Dunsby, Jonathan. 1983. "Music and Semiotics: The Nattiez Phase." *Musical Quarterly* 69: 27–43.

Eagleton, Terry. 1983. *Literary Theory: An Introduction.* Minneapolis: University of Minnesota Press.

Early, Gerald. 1992. "The Black Intellectual and the Sport of Prizefighting." In *Speech and Power: The African-American Essay and Its Cultural Content from Polemics to Pulpit,* vol. 1, edited by Gerald Early, 193–207. Hopewell, NJ: Ecco.

Eliade, Mircea. 1959. *The Sacred and the Profane: The Nature of Religion.* New York: Harcourt Brace & Company.

Ellington, Duke. 1939. "Duke Says Swing Is Stagnant!" *Down Beat,* February, 2, 16–17.

———. 1963. *The Great Paris Concert.* CD, Atlantic 304 2. Recorded 1, 2, and 23 February, Paris, France.

Elliott, David J. 1987. "Structure and Feeling in Jazz: Rethinking Philosophical Foundations." *Bulletin of the Council for Research in Music Education* 95: 13–38.

Ellison, Ralph. 1964a. "Blues People." In *Shadow and Act,* 247–58. New York: Random House.

———. 1964b. "On Bird, Bird-Watching, and Jazz." In *Shadow and Act,* 221–32. New York: Random House.

———. 1964c. *Shadow and Act.* New York: Random House.

———. 1964d. "The Charlie Christian Story." In *Shadow and Act,* 233–40. New York: Random House.

———. 1964e. "The Golden Age, Time Past." In *Shadow and Act,* 199–212. New York: Random House.

———. 1986. *Going to the Territory.* New York: Random House.

Erenberg, Lewis A. 1984. *Steppin' Out: New York Nightlife and the Transformation of American Culture, 1890–1930.* Chicago: University of Chicago Press.

Erlmann, Veit. 1993. "The Politics and Aesthetics of Transnational Musics." *World of Music* 35(2): 3–15.

Esman, Aaron M. 1951. "Jazz: A Study in Cultural Conflict." *American Imago* 8: 219–26.

Fabre, Geneviève, and Robert G. O'Meally, eds. 1994. *History and Memory in African American Culture.* New York: Oxford University Press.

Faulkner, Robert R., and Howard S. Becker. 2009. *"Do You Know ... ?" The Jazz Repertoire in Action.* Chicago: University of Chicago Press.

Feld, Steven. 1994a. "Aesthetics as Iconicity of Style (Uptown Title); or, (Downtown Title) 'Lift-Up-Over Sounding': Getting into the Kaluli Groove." In *Music Grooves: Essays and Dialogues,* edited by Charles Keil and Steven Feld, 109–50. Chicago: University of Chicago Press.

———. 1994b. "Communication, Music, and Speech about Music." In *Music Grooves: Essays and Dialogues,* edited by Charles Keil and Steven Feld, 77–95. Chicago: University of Chicago Press.

Finnegan, Ruth. 1989. *The Hidden Musicians: Music-Making in an English Town.* Cambridge: Cambridge University Press.

Florida, Richard, Charlotta Mellander, and Kevin Stolarick. 2010. "Music Scenes to Music Clusters: The Economic Geography of Music in the US, 1970–2000." *Environment and Planning A* 42: 785–804.

Floyd, Samuel A., Jr. 1995. *The Power of Black Music: Interpreting Its History from Africa to the United States.* New York: Oxford University Press.

———. 1991. "Ring Shout! Literary Studies, Historical Studies, and Black Music Inquiry." *Black Music Research Journal* 11: 265–87.

———. 1993. "Troping the Blues: From Spirituals to Concert Hall." *Black Music Research Journal* 13: 31–51.

Foucault, Michel. 1972. *The Archaeology of Knowledge.* New York: Pantheon.

———. 1973. *The Order of Things: An Archaeology of the Human Sciences.* New York: Vintage Books.

Fox, Aaron A. 2004. *Real Country: Music and Language in Working-Class Culture.* Durham, NC: Duke University Press.

Fox, Ted. 1986. *In the Groove: The People Behind the Music.* New York: St. Martin's Press.

Freedman, Samuel G. 2001. "Public Radio's Private Guru." *New York Times,* 11 November, Sec. 2: 1, 32.

Freeman, Phil. 2001. *New York Is Now! The New Wave of Free Jazz.* Brooklyn, NY: Telegraph Company.

Frith, Simon. 1987. "Towards an Aesthetic of Popular Music." In *Music and Society: The Politics of Composition, Performance, and Reception,* edited by Richard Leppert and Susan McClary, 133–49. Cambridge: Cambridge University Press.

Fuller, Hoyt W. 1971. "Towards a Black Aesthetic." In *The Black Aesthetic,* edited by Addison Gayle, Jr., 3–12. Garden City, NY: Doubleday.

Gabbard, Krin. 1995. "Introduction: The Jazz Canon and Its Consequences." In *Jazz among the Discourses,* edited by Krin Gabbard, 1–28. Durham, NC: Duke University Press.

Gans, Charles, and Greg Tusiewicz. 1978. "WRVR Goes Three-Form." *Jazz Forum* 53(3): 17.

Garofalo, Reebee. 1993. "Whose World, What Beat: The Transnational Music Industry, Identity, and Cultural Imperialism." *World of Music* 35(2): 16–32.

Gates, Henry Louis, Jr. 1988. *The Signifying Monkey: A Theory of African-American Literary Criticism.* New York: Oxford University Press.

Gavin, James. 2001. "The Most Democratic Music? Homophobia in Jazz." *JazzTimes,* December, 66–70.

Geertz, Clifford. 1973. "Thick Description: Toward an Interpretive Theory of Culture." In *The Interpretation of Cultures: Selected Essays,* 3–30. New York: Basic Books.

———. 1983. "Art as a Cultural System." In *Local Knowledge: Further Essays in Interpretive Anthropology,* 94–120. New York: Basic Books.

Gendron, Bernard. 1995. "'Moldy Figs' and Modernists: Jazz at War (1942–1946)." In *Jazz among the Discourses,* edited by Krin Gabbard, 31–56. Durham, NC: Duke University Press.

Gennari, John. 1991. "Jazz Criticism: Its Development and Ideologies." *Black American Literature Forum* 25: 449–523.

———. 2006. *Blowin' Hot and Cool: Jazz and Its Critics.* Chicago: University of Chicago Press.

Gerard, Charley. 1998. *Jazz in Black and White: Race, Culture, and Identity in the Jazz Community.* Westport, CT: Praeger.

Giddens, Anthony. 1979. *Central Problems in Social Theory: Action, Structure and Contradiction in Social Analysis.* Berkeley: University of California Press.

Giddins, Gary. 1993. "Shackling Surprise." *Village Voice,* 12 October, 78.

———. 1997. "Oxford and All That Jazz." *New York Times Book Review,* 26 October, 59.

———. 2001. "Signposts of Posthistory: The Best New Jazz CDs of the Year of Louis and Miles." *Village Voice,* 9 January, 100–101.

Gilroy, Paul. 1991a. "It Ain't Where You're From, It's Where You're At . . . : The Dialectics of Diasporic Identification." *Third Text* 13: 3–16.

———. 1991b. *"There Ain't No Black in the Union Jack": The Cultural Politics of Race and Nation.* Chicago: University of Chicago Press.

Gioia, Ted. 1988. *The Imperfect Art: Reflections on Jazz and Modern Culture.* Oxford University Press.

———. 1992. *West Coast Jazz: Modern Jazz in California, 1945–1960.* Berkeley: University of California Press.

Gitler, Ira. 1962a. "Racial Prejudice in Jazz, Part 1." *Down Beat,* 15 March, 20–26.

———. 1962b. "Racial Prejudice in Jazz, Part 2." *Down Beat,* 29 March, 22–25.

Godbolt, Jim. 1984. *A History of Jazz in Britain, 1919–50.* London: Quartet.

———. 1989. *A History of Jazz in Britain, 1950–70.* London: Quartet.

Goehr, Lydia. 1992. *The Imaginary Museum of Musical Works: An Essay in the Philosophy of Music.* Oxford: Clarendon Press.

Goldberg, Michael. 1991. "Biz Blasts New LP Chart." *Rolling Stone,* 11–25 July, 17, 19.

Gomes, Peter J. 1996. "Religion as Spectator Sport." *New York Times,* 28 November, Sec. A: 29.

Goodrich, Andrew L. 2001. "Jazz in Historically Black Colleges." *Jazz Education Journal* 34(3): 54–58.

Gordon, Robert. 1986. *Jazz West Coast: The Los Angeles Jazz Scene of the 1950s.* London: Quartet Books.

Gossett, Hattie. 1996. "Sugar Hill Groovin High." *Village Voice,* 5 November, 43.

Gottlieb, David. 1957. "The Neighborhood Tavern and the Cocktail Lounge: A Study of Class Differences." *American Journal of Sociology* 62(6): 559–62.

Gourlay, Kenneth A. 1978. "Towards a Reassessment of the Ethnomusicologist's Role in Research." *Ethnomusicology* 22: 1–35.

Gray, Herman. 1988. *Producing Jazz: The Experience of An Independent Record Company.* Philadelphia: Temple University Press.

———. 2005. *Cultural Moves: African Americans and the Politics of Representation.* Berkeley: University of California Press.

Graybow, Steve. 2001. "After Limbo, Columbia Jazz Renews Itself." *Billboard,* 24 February, 3.

Grazian, David. 2003. *Blue Chicago: The Search for Authenticity in Urban Blues Culture.* Chicago: University of Chicago Press.

Gridley, Mark C. 1987. "Trends in Description of Saxophone Timbre." *Perceptual and Motor Skills* 65: 303–11.

———. 1997. *Jazz Styles: History and Analysis.* 6th ed. Upper Saddle River, NJ: Prentice-Hall.

Gridley, Mark, Robert Maxham, and Robert Hoff. 1989. "Three Approaches to Defining Jazz." *Musical Quarterly* 73: 513–31.

Griffin, Marie P. 1985. "The Use of Audio-Visual Resources for Scholarly Research: A Jazz Archive as a Multidiscipline Resource." *Library Trends* 34(1): 111–27.

Guilbault, Jocelyne. 1993. "On Redefining the 'Local' Through World Music." *World of Music* 35(2): 33–47.

Gushee, Lawrence. 1981. "Lester Young's 'Shoeshine Boy.'" In *Report of the Twelfth Congress,* edited by Daniel Heartz and Bonnie Wade, 151–69 Philadelphia: American Musicological Society.

Gwaltney, John L. 1993. *Drylongso: A Self-Portrait of Black America.* New York: New Press.

Hall, Stuart. 1980. "Race, Articulation and Societies Structured in Dominance." In *Sociological Theories: Race and Colonialism,* 305–45. Paris: UNESCO.

Hannerz, Ulf. 1980. *Exploring the City: Inquiries Toward an Urban Anthropology.* New York: Columbia University Press.

———. 1992. *Cultural Complexity: Studies in the Social Organization of Meaning.* New York: Columbia University Press.

Hare, Nathan. 1992. "A Study of the Black Fighter." In *Speech and Power: The African-American Essay and Its Cultural Content from Polemics to Pulpit,* vol. 1, edited by Gerald Early, 158–66. Hopewell, NJ: Ecco.

Harris, Michael W. 1992. *The Rise of Gospel Blues: The Music of Thomas Andrew Dorsey in the Urban Church.* New York: Oxford University Press.

Hart, Antonio. 1994. Interview by author, Brooklyn, NY. 22 December.

———. 1995. Interview by author, Brooklyn, NY. 17 February.

Harvey, David. 1989a. *The Condition of Postmodernity: An Enquiry into the Origins of Cultural Change.* Oxford: Basil Blackwell.

———. 1989b. *The Urban Experience.* Baltimore, MD: Johns Hopkins University Press.

———. 2005. *A Brief History of Neoliberalism.* New York: Oxford University Press.

Hasty, Christopher F. 1997. *Meter as Rhythm.* New York: Oxford University Press.

Heath, Jimmy, and Joseph McLaren. 2010. *I Walked with Giants: The Autobiography of Jimmy Heath.* Philadelphia: Temple University Press.

Hebdige, Dick. 1979. *Subculture: The Meaning of Style.* London: Routledge.

Heckman, Don. 1990. "A Rising Generation of Talented Young Players Is Bringing New Fans to a Vital New Variety of Global Jazz." *Billboard,* 7 July, J1, 16, 18.

Helland, Dave. 1995. "Those Who Can, Teach." *Down Beat,* May, 22–24.

Hentoff, Nat. 1961a. "Jazz and Jim Crow." *Commonweal,* 24 March, 658.

———. 1961b. *The Jazz Life.* New York: Dial Press.

Herndon, Marcia. 1974. "Analysis: The Herding of Sacred Cows?" *Ethnomusicology* 18(2): 219–62.

Hine, Darlene Clark. 1989. "Rape and the Inner Lives of Black Women in the Middle West: Preliminary Thoughts on the Culture of Dissemblance." *Signs* 14: 912–20.

Hobsbawm, Eric, and Terence Ranger, eds. 1983. *The Invention of Tradition.* Cambridge: Cambridge University Press.

Hodeir, André. 1956. *Jazz: Its Evolution and Essence.* New York: Grove Press.

Hoffman, Lily M. 2003. "Revalorizing the Inner City: Tourism and Regulation in Harlem." In *Cities and Visitors: Regulating People, Markets, and City Space,* edited by Lily M. Hoffman, Susan S. Fainstein, and Dennis R. Judd, 91–112. Malden, MA: Blackwell.

Holt, Thomas C. 2000. *The Problem of Race in the 21st Century.* Cambridge, MA: Harvard University Press.

Hooper, Joseph. 1995. "A Saxophonist Who Doesn't Wear Armani." *New York Times,* 15 January, Sec. 2: 28–29.

Horn, David. 2002. "The Identity of Jazz." In *The Cambridge Companion to Jazz,* edited by Mervyn Cooke and David Horn, 9–32. Cambridge: Cambridge University Press.

Horowitz, Irving Louis. 1982. "On Seeing and Hearing Music: Eight Propositions in Search of Explanantion." *Annual Review of Jazz Studies* 1: 72–78.

Hudson, James R. 1987. *The Unanticipated City: Loft Conversions in Lower Manhattan.* Amherst: University of Massachusetts Press.

Hutchinson, Gregory. 1994. Interview by author, Brooklyn, NY. 8 November.

Hymes, Dell. 1964. "Introduction: Toward Ethnographies of Communication." *American Anthropologist* 66(6), part 2: 1–34.

Irvine, Judith T. 1979. "Formality and Informality in Communicative Events." *American Anthropologist* 81: 773–90.

Jackson, Travis A. 1992. "Become Like One: Communication, Interaction, and the Development of Group Sound in Jazz Performance." Master's thesis, Columbia University.

———. 1993a. "Transmission and Regeneration: Generational Interaction in Jazz Performance." *Middle Atlantic Chapter of the Society for Ethnomusicology Newsletter* 12(2): 4–6.

———. 1993b. "Veterans and Young Lions: The Role of Age in the Formation and Development of Small Jazz Groups." Paper presented at the Seventh International Conference of the International Association for the Study of Popular Music: Style and Identity, University of the Pacific, Stockton, CA, 11–15 July.

———. 1993c. "Where's Your Girl? African American Women and the Ritual of Jazz Performance." Paper presented at "Feminist Theory and Music: A Continuing Dialogue," Eastman School of Music of the University of Rochester, Rochester, NY, 17–20 June.

———. 1995. "A Jazzography." *New York Times Magazine,* 25 June, 32–33.

———. 2000. "Spooning Good, Singing Gum: Meaning, Association and Interpretation in Rock Music." *Current Musicology* 69: 7–41.

———. 2002. "Jazz as Musical Practice." In *The Cambridge Companion to Jazz,* edited by Mervyn Cooke and David Horn, 83–95. Cambridge: Cambridge University Press.

———. 2004. "'Always New and Centuries Old': Jazz, Poetry and Tradition as Creative Adaptation." In *Uptown Conversation: The New Jazz Studies,* edited by Robert G. O'Meally, Brent Hayes Edwards, and Farah Jasmine Griffin, 357–73. New York: Columbia University Press.

Jairazbhoy, Nazir A. 1977. "The 'Objective' and Subjective View in Music Transcription." *Ethnomusicology* 21: 263–73.

Jairazbhoy, Nazir A., and Hal Balyoz. 1977. "Electronic Aids to Aural Transcription." *Ethnomusicology* 21: 275–82.

Jameson, Frederic. 1971. *Marxism and Form: Twentieth Century Dialectical Theories of Literature.* Princeton, NJ: Princeton University Press.

Jarab, Josef. 1985. "Black Aesthetic: A Cultural or Political Concept." *Callaloo* 8(3): 587–93.

Jeffrey, Don. 1992. "Reissue Fever." *Billboard,* 4 July, J-4, 8.

Jeffri, Joan. 2003. *Changing the Beat: A Study of the Work Life of Jazz Musicians.* Washington, DC: National Endowment for the Arts, Research Division.

Jeske, Lee. 1980. "Imagine! All That Jazz, but No All-Jazz Radio Station Here!" *New York Times,* 20 September, 19.

Johnson, Bruce. 1993. "Hear Me Talkin' to Ya: Problems of Jazz Discourse." *Popular Music* 12(1): 1–12.

Jones, James T., IV. 1995. "Racism and Jazz." *JazzTimes,* March, 52–58, 61.

Joyner, David. 1997. "50 Years of Jazz Education at North Texas." *Jazz Educators Journal* 30(2): 53–62.

Julien, Patricia. 2003. "The Structural Function of Harmonic Relations in Wayne Shorter's Early Compositions: 1959–1963." Ph.D. diss., University of Maryland, College Park.

Judd, Dennis R., et al. 2003. "Tourism and Entertainment as Local Economic Development: A National Survey." In *The Infrastructure of Play: Building the Tourist City,* edited by Dennis R. Judd, 50–74. Armonk, NY: M.E. Sharpe.

Kahn, Ashley. 2000. *Kind of Blue: The Making of the Miles Davis Masterpiece.* New York: Da Capo.

Kalbacher, Gene. 1997. "Brad Mehldau." *Hot House,* January, 18.

Kater, Michael H. 1992. *Different Drummers: Jazz in the Culture of Nazi Germany.* New York: Oxford University Press.

Katz, Penny, and Sanna Longden. 1983. "The Jam Session: A Study of Spontaneous Group Process." *Social Work with Groups* 6(1): 37–52.

Keegan, Paul. 1994. "Come Blow Your Horn." *GQ,* June, 93–96.

Keepnews, Orrin. 1988. *The View from Within: Jazz Writings, 1948–1987.* New York: Oxford University Press.

Keepnews, Peter. 1979. "Why Big Record Companies Let Jazz Down." *Jazz,* Winter, 60–64.

Keil, Charles. 1991. *Urban Blues.* Chicago: University of Chicago Press.

———. 1994. "Motion and Feeling through Music." In *Music Grooves: Essays and Dialogues,* edited by Charles Keil and Steven Feld, 53–76. Chicago: University of Chicago Press.

Kelley, Robin D.G. 2009. *Thelonious Monk: The Life and Times of an American Original.* New York: Free Press.

Kelly, John D., and Martha Kaplan. 1990. "History, Structure, and Ritual." *Annual Review of Anthropology* 19: 119–50.

Kenney, William Howland. 1993. *Chicago Jazz: A Cultural History, 1904–1930.* New York: Oxford University Press.

Kernfeld, Barry. 1983. "Two Coltranes." *Annual Review of Jazz Studies* 2: 7–66.

———. 1995. *What to Listen for in Jazz.* New Haven, CT: Yale University Press.

———. 2006. *The Story of Fake Books: Bootlegging Songs to Musicians.* Lanham, MD: Scarecrow Press.

Kingsbury, Henry. 1988. *Music, Talent, and Performance: A Conservatory Cultural System.* Philadelphia: Temple University Press.

Kivy, Peter. 1990. *Music Alone: Philosophical Reflections on the Purely Musical Experience.* Ithaca, NY: Cornell University Press.

Kluckhohn, Clyde. 1942. "Myths and Rituals: A General Theory." *Harvard Theological Review* 35: 45–79.

Koch, Lawrence O. 1982. "Harmonic Approaches to the Twelve-Bar Blues Form." *Annual Review of Jazz Studies* 1: 59–71.

———. 1983. "Thelonious Monk: Compositional Techniques." *Annual Review of Jazz Studies* 2: 67–80.

———. 1985. "The Jazz Composition/Arrangement." *Annual Review of Jazz Studies* 3: 181–91.

Kofsky, Frank. 1970. *Black Nationalism and the Revolution in Music.* New York: Pathfinder Press.

———. 1977. "The State of Jazz." *Black Perspective in Music* 5: 44–68.

Koger, Terry. 1985. "Fifty Years of Down Beat Solo Transcriptions: A Register." *Black Music Research Journal* 5: 43–79.

Krebs, Harald. 1987. "Some Extensions of the Concepts of Metrical Consonance and Dissonance." *Journal of Music Theory* 31(1): 99–120.

Kruse, Holly. 1993. "Subcultural Identity in Alternative Music Culture." *Popular Music* 12(1): 33–41.

———. 2003. *Site and Sound: Understanding Independent Music Scenes.* New York: Peter Lang.

Kuhn, Thomas S. 1996. *The Structure of Scientific Revolutions.* 3rd ed. Chicago: University of Chicago Press.

Lakoff, George. 1987. *Women, Fire, and Dangerous Things: What Categories Reveal about the Mind.* Chicago: University of Chicago Press.

Larson, Steve. 1993. "Dave McKenna's Performance of 'Have You Met Miss Jones?'" *American Music* 11: 283–315.

———. 1998. "Schenkerian Analysis of Modern Jazz: Questions about Method." *Music Theory Spectrum* 20(2): 209–41.

———. 2009. *Analyzing Jazz: A Schenkerian Approach.* Harmonologia: Studies in Music Theory. Hillsdale, NY: Pendragon Press.

Lees, Gene. 1994. *Cats of Any Color: Jazz, Black and White.* New York: Oxford University Press.

Lefebvre, Henri. 1974. *La Production de l'Espace.* Paris: Anthropos.

Leonard, Neil. 1987. *Jazz: Myth and Religion.* New York: Oxford University Press.

"Letters." 1999. *New York Times,* 17 January, Sec. 2: 4.

Levenson, Jeff. 1992. "Who's Listening, Who's Buying?" *Billboard,* 4 July, J-2, 8.

Levine, Lawrence W. 1977. *Black Culture and Black Consciousness: Afro-American Folk Thought from Slavery to Freedom.* New York: Oxford University Press.

Lewis, George E. 2008. *A Power Stronger Than Itself: The AACM and American Experimental Music.* Chicago: University of Chicago Press.

Lii, Jane H. 1995. "God, Gospel and the Camcorder." *New York Times,* 26 March, Sec. C: 3.

Lincoln, C. Eric, and Lawrence H. Mamiya. 1990. *The Black Church in the African American Experience.* Durham, NC: Duke University Press.

Lipsitz, George. 1990. *Time Passages: Collective Memory and American Popular Culture*. Minneapolis: University of Minnesota Press.

List, George. 1963. "The Boundaries of Speech and Song." *Ethnomusicology* 7: 1–16.

———. 1974. "The Reliability of Transcription." *Ethnomusicology* 18: 353–77.

Lock, Graham. 1988. *Forces in Motion: Anthony Braxton and the Meta-Reality of Creative Music: Interviews and Tour Notes, England 1985*. London: Quartet.

Lopes, Paul. 2002. *The Rise of a Jazz Art World*. Cambridge: Cambridge University Press.

MacLeod, Bruce A. 1993. *Club Date Musicians: Playing the New York Party Circuit*. Urbana: University of Illinois Press.

Marcus, Greil. 1975. *Mystery Train: Images of America in Rock 'n' Roll Music*. New York: E.P. Dutton.

Margolis, Norman M. 1954. "A Theory on the Psychology of Jazz." *American Imago* 2 (Fall): 263–91.

Marks, Morton. 1974. "Uncovering Ritual Structures in Afro-American Music." In *Religious Movements in Contemporary America,* edited by Irving I. Zaretsky and Mark P. Leone, 60–134. Princeton, NJ: Princeton University Press.

Marsalis, Wynton. 1994. "Who Is Really Stupid?" *A Gathering of the Tribes* 4(1): 33–35.

Marshall, Christopher. 1982. "Towards a Comparative Aesthetics of Music." In *Cross-Cultural Perspectives on Music,* edited by Robert Falck and Tim Rice, 162–73. Toronto: University of Toronto Press.

Martin, Henry. 1996. *Charlie Parker and Thematic Improvisation*. Newark, NJ: Institute for Jazz Studies, Rutgers.

Masland, Tom. 1990. "Between Lions and Legends: Jazz's Lost Generation Is Stuck in the Middle." *Newsweek,* 24 February, 64–65.

Mazullo, Mark. 1997. "Fans and Critics: Greil Marcus's 'Mystery Train' as Rock 'n' Roll History." *Musical Quarterly* 81(2): 145–69.

McCauley, Michael P. 2005. *NPR: The Trials and Triumphs of National Public Radio*. New York: Columbia University Press.

McCormick, Moira. 1992. "Small Labels Show Marketing Finesse." *Billboard,* 4 July, J-19–20.

McCourt, Tom. 1999. *Conflicting Communication Interests in America: The Case of National Public Radio*. Westport, CT: Praeger.

McLeod, Kembrew. 2001. "'★1/2': A Critique of Rock Criticism in North America." *Popular Music* 20(1): 47–60.

McLeod, Norma, and Marcia Herndon, eds. 1980. *The Ethnography of Musical Performance*. Norwood, PA: Norwood Editions.

Meadows, Eddie S. 1992. "Africa and the Blues Scale: A Selected Review of the Literature." In *African Musicology: Current Trends, Volume 2,* edited by Jacqueline Cogdell DjeDje, 263–76. Los Angeles: African Studies Association Press.

Merriam, Alan P. 1964. *The Anthropology of Music*. Evanston, IL: Northwestern University Press.

Merriam, Alan P., and Raymond S. Mack. 1960. "The Jazz Community." *Social Forces* 38: 211–22.

Meyer, Leonard B. 1956. *Emotion and Meaning in Music.* Chicago: University of Chicago Press.

Michaels, Walter Benn. 1998. "Autobiography of an Ex-White Man: Why Race Is Not a Social Construction." *Transition* 7(1): 122–43.

Milkowski, Bill. 2001. "Family Jazz." *JazzTimes,* December, 72–79.

Mitchell, Charles. 1980. "Why It's So Hard to Find Jazz on the Radio." *Jazz* 4(2) (Spring): 48–54.

Monson, Ingrid. 1990. "Forced Migration, Asymmetrical Power Relations and African-American Music: Reformulation of Cultural Meaning and Musical Form." *World of Music* 32(3): 22–45.

———. 1991. "Musical Interaction in Modern Jazz: An Ethnomusicological Perspective." Ph.D. diss., New York University.

———. 1994. "Doubleness and Jazz Improvisation: Irony, Parody and Ethnomusicology." *Critical Inquiry* 20: 283–313.

———. 1995. "The Problem with White Hipness: Race, Gender, and Cultural Conceptions in Jazz Historical Discourse." *Journal of the American Musicological Society* 48: 396–422.

———. 1996. *Saying Something: Jazz Improvisation and Interaction.* Chicago: University of Chicago Press.

Moon, Tom. 1992. "New Artist Finally Getting a Break." *Billboard,* 4 July, J-4, 6.

Murphy, John. 1990. "Jazz Improvisation: The Joy of Influence." *Black Perspective in Music* 20: 7–19.

Murray, Albert. 1970. *The Omni-Americans: Some Alternatives to the Folklore of White Supremacy.* New York: Outerbridge & Dienstfrey.

———. 1976. *Stomping the Blues.* New York: McGraw-Hill.

Nattiez, Jean-Jacques. 1990. *Music and Discourse: Toward a Semiology of Music.* Princeton, NJ: Princeton University Press.

Navarro, Mireya. 2001. "Now Playing in Clubland: Hard Times." *New York Times,* 4 August, Sec. B: 1, 6.

Negus, Keith. 1992. *Producing Pop: Culture and Conflict in the Popular Music Industry.* London: Edward Arnold.

———. 1999. *Music Genres and Corporate Cultures.* London: Routledge.

Negus, Keith, and Michael Pickering. 2004. *Creativity, Communication and Cultural Value.* London: Sage Publications.

Nettl, Bruno. 1983. "I Can't Say a Thing Until I've Seen the Score." In *The Study of Ethnomusicology: Twenty-nine Issues and Concepts.* Urbana: University of Illinois Press.

———. 1995. *Heartland Excursions: Ethnomusicological Reflections on Schools of Music.* Urbana: University of Illinois Press.

Newsome, Sam. 1995. Interview by author, Brooklyn, NY. 5 February.

Nicholson, Stuart. 1990. *Jazz: The Modern Resurgence.* London: Simon & Shuster.

———. 2005. *Is Jazz Dead? (Or Has It Moved to a New Address).* New York: Routledge.

O'Meally, Robert G. 1994. "On Burke and the Vernacular: Ralph Ellison's Boomerang of History." In *History and Memory in African-American Culture*, edited by Geneviève Fabre and Robert G. O'Meally, 244–60. New York: Oxford University Press.

Ogren, Kathy J. 1989. *The Jazz Revolution: Twenties America and the Meaning of Jazz*. New York: Oxford University Press.

Oliphant, Dave. 1996. *Texan Jazz*. Austin: University of Texas Press.

Olson, Mark J.V. 1997. "'Everybody Loves Our Town': Scenes, Spatiality, Migrancy." In *Mapping the Beat: Popular Music and Contemporary Theory*, edited by Thomas Swiss, John Sloop, and Andrew Herman, 269–89. Oxford: Blackwell.

Omi, Michael, and Howard Winant. 1994. *Racial Formation in the United States: From the 1960s to the 1990s*. 2nd ed. London: Routledge.

Ong, Walter J. 1982. *Orality and Literacy: The Technologizing of the Word*. London: Routledge.

Orgill, Roxane. 1993. "Remastering Magic: A Miles Davis Classic Reborn." *Wall Street Journal*, 15 April, 12.

———. 1995. "Fewer Gigs Means Fewer Jazz Bands." *New York Times*, 6 August, Sec. 2: 28, 33.

Ortner, Sherry B. 1984. "Theory in Anthropology since the Sixties." *Comparative Studies in Society and History* 26: 126–66.

Ostransky, Leroy. 1978. *Jazz City: The Impact of Our Cities on the Development of Jazz*. Englewood Cliffs, NJ: Prentice-Hall.

Ottenberg, Simon. 1990. "Thirty Years of Fieldnotes: Changing Relationships to the Text." In *Fieldnotes: The Makings of Anthropology*, edited by Roger Sanjek, 139–60. Ithaca, NY: Cornell University Press.

Owens, Thomas. 1974. "Charlie Parker: Techniques of Improvisation." Ph.D. diss., University of California, Los Angeles.

Paikert, Charles. 1979. "Record Industry Drops but Jazz Plays On." *Jazz*, Fall, 44–45.

Palmer, Robert. 1985. "Jazz's Blue Note Label Comes Back to Life." *New York Times*, 10 February, Sec. 2: 23–24.

Pareles, Jon. 1984. "Jazz Swings Back to Tradition." *New York Times Magazine*, 17 June, 22–23, 54–55, 61–63, 66–68.

———. 1996. "Jelly Roll and the Duke Join Wolfgang and Ludwig." *New York Times*, 2 July, Sec. C: 11, 15.

Parker, Leon. 1998. Phone interview by author. 18 March.

Pearson, Nathan W., Jr. 1987. *Goin' to Kansas City*. Urbana: University of Illinois Press.

Pellegrinelli, Lara. 2000. "Dig Boy Dig." *Village Voice*, 14 November, 65–67.

Perlman, Alan M., and Daniel Greenblatt. 1981. "Miles Davis Meets Noam Chomsky: Some Observations on Jazz Improvisation and Language Structure." In *The Sign in Music and Literature*, edited by Wendy Steiner, 169–83. Austin: University of Texas Press.

Petlin, Jodi. 1995. Interview by author, New York, NY. 31 March.

Piazza, Tom. 1997. *Blues Up and Down: Jazz in Our Time*. New York: St. Martin's Press.

Pitts, Walter. 1988. "Keep the Fire Burnin': Language and Ritual in the Afro-Baptist Church." *Journal of the American Academy of Religion* 56(1): 77–97.

Pond, Steven F. 2003. "Jamming the Reception: Ken Burns, *Jazz*, and the Problem of 'America's Music.'" *Notes* 60(1): 11–45.

Porter, Eric C. 2002. *What Is This Thing Called Jazz? African American Musicians as Artists, Critics, and Activists.* Berkeley: University of California Press.

Porter, Lewis. 1985. "John Coltrane's *A Love Supreme*: Jazz Improvisation as Composition." *Journal of the American Musicological Society* 38: 593–621.

———. 1994–95. "The 'Blues Connotation' in Ornette Coleman's Music—and Some General Thoughts on the Relation of Blues to Jazz." *Annual Review of Jazz Studies* 7: 75–99.

———. 1998. *John Coltrane: His Life and Music.* Ann Arbor: University of Michigan Press.

Porter, Lewis, Michael Ullman, and Edward Hazell. 1993. *Jazz: From Its Origins to the Present.* Englewood Cliffs, NJ: Prentice-Hall.

Potter, Gary. 1990. "Analyzing Improvised Jazz." *College Music Symposium* 30(1): 64–74.

Powell, Richard J., ed. 1989a. *The Blues Aesthetic: Black Culture and Modernism.* Washington, DC: Washington Project for the Arts.

———. 1989b. "The Blues Aesthetic: Black Culture and Modernism." In *The Blues Aesthetic: Black Culture and Modernism,* edited by Richard J. Powell, 19–35. Washington, DC: Washington Project for the Arts.

———. 1994. "Art History and Black Memory: Toward a 'Blues Aesthetic.'" In *History and Memory in African-American Culture,* edited by Geneviève Fabre and Robert G. O'Meally, 228–43. New York: Oxford University Press.

Pressing, Jeff. 1982. "Pitch Class Set Structures in Contemporary Jazz." *Jazzforschung* 14: 133–72.

Pressman, Stuart. 1995. Phone interview by author. 31 May.

Primack, Bret. 1994. "Critical Analysis." *JazzTimes*, September, 34–39.

"Race & Jazz." 1996. *Commentary,* January, 13–21.

Racy, Ali Jihad. 1991. "Creativity and Ambience: An Ecstatic Feedback Model from Arab Music." *World of Music* 33(3): 7–27.

Radano, Ronald M. 1993. *New Musical Figurations: Anthony Braxton's Cultural Critique.* Chicago: University of Chicago Press.

"Radio Tries to Fill Its Jazz Void." 1980. *New York Times,* 27 November, Sec. C: 19.

Ramsey, Guthrie P., Jr. 1999. "Who Matters: The New and Improved White Jazz-Literati: A Review Essay." *American Music* 17: 205–15.

———. 2001. "Who Hears Here? Black Music, Critical Bias, and the Musicological Skin Trade." *Musical Quarterly* 85(1): 1–52.

Rasula, Jed. 1995. "The Media of Memory: The Seductive Menace of Records in Jazz History." In *Jazz among the Discourses,* edited by Krin Gabbard, 134–62. Durham, NC: Duke University Press.

Redman, Joshua. 1994a. *MoodSwing.* Warner Brothers 45643-2. Recorded 8–10 March 1994. New York, NY.

———. 1994b. Liner notes to *MoodSwing,* Warner Brothers 45643–2. Recorded 8–10 March 1994. New York, NY.

———. 1995a. Interview by author, New York, NY. 27 February.

———. 1995b. *Spirit of the Moment: Live at the Village Vanguard.* Warner Brothers. Recorded 21–26 March. New York, NY.

Reed, Harry A. 1979. "The Black Bar in the Making of a Jazz Musician: Bird, Mingus, and Stan Hope." *Journal of Jazz Studies* 5(2): 76–90.

Reeves, Scott D. 1989. *Creative Jazz Improvisation.* Englewood Cliffs, NJ: Prentice-Hall.

Reig, Teddy, and Edward Berger. 1990. *Reminiscing in Tempo: The Life and Times of a Jazz Hustler.* Metuchen, NJ: Scarecrow Press and the Institute of Jazz Studies.

Reisner, Robert. 1962. *Bird: The Legend of Charlie Parker.* New York: Citadel Press.

Rice, Timothy. 1987. "Toward the Remodeling of Ethnomusicology." *Ethnomusicology* 31: 469–88.

Richardson, Derk. 1990. "Reissue Mania: For Sheer Volume, It Looks Like the Biggest Year Yet." *Billboard,* 7 July, J-5, 8, 12, 18.

Richardson, Lynda. 2000. "Longing for Authenticity: Is the Jazz Really Jazz in Harlem Without the Locals?" *New York Times,* 16 November, Sec. B: 1, 6.

Rinzler, Paul. 1988. "Preliminary Thoughts on Analyzing Interaction among Jazz Performers." *Annual Review of Jazz Studies* 4: 153–60.

Roach, Joseph. 1996. *Cities of the Dead: Circum-Atlantic Performance.* New York: Columbia University Press.

Roach, Ronald. 1998. "Schools of Cool: Jazz Performance Education Providing a Different Kind of Gig." *Black Issues in Higher Education* 14(24): 16–22.

Roberts, John W. 1989. *From Trickster to Badman: The Black Folk Hero in Slavery and Freedom.* Philadelphia: University of Pennsylvania Press.

Roberts, Michael. 2002. "Papa's Got a Brand New Bag: Big Music's Post-Fordist Regime and the Role of Independent Music Labels." In *Rhythm and Business: The Political Economy of Black Music,* edited by Norman Kelley, 24–43. New York: Akashic.

Robinson, Greg. 1994. "Fred Hersch: Trials and Rewards." *JazzTimes,* September, 43–44.

Román-Velázquez, Patria. 1999. *The Making of Latin London: Salsa Music, Place and Identity.* Aldershot: Ashgate.

Rosenthal, David H. 1992. *Hard Bop: Jazz and Black Music, 1955–1965.* New York: Oxford University Press.

Rothman, Robin. 1999. "Sites Unscene." *Village Voice,* 28 September, 23.

Rudinow, Joel. 1994. "Race, Ethnicity, Expressive Authenticity: Can White People Sing the Blues?" *Journal of Aesthetics and Art Criticism* 52(1): 127–37.

Rudolph, Eric. 1996. "Jacky Terrasson: Capturing Jazz Piano with a 'Cello.'" *Mix,* June, 190, 194–96.

Russell, George. 1959. *The Lydian Chromatic Concept of Tonal Organization for Improvisation.* New York: Concept.

Sahlins, Marshall. 1976. *Culture and Practical Reason.* Chicago: University of Chicago Press.

Salamone, Frank A. 1988. "The Ritual of Jazz Performance." *Play and Culture* 1: 85–104.

Sales, Grover. 1984. *Jazz: America's Classical Music.* Englewood Cliffs, NJ: Prentice-Hall.

Sancton, Thomas. 1990. "Horns of Plenty." *Time,* 22 October, 64–71.

Sanjek, Roger. 1990. "A Vocabulary for Fieldnotes." In *Fieldnotes. The Makings of Anthropology,* edited by Roger Sanjek, 92–121. Ithaca, NY: Cornell University Press.

Schieffelin, Edward L. 1985. "Performance and the Cultural Construction of Reality." *American Ethnologist* 12: 707–24.

Schuller, Gunther. 1958. "Sonny Rollins and the Challenge of Thematic Improvisation." *Jazz Review* 1(1): 6–11, 21.

———. 1968. *Early Jazz: Its Roots and Musical Development.* New York: Oxford University Press.

———. 1986. *Musings: The Musical Worlds of Gunther Schuller.* New York: Oxford University Press.

———. 1989. *The Swing Era: The Development of Jazz, 1930–1945.* New York: Oxford University Press.

Seeger, Anthony. 1986. "The Role of Sound Archives in Ethnomusicology Today." *Ethnomusicology* 30: 261–76.

———. 1987. *Why Suyá Sing: A Musical Anthropology of a Amazonian People.* Cambridge: Cambridge University Press.

Seeger, Charles. 1958. "Prescriptive and Descriptive Music-Writing." *Musical Quarterly* 44: 184–95.

———. 1960. "On the Moods of a Music-Logic." *Journal of the American Musicological Society* 13: 224–61.

———. 1961. "Semantic, Logical and Political Considerations Bearing upon Research in Ethnomusicology." *Ethnomusicology* 5: 77–80.

———. 1969. "On the Formational Apparatus of the Musical Compositional Process." *Ethnomusicology* 13: 230–47.

———. 1977. "The Musicological Juncture: 1976." *Ethnomusicology* 21: 179–88.

Seremetakis, C. Nadia. 1991. *The Last Word: Women, Death, Divination in Inner Mani.* Chicago: University of Chicago Press.

Shank, Barry. 1994. *Dissonant Identities: The Rock'n'Roll Scene in Austin, Texas.* Hanover, NH: Wesleyan University Press.

Sharron, Avery. 1985. "The Mainstream of Conciousness: An Interactionist Analysis of a Phenomenological Concept." *Symbolic Interaction* 8(1): 47–62.

Shaw, Irwin. 1948. *The Young Lions.* New York: Random House.

Sher, Chuck, ed. 1988. *The New Real Book.* Petaluma, CA: Sher Music Co.

———, ed. 1991. *The New Real Book, Volume 2.* Petaluma, CA: Sher Music Co.

———, ed. 1995. *The New Real Book, Volume 3.* Petaluma, CA: Sher Music Co.

Shih, Hsio Wen. 1959. "The Spread of Jazz and the Big Bands." In *Jazz: New Perspectives on the History of Jazz,* edited by Nat Hentoff and Albert J. McCarthy, 173–87. New York: Holt, Rinehart, and Winston.

Sider, Gerald, and Gavin Smith, eds. 1997. *Between History and Histories: The Making of Silences and Commemorations.* Toronto: University of Toronto Press.

Sites, William. 1997. "The Limits of Urban Regime Theory: New York City under Koch, Dinkins, and Giuliani." *Urban Affairs Review* 32(4): 536–57.

———. 2003. *Remaking New York: Primitive Globalization and the Politics of Urban Community.* Minneapolis: University of Minnesota Press.

Slonimsky, Nicolas. 1947. *Thesaurus of Scales and Melodic Patterns.* New York: Scribner's.

Small, Christopher. 1987a. *Music of the Common Tongue: Survival and Celebration in Afro-American Music.* New York: Riverrun Press.

———. 1987b. "Performance as Ritual: Sketch for an Enquiry into the True Nature of a Symphony Concert." In *Lost in Music: Culture, Style and the Musical Event,* edited by Avron Levine White, 6–32. London: Routledge and Kegan Paul.

———. 1998. *Musicking: The Meanings of Performing and Listening.* Hanover, NH: Wesleyan University Press.

Smith, Gregory E. 1983. "Homer, Gregory, and Bill Evans? The Theory of Formulaic Composition in the Context of Jazz Piano Improvisation." Ph.D. diss., Harvard University.

Smith, Jonathan Z. 1987. *To Take Place: Toward Theory in Ritual.* Chicago: University of Chicago Press.

Soja, Edward W. 1989. *Postmodern Geographies: The Reassertion of Space in Critical Social Theory.* London: Verso.

Solis, Gabriel. 2009. "Genius, Improvisation, and the Narratives of Jazz History." In *Musical Improvisation: Art, Education, and Society,* edited by Gabriel Solis and Bruno Nettl, 90–102. Urbana: University of Illinois Press.

Spradley, James. 1988. "Adaptive Strategies of Urban Nomads: The Ethnoscience of Tramp Culture." In *Urban Life: Readings in Urban Anthropology,* edited by George Gmelch and Walter P. Zenner, 102–21. Prospect Heights, IL: Waveland Press.

Spring, Howard. 1990. "The Use of Formulas in the Improvisations of Charlie Christian." *Jazzforschung* 22: 11–51.

Stanyek, Jason. 2004. "Transmissions of an Interculture: Pan-African Jazz and Intercultural Improvisation." In *The Other Side of Nowhere: Jazz, Improvisation, and Communities in Dialogue,* edited by Daniel Fischlin and Ajay Heble, 87–130. Middletown, CT: Wesleyan University Press.

Starks, George L., Jr. 1993. "Jazz Literature and the African American Aesthetic." In *The African Aesthetic: Keeper of the Traditions,* edited by Kariamu Welsh-Asante, 143–57. Westport, CT: Greenwood Press.

Starr, S. Frederick. 1994. *Red and Hot: The Fate of Jazz in the Soviet Union, 1917–1991.* 2nd Limelight ed. New York: Limelight Editions.

Stebbins, Robert A. 1966. "Class, Status, and Power among Jazz and Commercial Musicians." *Sociological Quarterly* 7(2): 197–213.

———. 1968. "A Theory of the Jazz Community." *Sociological Quarterly* 9(2): 318–31.

Steedman, Mark J. 1984. "A Generative Grammar for Jazz Chord Sequences." *Music Perception* 2: 52–77.

Stein, Richard Leslie. 1977. "The Jazz Trumpet: Development of Styles and an Analysis of Selected Solos from 1924 to 1961." Ph.D. diss., University of Miami.

Stein, Stephanie. 1993. "Talent Scouting the New York Scene." *Down Beat,* May, 12.

Stewart, Alex. 2007. *Making the Scene: Contemporary New York City Big Band Jazz.* Berkeley: University of California Press.

Stewart, Milton L. 1979. "Some Characteristics of Clifford Brown's Improvisational Style." *Jazzforschung* 11: 135–64.

———. 1982. "Grid Notation: A Notation System for Jazz Transcription." *Annual Review of Jazz Studies* 1: 3–12.

———. 1986. "Player Interaction in the 1955–57 Miles Davis Quintet." *Jazz Research Papers* 6: 187–210.

Stokes, Martin. 1994. "Introduction: Ethnicity, Identity and Music." In *Ethnicity, Identity and Music: The Musical Construction of Place,* edited by Martin Stokes, 1–27. Oxford: Berg.

Stokes, W. Royal. 1991. *The Jazz Scene: An Informal History from New Orleans to 1990.* New York: Oxford University Press.

Stone, Ruth M. 1982. *Let the Inside Be Sweet: The Interpretation of the Music Event among the Kpelle of Liberia.* Bloomington: Indiana University Press.

Stowe, David W. 1994. *Swing Changes: Big-Band Jazz in New Deal America.* Cambridge, MA: Harvard University Press.

Strauss, Neil. 1996. "An Endangered Species: Rock Clubs in New York." *New York Times,* 23 October, Sec. C: 13, 18.

Straw, Will. 1991. "Systems of Articulation, Logics of Change: Communities and Scenes in Popular Music." *Cultural Studies* 5(3): 368–88.

Strunk, Steven. 1979. "The Harmony of Early Bop: A Layered Approach." *Journal of Jazz Studies* 6(1): 4–53.

———. 1988. "Harmony (i)." In *New Grove Dictionary of Jazz,* edited by Barry Kernfeld. New York: Macmillan.

Such, David G. 1993. *Avant-garde Jazz Musicians: Performing "Out There."* Iowa City: University of Iowa Press.

Sudhalter, Richard M. 1999a. "A Racial Divide That Needn't Be." *New York Times,* 3 January, Sec. 2: 1, 31.

———. 1999b. *Lost Chords: White Musicians and Their Contribution to Jazz, 1915–1945.* New York: Oxford University Press.

Sugrue, Thomas J. 1996. *The Origins of the Urban Crisis: Race and Inequality in Postwar Detroit.* Princeton, NJ: Princeton University Press.

Suhor, Charles. 1986. "Jazz Improvisation and Language Performance: Parallel Competencies." *Etc.* 43: 133–40.

———. 2001. *Jazz in New Orleans: The Postwar Years through 1970.* Lanham, MD: Scarecrow Press.

Suter, Bob. 1979. "How ECM Records Made Jazz Work for It." *Jazz,* Winter, 65–69.

Szwed, John F. 2000. *Jazz 101: A Complete Guide to Learning and Loving Jazz.* New York: Hyperion.

Tagg, Philip. 1982. "Analysing Popular Music: Theory, Method, and Practice." *Popular Music* 2: 37–69.

Tallmadge, William H. 1984. "Blue Notes and Blue Tonality." *Black Perspective in Music* 12: 155–65.

———. 1979. "Equipment Failure and Audio Distortion in the Acoustical Recording of and Remastering of Early Jazz." *Journal of Jazz Studies* 5(2): 61–75.

Tambiah, Stanley J. 1979. "A Performative Approach to Ritual." *Proceedings of the British Academy* 65: 113–69.

Taylor, Arthur. 1993. *Notes and Tones: Musician-to-Musician Interviews.* Expanded ed. New York: Da Capo.

Teachout, Terry. 1995. "The Color of Jazz." *Commentary,* September, 50–53.

Thomas, J.C. 1975. *Chasin' the Trane: The Music and Mystique of John Coltrane.* Garden City, NY: Doubleday.

Tirro, Frank. 1967. "The Silent Theme Tradition in Jazz." *Musical Quarterly* 53: 313–34.

———. 1974. "Constructive Influences in Jazz Improvisation." *Journal of the American Musicological Society* 27: 285–305.

———. 1977. *Jazz: A History.* New York: W.W. Norton.

Tomlinson, Gary. 1991. "Cultural Dialogics and Jazz: A White Historian Signifies." *Black Music Research Journal* 11: 229–64.

Trouillot, Michel-Rolph. 1995. *Silencing the Past: Power and the Production of History.* Boston: Beacon Press.

Tucker, Mark. 1991. *Ellington: The Early Years.* Urbana: University of Illinois Press.

———, ed. 1993. *The Duke Ellington Reader.* New York: Oxford University Press.

———. 1999. "Mainstreaming Monk: The Ellington Album." *Black Music Research Journal* 19(2): 227–44.

Tucker, Sherrie. 2000. *Swing Shift: "All-Girl" Bands of the 1940s.* Durham, NC: Duke University Press.

———. 2004. "Bordering on Community: Improvising Women Improvising Women-in-Jazz." In *The Other Side of Nowhere: Jazz, Improvisation, and Communities in Dialogue,* edited by Daniel Fischlin and Ajay Heble, 244–67. Middletown, CT: Wesleyan University Press.

Turino, Thomas. 1999. "Signs of Imagination, Identity, and Experience: A Peircian Semiotic Theory for Music." *Ethnomusicology* 43: 221–55.

———. 2008. *Music as Social Life: The Politics of Participation.* Chicago: University of Chicago Press.

Turner, Victor. 1969. *The Ritual Process: Structure and Anti-Structure.* Ithaca, NY: Cornell University Press.

———. 1974a. *Dramas, Fields, and Metaphors: Symbolic Action in Human Society.* Ithaca, NY: Cornell University Press.

———. 1974b. "Liminal to Liminoid, in Play, Flow, and Ritual: An Essay in Comparative Symbology." *Rice University Studies* 60(3): 53–92.

———. 1982. *From Ritual to Theatre: The Human Seriousness of Play*. New York: PAJ Publications.

Urban, Greg. 2001. *Metaculture: How Culture Moves through the World*. Minneapolis: University of Minnesota Press.

Van der Bliek, Robert. 1991. "Wes Montgomery: A Study of Coherence in Jazz Improvisation." *Jazzforschung* 23: 117–79.

Van Gennep, Arnold. 1960. *The Rites of Passage*. Chicago: University of Chicago Press.

Walser, Robert. 1995. "'Out of Notes': Signification, Interpretation and the Problem of Miles Davis." In *Jazz Among the Discourses*, edited by Krin Gabbard, 165–88. Durham, NC: Duke University Press.

———. 1997. "Deep Jazz: Notes on Interiority, Race, and Criticism." In *Inventing the Psychological: Toward a Cultural History of Emotional Life in America*, edited by Joel Pfister and Nancy Schnog, 271–96. New Haven, CT: Yale University Press.

Warren, Stacy. 1993. "'This Heaven Gives Me Migraines': The Problem and Promise of Landscapes of Leisure." In *Place/Culture/Representation*, edited by James Duncan and David Ley, 173–86. London: Routledge.

Washburne, Christopher J. 1991. "Communication as Composition: A Historical Perspective on the Music of Gil Evans." Master's thesis, Columbia University.

Waterman, Christopher A. 1990. *Jùjú: A Social History and Ethnography of an African Popular Music*. Chicago: University of Chicago Press.

Waters, Keith. 1996. "Blurring the Barline: Metric Displacement in the Piano Solos of Herbie Hancock." *Annual Review of Jazz Studies* 6: 19–37.

Waters, Keith J., and J. Kent Williams. 2010. "Modeling Diatonic, Acoustic, Hexatonic, and Octatonic Harmonies and Progressions in Two- and Three-Dimensional Pitch Spaces; or Jazz Harmony after 1960." *Music Theory Online* 16(3). http://mtosmt.org/issues/mto.10.16.3/mto.10.16.3.waters_williams.html.

Watrous, Peter. 1994a. "A Village Jazz Festival in Its Many Moods." *New York Times*, 21 September, Sec. C: 14.

———. 1994b. "Is Josh Redman a New Archetype?" *New York Times*, 20 November, Sec. 2: 38.

———. 1994c. "Jazz with Pizazz: A New Generation of Clubs." *New York Times*, 15 April, Sec. C: 1, 7.

———. 1994d. "Josh Redman, Bright Lights and All." *New York Times*, 5 December, Sec. C: 16.

———. 1994e. "Why Women Remain at the Back of the Bus." *New York Times*, 27 November, Sec. 2: 34, 40.

———. 1995a. "A Formula for a Whole New Sound." *New York Times*, 5 January, Sec. C: 11.

———. 1995b. "Jazz's New Fans Act as If It's Michael Jordan." *New York Times*, 23 April, Sec. 2: 32, 34.

———. 1996a. "A Fresh Cachet for Jazz in New York." *New York Times*, 1 February, Sec. C: 13, 16.

———. 1996b. "Album by Album, a History Emerges." *New York Times*, 21 January, Sec. 2: 32.

———. 1996c. "Quietly, Sorrowfully, A Jazz Club Dies." *New York Times,* 19 October, Sec. 1: 13–14.

Weinstein, Norman C. 1993. *A Night in Tunisia: Imaginings of Africa in Jazz.* New York: Limelight Editions.

Weisethaunet, Hans. 2001. "Is There Such a Thing as the 'Blue Note'?" *Popular Music* 20(1): 99–116.

Welburn, Ron. 1971. "The Black Aesthetic Imperative." In *The Black Aesthetic,* edited by Addison Gayle, Jr., 132–49. Garden City, NY: Doubleday.

———. 1986. "Duke Ellington's Music: The Catalyst for a True Jazz Criticism." *International Review of the Aesthetics and Sociology of Music* 17: 111–22.

———. 1987. "Jazz Magazines of the 1930s: An Overview of Their Provocative Journalism." *American Music* 5: 255–70.

Whitehead, Kevin. 1994. "Off Minor." *A Gathering of the Tribes* 4(1): 37.

Wildman, Joan. 1985. "The Evolution of Bebop Compositional Style: 'Whisperin'/'Groovin' High.' " *Annual Review of Jazz Studies* 3: 137–46.

Williams, James. 1994. Interview by author, New York, NY. 17 November.

Williams, James, and ICU. 1996. *Truth, Justice, and the Blues.* Evidence ECD 22142–2. Recorded 8–9 December 1994. New York, NY.

Williams, James Kent. 1982. "Themes Composed by Jazz Musicians of the Bebop Era: A Study of Harmony, Rhythm, and Melody." Ph.D. diss., Indiana University.

Williams, Kevin, and David Keen. 2009. *2008 Survey of Public Participation in the Arts.* Washington, DC: National Endowment for the Arts.

Williams, Martin. 1958. "Extended Improvisation and Form: Some Solutions." *Jazz Review* 1(2): 13–15, 49.

———. 1983. *The Jazz Tradition.* Revised ed. New York: Oxford University Press.

———. 1985. *Jazz Heritage.* New York: Oxford University Press.

Williams, Raymond. 1977. *Marxism and Literature.* Oxford: Oxford University Press.

Wilmer, Valerie. 1970. *Jazz People.* Indianapolis: Bobbs-Merrill.

———. 1980. *As Serious as Your Life: The Story of the New Jazz.* Westport, CT: Lawrence Hill.

Wilson, Olly. 1974. "The Significance of the Relationship between Afro-American Music and West African Music." *Black Perspective in Music* 2: 3–22.

———. 1985. "The Association of Movement and Music as a Manifestation of a Black Conceptual Approach to Music Making." In *More Than Dancing: Essays on Afro-American Music and Musicians,* edited by Irene V. Jackson, 9–23. Westport, CT: Greenwood Press.

———. 1992. "The Heterogeneous Sound Ideal in African-American Music." In *New Perspectives on Music: Essays in Honor of Eileen Southern,* edited by Josephine Wright and Samuel A. Floyd, Jr., 327–38. Warren, MI: Harmonie Park Press.

Wilson, Steve. 1995. Interview by author, New York, NY. 2 March.

Wilson, Steve (Quartet). 1996. *Four for Time.* Criss Cross 1115. Recorded 10 December 1994. New York, NY.

Winick, Charles. 1960. "The Use of Drugs by Jazz Musicians." *Social Forces* 7(3): 240–53.

Witmer, Robert, and James Robbins. 1988. "A Historical and Critical Survey of Recent Pedagogical Materials for the Teaching and Learning of Jazz." *Bulletin of the Council for Research in Music Education* 96: 7–29.

Woodard, Josef. 1990. "Indie Groundswell: Caught Up in Current Healthy Swing of Things." *Billboard,* 7 July, J-4, 14–15.

Woodward, Richard B. 1994. "Jazz Wars: A Tale of Age, Rage, and Hash Brownies." *Village Voice,* 9 August, 27–28, 30–34.

———. 2001. "Kind of Blue: Jazz Competes with Its Past, Settles for the Hard Sell." *Village Voice,* 16 January, 50, 53.

Wright, Richard. 1992. "High Tide in Harlem: Joe Louis as a Symbol of Freedom." In *Speech and Power: The African-American Essay and Its Cultural Content from Polemics to Pulpit,* Vol. 1, edited by Gerald Early, 153–57. Hopewell, NJ: Ecco.

"WRVR-FM Switches from Jazz to Country." 1980. *New York Times,* 10 September, Sec. C: 21.

Zabor, Rafi. 1997. *The Bear Comes Home.* New York: W.W. Norton.

Zukin, Sharon. 1995. *The Cultures of Cities.* Malden, MA: Blackwell.

———. 1997. "Cultural Strategies and Urban Identities: Remaking Public Space in New York." In *Cities in Transformation—Transformation in Cities: Social and Symbolic Change of Urban Space,* edited by Ove Källtorp et al., 205–17. Aldershot: Avebury.

Index

COVER DESIGNED BY
Sandy Drooker

TEXT:
10/13 Sabon

DISPLAY:
Sabon (Open Type)

COMPOSITOR:
Westchester

PRINTER AND BINDER:
IBT Global